While the Music Lasts

While the Music Lasts

The Representation
of Music
in the Works of George Sand

David A. Powell

Lewisburg
Bucknell University Press
London: Associated University Presses

Associated University Presses
440 Forsgate Drive
Cranbury, NJ 08512

Associated University Presses
16 Barter Street
London WC1A 2AH, England

Associated University Presses
P.O. Box 338, Port Credit
Mississauga, Ontario
Canada L5G 4L8

The paper used in this publication meets the requirements of the American National Standard for Permanence of Paper for Printed Library Materials Z39.48-1984.

Library of Congress Cataloging-in-Publication Data

Powell, David A.
    While the music lasts : the representation of music in the works of George Sand / David A. Powell.
        p.   cm.
    Includes bibliographical references and index.
    ISBN 0-8387-5474-0 (alk. paper)
    1. Sand, George, 1804–1876—Criticism and interpretation.   2. Music in literature.   I.   Title.

PQ2419.P65   2001
843'.8—dc21   00-068065

♫♫ Contents ♫♫

♫♫ Acknowledgments ♫♫

THE WORK INVOLVED IN PUTTING TOGETHER A BOOK ON AN AUTHOR as prolific as George Sand requires years of reading and analysis—critical, literary analysis, that is, although one might with reason advise other sorts. My labors have not been accomplished in isolation, and I wish here to extend my deepest gratitude to some of the people who have encouraged me and critiqued my work along the way. My most profound and sincere indebtedness devolves to Lucienne Frappier-Mazur, without whom I would probably never have completed the task. Her unending reassurance and critical eye, not to mention her model of excellence in scholarship and her generous and genuine friendship, have for many years provided me with an ever-bounteous source of inspiration and guidance.

To Simone Vierne, who from the outset expressed her support and interest in my work, I proffer indebtedness and appreciation. Her suggestions on this and other tasks, as well as the enthusiasm and ebullience she brings to all those she honors with her commentary, have always been a driving motivation for me.

Others who have read the manuscript of this book, but especially Frank Paul Bowman, warrant a special recognition for their time and patience. Also I offer my thanks to Dave Lalama for help in transcribing and formatting the musical quotations.

I am grateful to Hofstra University for funds from the HCLAS Research & Development Grants and from the President's Research Grants, which have allowed me to complete research in Paris. And I cannot neglect to thank the staff of Axinn Library at Hofstra, especially the Reference and Inter-Library Loan sections, for their devoted help.

And finally, to Thomas Pileggi, for his enduring tolerance and forbearance through countless conversations, travels, conferences, proofreading, and idle chatter about the Nohant author, I extend my most sincere gratitude, for this and for all the rest.

Notwithstanding the diligence and enterprise of these and several others, who devoted many hours to reading and rereading my manuscript, I alone am responsible for the persistent errors that it may contain.

♫♫ Abbreviations and References ♫♫

A	*Adriani*
C	*Consuelo*
CD	*Le Château des Désertes*
"Contrebandier"	"Le Contrebandier"
Corr	*Correspondance de George Sand*
CR	*La Comtesse de Rudolstadt*
DA	*Le Dernier Amour*
F	*La Filleule*
FC	*François le champi*
HV	*Histoire de ma vie*
J	*Jeanne*
LD	*La Daniella*
LV	*Lettres d'un voyageur*
M	*Malgrétout*
MA	*Le Meunier d'Angibault*
MD	*La Mare au diable*
MF	*Maître Favilla*
"Mouny"	"Mouny-Robin"
MS	*Les Maîtres Sonneurs*
NN	*La Nuit de Noël*
OA	*Œuvres autobiographiques.* The texts I have referred to include *Histoire de ma vie, Lettres d'un voyageur, Journal intime,* and *Entretiens journaliers du très docte et très humble Docteur Piffoël.*
"Orgue"	"L'Orgue du titan"
PF	*La Petite Fadette*
"Prima"	"La Prima donna"
RB	*Rose et Blanche*
"Rêveur"	"Histoire du rêveur"
S	*Spiridion*
SC	*Les Sept cordes de la lyre*
SJ	*Ma Sœur Jeanne*
V	*Valentine*

9

♫ ♫ ♫

References to *Consuelo* and *La Comtesse de Rudolstadt* will include page numbers preceded by a volume number, for example (*C*, 1:123).

In the case of "Histoire du rêveur," "La Prima donna," and *Rose et Blanche*, the texts I have quoted from do not exist in modern editions. The versions I have used are from nineteenth-century literary journals or reproductions of these editions. In all cases, I have respected the spelling and punctuation therein. I also respect the spelling and punctuation of Rousseau's texts.

♫ ♫ ♫

Abbreviations for works by other authors are limited to the following:

Doni	*Massimilla Doni*, Balzac
Dict	*Dictionnaire de musique*, Rousseau
Discours	*Discours sur l'origine des langues*, Rousseau
Musique	*Lettre sur la musique françoise*, Rousseau

While the Music Lasts

♫♫ Introduction ♫♫

THE STUDY OF THE REPRESENTATION OF MUSIC IN LITERATURE IS essentially a study of symbols, a semiotic investigation of the ways linguistic signs signify when they represent a nonverbal system. The crossing of literary and musical codes remains a thorny matter whatever the critic's standpoint on the semantic value of those codes. The question of whether music has or represents meaning continues a long debate, and the answer remains elusive. However, for George Sand—as indeed for the majority of nineteenth-century thinkers and writers—there is no question but that music does mean. My goal is not to determine whether music signifies or not. Rather, I shall examine the ways in which George Sand defines her own perceptions of music: of listening to music, of composing music, of performing music. Most importantly, I shall examine how she puts these notions to work in her fiction. Sand's representations of music extend from the microcosm of a musician's professional problems to the macrocosm of the place of art and the artist in society. Sand formulates her commentary in fictional contexts; thus my investigation will be one of literary criticism. By adding another system of signifying symbols to the analysis of literature, I shall be faced with a doubly complex construct. What I am looking at is, in fact, a double representation, a double system of symbols.

Paradoxically, while my literary analysis is complicated by the addition of a second semiotic system, Sand's universe flourishes thanks to this very admixture. Her language, where auditory images are just as common and important as visual ones, is rich with musical metaphors and her world is peopled with gifted musicians. Sand's musical upbringing and musician acquaintances obviously influenced her writing, but so did the place of music in mid-nineteenth-century French society.[1] Sand attempted a philosophy of music aesthetics, positing how music fits, or should fit, into the social structure based on her deep appreciation of what music can teach us. In developing her theories, Sand drew on the philosophical notions of her time, which she learned largely from her own reading of Rousseau and Diderot, but also through her association with Liszt, Pierre Leroux, Lamennais, and Chopin.

13

Perhaps the most elusive aspect of Sand's exploration of music involves the very hallmark of the art itself: its ineffability. Recognizing the challenge of translating music or musical effects into literary expression, poets often have recourse to techniques that replicate, to a certain degree, the sounds and the movements of music: onomatopoeia, alliteration, rhythmic movement, and the like. Prose writers rarely attempt to "reproduce" music, rather they describe it and its effect on the listener. Sand tackles the challenge of such a description, where music's expression and the listener's response are so abstract, so intangible that they seem to defy verbal articulation.

Music criticism emerges in the nineteenth century as a form of journalism as well as a commentary on aesthetics. The transposition of art criticism into prose fiction had already been a mainstay of the French tradition since Diderot. Romantic composers tried their hand at musical journalism; from Berlioz to Debussy, nineteenth-century composers provided reviews and opinions of current-day compositions and performances. A new language had to be developed, but the new discourse—so popular in contemporary periodicals—remained imprecise. This stream of critical prose enjoyed much success and was eagerly consumed by the public. The move into prose fiction was a logical and necessary one.

In an effort to convince her reading public that music was at once other-worldly and yet very much of this world, Sand often portrayed musicians as keepers of a divine language but also as less than perfect, with typical human failings. Her musical characters do not, for the most part, stand out from the general public; they can provide a model for readers. At the same time, Sand's accomplished musicians do represent an impressive level of sensibility, though they never lose their humanity. The creation of an attainable musical world helps Sand establish a more believable description of music insofar as the executors of this music are "real" people. Balzac and Stendhal write of the wonders of a certain soprano's voice, a disembodied sound that may inspire excesses of emotion but that could never represent an attainable model. Sand, on the other hand, presents musicians who encourage the reader to see the human side of artists while admiring their discipline and hard work.

The majority of texts in which Sand speaks about music are novels. Jean Cassou, in an enlightened article from 1961,[2] emphasizes the need to examine carefully the renewed energy of the second generation of romanticists, especially in the area of the new genres surfacing at that time, including "le roman noir, le roman feuilleton, le roman musical, le roman initiatique" ["the Gothic novel, the serial novel, the musical novel, the novel of initiation"], all of which are to be found, he says, in Sand's *Consuelo*. And Joseph-Marc Bailbé, in his landmark study,[3] explains the enormous influence on music of the artistic world of mid-nineteenth-century France, with an impressive census of works that classify as musical novels. I shall, therefore, without hesitation use the term "musical novel" or "musical text" to designate a work of prose fiction in which music occupies an important, if not the central, position, and where one or more of the principal characters is a musician. A refinement of this definition, with respect to Sand and to other contemporary authors, will emerge from this study.

The embedding of music in a work of literature is not new to the romantic period; Diderot's *Rameau's Nephew* (published in 1823 but written sometime between 1761 and 1774) and Heinse's *Hildegard von Hohenthal* (1795–96) provide excellent examples of such texts, from which romantic authors drew quite heavily. As romantic writers developed a heightened sense of emotion and enthusiasm, they leaned increasingly toward music as a sister art imbued with the capacity to express "pure" emotion. Even if music could not express precise emotions or ideas, it could represent essences and nuances of emotions in a way unknown to (or at least unsatisfying in) verbal art forms. Kant's and Herder's assessment of the qualities inherent in music easily passed into the realm of romantic individualism. Schopenhauer added precision to the appreciation of romantic undefined feelings and the response to music. The era of socialism displaced attention from the individual to society, with music mirroring that mode in Wagner and Kierkegaard.[4] The close relationship among the arts constituted a central point of interest for artists and journalists of the romantic period. Again at the end of the nineteenth century, writers incorporated music into their work with as much or perhaps greater fluidity and plurivocality than in the romantic era.

Serious interdisciplinary studies focusing on the critical aspect of literature and its relation to the other arts have formed part of professional criticism for more than half a century. Comparative investigations of the interrelations between music and literature have lagged behind those of literature and the other arts, especially comparisons with painting and architecture. We tend to trust our sense of vision more than our sense of hearing. The mystical aura that surrounds the world of music has also discouraged literary critics from delving into this domain. More recently, critics well versed in the technical and cultural aspects of music have developed complex methodologies for looking at music and literature. Some of these studies have enlightened our view of the ways literature uses music, but they often get caught up in technical jargon and pseudo-musico-logical analyses. They sometimes even attempt to set up a one-to-one relationship between musical and literary devices.

I do not subscribe to any one methodology; rather I look for the musico-literary key that the individual text dictates. Sand's use of music is so rich that each musical text hosts several musico-literary functions at the same time. Leo Treitler's commentary on music criticism, especially the convergence of history and criticism, has shaped much of my thinking regarding Sand's use of musical reference in her prose fiction.[5] The choices Sand makes—choice of musical works; choice of artist, performers; choice of styles and genres of music—reveal considerable information about her purpose and provide the reader with valuable criteria for evaluation. These criteria demand an analysis of the conflation of music and text and their relationship to Sand's world, leading to a complex critique of the work as a whole, which represents Sand's perception of the world. These musical works are the subject this book, and the musico-literary analysis they exact is determined by multiple factors involving the ritual of literature and the musical experience as they unfolded in the nineteenth century.

In *While the Music Lasts* I explore the widely varying functions of music in Sand's texts. While I shall not examine every mention of music in Sand's vast œuvre—to do so would be tedious and unproductive—I shall explore the various functions music performs, in terms of plot advancement, characterization, narrative structure, thematics, aesthetics, semiotics, political thought, the artist and society, and women artists. Such an array of domains will demand a variety of methodologies, including narratology, semiotics, reader reception theory, music history, musico-literary analysis, feminism, philosophy, and psychoanalysis. I do not pretend to establish a single methodology: that would limit my analysis and force it into a unidimensional mold. Rather, the eclecticism I bring to this study draws its inspiration from Sand's own wide range of interests and endeavors in both her writing and her personal life.

In like manner, the proponents of narratology have never to my knowledge undertaken an archeological examination of the function of musical elements in the structure of prose fiction. My study of Sand's texts will demonstrate that music and musical elements can serve to shape and advance the narrative, sometimes in imitation of musical development but more often as the impetus and model for the characters' actions. In such instances, Sand uses music to help formulate not only themes but also structures.

In order to examine fully George Sand's use of musical elements, in the representation of musical experiences as well as in characterization and plot structures, I focus principally on the function of these elements in her texts. While I will not ignore the music George Sand knew and heard, I will concentrate less on historical detail and more on structural and narratological function. I shall shift freely from analysis of musical form, precise musical references, and music history to the more abstract areas of the musical experience, especially the effects of listening to music. The ways these experiences affect Sand's characters and consequently influence the structure of her writings and their effects on the reader will provide a rich commentary of her work. The focus of my study is not music, rather George Sand's discussion about music in the context of her prose fiction. It is my hope that this study of George Sand's representation of music, the development of her thoughts concerning music, her use of musical elements to flesh out characters or to motivate action, will teach us more about the presence of music in French intellectual society in middle of the nineteenth century.

♫ ♫ ♫

> For most of us, there is only the unattended
> Moment, the moment in and out of time,
> The distraction fit, lost in a shaft of sunlight,
> The wild thyme unseen, or the winter lightning
> Or the waterfall, or music heard so deeply
> That it is not heard at all, but you are the music
> While the music lasts.
>
> —T. S. Eliot

T. S. Eliot, in "The Dry Salvages," the third book of his *Four Quartets*, posits the almost indefinable state where one fluctuates between heaven and earth, between reality and the ideal, as one listens to music. The listening experience remains one of the most difficult elements of music to discuss and continues to plague aestheticians, musicologists, philosophers, and writers of literature. The coincidence of time and timelessness to which Eliot refers represents the ineffable quality of music, the confluence of feelings, the epiphany of understandings that come together for only an instant—an instant that remains impossible to capture or recapture. As opposed to the idle pastimes in which "[m]en's curiosity searches past and future / And clings to that dimension," saints spend eternity, "a lifetime's death in love," seeking the "point of intersection of the timeless / With time." For most of us, however, that "moment in and out of time" comes shrouded in the myriad subtleties of nature, which we cannot pierce sufficiently with our human perceptions in a way that allows us to apprehend the mystical concept of art. When we do glimpse the meaning of the construct of time as it becomes an unearthly timelessness, we dare not discern it in the blinding "shaft of sunlight." We can smell the tantalizing odor of wild thyme, but we cannot quite spy it; we can feel the tension of lightning, yet we cannot find it in the winter sky, just as we cannot quite see what is hidden behind the cascade of a waterfall. These examples of human failing culminate in the experience of absorbing music so profoundly that we cease to hear, we only feel. And for that instant, we *are* music—while the music lasts.

George Sand remains fascinated her whole life by the impressions left by music, by the actual act of listening to music. For her, listening to music is an arduous occupation that requires concentration and focus. The residue of this effort enriches one's life beyond the experience of reading a book or looking at a painting. It approximates the most profound emotions of one's existence: love, death, and religion. Through the characters of her novels and plays, she examines and explores the possibilities of the musical experience as it influences our lives.

The memory of music, the remembrance of music heard, is an experience Sand will repeatedly try to incorporate into her works, a query she bequeaths to Proust. Through an examination of this experience she develops a lesson in human understanding that serves to shape her world. In like manner, music often structures her texts, and it is precisely this aspect I shall explore in this book. The human capacity, on the one hand, to relive and thereby, on the other, to anticipate emotions and feelings and even events through the personal experience of listening to music, even in the most social settings, provides Sand with material for delving into both the human psyche and the nature of human relationships. For Sand, anything is possible for humankind through a combination of compassion and understanding and a belief in progress. In this aspect of her ideology she announces herself as a true romantic. Music stands as a symbol of hope in Sand's universe, a universe that continues to improve and grow.

Music in the works of George Sand is not an unfamiliar topic among Sandists.[6] Thérèse Marix-Spire was the first to explore this theme in an orderly manner in her landmark book.[7] Hers is the only fairly thorough study of Sand's use of music in writing and her relationship to the musical world. She probes Sand's musical training as a girl, her musical acquaintances in early adulthood, and the musical references she uses in her writings up to 1838, which is to say up to the beginning of her relationship with Chopin. Her book, along with several additional articles, provides an invaluable source of information and a point of departure for the study of music in Sand's world. Marix-Spire's work remains, however, somewhat anecdotal and without any underpinning in musical analysis. It also stops just when Sand hits her musico-literary stride. This is one gap *While the Music Lasts* will fill.

A more recent book by Marie-Paule Rambeau perspicaciously examines the interrelations of Chopin's and Sand's art.[8] Rambeau's investigation takes up where Marix-Spire's leaves off. She establishes a critical equilibrium between the two artists, a balance this subject indeed requires. Her study is based on solid analysis of Chopin's compositions and Sand's writings of the period 1838 to 1847. Rambeau's book has opened a new direction in the analysis of music in Sand's works. Here the more technical interplay of music and literature comes forward, all the while not forgetting the symbiotic relationship of both arts and artists. Again, however, the corpus is limited to the dates the author imposed for the purpose of her comparative study.

Although recently several articles have brought to the fore Sand's abundant use of music,[9] none really demonstrates the degree to which she consciously weaves musical elements into her prose. *While the Music Lasts* will make a systematic analysis of the instances where Sand includes music to advance the plot, characterization, or themes, to delve into human emotions and psychology, and to define the role of music (and art) in society. Sand's principal goal is to express adequately in verbal language the experience one has when listening to or performing music. The nature of the musical experience, which remains somewhat mystical, serves as the basis of Sand's use of music and as the basis of this book.

If music can be found in much of Sand's prose, it cannot be marginalized as a simple *effet de réel.* On the contrary, I shall demonstrate that it remains an indisputably important element, one that serves a dynamic function in the texts. Music was such a driving, emotional force in Sand's life, from her early days at Nohant with her grandmother to her friendship with Liszt and her affair with Chopin, as well as her admiration from afar of Meyerbeer, Berlioz, Gounod, and Massenet, that it would be quite impossible to exempt music from a serious study of her artistic creation.

Even though music pervades much of Sand's output, I shall not attempt to examine all of her works. Indeed, even such important works as *Indiana, Lélia,* and *Nanon* will receive but a passing commentary. Inversely, I shall analyze several little-known novels, stories, and plays, as well as pertinent nonfiction works. This approach does not, however, misrepresent Sand's body of work, since the music element is present in all periods and genres of her production. Sand's musical works are sprinkled throughout her career, offering texts from the early, middle, and mature periods of her production. My study does not, all the same, skew or exaggerate the importance of musical elements in Sand's work. A careful investigation of the majority of works written during Sand's fruitful forty-five year career will promptly show the number of texts in which music springs to the service of literature.

In the first chapter, "Ballad and *Bildung*—Music and Narrative," I look at the important role of music in organizing plot and textual structure. The training and development of the musician in *Consuelo* and *Les Maîtres Sonneurs* provide a chronological and musical progression that parallels the philosophical and moral themes of these two important novels. As the protagonists of these novels grow artistically through their musical apprenticeship, they also grow morally and psychologically. The Bildungsroman structure provides Sand with a framework in which to present the growth of a musician, which is at once unique and universal. Travel, too, offers Sand an additional element with which to demonstrate the development of the musician in eighteenth- and nineteenth-century Europe. In *Adriani* Sand presents a musician who feels he has reached a plateau in his musical career and has begun to wonder whether the profession meets his own moral exigencies and personal goals. The conflict of the financial and moral demands of the musical world defines the narrative structure, which unfolds to unveil Adriani's musical ideals. The hero's discovery of love allows him to accede to a higher aesthetic plane of musical expression. And just as a love plot serves to complicate the situation in *Adriani*, it also becomes the running structural device in *La Dernière Aldini.* Here the hero's loves, spanning fifteen years and two heroines, mother and daughter, establish the action with the help of musical cues and associations. Sand also anticipates the nineteenth-century fascination with a total art form in the musico-theatrical experiences of *Le Château des Désertes*, where rehearsals for a performance of *Don Giovanni* structure the plot and the characters' relationships. This text also offers an important commentary on the performer's responsibility to her or his public.

In chapter 2, "Musical Language," I explore Sand's attempts to define a musical language and her discussion of music's ability to communicate. Various aspects of musical form and technique serve as springboards for this argument. Musical ornamentation, one of the defining tenets of baroque music but also an important element of bel canto singing that was beloved of the mid-nineteenth-century Parisian public, serves as the basis for discussion of the advantages and ills of (over)using fioriture, as we shall see in *Consuelo* and the "Lettre à Meyerbeer" from *Les Lettres d'un voyageur*. Sand displays her aesthetic ideals of simplicity while at the same time highlighting points of commonality between characters through discussions of musical techniques. The musician's ability to improvise and the effect of the improvisation on the listener also forge a unique relationship between characters. Consequently the novelistic structure in such works as *Consuelo, Les Maîtres Sonneurs, Les Sept Cordes de la lyre,* "Histoire du rêveur," and "Carl" is in part established through an appreciation of the musicians'/characters' improvisational skills. Music is also not exempt from the age-old query about the place of imitation in art. Several of Sand's works, principally "Carl," *Les Sept Cordes de la lyre*, and *Consuelo*, tackle the issue of the musical imitation of nature.

The question of communicative music as an imitation of language follows naturally. The role of memory in music leads to the analysis of the listener's participation in the musical act of listening. In "Le Contrebandier," *Les Maîtres Sonneurs* and *Consuelo*, memory establishes an evaluative tool with which to judge the musician's value. The power of music to evoke memories also provides many opportunities for Sand to exploit the powers of music in *Les Maîtres Sonneurs, Adriani,* "La Prima donna," and other texts. From these musical forms and techniques it is a short leap to the relationship between music and language. This argument, which grows largely out of the philosophical discussions of the Enlightenment, enjoys several sometimes contradictory manifestations in Sand's writings. We will see her change from the conception of a direct link between music and language in *Les Sept Cordes de la lyre*, to a somewhat modified view in "Carl," to a more multivalent but ambiguous interpretation in *Consuelo*. Sand will sustain the view of music as a communicator of emotions and nonmetaphysical ideas till the end of her life.

Chapter 3, "Love, Madness, and Music," examines the role and function of music in the love plots. Not unusual for prose fiction of the romantic period, many of Sand's love plots are born in the midst of music. However, Sand incorporates the musical element in such a way as to make it essential to the generation and development of the liaison. Rather than an addition of ambience, Sand integrates the functions of interpersonal relations and musical influence. I move from the tentative mixing of music and love in early texts, such as *Rose et Blanche* and *Valentine*, to more fundamental uses of music in the love plots of *La Dernière Aldini, Consuelo, Le Château des Désertes, Les Maîtres Sonneurs,* and finally *Adriani*. Music forms a basic element in the configuration of love plots in these novels. I make a brief comparison with Balzac's *Gambara* and *Massimilla Doni* to demonstrate the differences in the two authors' musical techniques.

Chapter 4, "The Musical Fantastic," examines Sand's use of musical elements to enhance the structure and function of the fantastic. With obvious links to E. T. A. Hoffmann, Sand creates mystical situations with unearthly characters through the medium of an other-worldly musical power. Some of these texts are playful, such as "Histoire du rêveur," "L'Orgue du titan," and "Carl"; others, for example, *Les Sept Cordes de la lyre* and *Maître Favilla*, contrive a complex mystical and metaphysical construct based on the characters' ability, or lack thereof, to *hear* music. As with Hoffmann, Sand always supplants her musical tales with a healthy dose of realism tempered by the characteristic *Unheimliche*. Sand posits the notion that music communicates, even though we do not know always *what* it communicates, which parallels the fantastic tendency to imply meanings that remain inarticulate or unarticulated. The proclivity of the music-lover to be deeply moved but not to be able to enunciate the precise emotion or idea communicated by music comes to the surface in these musical fantastic stories. And as always in the fantastic, the degree to which the musical effect is ethereal or real remains a constant of the genre.

Not unrelated to the fantastic, madness comes into the discussion in relation to music. At times the influence of music is beneficial, but often the superstitions associated with selling one's soul to the devil in exchange for musical talent, an especially Hoffmannesque theme, contribute an additional element of the Gothic or the fantastic to Sand's otherwise serious approach to the subject of music. Sand develops several characters, men and women, whose mental stability is now hindered, now abetted by music. Laure, in *Adriani*, Blanche, in *Rose et Blanche*, Gina, in "La Prima donna," but especially Hélène, in *Les Sept Cordes de la lyre*, succumb to the quasi-hysteria of musical madness. Albert and Zdenko, in *Consuelo*, and Joset, in *Les Maîtres Sonneurs*, derive from music a spiritual, social, and historical sense of purpose that often takes them out of their present context and thus removes them from the realm of the real. Music in Sand's universe often provides an escape from reality, similar to some forms of psychosis.

In chapter 5, "Folk Music," I explore the ethnomusicological contributions Sand makes to French literary tradition, especially in *Les Maîtres Sonneurs*, but also in *Jeanne, La Petite Fadette, François le champi, La Mare au diable,* and the musical aspects of some stage plays, *Claudie* and *François le champi*, the operatic setting of *La Petite Fadette*, and the informal theater at Nohant. Sand exploits peasant superstition through a commentary on the magical attributes of music. This and other magical aspects of music will be explored in the context of the rustic novels as well as in Sand's ethnological essays.

Chapter 6, "Musician, Public, and Society," examines the place of the musician in society. I identify Sand's thoughts on the musician's relationship to her or his public in "La Prima donna," *Lucrezia Floriani, Le Château des Désertes, Consuelo,* and in the "Lettre à Meyerbeer." Relationship to the public begs the question of what public. Sand's limited though significant dalliance in Saint-Simonism explains some of her definitions of music, art, the musician, and their place in society. Sand's so-called "socialist novels," which demonstrate the degree to which she approves and adopts the notions of such activists as Lamennais and Pierre Leroux, bear witness to the subtle manner in which music infiltrates Sand's whole corpus. The small but important place of music in the highly theoretical and socialist novel *Spiridion*, in contrast to the great importance of music in *Le Château des Désertes*, reveals some essential answers to the question of how all-pervasive Sand's use of music is. How, for example, does Sand explain the place of music in religion at the same time as she questions the very validity of organized religion? *Les Sept Cordes de la lyre*, Sand's most explicit manifesto of musical socialism, unveils a burgeoning yet naive belief in the power of music to "tame the savage breast." The socialist elements in *Consuelo* interact with the musical aspects of that novel to communicate a deep-felt assurance that a humanistic appreciation of music is essential to a successful application of socialistic constructs onto society. Sand's relationship with Franz Liszt sees the birth of a socialist dream of the curative and educative powers of music. This utopian view is revealed in the complementary efforts that resulted in Liszt's piano piece, "Fantaisie sur un thème espagnol," and Sand's short story, "Le Contrebandier."

Sand's definition of the female musician also constitutes an important segment of this chapter. I discuss the various women musicians in Sand's œuvre: Rose, Consuelo, Bianca Aldini, Lucrezia

Floriani, and others. Insofar as Sand defines music as a language, I shall explore the "linguistic" use women musicians make of music in Sand's universe. Such a gender-based description will naturally require a brief look at the use male musicians make of music. Joset, Albert, Zdenko, Adriani, Favilla, and several others provide enough masculine models to hold up in contrast to the female musicians. The latter usually show more humanity, and sometimes become the apostle of the male musician. This leads logically to a discussion of the role of women (musicians) in Sand's works. The thorny issue of Sand's feminism can be approached through music, and music adds a dimension to our understanding of this aspect of her writing. The treatment by nineteenth-century society of the female artist, especially as shown in *Lucrezia Floriani* and "La Prima donna," provides an opportunity to view Sand's reconciliation of the contemporary dialectic of woman and artist. The mature and progressive attitude of Cécilia, in *Le Château des Désertes*, offers a positive image for the female artist. Hélène's perception of music as language in *Les Sept Cordes de la lyre* demands a semiotic analysis of music-as-language in that work. More interesting, though, is the comparison of the rigid linguistic value Sand assigns music in this relatively early work with the more mature understanding of music she demonstrates in later works. Music often serves as a form of escape from a man's world or as an alternate means of communication when verbal language would mean tackling a man's world. Yet, we must be careful not to define music too easily as woman's *parole* in a domain of man's *langue*, for Sand's conception of the musician in society remains inclusive. Women musicians are in fact presented in Sand's world as privileged figures who experience music in a way men do not, or perhaps cannot.

While the Music Lasts establishes a thorough presentation of the important functions of music in the works of George Sand. This study will take Sand criticism into realms not fully explored elsewhere. Not just a study of music in literature, *While the Music Lasts* reveals Sand's aesthetics and her narrative techniques in a way that demonstrates the coupling and cooperation of thematic and structural elements to form the opus of the masterful writer who was George Sand. This book will serve students of George Sand, students of romanticism, and students of general musico-literary criticism alike.

1

♫♫ Ballad and *Bildung*—Music and Narrative ♫♫

J'écris sur la musique . . .

[I'm writing about music . . .]
—Letter to Casimir Dudevant, 21 February 1831

IN HER MUSICAL NOVELS GEORGE SAND ESTABLISHES A TIGHT PARAL-
lel between the development of characters, musical themes, and
musical symbolism on the one hand, and on the other the natural
progression of the narrative. As the plots progress, so do the characters' musical attributes and identifications. This simultaneous unfolding of musical and narrative structures creates a coherent text
unified around the representation of musical stimuli. The self-con-
sciousness of musical elements in these texts heightens their narrativity. Sand's Bildungsromane or *Künstlerromane* chronicle both
aesthetic and personal growth as well as the place of aesthetics, art,
and the artist in society. Far from a simple application of conventional musical allusions, this process represents a complex pairing
of musical and narrative structures and codes, enhanced by references to music history, musical forms, and often an exploration of
the professional musical world. Sand brings to these narratives an
intimate awareness of the experience of making and listening to
music.

Carolyn Abbate writes that "if we speak of music as 'narrative,'
we realize that the word is metaphorical. Yet since the nineteenth
century, musical works have been described as 'narrative' and the
word catches our attention."[1] Sand exploits our perceptions of the
narrative possibilities of music to enhance her own narratives. The
effect is double: not only is the absent music brought into play
through a verbal representation, but the desire for narrative on the
part of the nineteenth-century listener—and to a large extent today's listener, too—is activated by Sand's ability to combine her
own narrative with an evocation of music that carries its own poten-

25

tial narrative. The multiple narrative layers of Sand's texts thus engage the reader by appealing to more than one aesthetic expression. That music is not present but only represented complicates—in a good way—the artistic experience by increasing the polyphony of the text. Thus one representation is embedded within another, allowing the reader to flow between two intersecting worlds of illusion that progress simultaneously through their mutual narratological movements. Lucien Dällenbach provides a useful formula, based on Jakobson's, in his commentary on the structure of *mise en abyme*: "Once we realize that this *subject* [of the reflection] is an *utterance*—and more exactly a synecdochical utterance—we can relate the two aspects of reflexivity and suggest the following definition: a reflection is an utterance that relates to the utterance, the enunciation of the whole code of the narrative."[2]

The structure Dällenbach elucidates can be compared to Sand's interweaving of musical and literary narrative and/or representation, where any analysis must consider reflections of the utterance, reflections of the enunciation, and reflections of the whole code. What Dällenbach calls "triple meaning" applies to Sand's musical texts and helps to clarify the narratological function of the representation of music in these texts. So when a character discusses a work of music in some term of analysis or criticism, Sand is in fact commenting on the frame narrative and thereby encourages the reader to analyze the text as a whole.[3] The somewhat unstable movement between the music not heard and its narratological relation to the reader as presented by the narrator—a relation that Mieke Bal refers to as "focalization"[4]—results in a heightened awareness of narrative strategies, which Gerald Prince would term less readable or having less narrativity.[5] It is precisely this complex and sophisticated layering of narrative techniques, of codes, indeed of narratives that interests me in Sand's musical texts.

Sand uses a variety of techniques to weave musical concerns into the narrative, one of the most innovative being the commentary on student-teacher relationships in a young musician's musical and developmental training. In addition, the advantages of travel to an artist's growth contribute to the musico-literary construct that Sand judiciously integrates into the Bildungsroman. *Consuelo* (1842–44) and *Les Maîtres Sonneurs* (1853) demonstrate this process especially well and will be the focus of my investigation in this chapter.[6] Sand presents the musical world to which her young musicians aspire as at once calm and discordant. Her musicians are superior beings, guides, *vates* figures. Conversely, they are ordinary humans, replete with the same hopes and desires as everyone. Thus the musical protagonists must progress personally as well as artistically. Sand does not extol the mere presence of musical talent. It must first be recognized, respected, and desired; then it must be enhanced through discipline, learning, and understanding. This is the task of the true musician, a commitment to oneself and to society. In these novels, Sand guides her musicians through a detailed training process that cultivates them musically, psychologically, emotionally, and socially.

MUSICAL TRAINING: STUDENT AND TEACHER

The accomplished musician in Sand's universe represents sensitivity and romantic inspiration but also discipline and continual improvement. Hopeful musicians must undergo a process of rigorous training, submitting to the strict guidance of an austere yet devoted teacher. The teacher's role in the life trajectory of Sand's musicians affords insight into the dependency of the student on the teacher and the artist's simultaneous and paradoxical movement toward independence. This relationship provides a propitious environment in which to observe the musical evolution and personal growth that constitute a maturation process for these characters.

Components of musical training reflect essential elements of narrative structure, creating at once a narratological incentive for the unfolding of the musical themes and a musical incentive for the progression of the narrative. This combined progression tells the protagonists' stories at the same time as it teaches the reader about music and the musicians' role and comments on their emotional and psychological evolution in general. Sand presents all this before a musical backdrop, where she can advance her general notions of musical style and aesthetics.

The eponymous character of *Consuelo*, and Joset, the hero of *Les Maîtres Sonneurs*, are Sand's most accomplished musicians and typical of the musical and psychological development in her musical novels. They achieve a degree of artistry worthy of the admiration and respect of professionals and friends alike. We observe these artists' struggles and evolution as the action of their respective novels advances. From the beginning to the end of both *Consuelo* (including its sequel, *La Comtesse de Rudolstadt*) and *Les Maîtres Sonneurs*, these characters advance from amateurs to fledgling musicians and finally to mature and accomplished artists. Their musical development parallels their moral, spiritual, emotional, and political development.

Consuelo and La Comtesse de Rudolstadt

Sand starts off *Consuelo* by pairing the protagonist's personal and musical growth. As a young child, Consuelo traveled extensively throughout Europe with her mother, singing folk songs in exchange for room and board. Hearing her sing in the streets of Venice, Nicola Porporo takes her into one of the famous choir schools for young girls, *la scuola dei Mendicanti*. This stage of her (musical) development signals a departure from her upbringing by providing a sense of stability. Many of the girls in the choir school are not poor and come from good Venetian families.[7] Consuelo, on the contrary, is poor, Spanish, and probably of Moorish descent. This socioeconomic and racial difference earns her the status of stranger and the nickname of gypsy, or *bohémienne*.[8] But her dedication to singing and her speed and accuracy in learning music also set her apart from the others.

Consuelo's formal musical training occupies only about a sixth of the novel. Much of the instruction she receives from the famous Neopolitan composer and teacher Porpora precedes the opening of the narrative and is related through periodic exposition.[9] The general principle of this training is simplicity. Porpora explains to Zustiniani, the director of the San-Samuel theater in Venice who will offer Consuelo a singing contract (among other things!), that while he may have had reason to applaud "le *brillant*, le *cherché*, l'*habile*" [what's dazzling, contrived, skillful],[10] these qualities represent only secondary traits and are separated from true genius by an abyss. Many present-day singers, he goes on to say, excel in this "modern" genre, but they demonstrate bad taste, especially in sacred music. In particular, he criticizes the practice of Corilla, formerly his student and now prima donna at San-Samuel and seduced by Zustiniani's promises of fame and wealth. She has dedicated her fine voice to the splendors of ornamentation to please the ears of the general Venetian public. Sand sets the stage for the aesthetics of simplicity as well as for the moral rectitude and modesty of her heroine, for whom Corilla is the foil, by having Porpora describe Corilla's artistry thus:

> Les nymphes et les bergères peuvent roucouler comme les oiseaux, ou cadencer leurs accents comme le murmure des fontaines. . . . La Corilla excelle en ce genre: mais qu'elle veuille exprimer les émotions profondes, les grandes passions, elle reste au-dessous de son rôle; et c'est en vain qu'elle s'agite, c'est en vain qu'elle gonfle sa voix et son sein: un trait déplacé, une roulade absurde, viennent changer en un instant en ridicule parodie ce sublime qu'elle croyait atteindre. (*C*, 1:110)[11]

[Nymphs and shepherdesses coo like birds or pulse their tones like murmuring fountains. . . . Corilla outshines in this style; but if she were to try to express deep emotions or grand passions, she would offend her role; it would be futile for her to toss about and to puff up her voice and her bosom. A misplaced embellishment and a ludicrous run would instantly change what she is trying to attain into a ridiculous parody.]

The perfect student, in Porpora's eyes, is characterized by serious and patient intelligence, modesty to the point of effacing herself before the master, and a total absence of prior musical training. Consuelo belongs to this group.

Studieuse et persévérante, vivant dans la musique comme l'oiseau dans l'air et le poisson dans l'eau, aimant à vaincre les difficultés sans se rendre plus de raison de l'importance de cette victoire qu'il n'appartient à un enfant, mais poussée fatalement à combattre les obstacles et à pénétrer les mystères de l'art, par cet invincible instinct qui fait que le germe des plantes cherche à percer le sein de la terre et à se lancer vers le jour, Consuelo avait une de ces rares et bienheureuses organisations pour lesquelles le travail est une jouissance, un repos véritable, un état normal nécessaire, et pour qui l'inaction serait une fatigue, un dépérissement, un état maladif. (*C*, 1:83)[12]

[Determined and persistent, living in music like a bird in the air and a fish in water, willingly conquering problems without giving these victories any more importance than a child, but pushed inevitably to struggle against obstacles and to penetrate the mysteries of art with the same invincible instinct that makes seeds pierce through the heart of the earth and reach toward the light, Consuelo had one of those rare and blessed constitutions that experience work as a joy, a true respite, a necessary and normal state, and for whom inaction would be exhaustion, deterioration, a state of illness.]

This quotation, a single sentence replete with the natural metaphors and vaulting moral descriptions typical of the style Sand uses to describe her heroine, demonstrates the attributes she finds important for an artist, as well as Sand's devotion to the romantic precept of nature = good.

Sand comments on Consuelo's training in greater detail in the sections where she gives music lessons, invoking the familiar tradition of the student becoming the teacher. Consuelo first transmits her precepts of musical education to Anzoleto, her betrothed. He has just debuted at San-Samuel where he manages to succeed in dazzling the public despite the rough edges in his performance. Porpora tells him: "Tu te passionnes à froid; tu sais roucouler, gazouiller comme ces demoiselles gentilles et coquettes auxquelles on pardonne de minauder ce qu'elles ne savent pas chanter. Mais tu ne sais point phraser, tu prononces mal, tu as un accent vulgaire, un style faux et commun" [You become passionate in a detached way. You know how to coo and twitter like those nice and pretty young ladies whom we forgive for simpering what they can't sing. But you don't know how to phrase, your diction is poor, and you have a crude accent, a false and common style] (*C*, 1:60). Even though Porpora sees in him the native characteristics of a good musician, he predicts Anzoleto will never improve, as he possesses only "un feu qui n'éclairera rien de grand, un génie qui demeurera stérile . . . tu n'as pas le culte de l'art" [a flame that will never illuminate anything great, a genius that will always be sterile . . . you don't worship art] (*C*, 1:61).

Porpora uses the same denigrating vocabulary for Anzoleto as for Corilla. The contradictory language first offers ironic compliments, which are then quickly overturned by the biting tone of derogatory verbs for bird noises produced by silly girls. This judgmental discourse comes to an unambiguous conclusion with "vulgaire, faux, commun" [coarse, false, common]. As in the previously cited passage, the language of the pastoral genre provides a basis for criticizing the false but purportedly natural style of certain eighteenth-century composers who attempt to imitate nature but end up with a superficial rendition of nature, similar to the aristocracy's aping of pastoral lifestyle.[13]

Consuelo agrees with Porpora to an extent about Anzoleto's artistry. She convinces Anzoleto, however, through a detailed analysis of his faults, that he can improve if he will take stock of his performance. His main problem, she says, stems from a lack of preparation and an overzealous confidence in his virtuosity. He improves with Consuelo's help, but as her reputation grows faster than his, he begins to doubt the effectiveness of her instruction and to mistrust the goals of their common teacher. Spurred on by the vindictive jealousy of Corilla, whom Consuelo will soon replace as prima donna of San-Samuel, he returns to his flamboyant style. However, he can no longer impress the public. His relationship with Corilla preempts a return to Consuelo, which is analogous to his professional decline. Sand allows artistic concerns to determine the direction of the narrative.

Anzoleto's overconfident bravura demonstrates a trait Sand dislikes: arrogance. The goal of art, according to Sand, is not to use trickery to spark emotional reactions in the public, but rather to delve into the human soul and to stimulate an emotion or the memory of an emotion through sincere and virtuous artistry. Similar to Anzoleto, Célio, the protagonist of *Le Château des Désertes* (1851), is ever ready to dazzle the public and makes a spectacular but uninspired debut at the Vienna opera in *Don Giovanni*; "[il] se présenta avec un aplomb qui frisait l'outrecuidance" [he performed with a confidence that bordered on impertinence], and the public, although properly impressed, senses something not quite acceptable.[14] Failure before a public is an artist's worst fear, and Célio, like Anzoleto, waltzes right into his failure because he believes in his power to enchant the public. Admitting he performed badly, Célio maintains he was equal to the tastes of the Viennese public. However, Célio, as opposed to Anzoleto, is quite willing to delay his career by three years and undergo extensive training. Along with his friends and family, Célio will experience a slow and deliberate training in commedia dell'arte. In this method Célio is obliged to become aware of the interplay between characters and of the importance of the play, and thus to project his talents for the good of the whole and not just for his own reputation.

Musical education always parallels personal growth for Sand. After leaving Venice, Consuelo continues her training in Bohemia. This time it is not formal musical instruction but a fortuitous reintroduction to folk music. Zdenko, Albert's Bohemian faithful peasant companion, impresses Consuelo with his extensive knowledge of folk music. Zdenko's mysterious and spiritual relationship to Albert intrigues Consuelo as much as his familiarity with regional music and culture. He represents freedom through musical innovation, which the narrator, Consuelo, and Sand extol.[15] It is not an entirely guileless device on Sand's part to have Consuelo become intellectually interested in folk music in Bohemia. Here is how she explains to Amélie, Frederick II's sister, her interest in Bohemia:

> Dans notre langage d'artistes aventuriers, nous disons souvent *courir la bohême*, pour signifier qu'on s'embarque dans les hasards d'une vie pauvre, laborieuse et souvent coupable, dans la vie des Zingari, qu'on appelle aussi Bohêmiens, en français. Quant à moi, je partais, non pour cette Bohême symbolique à laquelle mon sort semblait me destiner comme tant d'autres, mais pour le malheureux et chevaleresque pays des Tchèques, pour la patrie de Huss et de Ziska, pour le Bœhmer-Wald, enfin pour le château des Géants, où je fus généreusement accueillie par la famille des Rudolstadt. (*CR,* 3:61)

> [In our wandering artists' language, we often say, "to lead a bohemian lifestyle," to mean that we set off on the chances of a poor, laborious, and often guilty life, the life of Gypsies, that are also called Bohemians

in French. As for me, I didn't set out for that symbolic Bohemia that I
seemed destined for, like so many others, but for the unfortunate and
chivalrous land of the Czechs, for the land of Huss and Ziska, for the
Bœhmer Woods, in short for the castle of the Giants, where I was gener-
ously welcomed by the Rudolstadt family.]

The overlap of musical and narrative development can be seen in
this trope, where Bohemia is on the one hand a geographical, concrete, historical reality, exotic for the French reader. On the other
hand, the metaphoric Bohemia, already common currency in
France, represents an artistic community and philosophy. The
growth Consuelo experiences in her rediscovery of folk music and
nature, all contrary to her experiences in Venice, parallels the development of the plot as she moves—physically, emotionally, and musically—away from the baroque stage of Venice and toward the
unsophisticated music of Bohemia. An interruption in the return to
simplicity through a series of experiences on the professional stage
in Vienna will punctuate this trajectory, but she will return to the
simple, the true, the pure.[16]

Consuelo again assumes the role of teacher, as tutor to Amélie de
Rudolstadt, Albert's cousin and fiancée.[17] Amélie shows no musical
talent, which only heightens Consuelo's need to find musical fulfillment elsewhere. Since her musical exchanges with Albert do not
fall into the category of teacher-student relations, I reserve that discussion for later.

After leaving the Rudolstadt home, Consuelo gives music lessons
to Joseph Haydn. The fictional Haydn, like Consuelo, was brought
up around music but without any formal musical training.[18] This
makes him a good candidate for a student of music according to
Porpora's definition. In this section Sand insists on positive rein-
forcement as well as on teaching by example rather than by theory,
evincing Sand's devotion to a humanistic education as opposed to
an academic approach. Somewhat reminiscent of Rousseau's
Émile, the mix of formal and informal education recalls Sand's own
upbringing, combining a tutor and her grandmother's musical
teachings alongside the informal learning she garnered from Berrichon neighbors and friends, and which she never ceased to appreciate. Consuelo asks to see Haydn's compositions and finds them
promising, but she encourages him to try his hand at improvisation.
Depending on how well he performs this musical exercise, she will
know whether he has true talent or just a good memory: "Elle re-
marqua avec plaisir qu'il n'était pas savant, et qu'il y avait de la
jeunesse, de la fraîcheur et de la simplicité dans ses idées pre-

mières" [She was pleased to note that he was not learned, and that there was a youthfulness, a freshness, and a simplicity in his raw ideas] (*C*, 2:51). The positive use of the term "simplicité" alongside the negative use of "savant" underscores Sand's scorn for theoretical training, a prejudice she inherited from Rousseau, at the same time as it recalls Porpora's abhorrence of improper instruction that would have to be undone. Theory, according to Sand, remains sterile without the irreplaceable and practical training of a musical gift that is honed through imitation and repetition.

This is not to say that Consuelo, or Sand, disapproves of learning theory. Her training with Porpora included some theory, but as a descriptive explanation rather than a prescriptive guide. She assesses her appreciation of theory thus: "Malgré mes longues et sévères études de contre-point avec un aussi grand maître que le Porpora, ce que j'ai appris ne me sert qu'à bien comprendre les créations du génie, et je n'aurai plus le temps, quand même j'en aurais l'audace, de créer moi-même des œuvres de longue haleine" [Despite the long and difficult hours I spent studying counterpoint with a teacher of the likes of Porpora, what I learned allows me only to understand creations of genius. And I no longer have the time, even if I had the audacity, to create long drawn-out works of my own] (*C*, 2:50). When Consuelo is later incarcerated in Spandau, she will have the time and will compose original music. Similarly, at the end of the novel in her wanderings with Albert and their children, she will compose. Nevertheless, it is her ear training and not her theoretical training that guides her in matters of composition as well as interpretation.

Sand's use of "audace" here suggests the perceived inappropriateness of Consuelo's composing, presumably because she is a woman. That she does compose later in the narrative, which is to say later in her musical, emotional, and psychological development, clarifies an aspect of Sand's statement of feminism. The contrast between the inexperienced Haydn, whose composition activity seems expected, and the well-versed and professional Consuelo, who dares not compose, is exacerbated by gender conventions. Sand thus prepares her reader's expectations for a shift later in the narrative.

Teacher-student relations surface in another passage of *Consuelo* through the parody of a music lesson with Count Hoditz. A kind but fatuous gentleman, Hoditz fancies himself a connoisseur of music and he mounts operas with his own orchestra. He proposes to employ Bertoni and Beppo (the pseudonyms Consuelo and Haydn respectively take on during their journey to Vienna) after a musical examination, to which he will subject only Consuelo. Though they realize the limitations of Hoditz's musical knowledge, they also recognize that a little flattery will earn them a hot meal and a night's lodgings.

Hoditz's exam consists in instructing Consuelo on how to produce a trill properly. Consuelo eggs him on, purposely stumbling over the ornament Hoditz illustrates for her. After mocking his methods for a quarter of an hour, Consuelo grows tired of the charade and produces the trill expertly. Hoditz is delighted at his ace pedagogy. While Hoditz does not perceive her mockery, he does recognize her true gender despite her masculine pseudonym and dress. The narrator invites the reader to share a privileged position among the musical elite by creating a vantage point from which to denigrate the musically limited autodidact representative of the many dilettanti in Sand's Paris.[19] The situation has a dual effect on the reader, who wishes to be included in the group of the musically informed but at the same time is aware of the possible condescension.

This parodic scene admirably displays Consuelo's training in and preference for simplicity. She refuses to take Hoditz's ideas on ornamentation seriously. The suitable role of the teacher is an important element of this scene. The teacher can command respect and thereby be successful, according to Sand, only when there is respect for and awareness of the student. This is not the case with Hoditz. In a parallel scene much later in the novel, when Haydn and Consuelo arrive in Vienna, Haydn feigns ignorance in music so that Porpora will take him on as a student. He is soon able to profit from Porpora's teaching, learning as much about pedagogy as about musical composition and execution. No details of Porpora's singing method are given, but Sand contrasts his pedagogy with the heavy and intellectual habits of contemporary German masters.[20] Her ironic treatment of German musicians, no less biting that her comments on French musical taste, are indicative of an overriding criticism of academic music and musical training that, according to Sand, tends to squelch native talent and inspiration. Moreover, the current debate in Sand's Paris over the relative value of German and Italian music is not really so far removed from the *Querelle des Bouffons* (the debate over the relative merit of French or Italian music in the early 1750s) or the battle between Gluckists and Piccinnists (the debate over the relative significance of German or Italian music in the 1760s) that riled mid-eighteenth-century Parisian audiences about the same time as the narrative action of *Consuelo*.[21]

Consuelo's musical experience and production takes another turn in the desolation of Spandau prison, where Frederick II has incarcerated her, ostensibly because she refused his advances but more likely because he suspects her of revolutionary intrigue. Her harpsichord and music have been brought to her, and she plays every day. In actual fact, it is at night that she most enjoys her music:

> Ses soirées, si redoutables d'abord, étaient devenues ses heures les plus agréables; et les ténèbres, loin de lui causer l'effroi qu'elle en attendait, lui révélèrent des trésors de conception musicale, qu'elle portait en elle depuis longtemps sans avoir pu en faire usage et les formuler, dans l'agitation de sa profession de virtuose. (*CR*, 3:146)

> [Her evenings, at first so dreadful, had become her favorite time of day; and the shadows, far from causing her the sort of terror she expected, revealed treasures of musical conception, which she had carried inside herself for a long time without being able to use or formulate them in the turbulence of her profession as a virtuoso.]

Creative impulse springs from the depths of Consuelo's soul, just as her musical expression surfaces from the darkness of the unlit cell at night. This romantic nod to the symbolic wealth to be found in darkness paves the way for the symbolism of light when, in the absence of any ink, she pricks holes in a piece of scored paper: when the light shines through the holes they will appear as musical notes. This illuminated musical writing—not to say a nineteenth-century version of an illuminated manuscript—symbolizes Consuelo's enlightenment in a context of physical, political, and spiritual darkness. Her enrichment is twofold, since she recognizes in music a source of calm amid political and personal turmoil, and at the same time she discovers her capacity for composition. It is important to remark that Consuelo has always felt she had the capacity to compose, but her professional responsibilities prevented her from developing that talent or even perhaps from realizing she had it. But the musical inventions are only as good as Consuelo's ability to seize and manipulate them with the trained and applied knowledge of the complete musician.

Finally, all Consuelo's musical training culminates in her role as Albert's interpreter at the end of *La Comtesse de Rudolstadt*. In the last thirty pages of the novel, she composes and plays the guitar. Even though she also articulates in verbal language what Albert expresses on the violin, the pastoral ballad that ends the novel, "La bonne déesse de la pauvreté," is ironically Consuelo's composition and Albert's lyrics. The panegyric extols the revelation that no man can destroy a muse's work if it speaks the truth. Consuelo is the incarnation of this goddess, this muse. The music she produces attests to the calm and individualistic nature of her musical training. It also bears witness to a life's devotion to musical expression and therefore to continual musical training. Her role will not die with her but will be reincarnated in others after her. The importance of poverty in the muse's role reflects Sand's devotion to "le peuple" and the need to reduce all acts of charity to a consideration of social progress through art.[22]

Les Maîtres Sonneurs

In contrast to the patchwork presentation of Consuelo's musical instruction, the description of Joset's training takes up a large part of *Les Maîtres Sonneurs*. Joset's early musical experiences include learning to sing by listening to his cousin, Brulette, and later teaching himself to play the reed flute and finally perfecting the bagpipes. Because of his social awkwardness, which manifests itself in a lack of communication skills, Joset wants to learn to express himself through music, and since he cannot sing, he turns to instrumental music. Joset's "formal" training begins when he leaves Berry to seek instruction on the bagpipes in the neighboring province of Bourbonnais.

Joset's training in Bourbonnais with Père Bastien represents a large portion of the novel (twelve of a total of thirty-two chapters, or more than a third of the novel). Just as for Consuelo, Joset's training never really ends as he continues to listen and learn. Throughout the novel Père Bastien watches and helps Joset grow as a musician while he himself lives vicariously through the younger bagpiper's creative and itinerant activity. He reveals in the last chapter that he shares Joset's love of performance and the conditions of the wandering musician: "Je vas musiquer un peu par les chemins avec Joseph, car il a besoin de cela, et moi, il y a trente ans que j'en jeûne" [I'm gonna make a little music on the road with Joseph, because he needs it, and I've deprived myself of it for thirty years].[23] The joy of seeing one's student progress and develop renews the teacher's own love of the art form and performance. Père Bastien's selfless devotion to Joset has rekindled his own love of bagpiping, which he left behind for the sake of his wife and the need for a stable, stationary life. Different from Porpora, whose own professional goals and the attempt to capitalize on Consuelo's burgeoning success in order to reestablish himself dominate his life and allow him less time and energy to devote to his students, Père

Bastien demonstrates the spiritual renewal teaching and music can provide.

Père Bastien offers the example of a conscientious and sensitive teacher. He tries to take Joset through the stages of training at a rhythm commensurate with his physical and musical capacities. Overzealous and eager to accede to a musical language he feels within him, Joset precipitates the process and falls ill. Despite the delay and clear risk to his health, he manages to get back on track and continue his apprenticeship. In his training with Père Bastien, Joset develops from a weak-lunged amateur to an accomplished bagpiper, the rival of the best pipers in the region. Moreover, he progresses quickly from a piper capable of reproducing the traditional tunes and improvisations of Berry and Bourbonnais to a more individualistic musician, more interested in creating his own improvisations than in endlessly repeating the received tunes of past generations. This creative impulse sets him apart from the other bagpipers, both Berrichon and Bourbonnais, and introduces a discussion of originality, memory, and the creative process.[24]

Bastien's dedication to teaching Joset remains foremost in his mind as he assesses his pupil's readiness to go off into the musical world. He has shared his stock of tunes with him, but he also senses Joset's need to invent new ones. "Je ne t'ai pas épargné la provision que j'ai dans la tête, et ce que tu auras retenu, tu t'en serviras s'il te plaît; mais, comme ton vouloir est de composer, tu ne peux mieux faire que de voyager un jour ou l'autre, pour tirer la comparaison de ton fonds avec celui d'autrui" [I haven't kept from you the reserve of tunes I have in my head, and you should feel free to use them if you wish. But as you are bent on composing, you can do no better than to travel one day or another to compare your own bank of tunes with other people's] (*MS*, 292–93). But what Père Bastien praises most, and what he encourages Joset to continue to develop, is the desire to go beyond the standard repertory of itinerant musicians' songs and to invent new tunes. This for him is the sign of an inspired musician, and it is in these terms he will compare Joset to his own son, who, although an excellent bagpiper, does not have the gift for original composition:

Mon fils Huriel a de l'esprit et du talent. Il a été reçu maître sonneur à dix-huit ans, et encore qu'il n'en fasse pas le métier, il en a la connaissance et la facilité; mais il y a une grande différence entre ceux qui retiennent et ceux qui inventent: il y a ceux qui, avec des doigts légers et une mémoire juste, disent agréablement ce qu'on leur a enseigné; mais il y a ceux qui ne se contentent d'aucune leçon et vont devant eux, cherchant des idées, et faisant, à tous les musiciens à venir, le cadeau de leurs trouvailles. . . . [Joset] sera un vrai maître sonneur des anciens temps, un de ceux que les plus forts écoutent avec attention et qui commandent des changements à la coutume. (*MS*, 389)

[My son Huriel has ideas and talent. He gained the rank of master piper at the age of eighteen; and even though he doesn't exercise the profession, he's knowledgeable about it and it's easy for him. But there's an enormous difference between those who can remember and those who can create: there are those who, with light fingers and a keen memory, recount what they've learned; but there are those who aren't satisfied with these lessons and go further, seeking ideas and making a gift of their discoveries for all musicians after them. . . . [Joset] will be a true master piper of yore, one of those whom the strongest listen to attentively and who command changes in tradition.]

According to Sand, inspiration cannot be taught; it is this gift that defines the true artist. Joset is capable of changing tradition and perhaps the world. Bastien's predictions for Joset's musical career not only acclaim his creativity but also exalt the forward movement of his composition. Future generations will profit from Joset's inventions, he says. Art promises to solve society's ills as it renews itself in the spirit of ancient times, thus moving at once backwards and forwards.

My term "formal training" requires a brief explanation. Consuelo's musical education at the Mendicanti school recalls the formal structure of the Paris Conservatoire. Joset's training, on the other hand, has nothing of that structure; Sand offers it in tacit contrast to the venerated institution of the Academy. Yet, Joset's training also stands in contrast to that of the other pipers, all who learned from their fathers. Sand's message on formal training is not so much contradictory as it is measured, minimizing the value of the Conservatoire and other such institutions, while at the same time prescribing the importance of formalized and coherent instruction.[25]

Marie-Paule Rambeau points out that several of Sand's male musicians are not formally trained: Carl ("Carl"), Stephen (*La Filleule*), and Albénib (*La Filleule*). Even Adriani (*Adriani*), she maintains, presents himself as a "musicien né."[26] While I take exception to Rambeau's discussion of Adriani here, another instance where the lack of formal training holds significance in *Adriani* does interest me. When Adriani hears Laure singing, he marvels at the simple beauty of her voice: "La plupart des cantatrices de profession sacrifient l'accent et la pensée aux tours de force, et, dans les salons de Paris ou de la province, la jeune fille ou la belle dame qui a su acquérir la roulade à force d'exercice éblouit l'auditoire en écrasant du coup la timide romance de pensionnaire" [Most professional singers sacrifice tone and thought for brilliance, and in Parisian or provincial salons, the girl or the beautiful lady who after much practice is able to succeed in producing a roulade blinds the audience while squashing the schoolgirl's cautious ballad].[27] Sand makes a plea for simplicity here, but also she adds a commentary on the state of training and the detriment it can have on native talent. Adriani has left the Capital and his profession because of a lack of sincerity on the part of the public in regards to art and performance. In Laure he rediscovers his natural love for music and musicality. Sand gives the inverse commentary on the qualities of Portia's voice ("Histoire du rêveur"), where the narrator assumes the singer is a peasant even though the voice demonstrates too well the discipline of a trained singer. *Teverino* offers a further example.

TRAVEL AND MUSIC

Another aspect of the musician's apprenticeship that Sand exploits in *Consuelo* and *Les Maîtres Sonneurs* is travel. Both Consuelo and Joset incorporate travel into their education in various ways and with varying results, revealing another insight into Sand's musical and narratological universe. Since antiquity travel has functioned in literature as a metaphor for life. And through the representation of travel, the reader strives to experience vicariously the growth of the protagonist. The significance of the metaphor lies in the route, not the destination. Sand writes that "l'art de voyager, c'est presque la science de la vie" [the art of traveling is almost the science of life].[28] Sand views travel and music as facilitators of self-awareness. Though she rarely traveled very far off the beaten path between Nohant and Paris, especially when compared with other contemporary French authors who ventured to the Near East and North Africa, George Sand nevertheless incorporated a flavor of wanderlust into her writing. From her early *Voyage en Espagne* and the more revealing *Voyage en Auvergne* (both written in 1829) through her late *Contes d'une grand-mère* (1873–76), travel figures as an important element in the Sandian universe.[29]

Romantic authors continued the late-eighteenth-century predilection for the travelogue as a vehicle for self-awareness. The romantics' view of music as a path to the human soul and as an interpreter of human emotions prompts the hypothesis that music is a guide and a facilitator of human growth. Sand's characters grow musically and personally through their travels.[30] Such growth creates a unifying intersection of the musical and psychological aspects of her narratives. It must also be remembered that novelistic travel as a narrative device moves the characters from one place to another, advancing the plot. Thus what we might call musical travel combines musical, psychological, and narratological elements of the text.

Consuelo and La Comtesse de Rudolstadt

Wandering throughout Europe with her mother, Consuelo learns not only a sense of practicality but also a wealth of folk songs from different regions and a respect for folk music. When she and her mother arrive in Venice, Consuelo is afforded a more intense musical experience. It is interesting that the stay in Venice also occasions Consuelo's introduction to academic music. There is a link between growth in academic music, a form that will be virtually disenfranchised by the end of the novel, and the absence of travel in the Venetian passage. This connection becomes obvious only after the heroine again begins her travels, this time as a series of escapes.

After the disappointment of Anzoleto's infidelity, Consuelo sets off in search of a change in several areas of her life. In addition, the challenge of a profession on the stage pits her love of music against moral questions that involve both her received ideas about the theater and her reaction to Anzoleto's behavior. She needs isolation to sort out whether the void she feels is Anzoleto's absence or an absence of love in general, as well as to determine her own feelings about the profession of musical performance. The move to Riesenberg represents at once a musical, psychological, and narrative advance in the novel.

While at Riesenberg, Consuelo learns about Bohemian folk music. Amélie de Rudolstadt instructs Consuelo in the history of the family and of the region, but she has little patience for local music or musicians. She translates one of Zdenko's songs for Consuelo, but has no appreciation for its musical worth. Even the quality of his voice fails to impress her: "Zdenko a eu, dit-on, une fort belle voix, mais il l'a épuisée à parler, à chanter et à rire" [They say that Zdenko once had a beautiful voice, but he wore it out by talking, singing, and laughing] (C, 1:282). Consuelo reacts quite differently to his voice: "Tout éteinte qu'elle est, elle me fait plus d'impression que celle des plus grands chanteurs" [As worn out as it is, it impresses me more than the voices of great singers] (*C*, 1:284). The discovery of Bohemian folk music revives Consuelo's own gypsy origins and an appreciation for the beauty of untrained voices. An epistemological awareness surfaces from the links between music and travel that Consuelo begins to recognize but will not fully assimilate and develop until the end of the novel.

Another journey Consuelo makes while in Bohemia, different in nature from the conventional sense of travel, takes her one step closer to understanding Albert and herself through music. Consuelo follows Albert, whose frequent and lengthy disappearances intrigue her, to a well below a rock named *Schreckenstein* (stone of fright), so called because it was an important site in the fifteenth-century Hussite uprising. When the water in the well recedes, revealing a stairway, Consuelo descends and comes to a series of three doors for which she has the keys. Consuelo enters what appears to be Albert's room, where she finds ancient music books with titles and lyrics in a Slavic language she cannot decipher. Then she hears the tones of a Stradivarius playing a melody unknown to her: "Jamais Consuelo n'avait entendu un violon si parfait, un virtuose si touchant et si simple" [Never had Consuelo heard such a perfect violin, such a moving and simple virtuoso] (*C*, 1:327). For Sand, modest and uncomplicated music is the only adequate medium of divine beauty and communication. And Albert's ability to communicate through simple music makes him Consuelo's exemplar of divine communication, just as the violin and the virtuoso are equated in this quote. Romantic concepts, yes, but also a Lerouican religious discourse. A second visit to the grotto after Anzoleto unexpectedly shows up at Riesenburg provides the opportunity for Albert to discuss theology and his notions on Calvinism, Lutheranism, Hussitism, Taboritism, the Eucharist, and Satan. Albert plays the same antique psalm that had mesmerized Consuelo before. Here the mystical nature of music in Consuelo and Albert's relationship becomes apparent.

Vertical travel rather than horizontal, and seemingly outside the boundaries of time, this journey typifies the metaphorical death and descent into hell of the traditional initiation rite. Drawn by her concern for Albert's well-being, Consuelo willingly faces certain danger, hoping to discover an answer to his apparent madness. She experiences a musical awakening that shatters her whole being, opens her eyes to Albert's pureness, and throws everything she has known into turmoil and question. At the culmination of the first descent into the grotto, Albert makes a declaration of love and a proposal of marriage, which Consuelo tries to parlay into a fraternal friendship. Frightened by the degree of Albert's attachment to her, Consuelo decides to flee. She fully realizes the position of Albert's family toward her because of her career on the stage. Their difference in social rank, evinced through music, is a typical Sandian element in the struggle for social equality. At Riesenburg, as before in Venice, she finds herself in the midst of a personal relationship that has progressed to an unanticipated state that she cannot cope with, and her solution is to leave.

Consuelo's departure from Riesenburg differs from her leaving Venice, however, since in addition to a need to escape she also experiences an ardent thirst for musical stimulation. Despite her renewed delight in traditional music, she realizes that she misses the music of her professional training. Remembering her mother's words, she admits that "ce bien-être c'était la contrainte, et ce repos, l'ennui, mortel aux âmes d'artiste. . . . Et . . . la contrainte m'y étouffe, et l'ennui m'y consume" [this well-being was constraining, and this peace was boring, which is mortal to an artist's soul. . . . And . . . constraint stifles me and boredom consumes me] (C, 1:393). She will seek out Porpora, who should be settled in Vienna by now, and take up her formal musical training again. She also feels an acute need for solitude to sort out her feelings about Albert and Anzoleto. The need to be alone is not unrelated to her need for autonomy, essential to artistic development, "ce besoin souverain et légitime, véritable condition du progrès et du développement chez l'artiste supérieur" [that sovereign and legitimate need, the unexaggerated condition of the superior artist for progress and development] (C, 1:393). This concatenation of romantic ethos, reminiscent of Madame de Staël's Corinne, reveals not only Sand's definition of the female artist, but also the tight weave of music and narrative.[31]

Consuelo's personal problems are not unrelated to her musical desires, since music is Consuelo's sole vehicle and outlet for passion. The passion Albert arouses in Consuelo does not equal that which Anzoleto inspires. Thus the need to travel, to escape, and to find solutions and gratification combine to make the trip to Vienna a personal quest where music provides both a substitute for passion and the means for sorting out her confusion. As she says later to Princess Amélie, "je regrettais ma profession, ma liberté, mon vieux maître, ma vie d'artiste, et cette arène émouvante du théâtre, où j'avais paru un instant pour briller et disparaître comme un météore" [I missed my profession, my freedom, my old teacher, my artist's life, and that touching arena that is the theater, where I had appeared for a moment only to shine and disappear like a meteor]

(*CR*, 3:65). Consuelo is determined to continue her musical training and to investigate further her vocation for a career on the stage. Her voyage from Bohemia to Vienna to rejoin her mentor represents the traditional travel quest of a hero in search of experience, training, and growth.

During her trip Consuelo encounters someone else looking for stability and a future in music: Joseph Haydn. The journey on foot with Haydn from Bœhmerwald to Vienna constitutes one of the most intriguing segments of *Consuelo* from the perspective of historical fiction as well as musical metaphors. Consuelo's musicianship and her devotion to a musical profession crystalize on several levels. First, her reputation has apparently spread throughout Europe since Haydn knows of her triumph. Second, Consuelo represents the consummate musician for Haydn, and she effectively assumes the role of his teacher, a more satisfying role than that of Amélie's tutor. Third, Consuelo becomes musically and psychologically more confident, and thus more aware of the importance of understanding and defining her own desires.

Haydn also profits from the trip to Vienna. He has set out to seek Porpora, and Porporina (tradition holds that a gifted student take a diminutive form of her or his mentor's name) falls onto his path like a godsend. He approaches her cautiously since her reputation and talent intimidate him, but also because his attraction to her makes him shy. She responds guardedly at first, then with increased confidence, seemingly unaware of his attraction to her. By the time they arrive in Vienna, Haydn has grown musically thanks to the lessons in composition and improvisation, voice, and Italian Consuelo gives him. Morally, he has learned to respect Consuelo's desires as well as her decision-making prowess, her ability to understand a situation and to act in their best interests.[32]

It is interesting to note here a significant and metaphoric overlap in musical and narrative development. Lessons in counterpoint parallel Consuelo's and Haydn's journey. The juxtaposition or the superimposition of two different but similar journeys, both moving in the same direction at different rates and having started at different places and points in time, destined to arrive harmoniously at the same destination at the same time and in similar circumstances, underscores the similarity of goal and technique that links the two musicians. Yet at the same time the contrary motion of their careers—one starts with practically no training and becomes a performing artist while the other comes from a musical background and turns to composition—allows for a depth and richness common to counterpoint. And throughout all this journey, Consuelo and Haydn discuss the famous exercises in Fux's book of counterpoint.

It is also not insignificant that the novel ends with travel. Consuelo, Albert, and their children wander around Bohemia preaching the promise of freedom and change, not so subtly predicting the French Revolution. Throughout the travels of the "perfect couple" and their children, music remains the principal means of communication. Thus music and travel continue to be linked. And as travel is a metaphor for life and music, the two are inextricably bound in the narrative. A secondary journey in the epilogue, that of Spartacus and Philon, accentuates this one. They search for Albert to tell them the secrets of the universe and will continue the geographical and spiritual journey of their mentor. A feeling of movement pervades the end of the novel, suggesting constant travel and an unending need to spread "the word."

In all instances of travel in *Consuelo* and *La Comtesse de Rudolstadt*, musical and moral growth combine to create an atmosphere of progress. Just as for Goethe's Wilhelm Meister, many of Consuelo's travels are occasioned by her profession. Thus musical and psychological growth coincide. A musician must travel to maintain her or his reputation, and the inevitable growth in matters both musical and personal comes naturally. Liszt and Viardot provided Sand with eminent examples of such professional travel even if Chopin did not. The combination of music and travel with the Bildungsroman, where travel is a standard device, provides a rich groundwork for the plot. The narrative progression advances quite naturally from the forward-moving tendencies inherent in travel and narrative linearity, all the while advancing the musical and emotional development of the characters.

Les Maîtres Sonneurs

In *Les Maîtres Sonneurs* travel also represents an important part of Joset's personal and musical growth. At the same time, however, it underscores the irony of his failure to mature. This in itself is a metaphor of his steady movement away from constancy. Joset's desire to leave familiar territory in order to learn better bagpiping techniques represents just as much a need to abandon a society where he does not fit in and where he does not want to fit in as it does a need to acquire a means of expression. Travel manifests a search for identity as well as a quest for the perfect music. In one way he succeeds, for he gains a confidence far beyond what he or anyone in Berry imagined possible. But despite the travel to master a musical expression, his search for Brulette's love remains a bitter failure.

That Joset travels to Bourbonnais to learn more sophisticated piping and musical techniques presents an interesting slant on the travel motif. Travel for peasants in the late eighteenth century[33] was a departure from the norm and thus the mark of an outsider or someone who endeavors to be an outsider. In many ways, Joset's pursuit of well-crafted bagpiping skills is an effort to be(come) different. He has always been different, although in a negative way because of his apparent slow-wittedness and his inability to express himself in verbal language. If he can acquire a superior language, not only superior to those who speak only a verbal language but also superior to those who speak a mediocre musical language, then he will have achieved a satisfying otherness as well as being able to please Brulette, he thinks. Since striving for superiority is often a sign of psychological otherness, the exoticism Joset seeks in travel results in a detrimental ostracism from both Brulette and music. The multiple complications of his separation provide a narrative network that traverses musical and moral developments.

The fatigue of travel complicates Joset's weak lungs, making him sick. The metaphor of sickness for overzealousness, very close to superciliousness, allows Joset to revert momentarily to the object of everyone's attentions. However, travel does eventually afford him an invaluable musical development. While Joset does overcome his physical impediment and improves his bagpiping techniques, his overconfidence undoes all the benefits of travel and training. Ironically, travel has led Joset to heightened musicality but at the same time alienated him from his ultimate goals: Brulette's love and the respect of the musical community.

This novel, too, ends with travel. After the double wedding, which formally excludes Joset from any amorous relationship, he and Père Bastien set off to travel and pipe together. For Bastien the departure represents a chance to regain a taste of the excitement of his youth. For Joset, the trip represents a different sort of journey, one far away from the disappointment for which he saw no other escape. He knows when he leaves the wedding party that he will not return. His final voyage again mixes his emotional life with music since he destroys his bagpipes, his most valuable possession, as he commits suicide.

Adriani and *Le Château des Désertes* also demonstrate the importance of travel in the process of self-discovery and musical development. Adriani leaves Paris, his profession, and his public to return to Rousseauian solitude in the countryside. He seeks separation and renewal with no thought of returning to the stage or his Parisian public. It is in the country that he learns to love, a discovery that represents an additional benefit for his musical expression. Célio, in *Le Château des Désertes*, leaves Vienna after an unsuccessful debut. He travels far from the musical center to the countryside near Briançon, where he learns, in quasi-seclusion and through assiduous training, that it is not his sole performance that counts. Rather, the relationship among all the characters on stage must be viewed as an organic structure in which he is but a single element.

In both instances movement from an urban cultural center to the countryside offers the protagonists an opportunity for renewal and maturation. Such an idyllic metaphor is not uncommon in the romantic novel, but Sand's innovation superimposes this romantic ethos on a profession that thrives in the city. It is fitting, therefore, that both heroes should return successfully to their respective capitals with a heightened appreciation for both their art and their personal relationships. In both cases travel represents less a metaphor for discovery than a flight from the ills of society toward the beneficence of nature and the value of self-awareness before being able to express emotions honestly to the public.[34]

It is clear now that the musical advancement of Sand's protagonists parallels their moral and psychological development. The evolution of a character in a novel, as she or he undergoes a series of trials and experiences, generates a heightened sense of self and confidence. The Bildungsroman furnishes the appropriate form to display the interplay of growth and musical experience. As it enhances the narrative progression in these novels, the Bildungsroman structure illuminates another aspect of Sand's use of music in prose fiction.

MUSICAL BILDUNGSROMAN

The Bildungsroman gained currency in France with the translation of Goethe's *Wilhelm Meisters Lehrjahre,* translated as *Les Années d'apprentissage de Wilhelm Meister* in 1802. As defined by the early nineteenth-century German critic Karl Morgenstern, the Bildungsroman "will justly bear [its] name firstly and primarily on account of its thematic material, because it portrays the *Bildung* of the hero in its beginnings and growth to a certain stage of completeness; and also secondly because it is by virtue of this portrayal that it furthers the reader's *Bildung* to a much greater extent than any other kind of novel."

The emphasis placed on reader reception in this definition springs largely from the concept of the novel as a teaching and moralizing tool. Morgenstern's definition places more importance on the structural and moral progress of the novel than on the character of the hero, interpreting the genre in largely didactic terms without any significant notion of individualism of style, character, or context. Goethe does portray an individual in a particular context, a character who, while perhaps not unique in characterization, does present a specific moral and psychological makeup. Wilhelm Dilthey's commentary on the genre a century later provides further considerations. "A regulated development within the life of the individual is observed, each of its stages has its own intrinsic value and is at the same time the basis for a higher stage. The dissonances and conflicts of life appear as the necessary growth points through which the individual must pass on his way to maturity and harmony."[35]

In addition to the heightened focus on the individual, Dilthey places attention on progress in development. Of primary importance here is a young hero who learns, through a series of experiences, to function effectively in society, a concept dear to Sand's socialist heart. The hero's training occupies center stage and provides the structure around which the rest of the novel is built. The word *Bildung* applies to both psychological development and to apprenticeship in a trade. The name of Goethe's title character suggests that he will become a "master" of his trade by the end of the novel, *Meister* being the last and highest stage of skilled training in the medieval guild system. While Goethe's hero does not, in fact, achieve this rank or degree of expertise, which underscores the ironic tone of the novel, nonetheless the proposition remains central to the genre. In *Consuelo* the heroine becomes a master of her art through rigor and training. Indeed, she surpasses the degree of mastery and moves on to more socialist concerns. In *Les Maîtres Sonneurs*—and here the term "master" reappears in the title—the hero will attain master status in the very real sense of the pseudo-guild system despite the ahistoricity of the context.[36] Both characters respond to the notion of superiority in radically divergent ways. Consuelo's musical mastery does not satisfy her desires, so she moves on to the socialist goals that Sand valued so much in the 1840s. Joset also achieves mastery, but as this does not satisfy his ultimate desire, he ends his life, the antithesis of Consuelo's idealism.

Sand's conception of idealism is a necessary part of any discussion of aesthetics. She inherits many of her ideas from German thinkers through Madame de Staël and Pierre Leroux. Yet, in this pre-1848 climate of socialism, idealism moves away from its abstract German origins and takes on an aspect of hopeful practicality. The sincere belief that an ideal can be achieved through education and honest work remains one of the staples of Sand's fiction, and this is most evident in her musical novels. Naomi Schor points out that Sand manages to restore the feminine in idealism as a viable representational mode.[37] This comment is especially true in the case of *Consuelo*.

In *Les Maîtres Sonneurs* Sand examines the place of idealism for a male hero whose arrogance gets in the way of reaching his ideal. That this novel is written after the disappointment of 1848 colors Sand's idealism, which in part explains this confusing combination of irony and idealism. The example of *Les Maîtres Sonneurs* does not support Schor's view that Sand's post-1848 idealism is more aligned with "the impotent and marginal position traditionally identified with femininity . . . more consoling than mobilizing, more regressive than progressive."[38] On the contrary, the idealism Sand presents in this novel does not suggest a utopia but encourages progress nonetheless. Sand's reflection is surely a reaction to the overconfident undertakings of her socialist colleagues in the period between February and June 1848. These two novels together permit an invaluable observation of Sand's philosophy of aesthetics and socialism, for here Sand presents both a positive and a negative manifestation of aesthetic idealism viewed through an ontological lens. The Bildungsroman provides her with the structure and themes necessary to analyze idealism as she sees it functioning in the artistic community.

Not only does the Bildungsroman genre lend itself perfectly to Sand's exposé of the musician, it also allows her to exploit her musical novels as a locus for working out her own aesthetics. A novel that closely studies an artist's development is typically termed a *Künstlerroman*, subsumed under the larger genre of the Bildungsroman. As in Tieck's *Franz Sternbalds Wanderungen*, or Novalis's *Heinrich von Ofterdingen*, or Proust's *À la recherche du temps perdu*, or Gide's *Les Faux-monnayeurs*, or Mann's *Tonio Kröger* and *Dr. Faustus*, or Joyce's *A Portrait of the Artist as a Young Man*, Sand's *Künstlerromane* represent the development of an artist into the stage of maturity where artistic destiny is recognized and mastery of craft is achieved.

Another important element of the Bildungsroman requires some attention, and here I refer to the *roman initiatique* (novel of initiation).[39] Sand's musicians not only train seriously and travel extensively in preparation for life, they also accede to a higher plane of understanding through art. And as this transcendental experience remains inexpressible in words, music serves to render it explicit. Music functions as the expression of the final stage of *Bildung*, completing the characters' initiation into a spiritual as well as a professional world.

Consuelo fulfills this model. Her visit to Albert's grotto and her meditations in the "château des *Invisibles*" provide the locus for her initiation and transcendence. Célio's and Adriani's maturations, though less spiritual than Consuelo's, undergo a similar process, as do Abel's (*Malgrétout*) and Jeanne's (*Ma Sœur Jeanne*). Joset's progression leads him to the threshold of transcendence, but he realizes he cannot step across and his initiation stalls there. Music provides these characters with a mode of expression just as ineffable as their transcendence.

Having moved rather quickly from a thematic to an ideological discussion of the genre, I would now like to comment on the structural elements that Sand exploits. As Martin Swales states, more modern analyses of the Bildungsroman have emphasized the self-reflective nature of the genre, the attention paid to the aesthetic, and narrative process. The problem with this approach, he continues, is that it tends to ignore the plot.[40] Swales posits a combined analysis that would account for both themes and aesthetics without sacrificing one or the other for the sake of an imposed sense of coherence that the genre does not necessarily convey. He further observes that writers of Bildungsromane, Goethe and Mann in particular, manipulate the reader's expectations, pretending to present a central character who will end up much better prepared for life and capable of facing important decisions, but who in fact represents a very human failing: the conflict between desire and experience. While life's lessons teach us certain ways of approaching problems, we do not always learn to set aside our own destructive desires. As we shall see, this is much more the case for Joset than for Consuelo, even though she is not exempt.

Sand uses the form and function of the Bildungsroman either wholly or partially in several of her texts, the most explicit examples being *Mauprat* and *Lettres à Marcie*, both published in 1837. But in *Consuelo* and *Les Maîtres Sonneurs* the Bildungsroman device stems logically from the protagonists' musical training, providing regular progression through the various stages of a career in the making. As Wilhelm Meister learns the ropes of the theater, albeit in a mediocre fashion, he also faces and resolves various issues in his own affective life. The German Bildungsroman crosses pragmatism with idealism. Sand's musical novels also mix music lessons with life lessons. Consuelo and Joset will encounter problems, and sometimes solutions, in their interpersonal relationships thanks to musical experiences. These problems seem on the surface to belong to the world of musical performance, but issues of jealousy, competition, arrogance, generosity, and altruism, which originate in their professional lives, also affect their personal lives and the lives of those around them. In both cases Sand creates a character who struggles with life, not just the life of a musician, but the quotidian problems of human existence. Herein lies Sand's innovation of the genre, for the solutions or attempts at solutions to such problems arise from the training and discipline Consuelo and Joset have received as musicians. As a result, the question of ontology surfaces. Both Consuelo and Joset wonder whether all their training is actually taking them in a productive direction. The answers are not clear, and it is even unsure, especially in the case of Joset, whether they find any solutions that benefit the reader.

The purposeful ambiguity of Sand's *Bildung* structure translates into a forced linearity. Both *Consuelo* and *Les Maîtres Sonneurs* are long novels (even though the former is almost three times as long as the latter), and both trace the central character's development.[41] Both Consuelo and Joset travel in pursuit of musical training at the same time as they run away from their problems. They leave their homes, encounter musical and personal experiences, grow in both domains, and end the novels having advanced as people and as musicians. Progress in musical training is essential to the sequential nature of Sand's Bildungsromane. It is important to note that unlike Goethe's hero, both of Sand's protagonists progress to a degree of mastery, establishing a clear direction and goal to the action.

Despite their thematic and structural similarities, *Consuelo* and *Les Maîtres Sonneurs* relay radically different lessons on the notion of development and maturity. Joset's progress comes to an abrupt halt, while Consuelo's continues beyond the close of the text. Consuelo learns her lessons better than Joset, for she moves into a calmer, happier phase of life. And yet, critics still disagree about the unity of the ending. But there is also critical ambiguity surrounding the ending of *Les Maîtres Sonneurs*, in that one wonders exactly what lesson, if any, Joset has learned. The reader of *Consuelo* is confident that hard work will lead to a better life, even if it means leaving the very profession that provided these lessons. The reader of *Les Maîtres Sonneurs* may wonder whether hard work might not also lead to bitter disappointment. Sand's lesson here, most likely colored by the disappointment of 1848 as well as her estrangement from Chopin, functions more as a cautionary tale than as a model. The reader is continually called upon to revise expectations. But never do the importance and power of musical training disappear. Thus development, progression, *Bildung*, training, and narrative combine with music to form Sand's musical version of the Bildungsroman.

Another element of the Bildungsroman structure that demands careful examination is the difference between the female *Bildung* in *Consuelo* and the male *Bildung*, especially in *Les Maîtres Sonneurs*. While I will discuss Sand's female musicians in chapter 6, their importance to the structure of the Bildungsroman genre demands a brief discussion here. As most recent studies of the female Bildungsroman have shown, the attempted replication of the male *Bildung* of the Wilhelm Meister type allows heroines to discover only the limitations of their developmental possibilities within the context of the social structure. Faced with such a negative realization, the heroine must choose between compromises: the relentless sublimation of her desires and aspirations, or the abandonment of those desires, usually resulting in suicide, as exemplified in the decisions of Emma Bovary and Edna Pontellier (Kate Chopin's *The Awakening*). Consuelo at once follows and deviates from this pattern, struggling with the options of compromise and abandonment of desire. Contrary to the examples Claire Marrone studies, in which she detects a distinction between male and female *Bildungen*, Consuelo does travel and does endure tests of courage.[42] This being said, she also experiences interpersonal relationships as an integral part of her growth and development, while totally eschewing "success in the domestic sphere."[43] This dilemma mirrors Sand's own feminist scramble to succeed within a male profession—all the while imposing a difference. Consuelo's devotion to music as an art form more than as a profession will have an essential bearing on her decisions. Herein lies Sand's contributions to the genre.[44]

Consuelo indeed begins the novel of her formation with an awakening caused by disappointment and disillusionment: Anzoleto's infidelity. Having allowed herself to believe that they would marry and form the perfect artist couple, Consuelo is jolted from this dream when she discovers that her own professional success has sparked Anzoleto's jealousy and betrayal. This series of events is occasioned by the vicissitudes of the musical profession, which advance the plot while providing ideal opportunities for psychological development. Without any professional aspirations, Consuelo flees Venice and her illusions of love. By leaving, she preserves at least the memory of her artistic dream, but at the same time she delays her entry into the world of secular musical performance. This departure affords her the time to meditate philosophical, aesthetic, and social transformation. That Consuelo is a woman enhances these possibilities in ways far subtler than a man's escape would have allowed.

Another of Sand's innovations of the Bildungsroman comes during Consuelo's initiation to the secret society of the *Invisibles,* in the role played by her confessor, Wanda. Consuelo has been encouraged to read the history and philosophy of the *Invisibles* and has been assigned a confessor. For the first several encounters, her confessor presents herself as a man, like the other initiators. On the morning of Consuelo's initiation, however, when the subject of her confession turns to commitment and divorce, the confessor reveals she is a woman and that she, too, married out of duty. She advises Consuelo not to let her sense of duty squelch her natural desires. Only now does Wanda reveal that she is Albert's mother and in the next three chapters she tells her story.

As Isabelle Naginski states, the confession of Consuelo to Wanda constitutes an important moment in the struggle between *savoir* (knowing) and *pouvoir* (being able).[45] One would be tempted to say she is not yet in a state of knowing since the identity of Liverani and Albert as one and the same will be revealed to her only the next day at her initiation ceremony. However, what she has learned is her capacity for love and desire. This she learns with Liverani (Albert's *Invisible* identity) in the romantically dangerous kidnapping-rescue and the subsequent nocturnal coach trip through Bohemia, not insignificantly just after an attempted rape. The difficult transition between *savoir* and *pouvoir* that Naginski discusses is represented by the period of reading and reflection in the chateau of the *Invisibles.* Curiously, music is all but absent during this period. Consuelo sings at the end only when she has decided to speak with the elders of the *Invisibles.* This turning point indicates she has advanced to a state of maturity in her political and emotional growth and is now ready to declare her freedom and independence.

Giving Consuelo a female spiritual guide upturns the traditional Free mason (and Catholic) structure of the *Invisibles.* And while it may seem that decisions of the heart remain the domain of women, Sand is careful to explain throughout this passage and to the end of the novel that in order for a woman to devote herself entirely to an ideal, be it political or aesthetic or both, she must be true to herself or else all future decisions and actions will be compromised. Suggesting that a woman's choice is always more difficult since her desires are traditionally subordinated to her duties and responsibilities, Sand begs the question of gender difference. Different but equal, Consuelo proves herself equipped with fortitude and decisiveness for the "masculine" tasks of study and contemplation. She may therefore proceed with the initiation.

This moral hurdle overcome, Consuelo is free to continue her development unfettered. The most striking event of her *Bildung*, leading to the conclusion of the novel, is the loss of her voice. The careful reader could have anticipated this twist as it does not come without warning. Several instances of laryngitis adumbrate the final loss of voice, which clearly represents a subconscious choice on Consuelo's part, neither a failure to commit herself nor a divine punishment. Here are the narrative circumstances: Consuelo receives word on the eve of a performance at the Vienna Italian theater that Liverani has been imprisoned in Prague for falsification of identity. When Consuelo asks Maria-Theresa for permission to miss a performance in order to go to her husband's side, the empress forbids it. She has already received word of Liverani's treacherous anti-Catholic and presumably anti-Austrian actions, and she pities Consuelo for being married to such a man. Consuelo's loss of voice is doubtless a manifestation of her subconscious desire to come to Albert's aid.[46]

The irony of Sand's bringing Consuelo through such rigorous musical training only to have her lose her voice requires a close examination. It is important not to read this event as the end of Consuelo's training. On the contrary, she will continue to exercise discipline in maintaining her musicianship. She may no longer aspire to a career on the stage, but her goals and ideals now form a new objective. Every detail from here to the end of the novel points to this turn of events as the only one possible for Consuelo. Her training and development have also led her in this direction, and the ending of the novel depends on this apparent peripeteia. Sand has taken the *Bildung* genre and rearranged it for her own purposes: moving the heroine beyond a simple story of training and professional success toward a goal of social progress. In *Consuelo* the movement toward ideals results irrefutably from musical training. This is Sand's essential innovation of the genre.

Nicole Mozet likens Consuelo's loss of voice to the indispensable condition of Sand's artist, which is to say an acceptance of her limits and a constant push toward those limits. "Renunciation of the desire for the impossible, the Sandian quest is an apprenticeship in human limitations. Like Consuelo, one must learn to sing with only a hoarse voice."[47] I agree with Mozet that Sand recognizes her limits. Her lifelong resolution to describe the musical experience without becoming frustrated at the impossibility of the task bears witness to this essential Sandian quality. However, the analogy of the hoarse voice (*voix cassée,* or "broken voice") leaves aside, on one hand, the significant detail that Consuelo's voice never lacked a superior quality; rather it remained a superb instrument whose apparent failure provided a solution, albeit a *deus ex machina,* in this time of need. On the other hand, if we read Mozet's analysis as applying the metaphor of the broken voice to Sand, she then also implies that Sand functioned with a flawed gift. Sand may have had doubts about her own artistry; her correspondence abounds with such uncertainty. Still, her acceptance of her limitations in no way restricted her abilities or her production. On the contrary, she embraced her limits and exploited them, thus discovering subtle intricacies of the human condition. Her own development becomes richer as she explores that of her (musical) characters.

Mozet underscores the truth of Porpora's prediction to Consuelo, that "le jour où tu te donneras à un mortel, tu perdras ta divinité" [the day you give yourself to a mortal, you'll lose your divinity] (*C,* 1:171). Paradoxically, in terms of Porpora's wishes, this is precisely the goal of the Sandian initiatory voyage, to lose divinity and to accept mortality and physicality and in turn sexuality.[48] For Mozet, Sand represents a liberating voice that refreshingly allows women to seek and find power and influence within a sexual and mortal existence.[49] Thus the goal of the artist is to accept one's limits—physical as well as moral, artistic as well as personal—in the neverending exploration of life. Such a sexually linked development could only be portrayed by a female protagonist.

Joset's development in *Les Maîtres Sonneurs* presents a still more complicated version of *Bildung.* He begins the novel an undeveloped and backward child. The stage is set to allow for substantial development. Joset's acquisition of knowledge and experience carries along with it, however, the suffering of a too-rapid discovery. Joset's musical development, like Consuelo's, parallels his moral development. But for Joset the former soon surpasses the latter and he remains unable to reconcile the two. His psychological development is stifled by his rapid and superior musical development, which leads to a haughtiness in music that he uses to compensate for his social and emotional awkwardness. The traditional Bildungsroman structure thus fails, as the hero does not successfully reach a state of maturity.

Joset's training, and therefore his *Bildung,* meets with an obstacle because he ignores Bastien's warnings about the lung power required for the larger Bourbonnais bagpipes. Such impatience is typical of Joset's frustration, clearly stemming from his early inability to communicate. This stands in stark contrast to his superior advancement in music as well as to Consuelo's reasonable progression. Halfway through the novel, Joset is restored to good health and is ready to advance in his training and *Bildung*. Joset's continued *Bildung* is thus anticipated, although the careful reader already senses failure.

The piping contest at the end of the novel, which determines that Joset will be given the rank of master piper, represents a complex network of desires, jealousies, and vengeance. It is an essential stage in Joset's *Bildung*. As opposed to Consuelo's initiation, and despite all appearances, music has little to do with Joset's contest and subsequently little to do with the deliberation and decision that follow. Joset is well aware of this, which fuels his already ripe lack of respect for the bagpipers' *confrérie* (brotherhood)].

The deliberations take place in the upper room of the inn. The religious connotations of the setting befit the mystical tenor of the ceremony. Theological analogies do not, however, go beyond this, in contrast to the highly religious staging of the initiation in *La Comtesse de Rudolstadt*. During the bagpipers' private deliberations, Joset becomes arrogant, as though his membership in the brotherhood were already assured, and he begins to vent his anti-brotherhood (read: antisocial) opinions, which come as much from his lifelong social exclusion as from Brulette's rejection. Carat, his rival, then counters by hurling the rumors that Charlot, the toddler who was mysteriously confided to Brulette's care, might be Joset's child.[50] Joset cannot tolerate the implications and, determined to settle the score, and agrees to an irregular initiation ceremony to prove himself.

The initiation takes place at midnight in the underground dungeon of an abandoned castle, approached through a cemetery. The Gothic atmosphere of the setting marries seamlessly with the traditional attributes of the initiation rite. The role of music in this ceremony is secondary but interesting. Once in the subterranean maze, Joset hears a constant drone of bagpipes reverberating against the stone walls of the caverns. The purpose of the musical din is to confuse the candidate and to elevate the level of his fear and anxiety. Such a superficial function of music underscores Joset's conviction that the brotherhood's appreciation of music does not portray a serious, artistic endeavor.

While the general guidelines of the traditional initiation rite are respected in both *Consuelo* and *Les Maîtres Sonneurs* (invitation and descent into hell; isolation and preparation; an induction ceremony), Consuelo's initiation comes to a fruitful conclusion and she becomes a productive member of the *Invisibles*. An interruption in the final stages of Joset's initiation disrupts the ceremony, and the results of the aborted initiation are inconclusive. Is Joset a true *maître sonneur*? Does he have the right to play in the designated areas of the *confrérie* that tested him? Will he be recognized by the other bagpipers? Consuelo's happy inclusion and worthwhile actions as a member of the *Invisibles* represent the inverse of Joset's unhappy and inconclusive initiation, which indirectly lead to his suicide.[51]

Suicide remained in 1853 a delicate subject. Sand has already seen her novel *Jacques* (1834) added to the Vatican Index because of the perceived exoneration of suicide. Several other commentaries on suicide surface in Sand's writing. While she describes an attempted suicide in *Indiana*, the despondency of the eponymous character of *Lélia* more explicitly portrays suicidal desire. She flirts with the idea again in 1862 with *Antonia* and 1866 with *Le Dernier Amour*. In *Lettres d'un voyageur* (1834–36) , especially letters 4 and 5, Sand writes that Germaine de Staël's *Réflexions sur le suicide* played a large role in her contemplations at that time. Sand states in this text that she will not commit suicide because of her children, and particularly because she lacks the courage.[52] Joset does not lack the courage, yet the resolution remains implicit and equivocal. Sand doubtless resisted making his suicide explicit for the sake of her readership and reputation. But the mystical cloud of possibilities in a rustic novel filled with evocations of the devil offers a fittingly obfuscated ending and at the same time avoids censorship. Nevertheless, there is no doubt that Joset committed suicide.

It is here that Joset's development parallels that of the traditional female *Bildung* protagonist. He first experiences difficulty in identifying his desire. When he discovers he loves Brulette, he determines to exploit music, which has already proven a special and private link between them. Throughout the training period, he sublimates his desire for Brulette, making music a servant to his love. Ironically, this is the attitude he disdains among the members of the bagpiping brotherhood, using music for a nonartistic purpose. When at the end he discovers he cannot have Brulette's love, and consequently that he has been using music as a mediation rather than for its own sake, he abandons all hope, which satisfies Cellier's definition of a failed initiation.[53] Symbolic of his disgust with his own treatment of music, he destroys his precious bagpipes. And finding no one else to blame for his disappointment in love and music, he takes his own life.

Suicide, then, remains a logical solution, a way out of a situation that would require compromise and sublimation of desire. Edna Pontellier and many others arrive at the same conclusion. If Sand ascribes a similar solution to a male hero, it is perhaps to demonstrate the very real instance of male suicide, a fact often neglected in portrayals of the nineteenth century.[54] The important difference between Edna and Joset is that Kate Chopin's heroine comes to her decision after thoughtful reflection. Joset, on the other hand, has not reached the stage of maturity that the Bildungsroman leads the reader to expect. Sand transposes and superimposes the traditional female Bildungsroman onto a male protagonist. Conversely, in *Consuelo* the success of the traditionally male Bildungsroman enjoys an appropriate application to a female protagonist. Sand has reversed the conventional gender markings of the genre.

While Sand was surely influenced by E. T. A. Hoffmann and Goethe in her amalgamation of musical narrative and Bildungsroman, she brings her own innovation to the genre by adding the initiation rite, reminiscent of the entry rites of the medieval guild system as well as that of secret societies.[55] In both *Consuelo* and *Les Maîtres Sonneurs* the procedure of initiation represents the culminating moment for both protagonists in their professional and personal lives, the instant when they must define their desires once and for all. In each case, the hero's musical and moral development has reached a decisive point, and the hero must verify her or his valor and fitness. In the case of Consuelo, the spiritual trial surpasses the aesthetic one, just as her gifts surpass those of artistic performance. In the case of Joset, his trial also transcends the realm of the aesthetic, yet the lesson he learns remains without a doubt wholly in the spiritual domain, eclipsing the aesthetic. Sand's innovation of the Bildungsroman comprises an additional twist in the switching of the conventional male and female *Bildung* endings. This is an illuminating example of Sand's feminism, of her desire to put a woman to an aesthetic and spiritual trial where she comes out victorious, strong, unadulterated, and successful on all counts.

Sand's message about the spirituality of music is clear. If she stages a trial for musicians that incorporates musical and spiritual elements, it is clearly to demonstrate her firm belief that art, and especially music, brings one closer to God. This artistic expression above all others requires that the musician prove her- or himself not only on the artistic level but also in matters of morality. If Sand does not put painters and writers, for example, up to the same standards in her fictional universe, the obvious conclusion is that she deems music closer to God than all other art forms.[56]

The admixture of travel and Bildungsroman proves profitable for

Sand's musical novels. There is no doubt that Consuelo's travels, both physical and metaphoric, have taken her from relative innocence and inexperience to confidence and maturity. Her *Bildung* has succeeded and she arrives at the end of the novel a fully developed and complete individual. Joset's journey has taken similar paths, yet he has not learned the same lessons. While failure is not unknown in the Bildungsroman, Joset's experience differs from Wilhelm Meister's. Goethe's hero fails in professional growth insofar as his theatrical experiences do not lead him to becoming a professional actor. But in terms of personal growth, he does mature and learn about himself and his desires and needs. Inversely, *Les Maîtres Sonneurs* presents an ironic Bildungsroman where the hero succeeds in the artistic sphere but fails in the professional and the personal. The importance of balancing musical talent and career with personal development parallels Sand's belief in the ability to care about someone other than oneself.

Sand's blend of music and narrative is not unique. Balzac also put music to the service of the narrative in several works. In *La Duchesse de Langeais* (1834) the hero becomes aware of his long-lost love when he hears an organ in a Mallorcan convent. Armand is convinced it is a Frenchwoman playing, who can be none other than the duchesse de Langeais: "il fut impossible de ne pas reconnaître une âme française dans le caractère que prit soudain la musique" [it was impossible not to recognize a French soul in the character the music suddenly took].[57] While nationalism is a typical product of the July Monarchy, the use of musicianship to identify a beloved person establishes an integral significance for music. At the end of the novel, when Armand de Montrivaut returns to kidnap Antoinette de Langeais from the convent, he again hears the organ. But this time it is not the same organist: "Terribles souvenirs pour Armand, dont l'amour refleurissait tout entier dans cette brise de musique, où il voulut trouver d'aériennes promesses de bonheur" [horrible memories for Armand, whose love blossomed fully once again in this musical breeze and where he wished to find elevated promises of happiness] (251). But the promises were empty, as the duchesse de Langeais was already dead.

Again in *Gambara* (1837) Balzac uses music to enhance the flow of the narrative, but we soon get bogged down in the exposition of Count Marcosini's interpretation of Beethoven and lose track of its role in the narrative. One is tempted to conclude that Balzac wanted to satisfy a public that was more and more accustomed to reading *La Gazette musicale* and had become conversant with, though not necessarily knowledgeable about, current trends in music. He proceeds in similar fashion in *Massimilla Doni*. Balzac and others exploited the wave of interest in the musical short story, especially under the July Monarchy, but these writers either excelled in literary style or in musical knowledge, rarely both.[58]

Sand inherits her technique of combining music and narrative structure from an author to whom she owes a great debt: E. T. A. Hoffmann. In almost every one of his pieces, from *Fantasiestücke* to *Kater Murr*, he weaves musical structure and sensibility through the narrative and the characters' portraits. No other author of the period so successfully combines music and literature. However, Hoffmann was also a musician. He worked as critic, composer, and conductor. His law studies and profession bored him, so he turned to writing. This distinguishes him from Sand, who has no pretensions to a musical career or even accomplished musical talent. Sand's descriptions of music in her prose benefits from the detachment of her amateur status. Her use of music remains less emotionally charged but better suited to the literary structure of her writing. Of paramount importance is Sand's development of the concept of music as language, a notion that Hoffmann clearly embraces but less explicitly than Sand. The paradox of music considered as language and the impossibility of expressing the musical experience in verbal language will never cease to frustrate Sand but also inspire her to investigate this most intriguing aspect of her musical musings.

Sand's artful intertwining of music with narrative structure renders her unique among romantic writers. Her technique of making music an integral element of the narrative would later find a comfortable place in the works of Romain Rolland, whose *Jean-Christophe* exemplifies the central role of music and the musician in plot, characterization, and theme. Thomas Mann also exemplifies the admixture of music and narrative, especially in *Buddenbrooks* and *The Magic Mountain,* where the musical sensibilities of the characters demand a subtle interlocking of musical references, political allusions, and plot development. Similarly, Proust will know how to incorporate music into his novel to the benefit of plot, theme, characterization, and the satisfaction of the reader.[59]

2

♫♫ Musical Language ♫♫

La musique, c'est l'imagination même.

[Music is imagination itself.]
—*Adriani*

INCORPORATING MUSICAL TERMINOLOGY INTO A LITERARY TEXT, A tradition inherited from eighteenth-century writers such as Diderot, had become commonplace by the 1830s.[1] Stendhal had been writing about music for some time and Balzac had already expressed a desire to write a musical novel. Sand's familiarity with music was profound and sensitive. Sand demonstrates in her musical texts that musical forms and techniques can be represented in literature in an attempt to reproduce reactions in readers similar to those we experience when listening to music. She skillfully weaves allusions to musical processes into her prose with full knowledge of their musical function and artful exploitation of their metaphoric ramifications. I shall examine how Sand applied several musical techniques to literary texts.

Music and literature seem to contradict each other by the nature of the "language" each uses to express itself, one elusive and victim to time, the other concrete and conducive to reflection since unrestricted by time. Sand's primary challenge in her musical works is to portray the effects and meaning of music and the musical experience in literary writing, to represent a nonverbal art form in a verbal form. As she adopts musical devices and gives them a new dynamic in literature, she creates a new art form, a paradoxical form in which she claims the independence of both forms, and especially the independence of music from language. Paradoxically, it is through language that she combines the two so as to lead the reader into a world of artistic experience where the distinction between music and literature becomes blurred. Sand's experiments in musico-literary expression announce the dream of complete union of music and poetry that will later become commonplace for poets such as Mallarmé and Verlaine.

For her aesthetic experiments, Sand has to invent a new discourse that attempts to "translate" music into verbal language. Such a presumption supposes that music itself is a language. Sometimes implicitly but often explicitly she engages the reader in an exploration of the notion of language and meaning. While she inherits many of her arguments from the theoreticians of the Enlightenment, she clearly advances a romantic sense of progress and individuality. Although she claims for music the ability to communicate metaphysical ideas in early works, in later works Sand modifies her definition of art to incorporate a human(istic) element, a construct of communication that exists as an exchange between people, a sharing of ideas and emotions. Art, then, exercises a more social function, a mode of intercourse that resembles a collective language.

Two of the musical techniques Sand exploits abundantly in her works are ornamentation and improvisation. Sand is intimately familiar with both. Her musician characters comment abundantly on these techniques, whose social implications become clear through their function in the narrative. Sand also tackles the important issue of memory in music, the memory of the musician as well as the memory of the listener. This significant element of the musical experience is not commonly seen as a technique of music, but its significance cannot be ignored. The function of memory in both ornamentation and improvisation, indeed in the whole musical experience, occupies a fundamental position in Sand's exploitation of music as a communicating phenomenon. The constituent question of imitation also enters into the neoclassical discussion of how art imitates nature. Similar to what Madame de Staël does in *Corinne*, for example, Sand will interpret numerous instances of the sounds of nature as "music." Just as she modifies her notions of music and language, Sand also adjusts her concept of imitation in music and art. Finally, the notion of whether all these musical considerations lead to the notion of a musical language demands an examination of Sand's linguistic presentation of music. This discussion allows her to address the question of musical language and the unresolved query of whether music signifies.

ORNAMENTATION

My discussion of musical ornamentation concerns the embellishments and decorations of a melody insofar as they constitute a basis for aesthetic and cultural commentary in a literary text. Sand's understanding of musical ornamentation originates with her exposure

to Italian baroque singing technique from her grandmother and
Pauline Viardot. Virtuosity and imagination work together in this
style to produce a feeling of wonderment, and it is this baroque
quest for wonder that Sand inherited from her grandmother that ap-
pealed to seventeenth- and eighteenth-century sensibilities. Viardot's performance of baroque music was powerful, but she
preferred bel canto, a lyrical style that flourished in Paris at the beginning of the nineteenth century, especially with Rossini's success
there. Viardot's use of ornaments was calculated and never exaggerated. In "Le Théâtre italien de Paris et Mlle Pauline Garcia"
(1840) Sand remarks that the singer always used an ornament with
good reason and never corrupted it.[2] Musset wrote in *Revue des
deux mondes* that she did not succumb to the conventional, as her
sister had. "Il est temps qu'on nous débarrasse de la maladie des
effets" [It is high time we were delivered of the mania for effects].
Musset will praise Viardot again several months later in the same
publication, when he hears her sing in *Otello*: "Quand la phrase
simple arrive, on est à l'opéra; mais, dès que la difficulté se pré-
sente, on est au concert" [When there is a simple phrase, we are at
the opera; the moment difficulty appears, we are at a concert].[3]
Musset's distinction between "opera," an experience of profound
sincerity and emotion, and "concert," a display of virtuosity, sus-
tains the current argument for simplicity in performance. Explicit
echoes of these discussions can be found in *Consuelo*.

During the romantic period, ornamentation went from being the
demonstration of a singer's spontaneous and individual imagination
and technique to a more standardized and controlled display of virtuosity. Performers only rarely improvised their ornaments at this
time. Popular legend assigns this standardized, composed expression of ornaments to Rossini and his disgust with performers' over-
wrought interpolations. Even though he may have tried to exercise
some control in these matters, the lyrical *Geistzeit* of the early nineteenth century was propitious to the abandonment of formulaic fioriture in favor of passionate expression. The concertgoing public of
the 1830s and 1840s, now tired of facile displays of virtuosity,
began to expect something more sincere and honest, which is not to
say they wished to do away with ornamentation. Balzac describes
one such reaction in *Massimilla Doni*, where Capraja extolls the
wonders of flamboyant runs: "La roulade est donc l'unique point
laissé aux amis de la musique pure, aux amoureux de l'art tout nu"
[The run is then the only aspect left to the friends of pure music,
to the lovers of unadulterated art]. The duc de Cataneo contradicts
Capraja's passionate kudos: "Il existe en musique un pouvoir plus

magique que celui de la roulade. . . . L'accord de deux voix ou d'une voix et du violon, . . . nous mène plus avant dans le centre de la vie" [In music there is a force more magical than the run. . . . The harmony of two voices or of one voice and a violin, . . . leads us beyond to the center of life].[4] Cataneo represents the progressive attitude of the time, a growing weariness of unwarranted virtuosity. Sand takes this position much further than Balzac, incorporating it into the narrative structure as well as into the characterization of the heroine in *Consuelo*. She also exploits it in *Le Château des Désertes* and with more extensive implications in *Les Maîtres Sonneurs*.

As romantic audiences demanded sincerity in art, they also demanded stories that more directly portrayed their lives. Gone were the noble ideals of the classical age. The public wanted love stories in an everyday context. And with this shift in emphasis came a change in musical exigencies. The melody itself, without the trappings of virtuosic ostentation, once again became important. Audiences wanted to see and hear love and passion, torture and revenge, no longer in the context of *Phèdre* and *Le Cid*, or *Orphée* and *Rinaldo*, but something more contiguous. The movement away from ornamentation, though not sudden and immediate, plunged the Parisian music-listening public into a new quarrel between the adherents of stylized virtuosity and those of the simpler bel canto style.[5] This debate had nothing of the fervor of the eighteenth-century *Querelle des Bouffons* or the conflict between Gluckists and Piccinnists. Nonetheless it occupied the minds of concertgoers and readers of musical journals.[6] Sand reflects this shift in her texts and in her commentary on musical expression.

Dilettante praise of ornamentation amused Sand, and she did not hesitate to mock such appreciation. In *La Filleule* (1853), the duchess de Florès, who holds musicales in her Parisian salon, is impressed by a fancy run. In the same novel, a retired professional musician, Schwartz—patterned after Balzac's Schmuck in *Le Cousin Pons*[7]—plays some Bach for his neighbor Stéphen and his friends. Roque, a pedantic friend, begins to harangue on the qualities of "modern" music, as opposed to the melodies and harmonies of the previous century. (The scene takes place in 1832.) He bases his commentary on the assumption that they are listening to Bellini! By introducing the confusion of Bach and Bellini, Sand derides the pseudo-sophistication of certain Parisian concertgoers and a bourgeois taste that willingly equates good with new in matters of art.

Rossini brought ornamentation into a realm of useful artistry and restricted vocalise singing. That he wrote out the ornaments demon-

strates the importance of their occurring in certain places, in particular ways, and with specific effects. The point was not to abandon
embellishments, but to use them more sparingly and judiciously.
For Parisian audiences, one of the most noteworthy aspects of Italian operatic style, especially the Neapolitan style of the seventeenth
and early eighteenth centuries, was fioritura. In letters about *Alceste*
and in his preface, Gluck insisted on acting as an essential element
of the singer, suggesting a degree of emotional engagement on the
singer's part that would justify audience response, in both the eighteenth and the nineteenth centuries.[8] And this technique, which in
the baroque age served to enhance the melody as well as to display
a singer's talents, was transformed in the early romantic period into
a device to showcase virtuosity. A post-Revolutionary public that
needed more human heroes applied those same needs to music,
where performers became superior beings who could dazzle audiences with mysterious and marvelous techniques.

It cannot be ignored that the French Revolution also had an effect
on singing in Paris because the exaltation of royalty no longer interested the public. The so-called search for veracity claimed by post-
1789 generations caused further distrust of the ornamentation of the
baroque style. Now, Meyerbeer and Donizetti looked for less
adornment and more substance. Soon we see the trend turn to *opéra
lyrique*, which ensured a dominion of melody over harmony and a
weakening of the tendency for ornamentation. By the mid-nineteenth century, when a taste for realism had infiltrated the theaters,
the place of baroque-style ornamentation was weakening. Little of
the mystical and fantastic fioriture of earlier times induced contemporary audiences to believe the action these musical fantasies attempted to depict. The new opera claimed to present realism in
characterization and emotion.[9] Yet, the desire to go beyond the real
world still spurred the public to seek illusion in the theater, which
explains in part the popularity of Verdi and Wagner.

At the same time, the fervor for virtuosity was still apparent.
Liszt, Thalberg, and Paganini were performers the public wanted to
see as well as hear. Although contemporary virtuoso music did not
pretend to communicate profound thoughts, romantic individualism
found its place in virtuosity as each performer attempted to outdo
the other. Virtuosity under the July Monarchy was almost exclu-
sively the domain of instrumental music, which separated it radically from baroque practices. Paris audiences willingly gathered,
most notably in private salons, to observe—or more frankly to be
observed observing—a musician's astonishing flexibility and sup-
pleness.[10] The persistent struggle during Restoration and July Mon-

archy Paris between the popularity of Beethoven and that of Rossini provides some explanation of the apparent contradiction in musical tastes.

What is intriguing about Sand's portrayal of musical style in *Consuelo* is her successful, albeit anachronistic, mixture of eighteenth- and nineteenth-century musical and artistic ideals. While there can be no doubt that the French music-loving public of the romantic age adored Italian music, the heavy presence of Italy in Sand's *Consuelo* goes far beyond a love for Rossini. Indeed, setting the opening of the novel in Venice and then exhibiting Italian composers at the Austrian and Prussian courts in *La Comtesse de Rudolstadt* demonstrate the eighteenth-century tendency for cosmopolitan and Italian tastes. Against an Italianate backdrop, Sand sets the stage to explore a musical language based on simplicity.

Steeped in the music and style of eighteenth-century Italian composers, Sand nonetheless promotes Consuelo as an artist of simplicity and purity. Simplicity is Sand's catchword.[11] It resounds in the mouths of all the main characters in *Consuelo*. The expression clearly represents an anti-baroque sentiment, one that is only just beginning to gain currency in an eighteenth-century setting but that also reflects the feelings of Sand's contemporaries. She superimposes the romantic interest in bel canto and virtuosity on the waning of baroque and the advent of classical style in the mid-eighteenth century. The transition from high baroque to romantic musical styles (bypassing classical), which spans nearly three-quarters of a century, finds telescoped concentration in the narrative of *Consuelo*. The result is an apologia for simplicity in music.[12]

Consuelo accepts Porpora's approach to music not only because it pleases her aesthetically, but also because in so doing, she aligns herself with her mother's teachings: "Dieu m'a inspiré d'être modeste et simple. Ma mère est venue me voir en rêve, et elle m'a dit ce qu'elle me disait toujours: Occupe-toi de bien chanter, la Providence fera le reste" [God inspired me to be modest and simple. My mother came to me in a dream and told me what she always had: Mind that you sing well, Providence will do the rest] (*C*, 1:98–99). Consuelo carries her preference for simplicity over to all sectors of her life. She does not want to wear fancy costumes when performing on stage. She insists on performing her first solo appearance in a black mourning dress, a respectful outfit and her best. At first Anzoleto is convinced this will ruin her chances to stir the impresario; "Mais quelle miraculeuse transformation s'était opérée dans cette jeune fille tout à l'heure si blême et si abattue, si effarée par la fatigue et la crainte!" [But what a magical transformation had happened to this young lady, just a moment ago so pallid and worn out, so alarmed by fatigue and fear] (*C*, 1:100).[13]

In her lessons with Amélie de Rudolstadt, Consuelo continues to promote simple melodies. They provide the best training and this style must be mastered before attempting ornamented melodies.

> Amélie voulut faire à sa tête, comme à l'ordinaire, en chantant des cavatines à grand effet; mais Consuelo, qui commençait à se montrer sévère, lui fit essayer des motifs fort simples et fort sérieux extraits des chants religieux de Palestrina.[14] La jeune baronne bâilla, s'impatienta, et déclara cette musique barbare et soporifique. (*C*, 1: 255)

> [As usual, Amélie wanted to have her own way and sing exciting cavatinas. But Consuelo, who was starting to become harsh, had her try some very simple and serious motifs, excerpts from Palestrina's religious songs. The young baroness yawned, became impatient, and labeled this music primitive and soporific.]

Consuelo insists on the importance of simplicity in music by demonstrating how it is done. She has not sung since her arrival at Riesenberg, and as we have already seen, the effect is momentous. Amélie remains "à la fois ravie et consternée" [at once thrilled and dismayed], realizing how little she knows of music. Albert appears as if out of nowhere and falls to his knees, speaking to the young voice teacher in Spanish and calling her Consuelo, a name no one at Riesenberg knows.

The dichotomy between sacred and profane music also plays an important role in Sand's aesthetics of simplicity. Sand's Porpora claims to disdain profane music, but less for moral than for aesthetic reasons. He finds that profane music panders to the frivolous desires of the public and quickly ruins a singer's voice. Yet, he recognizes that there is perhaps a place for such music. A former pupil of Porpora's, Farinelli,[15] has gone on to glory singing opera replete with fioriture. Anzoleto reminds him, "Votre seigneurie réprouve ces traits et ces ornements difficiles qui ont cependant fait le succès et la célébrité de son illustre élève Farinelli?" [Does my lordship disapprove of these difficult ornaments, which have brought success and fame to his illustrious pupil, Farinelli?] (*C*, 1:109). Porpora is forced to admit how much he admires his former student's abilities in this domain, but reserves judgment: "Je ne les réprouve qu'à l'église. Je les approuve au théâtre; mais je les veux à leur place, et surtout j'en proscris l'abus" [I disapprove of them only in church: I approve of them in the theater; but I want them in their place, and above all, I forbid that they be overused] (*C*, 1:109).

Consuelo's first musical stirrings arise from church music. She meets Anzoleto as she sings to the Virgin, and her training with Porpora is strictly in sacred music. As for her ability to sing profane music, the issue becomes a complicated matter of pride. Zustiniani wants to hear how she manages operatic music as he is interested in hiring her for his theater. Partly to help her show off and partly because of the rancor he feels toward both his teacher and the theater director, Anzoleto assures them that his fiancée can perform on stage alongside the best of them. Porpora, too, is curious to see whether his protégée can manage operatic style with taste. Thus three men urge Consuelo to try her hand at secular opera for their own agendas; Consuelo's only wish is to please them all. The challenge carries high risks for all concerned, but Consuelo agrees to try her luck singing from Galuppi's *La Diavolessa*.

That Galuppi's opera was composed only in 1755, making it impossible for Consuelo to sing it in 1743, is hardly important. Sand takes several such liberties with historical accuracy in her novel. What is important is the choice of an opera buffa, where the music of the heroine is replete with ornaments that are designed to dazzle the audience, and Consuelo performs it perfectly, adding inventions of her own to display her coloratura expertise. Consuelo shows herself capable of singing nonsacred music, and so begins her involvement with the professional world of performing artists and its attendant politics. It is not insignificant that her first foray into comic opera should be singing the role of a female devil!

Sand accents the insistence on the virtues of simplicity by presenting other characters who, while excellent musicians in a technical sense, cannot appreciate the simple beauties of an unadorned melody. Anzoleto and Corilla quickly learn the public's penchant for ornamentation and opt to satisfy public taste. Anzoleto has a facility for ornamentation that saves him from many an awkward moment. His training is minimal and unprofessional and he often fails to understand the intentions of the composer, but he always emerges triumphant thanks to impressive ornaments. "Il manqua des effets que le compositeur avait ménagés; mais il en trouva d'autres auxquels personne n'avait songé. . . . Pour une innovation, on lui pardonna dix maladresses; pour un sentiment individuel, dix rébellions contre la méthode" [He blundered effects that the composer had carefully molded, but he found others that no one had thought of. . . . For one innovation he was pardoned ten blunders; for one individual feeling, ten assaults against technique] (*C*, 1:56). The importance of the conventional method underlines the place of dogma in musical training, a rigid though ever-changing policy of performance.

With a hearty little dose of sardonic irony, Porpora offers the conviction that Anzoleto can overcome these defects, but he doubts this will ever come to pass:

> tu as de quoi les [les défauts] vaincre; car tu as les qualités que ne peuvent donner ni l'enseignement ni le travail; tu as ce que ne peuvent faire perdre ni les mauvais conseils ni les mauvais exemples, tu as le feu sacré . . . tu as le génie! . . . Hélas! un feu qui n'éclairera rien de grand, un génie qui demeurera stérile . . . car, je le vois dans tes yeux, comme je l'ai senti dans la poitrine, tu n'as pas le culte de l'art, tu n'as pas de foi pour les grands maîtres, ni de respect pour les grandes créations; tu aimes la gloire, rien que la gloire, et pour toi seul. (C, 1:61)

> [You have what it takes to conquer your faults, because you have qualities that neither instruction or experience can provide. You have what neither bad advice nor poor example can take away: you have the sacred flame, you have genius! Alas, a flame that will never illuminate anything great, a genius that will remain sterile; because, I see it in your eyes just as I felt it in my breast, you don't worship art, you have no praise for the great masters nor any respect for great compositions; you love only glory, nothing but glory, and for you alone.]

The stinging twist in Porpora's commentary underscores Sand's notion that all the talent and all the training in the world will not counteract a self-centered artist's egotistical need for fame and popularity. To give in to the desires of the public rather than to offer them the standards of good taste will always reduce the gifted musician to the rank of a servant of the people.

Consuelo shares Porpora's attitude toward Anzoleto's talent, but she offers encouragement and practical lessons. They debut together at the San-Samuel theater in Gluck's *Ipermnestre*. Consuelo is warmly embraced; Anzoleto is politely received, but clearly only in sympathy with Consuelo's reception. After the performance, she reprimands him for his lack of discipline and integrity: "Je te l'ai toujours prédit, tu préfères les résultats de l'art à l'art lui-même" [I've always told you that you preferred the effects of art to art itself] (C, 1:158). Anzoleto benefits from lessons with Consuelo until Corilla convinces him that his new style lacks brilliance. He is easily seduced into abandoning Consuelo's advice, and also Consuelo, and forges his career and his life to comply with the ideals and the multiple seductions of Corilla. "Anzoleto, chanteur incomplet et tragédien médiocre, avait les instincts d'un bon comique" [An unaccomplished singer and a mediocre tragic actor, Anzoleto had the instincts of a good comic actor] (*C*, 1:458). This will remain the author's judgment of the talented singer.

Célio, in *Le Château des Désertes*, makes a similarly disastrous debut because of his overzealous desire to please the public. He, too, is gifted and technically proficient. However, his thirst for public approbation outweighs his good taste, and he finds it more satisfying to provide brilliance than to remain true to the indications in the music. His ability to use ornamentation to cover up a lack of emotion and purity in musical expression, however, does not succeed as well as Anzoleto's, and he is obliged to leave Vienna to further his training before appearing in public again. Fortunately he understands his mistake and manages to curb his vanity.

Humor also helps Sand to clarify her position on ornamentation in *Consuelo*. The scene of the singing lesson with Count Hoditz that I have already discussed provides an excellent example of Sand's satire. In a parallel but more serious lesson, Consuelo discusses the purity of musical style with Haydn. As a budding composer, he is eager to try out all his gifts, but Consuelo cautions him against taking the easy road and producing only what he knows he can do well. Warning Haydn against being satisfied with "la musique tranquille" [calm music], she explains that tranquility only produces a calming and satisfying effect when it follows turmoil: "la pureté du ciel ne nous frappe que parce que nous l'avons vu maintes fois sillonné par l'orage" [the pureness of the sky only catches our attention because we've seen it crisscrossed so often by stormy weather] (*C*, 2:118). This commentary is obviously aimed at the formulaic writing of the late baroque composers, where "tranquille" means standard and unoriginal. What Sand calls "tranquille" is less "calm" and "soothing" than "easy" and "expected."

Corilla, trained by Porpora and seduced to the theater by Zustiniani, shows a great facility for ornamentation. Porpora has no time or respect for her now that she has given in to the public affinity for such fioriture, although he places the bulk of the blame on the theater director and by extension on the theater itself: "N'est-ce point une désolation, une honte de voir cette Corilla, qui commençait à comprendre grandement l'art sérieux, descendre du sacré au profane, de la prière au badinage, de l'autel au tréteau, du sublime au ridicule, d'Allegri et de Palestrina à Albinoni et au barbier Apollini?" [Is it not a pity, a shame to see this Corilla, who was just starting to understand a great deal about serious art, fall from the sacred to the profane, from prayer to banter, from the altar to the stage, from the sublime to the ridiculous, from Allegri and Palestrina to Albinoni and Apollini the barber?] (*C*, 1:49).

Corilla recognizes later that Consuelo's style has remained pure and beautiful while hers has become common and expected. When the two sopranos sing together in Vienna later in the novel, Corilla compliments her rival. She asks Consuelo how to execute a particular ornament, a secret one usually never shares with another singer. Consuelo teaches her the figure and gives her permission to use it. This sign of camaraderie and artistic sisterhood, although it does not lead to a significant relationship, is indicative of Consuelo's generosity as well as Sand's entreaty for the appropriate use of embellishment.

While Sand is measured in her discussion of musical aesthetics in prose fiction, she is often more explicit in her nonfiction. In an open letter written to Giacomo Meyerbeer, number 11 of *Les Lettres d'un voyageur* (1834–36), she addresses two essential issues of the music profession: common sense and criticism. Sand had recently seen a production of Meyerbeer's *Les Huguenots*, which impressed her despite her assurance that nothing could surpass his *Robert le diable*. Sand praises Meyerbeer's ability to produce characterizations through simple music and ignoring for the most part the musical conventions of the time. This is what she calls common sense, to opt for a type of aria that fits the dramatic action. She abhors the usual acceptance of separating drama from music for the sake of conventions, the typical recitative/aria alternation. She distinguishes a "musique de musicien" [musician's music] from a "musique de littérateur" [literary author's music], a trap Meyerbeer manages to avoid, she says. Her commentary on criticism refers to the practice of punctuating the dramatic flow of an opera with set musical pieces which may or may not fit into the narrative. Sand insists there should be only one type of dramatic music: "une musique de passion vraie et d'action vraisemblable où le charme de la mélodie ne doit pas lutter contre la situation et faire chanter la cavatine en règle, avec *coda* consacrée et *trait* inévitable, au héros qui tombe percé de coups sur l'arène" [a music of true passion and realistic action, where the charm of the melody must never fight against the matter at hand and produce a cavatina sung to the hero fallen from wounds received in the arena according to the rules with the ritual coda and the inevitable ornament].[16]

Sand details important aspects of her aesthetic ideals. Music must speak to the passions in a sincere and profound way. As she says in the voice of the narrator in *Consuelo*, "On a dit avec raison que le but de la musique, c'était l'émotion" [it has been said, and rightly so, that the goal of music was emotion] (*C*, 1:417). Although this is not a new concept in music interpretation, it remains one of the most prominent ideals of music for the romantics in general, and for George Sand in particular. At the same time, she pleads for verisimilitude on the stage. The period of the realist theater has started and Sand finds herself intrigued by the new playwrights' success, especially Hugo and Dumas. Interesting is Sand's position on the cusp between romantic and realist approaches to art, maintaining the need for passion yet without relinquishing the believable. Sand will always hover between these two schools of aesthetics.

In addition to these general comments on the performing arts, Sand offers in her letter to Meyerbeer some advice about musical composition.[17] She decrees against unnecessary and ill-placed ornaments that detract from the dramatic action. Sand contends that music does not have to be slighted in favor of realism, that both can and should coexist, but within the proportions of common sense. She illustrates her commentary with remarks on the use of the coda.

The coda is a closure device at the end of a movement or an aria whereby the main theme is restated in such a way as to signal the end. In baroque style, the coda often concludes with a difficult embellishment on the penultimate note, the leading tone, which enjoins the public to anticipate the impending resolution. The embellishment, often ending in a trill or sometimes a more complicated series of runs or a full-blown cadenza, serves largely to demonstrate the abilities of the singer. By this point in the aria, the audience knows that the piece is ending and is no longer paying much attention to the dramatic aspect but devoting its attention to the virtuosity of the soloist. The passage lays bare Sand's musical criticism and uncovers another detail of her (musical) aesthetics.

Pourquoi cette forme consacrée, pourquoi cette *coda*, espèce de cadre uniforme et lourd? pourquoi ce *trait* . . . ? pourquoi cette habitude de faire passer la voix, vers la fin de tous les morceaux de chant, par les notes les plus élevées ou les plus basses du gosier? . . . Ne viendra-t-il pas un temps où le public s'en lassera . . . ? Il paraît que le vulgaire chérit encore ce vieil usage, et ne croit pas qu'il y ait scène terminée là où il n'y a pas quatre ou huit mesures banales de psalmodie grossière, qui ne sont ni mélodie, ni harmonie, ni chant, ni récitatif. (*LV,* 2:928–29)

[Why this ritualized form, why this coda, a kind of unvarying and heavy frame? why this ornament . . . ? why this habit at the end of all vocal selections of forcing the voice to the highest or the lowest notes of the throat? . . . Will there not come a time when the public will tire of it . . . ? It seems that crude people still cherish this old-fashioned custom and think that a scene isn't finished so long as there haven't been four or eight insipid measures of crude droning, which are neither melody, harmony, song, nor recitative.]

Even though Sand claims not to be offering Meyerbeer any advice, her language leaves no doubt as to her opinion and recommendation. The vocabulary of this passage points to a disdain for the composer as well as for the public in these matters. Everything here points to Sand's condemnation of a convention that allows dazzling music to overshadow dramatic action. One can understand Sand's attitude in the midst of a dramatic scene where the attention should be drawn to the story while the ear is constantly being reminded that this is a rigidly formulaic piece of music.[18]

The real subject of Sand's letter to Meyerbeer is the opera *Les Huguenots*. She turns her attention to Protestantism, a preoccupation that will engage her for years to come.[19] She implicitly suggests that Meyerbeer's insight into the Protestant plight depicted in Scribe's libretto might have had an influence on the simplicity of his approach to the music. She praises his invention and his inspiration: " 'Ô musicien plus poète qu'aucun de nous, dans quel repli inconnu de votre âme, dans quel trésor caché de votre intelligence avez-vous trouvé ces traits si nets et si purs, cette conception simple comme l'antique, vraie comme l'histoire, lucide comme la conscience, forte comme la foi?" [Oh musician more poet than any one of us, in what unknown recess of your soul, in what hidden treasure of your intelligence did you find these ever so clear and pure ornaments, this concept as simple as tradition, as true as history, as limpid as the conscience, as strong as faith?] (*LV*, 2: 921). This vocabulary differs radically from the tone she uses to decry misplaced and exaggerated ornamentation.

The commentary on the possibility of a Protestant origin of the music's simplicity leads Sand to contemplate briefly a remark she reports here: "On a dit à propos des *Huguenots* qu'il n'y a pas de musique protestante, non plus que de musique catholique" [It's been said about *Les Huguenots* that there is no such thing as Protestant music, no more than there is Catholic music] (*LV*, 2:923). She does not ignore the beauty of "cette œuvre catholique de *Robert*" [this Catholic work that is *Robert* (*le diable*)] (*LV*, 922), which she extols as one of his finest works. On the other hand, in *Consuelo* Sand will have Albert say that he fears Porpora confuses religious sentiment in music with human thought, that he hears sacred music too much as a Catholic (*C*, 1:386). These statements offer less a contradiction than an allowance that Albert's religious adherence cannot be easily defined, nor can the spiritual inspiration of music.

Whether giving advice to Meyerbeer or portraying eighteenth-century music as overly embellished, Sand's insistence on judicious and sparing use of ornamentation is clear. Ornamentation clearly has its place in Sand's musical universe, but she transmits the lessons of moderation she learned from Pauline Viardot to her own reading public.

IMPROVISATION

Another musical device Sand exploits in her musical works is improvisation. Not unrelated to ornamentation, improvisation is the modification of an established melody by a change in rhythm, tempo, mode, and the like. While improvisation is at the source of baroque singing, by the nineteenth century it had become more the domain of instrumental music, especially of keyboard music. George Springer cites improvisation, along with variation and virtuoso performance, as proof of music's greater tolerance for deviation in comparison to language.[20] Sand recognizes this flexibility and exploits it in her musical works. Evidence of the importance of improvisation to Sand's aesthetic observations can be found throughout her career.

Improvisation appears throughout Sand's œuvre. Her grandmother most certainly exposed her at an early age to baroque music practices, which encouraged spontaneous and often spectacular displays of virtuosity and where the focus was on music becoming rather than music being. Sand was convinced of the genius inherent in the ability to improvise, as she says repeatedly in *Consuelo* and *Les Maîtres Sonneurs*. When Consuelo first meets Haydn, who plays some of his compositions for her, her response suggests that while his pieces are solid, he needs to learn to improvise and to hazard an independence of expression: "Essayez-vous à improviser, tantôt sur le violon, tantôt avec la voix. C'est ainsi que l'âme vient sur les lèvres et au bout des doigts" [Try your hand at improvising, now on the violin, now with the voice. That's how the soul comes to the lips and the fingertips] (*C*, 2:50–51). Hadyn has been studying from Fux's book on counterpoint, *Gradus ad Parnassum*, which Consuelo feels has perhaps limited his inventiveness. The soprano insists on the importance of "pure" music, music which comes from the soul and therefore represents its divine origins. As Sand states in the seventh of the *Lettres d'un voyageur*, music is "la langue divine perfectionnée" [divine language perfected] (*LV*, 2:819). And in *Les Maîtres Sonneurs* Père Bastien tells the narrator that although his son is an excellent musician, he cannot improvise beyond the familiar exercise of a master piper, whereas Joset displays the gifts of a true musician since his improvisations show originality. And in *La Filleule*, Stéphen is asked to play a Bach fugue, but when he admits to not knowing the ending, his friend Schwartz encourages him to play it anyway; "tu improviseras la fin et tu partiras de là pour le pays de ta fantaisie" [you'll improvise the ending, and from there you'll take off for the land of your fancy].[21]

Sand's first explorations into improvisation, literary and musical, revolve around her invention of a childhood deity, Corambé. The androgynous creature spoke to little Aurore in poems and songs, repeated and altered time and again in the spirit of improvisation. She took great solace in composing these variations. Notwithstanding the fact that Sand wrote her memories of Corambé at the age of fifty, perhaps imposing a musical interpretation that may have been only subjacent at the time, the origins of her appreciation for improvisation may well reside in Corambé.[22]

Little Aurore also improvised in another narrative form, as she relates in her autobiography. As a child she would build a small enclosure with four chairs in her mother's apartment in Paris. Ensconced in the protective cavern, she would invent stories. She repeated them over and over until her mother knew them by heart as well as Aurore.

[J]e composais à haute voix d'interminables contes que ma mère appelait mes romans. Je n'ai aucun souvenir de ces plaisantes compositions, ma mère m'en a parlé mille fois, et longtemps avant que j'eusse la pensée d'écrire. Elle les déclarait souverainement ennuyeuses, à cause de leur longueur et du développement que je donnais aux digressions. C'est un défaut que j'ai bien conservé, à ce qu'on dit. (*HV,* 1:541–42)[23]

[Aloud I composed unending stories that my mother called my novels. I have no memory of these amusing compositions; my mother talked about them a thousand times, and long before I thought about writing. She proclaimed they were intensely boring because of their length and the degree to which I developed the digressions. That's a flaw I've indeed kept, or so I'm told.]

In another autobiographical text, Sand recounts how while visiting at Nohant Liszt would improvise at the keyboard:

J'aime ces phrases entrecoupées qu'il jette sur le piano et qui restent un pied en l'air, dansant dans l'espace comme des follets boiteux. . . . J'aimerais mieux croire qu'il se promène dans la chambre sans composer, livré à des pensées de tumulte et d'incertitude. Il me semble qu'en passant devant son piano, il doit jeter ces phrases capricieuses à son insu en obéissant à son instinct de sentiment plutôt qu'à un travail d'intelligence.[24]

[I like these broken phrases he tosses out on the piano that hover one foot in the air, dancing in space like limping sprites. . . . I'd rather think he's wandering around in his room not composing, lost in thoughts of tumult and uncertainty. I imagine that as he walks past the piano, he must toss off these whimsical phrases unwittingly, obeying his instinct for feeling rather than an intellectual chore.]

Unsure whether Liszt is improvising or trying to work out a compositional problem, Sand invents or improvises her own context for the event, preferring to think of the musician as responding to random but not arbitrary musical thoughts rather than performing a rational, well-thought-out composition. She has recourse to dance imagery in an attempt to visualize or perhaps to reify music. Since Liszt played more improvisations than original compositions, and since Sand's exposure to actual musical creation at this time was based almost solely on Liszt's music, Rambeau suggests that Sand concluded musical creation was less intellectual than literary creation.[25] In this case, musical improvisation for Sand would be less inspiring but more inspired than literature. I am not convinced this continues to be the case later on, especially in the rustic novels.

Sand's "Une Causerie d'artistes en 184 . . . ," in *Impressions et Souvenirs*, describes how Chopin was capable of blocking out conversation and social intercourse by improvising at the piano. Stéphen, in *La Filleule*, also improvises at the piano without knowing much what he is doing. It is more a diversion or an attempt to remove himself from a company of people who fail to deflect his attention from his lovelorn melancholy: "Stéphen s'oubliait au piano et improvisait sans le savoir" [Stéphen lost himself at the piano and improvised without knowing it] (*F*, 78). Later, Stéphen comes home from his beloved's frustrated that he has not made his feelings known to her. He pours out his feelings in improvisations at the keyboard. His friend Roque agrees to help him out of his financial difficulties, provided that Stéphen cease his infernal melancholy, including his nocturnal improvisations. Many of Roque's character flaws are conveyed through musical examples that display his ignorance in such matters.

The most overt use of improvisation in Sand's œuvre is in "Le Contrebandier" (1837). Writing in response to a challenge that words could not render the feelings evoked by a piece of music, Sand fashions "Le Contrebandier" after Liszt's piano piece, itself modeled on a popular Spanish song and composed in memory of

Maria Malibran. Dedicating his piece to Sand, Liszt took his inspiration for *Rondeau fantastique sur un thème espagnol* (1836)[26] from a song made popular by Manuel Garcia, Pauline Viardot and Maria Malibran's father, "El Contrabandista." The lyrics tell the romantic story of a border outlaw who derives as much pleasure from evading the authorities as from making money. Liszt elaborates on the themes of the Spanish song, indeed his version is over six times as long as the original. The term "fantastique" in Liszt's title indicates his deviation from the standard rondo form, although he does return to the first theme after each variation. Liszt developed only one new thematic group; all other additions are virtuoso passages and dramatic modulations. The term "theme and variations" does not apply here since the changes from one version to the next are slight and involve mainly decoration and a small number of rhythmic or tonal changes.[27]

Sand elaborates on Garcia's lyrics as much as Liszt does on his music. But it is the musical form that remains the structural basis for the short story. In the foreword, she defines the form in operatic terms, "airs," "recitatives," and "choruses." She provides commentary on Liszt's piece as well as on the Spanish song, and from there she proceeds to discuss the marriage of music and poetry: "Les paroles de cette chansonnette sont admirablement portées par le chant, mais elles sont insignifiantes séparées de la musique, et il serait impossible de les traduire mot à mot" [The words of this little song are admirably conveyed by the music, but they are insignificant if separated from the music, and it would be impossible to translate them word for word].[28] The paradox of Sand's text, a narrative inspired by a piece of music without words, itself inspired by a song with lyrics, provides a fruitful confusion of music and text.[29]

The structure of Sand's "Contrebandier" loosely follows a rondo structure.[30] She begins by giving a description of Liszt's piece, which will serve at once as backdrop and refrain. After a brief explanation of how she came to write the story, she gives an outline. The structure and content of the story are ingeniously interwoven, demonstrating an original albeit unsubtle melding of two art forms. The protagonist, an unknown Traveler, interrupts an engagement celebration. The group wishes to know who he is, and he teases by saying he knows one of their regional songs, adding to the mystery of his identity. They challenge him, and he begins to sing a song, pretending to have forgotten the original version. His nine variations all begin with the same formula: "Moi qui suis . . ." [I who am . . .]. This series spins a musical yarn. His variations include various professions or stations of life that happen to represent those present: "Moi qui suis jeune chevrier, amant infortuné, aventurier, etc." [I who am a young goatherd, jilted lover, adventurer, etc.]. The variations replicate in a certain fashion the style of the rondo form, where the refrain is followed by first one variation, the refrain again, then another variation, and so forth (ABACADA . . .). They also underscore the irony of the Traveler's message: life is not so simple and joyous, because I know who you are and you don't know who I am . . . and yet, you do! The final variation, "Moi qui suis poète" [I who am a poet], combines all the other professions into a single one, which must be seen at once as superior to all the others and yet human and earthbound. Only at the end does he come to the original version, "Moi qui suis contrebandier" [I who am a smuggler], at which point the groom recognizes him as a well-known bandit and smuggler.

The musical form Sand imposes on her story vacillates between rondo form and theme and variations. As in Liszt's piano piece, the various versions of the main theme do not deviate radically from the original. Rather they modify as they add piecemeal to the information that has been withheld, although the singer's information is not necessarily reliable. The identification between "smuggler" and "poet" does not surprise the reader of romantic fiction. When the Traveler finally does sing the original version of the song, the group realizes that he has been feigning a lapse of memory. Liszt achieves a similar effect in his piece by introducing modulations of the first period of the theme in the coda. The listener already knows the second half, but tension is heightened by its continual suspension. And just as Sand has the original version of the song repeated at the end by the Traveler and not the character who first introduced it, that is, the Child, Liszt repeats the main theme in a different key and constructs it on the second theme of the original song, unusual for rondo style. The reader and the listener can react not only to a repetition, but they also observe a totally new aspect to the recapitulation thanks to the changes of key and annunciator respectively. The irony of the Traveler's coup provides an additional innovation, an element inspired by Liszt's fantasy.

"Le Contrebandier" suffers from a lack of generic identity. The reader does not know what it is and therefore cannot know what to expect. Sand gives her own makeshift term to the text, "drame lyrico-fantastique," which suggests an uneasiness with the form along with a desire to promote its innovativeness. In Sand's defense, it must be said that Liszt's *Rondeau fantastique* also does not have a consistent form, and in that respect she fulfills her goal to emulate it. The text belongs more to the prose poem than to the short story form by the nature of the tone and form. The structure clearly carries more importance than the narrative. Some critics have suggested that the foreword, where Sand discusses the form and the inspiration for the text, has more significance than the actual text. Sand's story fails because, unable to establish itself as a new or intermediary form, it falls back into the literary mode. At the same time, it lacks sufficient narrative qualities and literary structure and complexity of theme and characterization to satisfy the demands of literary convention. While to be commended for the noble attempt at a new form, Sand will not repeat this foray into a new musicoliterary genre. Bailbé states that the marriage of the arts can lead to satisfying results, but one art form cannot replace the other.[31] We must see "Le Contrebandier" as an innovative text that opens discussions of discovery in aesthetic considerations more than anything else. And to that end, Sand's text serves as an eye- and earopener for such issues in musico-literary criticism.

The admixture of improvisation and contraband finds another expression in *Teverino* (1845). The title character is again of unknown origin—maybe poor, maybe noble—who sings with the beautiful voice of a professional. The first song quoted in the narrative, translated liberally by the narrator from Italian into French, tells the tale of a indigent wanderer who commands nature in contrast to the stilted culture of the nobility to whom the song is addressed.[32] Teverino's gift as an improviser, both in music and in verse, thus not very far removed from Staël's Corinne, also portrays his changing character, since he disguises himself several times throughout the novel—as a vagabond, as a nobleman, as an amateur singer, as a professional singer, as a novice monk—to the point where the reader is never sure of his origins. He reveals at the end of the narrative that he was befriended by a border smuggler, the brother (absent in the narrative) of the peasant girl, Madeleine, with whom he is in love. In as much as his costumes change as frequently as his improvisations, Teverino must be seen as another manifestation of Sand's "contrebandier."

Sand exploits the practice of improvisation most fully in her discussions of folk music. She calls improvisation in folk music "musique naturelle" and focuses on the difference between written music and music that is performed, repeated, and passed down orally without the so-called benefit of a written form. Popular music or folk music valorizes a means of expression that is open to all, regardless of education and cultural training. It is not restricted to an elite who have learned the various codes of an academic discourse. It represents a natural expression of the people.

The Berrichon author prizes the spontaneity of folk music and applauds the ability of a folk musician both to create on the spot and to remember improvisations of a previous occasion or of another musician. The exact nature of improvisation in folk music remains obscure in *Consuelo*, but it is an obscurity that enhances the value of the element. When Consuelo inquires of Amélie de Rudolstadt whether Zdenko is improvising, Amélie shows indifference and possibly jealousy at Consuelo's interest. Amélie does admit, however, to Zdenko's limitless prowess and originality, lending credence to the narrator's appreciation of his abilities. Later Amélie will admit that Zdenko never repeats a song the same way twice, "je suis persuadée que ce sont des improvisations, et je me suis bien vite convaincue que cela ne valait pas la peine d'être écouté, bien que nos montagnards s'imaginent y trouver à leur gré un sens symbolique" [I'm convinced that they're improvisations, and I was sure they weren't worth listening to, even though the mountain folk believe there is a symbolic meaning to be found in them] (*C*, 1: 284). The value of Zdenko's gift for improvisation is not only a mystery but also a source of mysticism. Amélie's disdain displays more ignorance than aesthetic judgment.

One episode between Consuelo and Zdenko involving improvisation warrants commentary. Intrigued by Zdenko's singing and convinced he could lead her to Albert, Consuelo finds Zdenko and asks him, in German, to sing some Bohemian songs for her.[33] Zdenko agrees to sing for her, but says she must provide the first line of the song. She offers him a line she remembered hearing him sing, but he wants to teach her another one, true to his nonrepetitive reputation, and again asks for another opening line. Although the exchange finishes badly, as it almost always does with Zdenko and Consuelo, the structure of the scene recalls salon customs of the time, where the soloist requests a musical phrase from someone in the audience on which she or he improvises. In any case, Sand reinserts a well-known practice into a very different context, successfully producing a scene that is at once familiar and strange for the nineteenth-century reader.

The very notion that improvisation represents a deviation from an established melody leads Sand easily and logically to a statement of freedom, a need to affirm the ability to deviate according to one's own ideals so long as they are moral and ethical. *Consuelo* is nothing if not a text about freedom and a declaration of independence. Sand manages to communicate the ability to deviate from convention in an artistic context by presenting various musicians who diverge from the straight and narrow by way of their aesthetic expression. In this manner Sand uses improvisation as an important metaphor for freedom and the search for freedom. It is significant that Consuelo's apprenticeship in improvisation comes not from her revered and famous mentor, Porpora, who maintains rigid control over her musical development, but from the popular and possibly mad Zdenko. Only in Spandau does Consuelo venture independently into the serious application of improvisation, despite her advice to Haydn of several hundred pages earlier. The gulf that separates academic training from popular apprenticeship begins to creep into the narrative, and Consuelo deplores the perceived insistence on one to the detriment of the other. From this point on Consuelo will try to reconcile the two sides of her musical experience, a struggle in which Albert will be of some help.[34]

In *Les Maîtres Sonneurs* Sand further explores the vital role improvisation plays in folk music. Her investigation into this technique contributes as much to the narrative and to the characterization of Joset as to the cultural history she documents, albeit with embellishment. Bagpipers, like most folk musicians, rely heavily on their ability to improvise. According to Sand, however, while tunes and improvisations make up the repertoire one acquires on the road to becoming a master piper, original invention does not enter into the game. Some individuality is, of course, tolerated and indeed encouraged in the repetitious manipulation of folk airs, but the limits are strongly felt and firmly adhered to. In some ways, the differences between folk improvisations and those of bel canto are few and subtle.

The degree of Bastien's respect for Joset is clear. He recognizes his talent and encourages him to develop it. Others in the novel have the same respect, albeit guarded, for Joset's powers of inventiveness. He displays two areas of creative ability: improvisation on traditional tunes and invention of new tunes. In neither case do the other characters know how to react: to shun the difference or to allow their curiosity free rein.

Il le [l'air] joua d'abord tel que nous le connaissions, et ensuite un peu différemment, d'une façon plus douce et plus triste, et enfin le changea du tout au tout, variant les modes et y mêlant du sien, qui n'était pas pire, et qui même semblait soupirer et prier d'une manière si tendre qu'on ne se pouvait tenir d'en être touché de compassion. Ensuite, il le prit sur un ton plus fort et plus vif, comme si c'était une chanson de reproche et de commandement, et Brulette . . . recula comme effrayée de la colère qui était marquée dans cette musique. (*MS*, 414–15)

[First he played the tune the way we knew it, then a bit differently, sweeter and sadder, and finally he changed it altogether, varying the modes and mixing them up with his own, which was no worse, and which even seemed to sigh and pray so gently we couldn't help but be touched with compassion. Then he played it on a stronger and quicker tone, as if it were a song of reproach and command, and Brulette . . . backed away as if in fear of the wrath that marred this music.]

This passage points out the multiplicity or polyvalence—dare I say polyphony?—with which Sand shows the effects of music on her characters. Tiennet's first-person plural indicates a collective mistrust of Joset's playing style, a mistrust that originates in difference. The degree of emotion in Joset's interpretation is especially palpable for Brulette. At the same time as the author suggests a movement away from such individualized music, and therefore away from Joset, she also exhorts approbation and respect for the musical abilities of this anticonformist character. Sand paints a individual who at once attracts and repels, which makes a strong commentary on the artist's role in society.

A key passage in Sand's description of folk music plays on terminology familiar to her Parisian readers but foreign to the peasant characters of her novel. Père Bastien establishes the figure of the calm, mature musician who knows the power and dangers of music. He also offers explanations of the creative freedom inherent in Bourbonnais music:

La musique a deux modes, que les savants, comme j'ai ouï dire, appellent majeur et mineur, et que j'appelle, moi, mode clair et mode trouble; ou si tu veux, mode de ciel bleu et mode de ciel gris; ou encore mode de la force ou de la joie, et mode de la tristesse ou de la songerie. Tu peux chercher jusqu'à demain, tu ne trouveras pas la fin des oppositions qu'il y a entre ces deux modes, non plus que tu n'en trouveras un troisième; car tout, sur la terre, est ombre ou lumière, repos ou action. Or, écoute bien toujours, Joseph! La plaine chante en majeur et la montagne en mineur. (*MS*, 293–94)[35]

[Music has two modes, which I've heard learned people call major and minor, and which myself, I call clear and murky; or if you prefer, blue sky and grey sky; or rather the mode of power or joy and the mode of sadness or daydreaming. You can search till the cows come home, but you'll find no end to the contrasts between these two modes, no more than you'll find a third. Because everything on earth is shadow or light, rest or bustle. So always listen well, Joseph. The plains sing in a major key and the mountains in a minor key.]

Léon Guichard points out that Sand would have been more in keeping with the traditional understanding of musical modes had she assigned the minor to the Berrichons, since they have a slow and heavy temperament, and also often transform tunes that come to them in a major key to a minor one.[36] On the contrary, if Sand chose to characterize Bourbonnais music as minor, it was most likely because that mode, which conventionally connotes darkness and mystery, corresponded better in her mind to the geography and temperament of that province as she portrays it in her novel. The major mode translates more readily for her into the straightforward and simple disposition of the geography and character of Berry.

The concerted effort to steer away from academic musical terminology underlies another of Sand's goals: to establish folk music as a separate but equal entity. Whereas Père Bastien tries to emphasize the diversity of appellations, Sand is obliged to use the terms "major" and "minor" for her reading public. This compromise corresponds to the general principle she adopts in attempting to introduce a regional flavor in the language of her novel—an important feature of the rustic novels—all the while including explanations for the Parisian reading public.[37] The assessment that no other modes exist is, of course, faulty. I assign this detail not to Sand's ignorance of traditional modes in ancient, medieval and Renaissance music, but rather partly to the "modern" tendency, from the baroque through romantic periods, to reduce the various modes to two, and partly to her need to establish a clear dichotomy, not only for the symbolic and geographic distinction she was drawing but also for the romantic duality to which she so willingly subscribed. One senses, in fact, an avoidance of strict musicological terminology in an effort to situate folk music outside the realm of academic music and thus outside its restrictive definitions.

It is not without interest that Sand writes this novel about a musician-hero who concentrates so much on his music and so little on interpersonal relations just five years after her split with Chopin. Salomon and Mallion in their edition of the novel, and Rambeau in her commanding comparison of the two artists, as well as several other critics, compare Joset's selfishness and egotism with Chopin's. This commentary goes beyond idle biocritical curiosity as the contrast between Joset and Consuelo specifically targets the play of arrogance and selfishness on the one hand and modesty and generosity on the other. The reflection of Chopin in Joset and even in Anzoleto seems, therefore, not without significance in understanding Sand's portrayal of extremely talented but self-involved musicians, whose art cannot replace the value of interpersonal skills. In *Les Maîtres Sonneurs* Sand seems to be drawing a type of musician she respects immensely for his musical prowess and his determination to pull himself up from a background devoid of musical training, yet one she pities on a personal level. And it is through Joset's facility with improvisation that the reader can appreciate at once his talent and his impertinence. Rambeau posits that it is the linking of traditional art and the "magic of improvisation" that form Sand's image of the inspired musician.[38]

Improvisation also plays a decisive part in the characterization of Angelin in "L'Orgue du titan" (1872). In the frame story the protagonist recounts the pain he endures whenever he plays a particular set of improvisations. Sand begins the story thus: "Un soir, l'improvisation musicale du vieux et illustre maître Angelin nous passionnait comme de coutume, lorsqu'une corde de piano vint à se briser avec une vibration insignifiante pour nous, mais qui produisit sur les nerfs surexcités de l'artiste l'effet d'un coup de foudre" [One evening the musical improvisation of the elderly and illustrious master Angelin fascinated us as always, when a piano string broke with a vibration that to us was insignificant but which had the effect of a thunderclap on the artist's overexcited nerves].[39]

Three aspects of this opening sentence arrest our attention. First, Sand puts "l'improvisation" as the subject of the verb instead of the performer of the music. Such a stylistic nuance indicates the importance of music and the musical form for the story. Second, that the piano string breaks, causing Angelin acute pain even though it remains barely perceptible for his companions, points to the psychological nature of the story. The import of the term "vibration" for both music and emotions intensifies the gulf that separates the pianist from his friends. Third, the comparison of the thunderclap establishes a firm adumbration for the natural explanation in the rest of the story, where we learn that a thunderclap followed by an avalanche of rocks accompanied the original occurrence of the pain resulting from these variations. Taken all together, the elements of this first sentence disclose the essence of the tale, including the fantastic hesitation between a logical explanation housed in reality and an other-worldly sequence of events that seems to repeat itself mysteriously.

The pianist continues to explain his pain: "Ceci m'arrive quelquefois quand je joue le motif sur lequel je viens d'improviser. Un bruit imprévu me trouble et il me semble que mes mains s'allongent. C'est une sensation douloureuse et qui me reporte à un moment tragique et pourtant heureux dans mon existence" [This sometimes happens to me when I'm playing the motif I've just been improvising on. An unexpected noise agitates me and I feel my hands growing longer. It's a painful sensation that takes me back to a tragic and yet happy moment of my life] ("Orgue," 107). Improvising thus connotes a transgression, something for which Angelin feels he was once punished, and he continues to be punished or to punish himself for the same improvisations. Yet the experience also represents happiness for him. The apparent contradiction epitomizes art as a source of both joy and pain at the same time as it manifests the hero's guilt through the use of a musical symbol.

The protagonist in "Histoire du rêveur" (1829) also experiences his musical fantastic through improvisation. The first time he hears a mysterious voice that intrigues him, he listens closely to the words: "c'était une poésie enthousiaste et sauvage qui portait le caractère de l'improvisation" [it was an enthusiastic and wild poetry that conveyed the character of improvisation].[40] Here the notion of improvisation recalls Madame de Staël's Corinne, who spontaneously produces a lyrico-poetical creation based on an often abstract idea. The sense of the word "enthusiastic" evokes Staël's use of the term in De l'Allemagne, an impassioned and near-ecstatic abandonment to an Ideal. Sand's unknown singer continues to "speak" a musical language, further promoting the notion of improvisation as well as that of communication through music. Later in the story the singer will enter into dialogue with the Spirit of Mount Etna, also expressed in improvisational terms. The protagonist will attempt, in vain, a musical dialogue wherein he improvises his discourse.

At the end of "Histoire du rêveur," Portia, the revered soprano who is the unknown singer of the beginning of the tale, sings a simple Venetian song with three verses. The narrator comments on her changes in the music from one stanza to the next:

> Portia chanta le premier couplet avec une simplicité pure et suave. Au second elle altéra le thème pour suivre ses inspirations et l'on se crut transporté sur les flots de Venise. On écouta le doux murmure des vagues et le refrain lointain du barcarole. Au troisième, elle reprit le thème, mais elle lui donna une autre expression. La douleur, l'amour, le reproche s'y montrèrent avec énergie, l'abattement mélancolique de ses derniers accens s'empara de tous les cœurs. ("Rêveur," 35)

> [Portia sang the first verse with a pure and exquisite simplicity. For the second she altered the theme according to her inspiration and we felt transported onto the waters of Venice. We listened to the soft murmuring of the waves and the far-off refrains of the barcarole. For the third, she returned to the theme, but she gave it another expression. Pain, love, and reproach emerged energetically, and the melancholy despondency of the final notes took hold of our hearts.]

Even though Sand's expression in matters of music and her notions of musical language are still in a state of infancy, improvisation and the development of the melody from one verse to the next unmistakably announce a serious regard for the performer's ability to manipulate a melodic line. Moreover, the ability to improvise maintains an important power and control over the listener.

Improvisation in *Les Sept Cordes de la lyre* (1839) again recalls Staël's Corinne. The lyre, an actual character in the closet play, sounds by itself and improvises musically on various concepts and metaphysical problems. This voice that expresses the important notions of the text sometimes calls itself "la voix de la lyre" [the voice of the lyre], sometimes "les chœurs des esprits de l'Harmonie" [the chorus of the spirit of harmony], "l'esprit de la lyre" [the spirit of the lyre], or even "le chœur des Esprits célestes" [the chorus of celestial Spirits]. Changing appellations so often does not suggest instability; on the contrary, it advances the notion that the spirit of music, the pipeline to God, surrounds us and all we have to do is learn to listen. This displays another sort of improvisation, that of antiphonal exchange where various voices share and compete with the same musical material. Once Hélène, the heroine, begins to emerge from her naivete and to explore the inferences between music and madness that pervade the text, she also begins to contemplate the power of music and its effect on the human psyche. Albertus, her tutor and a philosopher, calls her "une pure et belle improvisatrice" [a pure and beautiful improviser],[41] although he acknowledges that she has no superior intelligence. As we move toward the end of the text, the lyre and its analogues become more articulate about the nature of music and about the need to listen with a pure heart. Music, unlike philosophy, goes beyond intellectual training; it requires sincere and heartfelt compassion. Only with an honest and open-minded approach, which is to say with the spirit of improvisation, can one hope to understand the message of love that music alone can express. Brian Juden posits that the text "represents the unison of the arts under the aegis of love in a single symbol."[42]

Literary improvisation of the type Staël's Corinne proffers also causes Sand to consider the disadvantages of improvisation. In her *Entretiens journaliers* she recounts an evening at her home when several Polish emigrants have come together. A young and not untalented poet recites a piece in verse he has written in praise of Mickiewicz, bemoaning the fact that he has not yet become a great poet. The famous Pole stands up and answers him in improvised verse about the hard work required to become a praiseworthy poet.

Sand comments more on the effect of the improvisation than on the phenomenon itself. She finds that those who fall into a sort of delirium witness not so much an appreciation of artistic prowess as a manifestation of ecstasy. These exalted feelings, much exaggerated of late, she writes, are symptomatic of the loss of and the simultaneous need for religion.

> Entre la raison et la folie, il y a un état de l'esprit qui n'a jamais été ni bien observé ni bien qualifié et où les croyances religieuses de tous les temps et de tous les peuples ont supposé l'homme en contact direct avec l'esprit de Dieu. . . . Ce miracle éternel, qui est dans les traditions de l'humanité ne pouvait se perdre avec la religion. Il lui a survécu, mais au lieu de s'opérer de Dieu à l' homme dans l'ordre métaphysique, il s'est passé d'homme à homme par l'opération des fluides nerveux, explication beaucoup plus merveilleuse et moins acceptable en philosophie que toutes celles du passé. (*OA*, 2:1008–9)

> [Between reason and madness, there's a state of mind that has never been well observed or described and where religious beliefs of all times and of all peoples have supposed that man was in direct contact with God. . . . This eternal miracle, which is in line with the traditions of humanity, could not be lost along with religion. It outlived it, but instead of being transmitted from God to man in a metaphysical order, it went from man to man by the process of nervous fluids, a much more marvelous explanation and much less acceptable in philosophy than all those of the past.]

This is clearly Sand's condemnation of the public's facile response to an artistic performance. We cannot overlook the blurry line that separates reason from madness, always important in romantic fiction and especially in Sand's musical fantastic. Sand remains severe and demanding in these matters. The art of improvisation represents for Sand the sign of a true artist, so long as it is not done merely for the entertainment of an avaricious and dilettante public or for the self-aggrandizement of the artist.

MEMORY AND MUSIC

Sand frequently evokes the role of memory in the appreciation, effect, and representation of music. She was vastly impressed by the prodigious memory of Chopin, Liszt, and others and often highlights this trait as an important quality for a musician. Memory emerges in her writing as an important element in musical concerns, sometimes in terms of training, sometimes in performance technique, and always in its effect on the listener. The role of memory in nineteenth-century music performance and concert attendance carries an additional burden in that the public often heard a new piece only once and remembered it from that performance or from a piano transcription, as opposed to today's habit of relying on the possibility of endless electronic repetition. The function of memory in the music listening experience does not necessarily involve a conscious effort; it is a fairly automatic response. On the contrary, cognitive intrusion would alter and disturb the role of the memory in the musical experience, as Sand sees it.[43] She is aware of the instinctive role of memory in the musical experience and exploits it in all her musical novels.

An essential passage on musical memory in *Consuelo* occurs during the heroine's stay at Spandau. While the king allows her a harpsichord, he will permit neither candles nor writing implements, so she cannot write down her compositions and improvisations. Consuelo perseveres, however, and manages to exercise her training and discipline to produce and retain simple and beautiful pieces. When her harpsichord is removed at the end of the opera season, she must focus even harder to remember her inventions, which now become simpler. It is at this moment that she begins to see the fruits of combining improvisation and composition, thus joining two methods for which she received no training. A period of new musical expression dawns for Consuelo while she is in prison, again proof of the romantic adage that repression spawns creativity.[44]

In *Consuelo* the narrator sanctions different levels of musical memory. One, which recurs frequently throughout the novel, is the memory of Consuelo's mother and the songs she taught her during their travels through Europe. These musical memories help Consuelo to understand her origins and to connect with Zdenko. They also offer her an alternative musical expression quite different from the academic music for which Porpora trains her. She moves from a formal musical preparation that has all but obliterated her memories of this maternal music to a renewed appreciation of folk music. At the end of the novel she fully embraces and practices folk music and improvisation.

Consuelo's first exposure to Zdenko is established through musical memory. He sings some Bohemian folk tunes that she asks Amélie de Rudolstadt to translate for her. She is impressed by his voice and wishes to know whether he is repeating ancient songs or improvising new ones. Amélie, who is singularly unimpressed by any of this, replies, "Qui peut le savoir? Zdenko est un improvisateur inépuisable ou un rapsode bien savant" [Who can tell? Zdenko

is either an inexhaustible improviser or a very learned rhapsodist]
(*C*, 1:282). The term "rapsode" refers to medieval jongleurs. The
allusion is flawed because the culture and training of the jongleurs
contrasts with the natural, untrained gifts of Zdenko; but the similarity of seemingly endless improvisations springing spontaneously
from an exceptional memory fits the context. What Amélie does
respect in Zdenko—and Sand will show this aspect of his talents on
several occasions throughout the novel—is his prodigious memory.
He remembers so many folk tunes that it staggers Albert, who has
written many of them down.[45] Consuelo hears and retains Zdenko's
songs, proof of her own excellent musical memory, and repeats
them to the amazement of both Albert and Zdenko. She thus returns
to her folk origins in a musical way as well as demonstrating musical mastery in a domain that, by its placement in the novel later in
her *Bildung*, after the apprenticeship in Venice, suggests a greater
importance of musical memory for folk than for academic music.

The function of musical memory in *Consuelo* also provides a
convenient method of retrospective narrative. Musical memories
allow Consuelo to remember her mother; Anzoleto to remember
when he first met Consuelo, and Albert to remember his first encounters with Zdenko as well as his first encounter with Consuelo
and her mother over a decade earlier.[46] Folk music serves this function for Consuelo, Albert, and Zdenko, religious songs for Anzoleto. It is not generally uncommon to revisit a previous situation or
the memory of a particular person while listening to a specific piece
of music. Sand takes the simple procedure that affects everyone and
makes it work on a narrative level.

In the case of Zdenko and Albert and, to a lesser degree, Consuelo and her mother, glimpses into the past occasioned by popular
music provide an important element of Sand's message of egalitarianism. The memory of folk music remains more charged with significance than that of baroque ornaments, and the historical
references that inevitably follow such folk memories point to a decided effort to reach into the past of a forgotten people and to make
their struggle relevant again. The struggle that is being resuscitated
here is that of the ancient Bohemians; Zdenko's musical memory
represents Old Bohemia and allows Albert to appreciate the distant
religious and social conflict of Bohemian Protestants against Austrian Catholics. Albert's madness results directly from the insincerity and dishonesty of the discord.[47] At the same time Sand
implicitly evokes the contemporary social dissatisfaction in France
of the July Monarchy and holds up the peasantry, symbolized by its
folk music, as the disenfranchised.

Ethnic music also figures in *La Filleule* (1853). The title character, Moréna, and her brother/husband, Algénib, are *gitani*.[48] Algénib defines himself in part through the music of his people, which
he learned from his stepmother. He wishes to share his culture with
Moréna, whose heritage has been hidden from her, and insists she
learn the language, the songs, and the dances of their tribe. Thus
the transmission of culture is effected through the memory of those
elements that define a people. Algénib sings quite well and makes
a stirring impression with his native songs in a Parisian salon.
While the quality of his voice remains uncontested, the musicality
of his songs comes under some scrutiny by those aristocrats unused
to non-Western harmonies.

Another instance of memory and non-Western music surfaces
when Stéphen, Moréna's adoptive French father, writes from Ma-
nilla that he will bring back some Hindu, Chinese, and Japanese
melodies. He prefers to store them in his memory and to interpret
them for his musician friend Schwartz when he returns rather than
attempt a translation in writing doomed to failure (*F*, 135). Here the
notion of the inability of Western musical notation to represent non-
Western sounds recalls Sand's treatment of a similar matter in the
rustic novels, which I shall discuss later. More important than the
inability of standard musical notation to render these tunes is the
importance of the memory in the transmission of cultural material,
especially music. Memory stands out as the most reliable tool, accessible to more people because of illiteracy and infinitely more
adaptable and fluid, due partly to unreliable memory and partly to
the lack of a notion of a fixed version. Memory of music thus defines folk music and culture in a way academic music cannot hope
to attain.

The respect Sand shows for musical memory stands in contrast
to the traditional concept of mental faculties. Zdenko fulfills the
role of the wise fool, uttering to Albert the ominous prediction that
Consuelo will be the cause of a major change in their lives. Similarly Joset, in *Les Maîtres Sonneurs*, has the reputation of having
"une petite folleté dans la tête depuis qu'il est au monde" [a little
craziness in his head since he was born] (*MS*, 39); but his great
memory of local songs earns him the respect of the principal characters of the novel. Thus folk music, or more precisely the memory
of folk music, provides a more reliable measure of a character's
worth than traditional impressions of intelligence. These characters
display a sixth sense that manifests itself in music.

Another instance where Sand combines musical memory and
emotional instability occurs in *Les Sept Cordes de la lyre*, where

Hélène's history of madness is constantly linked with music and the memory of music. Her father, also reputed to have been mad, bequeathed the lyre to her. Her sole inheritance, it was not to be played for fear of awakening dangerous memories: "Il est de la nature de ces maladies de recommencer avec les causes qui les ont fait naître" [It is the nature of these disorders to start up again with the causes that brought them about in the first place] (*SC*, 79). Later Hélène will state more explicitly the link between the lyre and her madness: "N'y touchez plus jamais, Hanz. C'est mon héritage. On appelle cela *la folie*" [Don't ever touch it again, Hanz. It's my heritage. They call it *madness*] (*SC*, 100). Then she compares the lyre to the sacred host. Here the influence of Leroux and Lamennais is evident in the religious connotations Sand weaves into discussions about music, especially early in her career.

Musical memory contributes considerably to the artistic activities in *Le Château des Désertes* insofar as the majority of the narrative revolves around interpreting and reproducing in commedia dell'arte style three different versions of the Don Juan myth.[49] As with any representation of commedia dell'arte, the actors' memories are essential since each one must remember what has been said so as to be able to react in a logical fashion and at the same time remember the plot outline. This demands different skills from those traditionally involved in an actor's memorization of a script. The role of the memory is important as it constantly forces the actors to combine efforts and to work together and serves as a support for the collective effort of the theater, and therefore for the collective in general. However, the nature of the memory Sand extols here differs from that in other novels since it relies on improvisation. While the memory maintains continuity in the dialogue and plot, the dramatic progression of the play relies solely on spontaneity: "Ne vous attachez pas aux mots. Au contraire, oubliez-les entièrement: la moindre phrase, retenue par cœur, est mortelle à l'improvisation" [Don't get attached to words. On the contrary, forget them altogether; the simplest memorized phrase is deadly to improvisation] (*CD*, 119).[50]

A painful memory recalled by music evinces another aspect of musical memory, one that bears witness to the power of music to evoke emotion, suffering, and memory. Such is Angelin's lot in "L'Orgue du titan." He feels such guilt from having abandoned his master to supersede him in the musical world, that the very memory of that decisive event, always evoked by the same musical improvisation, causes him physical and emotional pain. The swelling of Angelin's fingers symbolizes guilty pride.[51] Note also that not just the memory of a melody, but of improvisation on that melody, a musical manipulation that itself requires memory on the performer's and the listener's parts, evokes the pain of remembrance.

Music evokes a memory of love in *Le Dernier Amour* (1866) when the narrator hears Félicie, his beloved, playing the same tune he heard her play when he first realized he loved her. However, hearing this tune a second time just at the moment when he is beginning to admit his jealousy elicits the pain of faltering love. It is the double cognizance of past felicity (the irony of the heroine's name is not unappreciated) and the present lack of conviction in his love that the music elicits. "Je me rappelai les circonstanaces où cette magie s'était emparée de moi, je revis le paysage où j'étais. . . . j'étreignis la femme, je crus étreindre l'amour. Mais ce n'était que le rêve, l'amour physique qui fait sentir plus odieusement l'absence de l'amour moral. Le réveil fut affreux" [I remembered the circumstances where this magic took control of me; I could see the countryside where I was. . . . I hugged the woman, thinking I was hugging love. But it was only a dream, physical love that displays more odiously the absence of emotional love. Waking up was horrible].[52]

Les Maîtres Sonneurs privileges invention over memory, without diminishing it. This is a principle Joset assimilates perhaps too well since it causes him to consider himself superior to other pipers, whose originality does not go beyond improvising on existing tunes. Lionel Dauriac tells us that when the memory works, all the while intellectually unaware that it is working, it produces similar music; but when it produces different music, there is a function of disassociation that is no longer a function of memory but of imagination, and that is the manifestation of genius.[53]

Dauriac would have us believe that Joset and his ilk offer no verisimilitude. Different from the critiques of G. Guillaume and L. Charles-Dominique,[54] here the issue is not one of historicity but of the nature of memory, genius, and music. The very concept of genius being problematical at best, I prefer merely to observe Sand's commentary of the function of memory in the creative process. For her, the manifestation of the memory plays a key role in the creation and the re-creation of music and signals an alternate mode of reflection, different from and superior to intellectual activity.

The academic world of music also relies heavily on the memory of its performers. In *Consuelo* frequent reference is made to the importance of Consuelo's, Corilla's, and Anzoleto's memory. Célio's memory also impresses the narrator of *Le Château des Désertes*. It is also not surprising that Lucrezia Floriani, Célio's mother, had an impressive memory. In all cases Sand's opinion of the performer's memory commands respect but also caution: one must not complacently rely on a good memory to be an excellent musician, rather one must take that gift, like musical talent, as a beginning.

The role of memory in the reception of music is another aspect of the musical experience Sand considers. The listener is vital to the musical exchange. The composer relies on the listener's memory to apprehend the various structures of the composition. When contemplating the structure of a piece, the composer considers the public's reception in determining, for instance, whether to repeat a phrase, how often to repeat it, when to alter it, when to return to it. While in most musical forms the nature of repetitions is highly conventional, these and other decisions do often depend on the composer's appreciation of the listener's memory. Keeping in mind that music is a time-bound art that cannot be stopped and rewound, repetitions and other devices that stimulate the memory are essential to composer and public alike.

Sand highlights the public's memory in several examples: *Adriani, Le Château des Désertes, Consuelo, La Filleule, Malgrétout*, but most notably in *Les Maîtres Sonneurs*. The flute scene in the fourth *veillée* affirms the degree to which Joset's music affects Brulette through her memory. Brulette weeps and says she does not know why she is crying, simply that she cannot help herself. She then enters into a narrative of her memorial reactions to Joset's music. "Tu me paraissais comme dans l'âge où nous demeurions ensemble. . . . J'ai vu aussi, dans ma songerie, ta mère et mon grand-père assis devant le feu, et causant de choses que je n'entendais point, tandis que je te voyais à genoux dans un coin, disant ta prière, et que je me sentais comme endormie dans mon petit lit" [You appeared to me at the age you were when we lived together. . . . In my day-dreaming, I also saw your mother and my grandfather sitting by the fireplace, talking about things I couldn't understand, while I saw you on your knees in the corner saying your prayers; I could feel myself falling asleep in my little bed] (*MS*, 117–18). All her reactions are based on memories of their past together, of the happy and simple times they spent beside each other as children. Joset has managed to communicate these memories through music, and Brulette has understood them. In the seventh of the *Lettres d'un voyageur*, written to Liszt, Sand exhorts a similar use of music to evoke memories: "improvisez-moi sur le piano ces délicieuses pastorales qui font pleurer le vieux Everard et moi, parce qu'elles nous rappellent nos jeunes ans, nos collines et les chèvres que nous paissions" [improvise for me on the piano those delightful pastorals that make poor Everard and me cry because they remind us of our youth, our hills, and the goats we put out to graze] (*LV,* 2:846).

In *Consuelo*, especially in the Bohemia section, Sand uses a different approach to the receiver's memory. Here musical communication is of two sorts: public and private. When Consuelo arrives at Riesenberg, Albert remains aloof and uninterested. Not until he first hears her singing during a lesson with Amélie does he acknowledge her presence, and then he appears to recognize her as a savior sent to him: "la figure pâle et pensive d'Albert . . . resta immobile et singulièrement attendrie jusqu'à la fin du morceau. . . . Albert, pliant les deux genoux et levant vers elle ses grands yeux noirs ruisselants de larmes, s'écria en espagnol sans le moindre accent germanique: 'O Consuelo, Consuelo te voilà donc enfin trouvée!' " [Albert's pale and pensive face . . . remained motionless and strangely touched until the end of the music. . . . Bending his knees and raising toward her his large, black eyes streaming with tears, Albert cried out in Spanish without the least trace of a German accent: "Oh Consuelo, Consuelo, finally I've found you!"] (*C*, 1: 256). Albert's sincere and profound outpouring, clearly resulting from Consuelo's music having stimulated and articulated a profound memory, exhausts him and he faints. Consuelo has never before seen such emotion from him.

The stimulation of Consuelo's voice affects Albert more than the piece she sings. He remembers the promise of a *consolation* that he thought forgotten but now recognizes in the voice of the singer. Recognition, like memory, supposes prior knowledge. Later music will have a similar effect on Consuelo when she descends into the grotto. She hears the sounds of Albert's Stradivarius. Although she does not recognize the melody, she understands intuitively why Albert "l'avait si bien comprise dès la première phrase qu'il lui avait entendu chanter" [had understood her so well from the first phrase he heard her sing] (*C*, 1:327).

Musical memory also has quasi-medicinal consequences in the case of Albert. After his long discussion with Consuelo in the grotto when they discover all they have in common, his general state of health improves. If ever he feels depressed, Consuelo sings for him, and that cures him: "Elle se mettait à chanter et aussitôt le jeune comte, charmé et subjugué, se soulageait par des pleurs, ou s'animait d'un nouvel enthousiasme. Ce remède était infaillible" [She began to sing and immediately the young count, enchanted and captivated, was calmed by his tears or became animated with renewed enthusiasm. This remedy was infallible] (*C*, 1:384). Similarly, Brulette was able to awaken Joset from his mental wandering by singing to him (*MS*, 67).

An equally painful yet curative consequence of music and musical memory occurs in *Adriani* (1854). Laure, suffering from her recent widowhood, sings the gondolier's aria from Rossini's *Otello*: "Nessun maggior dolor." Adriani hears her and responds in song, but her anguish is too great to allow him to continue. Later Adriani plays it on her piano, not realizing she is in the room, again awakening Laure's pain. Throughout the novel Laure struggles with her memories. She discovers that her love for her dead husband is misplaced since he married her for position and money. Now afraid of relationships and of her own feelings, she hesitates to trust her emotions and her emotional responses to the feelings music evokes.

Memory of music is an integral part of Sand's representation of the musical experience. From the perspective of the musician, the composer, the listener, and by extension the reader, memory is constantly used and continually needed for a successful musical exchange. The intercourse between the various participants in musical communication involves the memories of each, either conscious or unconscious, and at the same time results in the construction of new memories. Sand brings us back to a basic element of music listening: tunes remind us of people, events, and times. And these associations reemerge at the sound of that music. The Proustian phenomenon of a memory evoked by the senses comes to life again and again in Sand's musical works.[55]

MUSIC AND MIMESIS

A discussion of music's ability to evoke the emotions and its tendency to speak to a profound level of the human psyche begs a discussion of the purpose of music, indeed, of all the arts. Sand was familiar with the notions of Plato, Pythagoras, Saint Augustine, Kant, Hegel, Herder, and Friederich Schlegel, and was conversant with the writings and ideas of Rousseau and the Encyclopédistes, who in turn were acquainted with the more specifically musicological writings of Quinault, Rameau, Mattheson, Du Bos, Batteux, Morellet, and Chabanon, to name only the best-known music aestheticians. Even though she embraces the Platonic notion of artistic mimesis, which does not copy mindlessly for the sole purpose of replication but attempts to see beyond the external and to demonstrate how the internal is communicated, most of Sand's aesthetic concept of mimesis was formed and informed by thinkers in the

Age of Reason, whose explanations of music most often led away from feelings and toward a rational definition. The notion of the imitation of feelings came under scrutiny by some eighteenth-century thinkers, and in the place of "feelings" the term "expression" surfaced, although it is hardly a less ambiguous term. For many theorists, rather than feelings themselves it was their objective manifestation in impassioned utterances and in vocal cries that became the model for musical imitation. Charles Batteux used the term "expression" in place of "imitation," providing another judicious dose of imprecision. André Morellet adopted a similar postulate when he wrote that imitation and expression are identical. Other noted contemporary theorists, such as Michel-Paul de Chabanon, rejected the notion of musical mimesis, stating that the other arts produce faithful images while music does not, making it less an art of imitation than the others. Music is not, he maintained, an imitation of human speech. James Beattie pointed out that, while there may be some imitation in music, it is not the important aspect of the musical experience, which is pleasure, distinguishing clearly between imitation and expression. Friederich Schlegel agreed that imitation is not the highest principle of music.[56]

George Sand valiantly undertakes to argue the issue of music's purpose. Her ideas change somewhat across time, but she usually locates her discourse in an analysis of imitation. In the famous letter to Meyerbeer (*LV,* 12), she juggles her notions on this question:

> Je reste convaincu qu'il est au pouvoir du plus beau de tous les arts de peindre toutes les nuances du sentiment et toutes les phases de la passion. Sauf la dissertation métaphysique . . . , la musique peut tout exprimer. . . . Il n'est pas besoin d'une mélodie complète; il ne faut que des modulations pour faire passer des nuées sombres sur la face d'Hélios et pour balayer l'azur du ciel, pour soulever le volcan et faire rugir les cyclopes. . . . [C]omment croirais-je que la musique est un art de pur agrément et de simple spéculation, quand je me souviens d'avoir été plus touché de ses effets et plus convaincu par son éloquence que par tous mes livres de philosophie? (*LV,* 2:923–26)

> [I remain convinced that it is within the power of the most beautiful of all the arts to paint all the shades of feeling and all the phases of passion. Except for the metaphysical essay . . . , music can express anything. . . . It doesn't need a complete melody; it only needs modulations to send dark clouds over the face of Helios and to brush away the blue of the sky, to stir up the volcano and to make the Cyclopes blush. . . . How could I believe that music is purely an art of entertainment and simple speculation when I remember being more touched by its effects and more convinced by its eloquence than by all my philosophy texts?]

Sand frequently depicts the noises of nature as music, sometimes hinting at imitation in music. One of the richest passages of this sort can be found in the "Avant-Propos" of *François le champi*. It presents the wonders of nature and the limitations of art in transmitting its beauty to the public. Sand attempts a description of the Berrichon landscape—a representation that is rife with musical metaphors and images.

> Nous-mêmes, mon ami et moi, nous marchions avec une certaine précaution, et un recueillement instinctif nous rendait muets et comme attentifs à la beauté adoucie de la nature, à l'harmonie enchanteresse de ses derniers accords, qui s'éteignaient dans un *pianissimo* insaisissable. L'automne est un *andante* mélancolique et gracieux qui prépare admirablement le solennel *adagio* de l'hiver.[57]

> [My friend and I were walking rather cautiously and an instinctive contemplation kept us quiet and sort of attentive to the toned down beauty of nature, to the enchanting harmony of its last chords that faded in an elusive *pianissimo*. Autumn is a melancholy and gracious *andante* that delightfully prepares the solemn *adagio* of winter.]

Sand rarely uses technical musical terms such as these; she leaves that technique, too often superficial, to other authors. The italics underscore the foreignness of the terms, not only because they are Italian words but also because they represent a network of musical vocabulary quite foreign to the peasant context of the novel. All the musical terms tend toward the calm, the slow, the gentle, in rhythm and in manner. The sight Sand and Rollinat are taking in here reflects the salubrious qualities of the Berrichon countryside Sand wishes to convey.

Sand continues to remark on the musicality of nature:

> Cette nuit d'octobre,[58] ce ciel incolore, cette musique sans mélodie marquée ou suivie, ce calme de la nature, ce paysan qui se trouve plus près que nous, par sa simplicité, pour en jouir et la comprendre sans la décrire, mettons tout cela ensemble, et appelons-le *la vie primitive*, relativement à notre vie développée et compliquée, que j'appellerai *la vie factice*. (*FC*, 206)

> [This October night, this colorless sky, this music without a defined or sustained melody, this calm nature, this peasant who by his simplicity is better able than we to find joy in nature and to understand it without describing it—let's put all that together and call it *primitive life*, as opposed to our cultivated and complicated one that we'll call *contrived life*.]

The metaphor of the tuneless melody underscores the ineffable beauty and calm of nature by the modification of two qualifying adjectives: "no *defined* or *sustained* melody." Not the grouping of sounds one would normally call a melody in a strictly academic sense, the ethereal tune lilts through the air, remaining aloof and difficult to perceive or catch; note the use of "insaisissable" in the previous quotation. A parallel metaphor applies visually in the phrase "ce ciel incolore," which describes not the total absence of color, but a muted color, one almost too subtle to describe.

Sand's antithesis of "la vie primitive" and "la vie factice" is a mainstay of her aesthetic criticism. The author privileges peasant music in these novels as a source of poetic language, different from and equal to the academic music of the Capital. She often states that she finds popular art superior to high art, "car le paysan le plus simple et le plus naïf est encore artiste; et moi, je prétends même que leur art est supérieur au nôtre" [because the simplest and the most naive peasant is still an artist; and I would even claim that his art is superior to ours] (*FC*, 210–11). Sand had long defended the poets of the people. In 1842 she published her essays: *Dialogues familiers sur la poésie des prolétaires*.[59] Not surprisingly *Consuelo*, which she was writing at the same time, also contains pertinent passages on the aesthetic and moral worth of popular music and poetry. Her principal goal is to enunciate the beauty of popular art and to make it accessible, in all senses of the term, to the Parisian public. Sand does acknowledge that pastoral life has long been a hobby and a source of curiosity for the aristocracy. She wishes to demonstrate the falseness of that image and to contrast it with the truth and beauty the provinces have to offer.[60]

Music is for Sand an imitation, not an imitation of nature as we perceive it, but of the essence underneath and beyond what we perceive. The reservation for metaphysical communication she expresses here is not a constant in her writings, for she did attempt to portray an exchange of philosophical ideas through music in *Les Sept Cordes de la lyre*, written three years later than the letter to Meyerbeer. Her notions of musical mimesis change throughout her early writings, filtering out metaphysics and focusing on the essential communication of profound human and divine thought.

Convinced that music can and does convey meaning, she presents in *Les Sept Cordes de la lyre* (1839) a situation wherein music communicates among only those who are pure of heart. Hélène and Méphistophélès stand at the antipodes of this spectrum with Albertus wavering somewhere in between. As each character of the play encounters the lyre and attempts to understand its music, its powers and significance become apparent. One of the most interesting scenes, and certainly the most amusing, brings together a musician, a poet, a painter, and an art critic (act 1, scene 7). These professionals examine the lyre with curiosity and claim to have a desire to understand it. In truth they are interested only in their own reputations and their supposed superiority over one another. The artists make pronouncements about the nature of art, demonstrating Sand's distrust of "professional" artists who are more interested in themselves than in art. On the matter of mimesis, the painter berates his colleagues by accusing them of blind replication: "[H]abitués que vous êtes à copier servilement, vous criez à la bizarrerie et à l'exagération lorsque, dans l'imitation d'une œuvre d'art, vous voyez le génie de l'artiste surpasser son modèle" [Accustomed as you are to slavishly copying, you impute eccentricity and exaggeration when in the imitation of a work of art you see the genius of the artist surpassing his model] (*SC*, 93). The distinction between "modèle" and "une œuvre d'art" underscores the dialectic surrounding the question of mimesis. Sand suggests that interpretation and not mere reproduction defines art. Here the painter appears to represent Sand's attitude toward the role of imitation, but later he, too, will be severely criticized by the others, showing Sand's characteristic self-doubt.

In the fourth act Sand attempts to have music represent and interpret the physical world. Hélène has taken the lyre and climbed to the top of the cathedral, from where she can observe the village, that is, the real world in all its crudeness. She tunes the lyre, which begins to play for her, interpreting all she sees: "Ce que tu vois, c'est l'empire de l'homme; ce que tu entends, c'est le bruissement de la race humaine. . . . Vois quelle est la grandeur et la puissance de l'homme! Admire ses richesses si chèrement conquises, et les merveilles de son infatigable industrie!" [What you see is the dominion of man; what you hear is the rustling of the human race. . . . See the grandeur and the strength of man! Admire the wealth he has so dearly acquired and the wonders of his indefatigable work!] (*SC*, 156). Music transforms the vision of the world into a grandiose spectacle, but one riddled with irony in the face of an impending industrial age that Sand mistrusts.

Hélène's experience atop the cathedral suffices to teach her both the wonders and the dangers of society. And she learns this lesson through music. But she remains suspicious: "Je ne vois au-dessous de moi que les abîmes incommensurables du désespoir, je n'entends que les hurlements d'une douleur sans ressource et sans fin!" [I see below me only infinite abysses of despair; I hear only the wailing of a pain without support or break!] (*SC*, 158). These words, which combine space and sound, society and art, are the music Hélène produces when she plays the lyre. They are music just as the Spirit's words are to be understood as music. The reader is meant to be "hearing" music and thereby to understand the Spirit's thoughts. But the only way to transfer this communication to the reader is to "translate" it into words. Sand thus demonstrates an essential failure of language in representing music.

Sand's quirky use of music in *Les Sept Cordes de la lyre* provides an insight into her belief, at least in 1839, that music could communicate precise ideas to those who had the gift and the training to receive them. The rude lesson to which Hélène is subjected affords her a heightened awareness and a loss of naivete. In the fifth act, her despair turns to gratitude as she falls in love with the Spirit of the Lyre. Here it is Hélène's Spirit who "speaks" through music as she plays the lyre. The thoughts she expresses in music are of love and devotion. At the same time, Albertus begins to see there is something else in the world besides philosophy and the scientific method: "Hélène, les sons puissants que tu viens de me faire entendre ont ouvert mon âme aux harmonies du monde supérieur" [Hélène, the powerful sounds you've just played for me have opened my soul to the harmonies of a superior world] (*SC*, 183). For the first time he begins to understand and feel love. But Hélène cannot relinquish her mystical relationship with music in favor of Albertus. She goes off with the Spirit of the Lyre to another world. Albertus has learned a great lesson: "la lyre est brisée, mais l'harmonie a passé dans mon âme. Allons travailler!" [the lyre is broken, but harmony has passed into my soul. Let us go work!] (*SC*, 189).

These final words of the text, which exhort his students to Voltairian productivity, show that Albertus has grown and become a worthy character. Méphistophélès wins nothing, nor do the students (although Hanz was already enlightened from the beginning). Only Hélène and Albertus have made progress and look to the future with hope. The imitation of the industrial world as well as that of human language considerably extends the conceit of musical communication, which Sand did not intend to be taken too seriously here. She does not even attempt a fantastic presentation of the phenomenon. But she does attempt in this text to provide an aspect of music that remains inexpressible, a belief that music has communicative powers beyond the conventional notion of language.

Again in the "Avant-Propos" of *François le champi* and in *La Filleule*, Sand suggests music as an imitation of nature. To her friend François Rollinat, she writes, "l'art est une démonstration dont la nature est la preuve" [art is a demonstration of which nature is the proof] (*FC*, 209), and four years later the protagonist of *La Filleule* states, "[ces transitions musicales] sont dans la nature, et . . . la nature ne peut pas ne pas avoir raison" [these musical transitions are in nature and . . . nature cannot not be right] (*F*, 80). In these discussions, however, especially the one in *François le champi*, Sand describes a spirituality that is reflected in nature and then reflected in music. Such a triple-leveled correspondence establishes a metaphysical construct where music imitates not so much nature but the natural manifestations of God. She sees music less as an Aristotelian mimesis than as a further manifestation of God.

There is a hint in *Les Maîtres Sonneurs* that Joset expects music to communicate not only his intimate thoughts but also the intricacies of nature. After Joset plays the reed flute and Brulette understands his thoughts, she cautions him from being too quick to assume that a musical communication based on imitation will always occur so easily. She remembers when they were children that Joset told her to listen carefully to the sounds of nature and to try to remember them:

> Alors, moi, j'écoutais bien fidèlement, et je n'entendais que le vent qui causait dans les feuillages, ou l'eau qui grelottait au long des cailloux; mais toi, tu entendais autre chose, et tu en étais si assuré, que je l'étais par contre.
>
> Eh bien! mon garçon, conserve dans ton secret ces jolies musiques qui te sont bonnes et douces; mais n'essaye point de faire le ménétrier, car il arrivera ceci ou cela: ou tu ne pourras jamais faire dire à ta musette ce que l'eau ou le vent te racontent dans l'oreille; ou bien, si tu deviens musiqueux fin, les autres petits musiqueux du pays te chercheront noise et t'empêcheront de pratiquer. (*MS*, 112)

> [As for me, I listened faithfully and all I could hear was the wind talking in the leaves, and the water gurgling over the pebbles; but you, you heard something else, and you were so sure of it, that I became sure of it too.
>
> So, my dear boy, keep your secret of pretty music that is so good and sweet for you; but don't try to be a minstrel, because one of two things will happen: either you'll never be able to make your bagpipes say what the water or the wind was whispering in your ears, or else, if you become a good musician, the other little musicians around here will make trouble for you and will prevent you from playing.]

Brulette's warning, although intended to alert Joset to the danger of his plans, admits to the possibility of reproducing nature in music. Sand nods to the Platonic distinction between replication and interpretation, although this time from the receiver's perspective and not from the artist's. The double warning—either you will never be able to imitate what you hear in nature, or if you can, you will incur the wrath of those professional pipers who cannot—announces a tension that will play out in the development of the narrative. Imitation or mimesis therefore presents a delicate goal to pursue for the artist, especially for the musical artist. How closely can one hope to imitate nature? How much can one go beyond the representation of nature to express an interpretation? And how will this affect one's relations with other musicians, especially with folk musicians?

In *Consuelo* Sand toys with the concept of imitation without making a definite pronouncement. Talking about the emotional import of music, the narrator outlines the various areas where music can be communicative:

> Aucun autre art ne réveillera d'une manière aussi sublime le sentiment humain dans les entrailles de l'homme; aucun autre art ne peindra aux yeux de l'âme, et les splendeurs de la nature, et les délices de la contemplation, et le caractère des peuples, et le tumulte de leurs passions, et les langueurs de leurs souffrances. . . . [La musique] crée même l'aspect des choses, et, sans tomber dans les puérilités des effets de sonorité, ni dans l'étroite imitation des bruits réels, elle nous fait voir, à travers un voile vaporeux qui les agrandit et les divinise, les objets extérieurs où elle transporte notre imagination. (*C*, 1:417–18)

> [No other art can so sublimely and so viscerally awaken human feelings; no other art can paint for the soul's eyes the splendors of nature, the sensitivity of contemplation, the character of a nation, the turmoil of passions, and the weariness of suffering. . . . Music creates the very appearance of things, and without falling into the childishness of sound effects or the strict imitation of real sounds; it transports our imagination to the external objects that it shows us through a gossamer veil that enlarges and deifies them.]

Sand's voice sounds clearly in the narrator's thoughts. Musical composition suggests the emotions evoked by the artist, as opposed to imitative harmony that translates external sounds. This notion of mimesis, integral to Sand's presentation in *Consuelo*, comes to Sand in large part from Chopin. Certainly Sand disapproves of the "puerile" manifestation of the sounds of nature in music, which a momentary resurgence of programme music did allow for in the middle of the century. Sand distinguishes between such superficial attempts at mimesis and a more sophisticated, more intimate duplication of the essence of nature. This notion of mimesis rejoins that of Rousseau, who believed that the musician does not represent things but excites the emotion we feel when we see them. The subtle shift from the imitation of actual nature to the imitation of the feelings nature produces explains Sand's appreciation of the imitative powers of music.[61]

Thus imitation or mimesis in its most narrow sense has no place in Sand's aesthetics. She admits it as part of the contemporary discourse about music and refutes it continually in her works on music. Rather Sand postulates a spiritual interpretation of nature—in wind, water, sun, flowers, and the like—as well as of human nature—feelings, emotions, relationships. All these manifestations of nature can be perceived through music. Such musical mimesis brings us closer to understanding God and the ineffable aspects of the universe. One cannot hope to achieve this imitation or even to understand it without an openness of mind and heart, an inherent ability to listen, to see, to sense—musical talent—and the willingness to work toward the perfection of this quality and toward its virtuous application—musical training.

MUSIC AS LANGUAGE

If one accepts that music is an imitation of human speech—not an assumption I endorse, but one that gained currency in the late eighteenth and early nineteenth centuries and that Sand inherited from Rousseau and similar thinkers—it is a small leap from imitation to the communicative powers of music. It is difficult to discuss one and not the other. Sand flirts with several theories and sometimes adopts contradictory hypotheses. But one notion remains constant: she firmly believes in the ability of music to communicate. She writes to Meyerbeer, "la musique peut tout exprimer" [music can express anything] (*LV*, 2: 923) and to Pauline Viardot, "la musique, cette langue la plus parfaite de toutes" [music, this most perfect of all languages] (*Corr*, 9: 63). Consuelo says to Albert, "la musique est un langage plus complet et plus permanent que la parole" [music is a more complete and more permanent language than words] (*C*, 1:385). Sand's increasing awareness of both language and music, will allow her to understand the communicative powers of music and paradoxically to accept a less articulate definition of musical language, one that works for her purposes and for the purposes of her fiction.

The most direct influences on Sand about the notion of the language of the arts are to be found in the Enlightenment, particularly in Rousseau. His *Discours sur l'origine des langues* (1768) reveals many of the ideas and perspectives of his day, ideas that Sand found central to her own aesthetic. Writing of the original human language, Rousseau posits that it would have had numerous vowels and few consonants, but many inflections. The voice, the sounds, the accent, the rhythm—all these conventions constituted the original language, which suggests that "l'on chanteroit au lieu de parler"[62] [people would sing rather than speak]. The need to express emotions, especially passion and fear, he continues, caused humans to produce various sounds that communicated those emotions: "ainsi les vers, les chants, la parole, ont une origine commune" [thus verse, songs, words all have a common origin] (*Discours*, 410). For Rousseau, then, poetry, music, and language—all expressions of human emotion—came into existence at one and the same time. When the human voice produces a melody, it imitates the accents of language, with all its stylistic and emotional input. Furthermore, the music generated by the human voice communicates better than verbal language. "[La musique] n'imite pas seulement, elle parle; et son langage inarticulé, mais vif, ardent, passionné, a cent fois plus d'énergie que la parole même" [Music doesn't just imitate, it speaks; and its inarticulate but vivid, fiery, and passionate language has a hundred times more energy than words] (*Discours*, 416). This recalls the Platonic distinction between real and false imitation, where musical imitation would not be false but would speak in a nonverbal language characterized by more passion and energy than verbal language.

But while Rousseau views music and language as originating and developing together, he also recognizes that they diversify, which announces the demise of both.

A mesure que la langue se perfectionnoit, la mélodie, en s'imposant de nouvelles règles, perdoit insensiblement de son ancienne énergie, et le calcul des intervalles fut substitué à la finesse des inflexions. . . . L'étude de la philosophie et le progrès du raisonnement, ayant perfectionné la grammaire, ôtèrent à la langue ce ton vif et passionné qui l'avoit d'abord rendue si chantante. (*Discours*, 424)

[As language was perfected, melody lost some of its archaic energy by taking on new rules, and the calculation of intervals replaced the delicacy of inflections. . . . The study of philosophy and the progress in reasoning, having perfected grammar, took away the vivid and passionate tone that had made language so lilting.]

Throughout the grand period of Greek theater, the marriage of poetry and music still bore witness to the mutual dependence of the two art forms; but with the Roman period, Rousseau continues, a separation resulted from the efforts to dramatize language. And to compensate for the loss of melody and its relationship with language, musicians began to invent other devices, such as descant and counterpoint, in order to re-create the melodic pleasures of music.[63]

Rousseau's ideas about language and music are well developed and clear even if somewhat opinionated. For example, his belief in the complete amusicality of the French language, on which he expounds at great length in *Lettre sur la musique françoise* (1753), expands on his opinions about the close ties between language and music. Italian, claims Rousseau, is the only European language adaptable to music. "La Musique Françoise ne sçait ni peindre ni parler" [French music can neither paint nor speak].[64] The metaphor of painting puts Rousseau's comments among those of many other theoreticians of his day.[65] But the speaking metaphor distinguishes him, along with Diderot and d'Alembert, from other writers. It is especially in dramatic music that Rousseau sees the importance of music and language working together. The movement from language to music and from music to language cannot survive endless arias because one loses the illusion, "car il y a une sorte de vraisemblance qu'il faut conserver, même à l'Opéra, en rendant le discours tellement uniforme, que tout puisse être pris au moins pour une langue hypothétique" [because there is a kind of realism that must be kept, even at the Opéra, by making speech so uniform that everything can be seen as at least a hypothetical language] (*Musique*, 319). He concludes, "que les François n'ont point de musique et n'en peuvent avoir, ou que si jamais ils en ont une, ce sera tant pis pour eux" [that the French have no music and can have none, or if ever they did, it would be too bad for them] (*Musique*, 328). He continues in a footnote to say that he would rather keep the bland melodies of the French than to try to impose the French language on Italian melodies (*Musique*, 328n).[66]

Needless to say, Rousseau did not endear himself to French composers or musicians of his day. What interests me chiefly is his insistence on the unity of music and language, the continued and coherent way he mentions them together, without any possibility of separation. Curiously, nowhere in his discussion does Rousseau mention the amusicality of French for his own compositions. On this matter he focuses more on authenticity of authorship, since he felt beleaguered by accusations that he had stolen parts of his opera *Le Devin du village*.[67]

Generally speaking, thoughts on imitation and language overlap since many thinkers of Rousseau's and Sand's periods felt that music originated in human speech. Music would then be an attempt, most likely but not necessarily conscious, to imitate the sounds of the human voice. The marriage of music and words enjoys a brief discussion in *Adriani*, when Baron West, an unsuccessful poet, implores the title character to put his poetry to music. Vaguely reminiscent of the argument Richard Strauss would use for *Capriccio* (1940), this passage presents Sand's notion of the highly expressive capacity of music, whereby overly descriptive poetry detracts from the musical possibilities: "Quand vous me peignez en quatre vers l'alouette s'élevant vers le soleil, à travers les brises embaumées du matin, vous faites une peinture qui ne laisse rien à l'imagination. Or, la musique, c'est l'imagination même" [When you describe in four lines of poetry the flight of a lark toward the sun, rising through the perfumed morning winds, you make a painting that leaves nothing to the imagination. But music is imagination itself] (*A*, 115). Suzanne Langer concurs on the impossibility of such a union.[68]

Adriani assures his friend that a simple line is quite enough for him to conjure the multitude of musical images that he can apply to that feeling. If the poetry is too powerful, it destroys any hope of interesting, beautiful music: "les mots écrasent l'esprit de la mélodie, et la forme emporte le fond" [words crush the spirit of the melody, and form overshadows content] (*A*, 114). In this last comment, Sand posits a surprising argument, for normally one would expect the lyrics to represent the content and the music the form. Just the opposite is true in Sand's eyes, demonstrating her notion that music communicates a meaning no matter how inexplicable. Essential communication comes from or through the music; the words are little more than a vehicle for the music. Sand thus moves away from Rousseau in giving a privileged place to music over language. Music is not for her an imitation of language but something far more profound and meaningful, which comes from the soul, that is to say from God. Hence the belief in music as "le langage divin."

Adriani, who writes both poetry and music, maintains that the best method is to start from a simple thought, leaving room for the music to embellish its own "ideas." "La musique peut exprimer des idées aussi bien que des sentiments, quoi qu'on en ait dit" [Music can express ideas as well as feelings despite what has been said] (*A*, 114). The narrator seconds and develops this commentary in the next sentence: "[P]as plus qu'Adriani, nous ne voyons bien la limite où le sentiment devient une idée et où l'idée cesse absolument d'être un sentiment" [No more than Adriani can we clearly discern the boundary where feeling becomes idea and where idea completely ceases to be a feeling]. Sand manages in this brief observation to restate her notion of simplicity of expression and the consciously blurry distinction between verbal and musical languages. At the same time she levies a neat attack against current-day positivism and the fad of scientific nomenclature. The underlying message is multiple and treats not only the aesthetics of expression but also the sociological impact of progress.

In a similar vein, Sand wrote to Pauline Viardot in 1849 about her thoughts concerning memory and music and the frustration she felt at her own inadequacy in music:

> Nous autres ignorants dans cet art divin, nous sommes absorbés par la mélodie, par le chant proprement dit, et nous ne saisissons pas du premier coup tous les éléments du poème musical. . . . Ah! que je voudrais parfois avoir quinze ans, un maître intelligent, et toute ma vie à moi seule! Je donnerais mon être tout entier à la musique, et c'est dans cette langue-là la plus parfaite de toutes, que je voudrais exprimer mes sentiments et mes émotions. Je voudrais faire les paroles et la musique en même temps. Mais c'est un rêve comme celui qu'on ferait d'une île enchantée au moment où la mer va vous avaler à tout jamais. (*Corr*, 9:63)

> [Those of us who are uneducated in this divine art are preoccupied by the melody, by the song as such, and we cannot at first grasp all the components of the musical poem. . . . Oh, how I would sometimes love to be fifteen, to have an intelligent teacher, and my whole life to myself! I would give my whole being to music, and in that language, the most perfect of all, I would express my feelings and my emotions. I would write the words and the music at the same time. But this is a dream like one you might have about an enchanted island when the sea is about to swallow you up for ever.]

The metaphor of the sea for music or for being lost in music prefigures Baudelaire's sonnet "La Musique": "La musique souvent me prend comme une mer! . . . calme plat, grand miroir / De mon désespoir!"[69] [Music often takes me like the sea! . . . calm, flat, large mirror / Of my despair!]. Sand's desire for musical talent often defeats itself in the chagrin of ineffectiveness vis-à-vis the musicians she knows.

Sand first hints at the expressive qualities of music in *Rose et Blanche* (1830). Rose, the young daughter of a professional actress, has been sold to Horace, who entrusts her to his sister in order to remove her from the immoral life of her mother and the theater. In a convent Rose reveals herself an excellent singer despite a lack of training. "En peu de mois, elle acquit une méthode excellente, et sa voix, brisée aux études et aux roulades, prit encore plus d'extension et de légèreté" [In just a few months, she acquired excellent technique, and her voice, hoarse from practice and runs, gained even more range and lightness]. Abandoning ostentation, Rose recovers the natural beauty of her voice, but she lacks the one thing that would make her a great musician: "Il lui manquait *ce feu sacré* qui fait de la musique un langage de l'ame bien plus qu'un plaisir des sens"[70] [She lacked *the sacred fire* that makes music a language of the soul much more than a pleasure of the senses]. The connotation is clear that music has divine origins and that not everyone imbued with musical talent will develop into a great musician. The juxtaposition of "musique" and "langage" is not coincidental. Sand begins already in 1830 to untangle the association of divine inspiration and musical talent, resulting in a divinely inspired language. It is this expressive element that makes music mystical for Sand.

In "La Prima donna" (1831), written, like *Rose et Blanche,* in collaboration with Sandeau, Gina experiences and transmits the experience of musical ecstasy. But when she marries an aristocrat, her singing days end. Her new social status forbids her to sing and she withdraws from public life. As a result her health fails and she is near death. She explains to no one what is ailing her, remaining silent about her feelings. Her lack of language is directly related to the lack of music. The narrator, Valterna, finally convinces the doctor of the true cause of Gina's malaise. Together they persuade her husband to allow her to perform once again. It is while singing Juliet's final aria in Zingarelli's *Giulietta e Romeo* that Gina expires, having perfectly executed the role. Language returns to Gina only through music. The musical experience communicates such energy that the only narrative possibility is for Gina to sing superbly and die. That she should die instead of abandoning her husband and returning to the stage shows perhaps as much Sandeau's hand in the writing as it does Sand's hesitation in such matters at this date.[71]

In *Les Sept Cordes de la lyre* Sand begins to present her ideas of music and language with a more theoretical discourse. Music and poetry intermingle in this text, as the conventional symbol of the lyre demands. Accordingly, much of Sand's commentary on "la langue universelle" [the universal language] applies to art in general. Her concerns about art and language are not original, but her application of the question provides a mystical perspective of the place of art in society reminiscent of Leroux and Ballanche. Like Plato, Sand's philosopher in this text, Albertus would rather see music banned from his universe. He finds no utility in it, and without usefulness it has no reason to be. His definition of music in the second act testifies to the limits of scientific and metaphysical training:

La musique est une combinaison algébrique des divers tons de la gamme, propre à égayer l'esprit d'une manière indirecte, en chatouillant agréablement les muscles auditifs; chatouillement qui réagit sur le système nerveux tout entier. D'où il résulte que le cerveau peut entrer dans une sorte d'exaltation fébrile, ainsi qu'on l'observe chez les dilettanti. . . . La musique peut exprimer des sentiments . . . mais rendre des idées . . . mais seulement peindre des objets . . . c'est impossible! A moins qu'elle ne soit une magie, comme plusieurs le prétendent. (*SC*, 113)

[Music is an algebraic combination of various tones of the scale, likely to amuse the mind indirectly by pleasantly tickling the auditory muscles, a tickling that acts on the whole nervous system. From which it follows that the brain can enter into a sort of febrile exaltation, as can be observed in dilettanti. . . . Music can express feelings, but as for depicting ideas, even painting objects, that's impossible! Unless it is a sort of magic, as some claim.]

The derogatory terms in this passage clearly indicate Albertus's dismissal of music. Hanz, the only one of Albertus's students who can appreciate music, contradicts him: "Ce sont les éléments simples et connus dont la combinaison devient un mystère, une magie si vous voulez: la langue de l'infini!" [It is simple and well-known elements that combine to become a mystery, a kind of magic if you like: the language of infinity!] (*SC*, 113–14). By using the same terms of mysticism as his teacher, Hanz turns Albertus's argument on itself and thus successfully refutes the philosopher's condemnation of music. He continues his challenge directly: "Maître, vous croiriez à la magie plutôt qu'à la musique" [Master, would you rather believe in magic than in music?] (*SC*, 114).

In his attempts to seduce Albertus into deceiving Hélène, Méphistophélès produces documents supposedly written by Tobias Adelsfreit, Hélène's grandfather and the maker of the lyre. He gives the falsified manuscript to Albertus to confuse him. He reads: "Un temps viendra où les hommes auront tous l'intelligence et le sentiment de l'infini, et alors ils parleront tous la langue de l'infini: la parole ne sera plus que la langue des sens; l'autre sera celle de l'esprit" [A time will come when all men will have the intelligence and feeling of infinity, and then they will all speak the language of infinity: words will then be no more than the language of meaning; the other one will be that of the spirit]. Not sure he understands, Albertus questions Méphistophélès, "Qu'entend-il par l'autre? . . . La musique?" [What does he mean by the other one? . . . Music?].

The devil is pleased with his victim's progress, "Tout être intelligent sera une lyre, et cette lyre ne chantera que pour Dieu. La langue des rhéteurs et des dialecticiens sera la langue vulgaire" [Every intelligent being will become a lyre, and this lyre will sing only for God. The language of rhetoricians and dialecticians will be the trite language] (*SC*, 121).

This passage presents a revealing comparison between verbal language and music, wherein the former is subjugated to the realm of the senses, therefore vulgar and banal, while the latter accedes to the level of the spirit. The use and the repetition of the term "l'autre" suggests in addition a transcendence of earthly existence and understanding that, according to Sand, is possible only through music. The style and content of the document rings true, but the reader is quick to suspect its inauthenticity. Méphistophélès's goal is not to convince Albertus of the authorship of the false documents, but to seduce him into examining the lyre. During this examination, Albertus would clumsily destroy the lyre, thus giving Méphistophélès control over it, over Hélène, and ultimately over music.

The fourth act provides perhaps the most explicit exposition of music as language. In all scenes where the Spirit of the Lyre "speaks," we are clearly to understand that the lyre produces its own music that the reader and Hélène understand in the verbal language of Sand's text. Wilhelm, another student in philosophy, observes: "Jamais la lyre n'a été plus sonore, jamais le chant n'a été plus mâle, et l'harmonie plus large ou plus savante" [Never has the lyre been more sonorous, never has the song been more masculine, the harmony more abundant or more enlightened] (*SC*, 157). Even though the lyre is now missing four strings, its music is still beautiful. Wilhelm appreciates the beautiful music of the lyre, though he does not seem to understand it in the same way Hélène does.

The troubling use of "mâle" can be explained as Sand's attempt to destroy the conventional association of music with women. By labeling this music serious and strong, although its strength is a virile one, she reverses the stereotypically gendered association of serious thought and men, since Hélène is the only one to understand it. Sand has used the term "mâle" elsewhere to describe music characterized as energetic and vigorous. Sand's comment offers subterfuge and irony as well as an assurance of force. It is at this moment, however, that Albertus admits, "Oui, maintenant enfin, je comprends le langage de la lyre" [Yes, now I finally understand the language of the lyre] (*SC*, 157). His emotional apprenticeship has not been in vain and he now begins to recognize Hélène as an individual capable of her own thoughts and decisions. He interprets the tones of the lyre's music with a burgeoning sensitivity, "Le rythme est lugubre et la mélodie déchirante! Voyez comme Hélène souffre" [The rhythm is gloomy and the melody agonizing. Look how Hélène is suffering] (*SC*, 159). But Hélène cannot accept the hopeful message of the lyre. All she sees is suffering and destruction. "La Providence est muette, elle est sourde, elle est impotente pour les victimes, elle est ingénieuse et active pour servir les desseins de la perversité" [Providence is mute and deaf; she is powerless to help victims, ingenious and active in serving the designs of perversity] (*SC*, 161). And she throws the lyre to the ground far below, upon which onlookers remark, "La musique a cessé!" [The music has stopped!] (*SC*, 162).[72]

In their discussion of what has just happened, Albertus and Méphistophélès exchange notions about the state of the world. Surprised that the devil seems to have understood the music, Albertus asks him whether he could interpret its message. Méphistophélès tries to confound Albertus: "N'a-t-elle pas chanté aujourd'hui les merveilles et les misères de la civilisation? Tandis que la lyre disait la grandeur et le génie de l'homme, Hélène ne disait-elle pas ses crimes et ses malheurs?" [Did (the music) not sing of the marvels and the miseries of civilization today? While the lyre spoke of the greatness and the genius of man, did Hélène not speak of its crimes and problems?] (*SC*, 167). The dialectic this exchange represents in its interpretation of contemporary French society reveals more about Sand's uncertain worldview than about her wariness of philosophy. That the dialectic is expressed in music "translated" into philosophical terminology brings her concept into Albertus's discursive realm. Not only does this scene provide an ironic, indeed cynical view of modern society and industrial progress, and not only is this view expressed in music, but the mode of presentation resembles a discourse familiar to the philosopher, thus enabling him to appreciate the argument and thus to understand music.

Finally Albertus has learned music's power to communicate. And as he realizes his need for love, he admits to understanding Hélène's message and that of the lyre: "Hélène, les sons puissants que tu viens de me faire entendre ont ouvert mon âme aux harmonies du monde supérieur" [Hélène, the powerful sounds you've just shared with me have opened my soul to the harmonies of the superior world] (*SC*, 183). Hélène chooses to leave Albertus in favor of music and the Spirit of the Lyre. Although disappointed, Albertus is content to have learned a valuable lesson and to have developed a valuable talent. One final warning the Spirit of the Lyre shares with Hélène concerns the failings of interpretation: "Ecoute la voix qui chante l'amour, et non pas la voix qui l'explique" [Listen to the voice that sings of love and not the voice that explains it] (*SC*, 184). The antithesis of "chanter" and "expliquer" parallels that of music and verbal language: one *speaks* an ineffable truth and the other attempts an interpretation by and for uninitiated humans.[73]

In "Carl" (1843), Sand again represents the communicative powers of music. This time she highlights the psychological aspect. The narrator's close friend, a composer, has died and on his deathbed he sang a familiar song of his own composition. The narrator's memories of the friend are tightly linked to this tune. He suffers from fevers and disorientation, but this is not the same suggestion of madness we find in *Les Sept Cordes de la lyre*. For the narrator in "Carl," music represents something personal and intimate that he is not eager to share with his young companion, also named Carl. Not until he discovers the depth to which the young Carl also understands music will he confide his musically evoked feelings to the boy. The way music serves as the vehicle for metempsychosis in this tale suggests another aspect of musical powers that Sand does not pursue in other texts but that remains one of the more interesting aspects of the story. Communication between the narrator and the young Carl occurs by the grace of music much more than through words. The existence of printed music in the text heightens the importance of music in the relationship as well as in the narrative.

Sand's presentation of music as language offers a slightly different and more subtle version of its communicative powers in "Carl" than *Les Sept Cordes de la lyre*. Using techniques commonly found in the fantastic tale, Sand provides details that place the narrator's perception of music directly on the line of demarcation between illusion and reality: his grief at having lost his best friend, his feverish state, his being lost in the snowy mountains with a halfwit boy. These circumstances mitigate the veracity of his musical perception. Yet the experience seems so real and has such an effect on him, the reader willingly accepts the narrator's intuitions.[74]

Essentially Carl's melody urges the narrator to keep his friend's spirit alive through music. And this is just what he does. During the feverish dreams in which he hears the melody, he recollects his dear friend. When he meets the young Carl and discovers his name and his musical gift, he derives new meaning from the melody. When the narrator finds out that Carl-the-boy knows the dead Carl's melody because he previously heard the composer humming it during his stay at Carl's father's inn, he is convinced of a mystical connection between the two Carls. He constantly resuscitates the dead friend's spirit through this music. Finally, he insures that his friend's memory will continue to live through music by providing for the young Carl's musical training. Musical metempsychosis reflects Sand's reading of Leroux as well as a familiarity with Swedenborg's belief in the transforming powers of music. But more importantly, the tale contributes to Sand's explanation of the ability of music to carry information from one person to another, from one generation to another, from one social class to another.

Consuelo presents a plethora of examples demonstrating Sand's belief that music can and does communicate as a language. Having lived with Chopin for five years by the time she is writing this novel, Sand has become quite articulate about her musical sensitivity. Consuelo was to be her most gifted and most complex musical character. Music always represents calm and security for the heroine, from the cosseting memory of her mother to her nurturing relationship with Albert. While she does not refer to music as a language in the beginning of the novel, this soon becomes a catchphrase and Consuelo and Albert will frequently allude to the "divine language." It seems that Albert's mystical influence helps Consuelo to voice more precisely her feelings about music, about its role in society and in her life.

Communication, or rather a decided effort at "miscommunication," represents one of the most important issues for the Rudolstadt family. They have expended much energy covering up their Protestant and Bohemian origins, to the point where even among family members no allusions are permitted. Albert, who is most affected by the total rejection of his heritage, responds to this silencing of his background by removing himself from his family in every way. It is only when Consuelo arrives at Riesenberg and Albert hears her sing for the first time that he seems to come alive, enthralled with the beauty of her voice. He speaks to her in Spanish and calls her Consuelo. This scene constitutes the first sign of any interest in life on Albert's part. Consuelo's voice clearly "speaks" to his soul. And the juxtaposition of the musical awakening and the use of Spanish places an obvious emphasis on language as a private code between two people, thus prefiguring the mystical code music will have in this relationship.

Consuelo's voice continues to awaken Albert from his recurrent lethargy. Whenever she notices him withdrawing, she sings. The effect is immediate and profound:

Consuelo, tu connais le chemin de mon âme. Tu possèdes la puissance refusée au vulgaire, et tu la possèdes plus qu'aucun être vivant en ce monde. Tu parles le langage divin, tu sais exprimer les sentiments les plus sublimes, et communiquer les émotions puissantes de ton âme inspirée. Chante donc toujours quand tu me vois succomber. Les paroles que tu prononces dans tes chants ont peu de sens pour moi; elles ne sont qu'un thème abrégé, une indication incomplète, sur lesquels la pensée musicale s'exerce et se développe. Je les écoute à peine; ce que j'entends, ce qui pénètre au fond de mon cœur, c'est ta voix, c'est ton accent, c'est ton inspiration. La musique dit tout ce que l'âme rêve et pressent de plus mystérieux et de plus élevé. (*C*, 1:384–85)

[Consuelo, you know the way to my soul. You possess the power refused to the common, and you possess more than any living being in this world. You speak the divine language, you know how to express the most sublime feelings and how to communicate the powerful emotions of your inspired soul. So, always sing when you see me collapsing. The words you utter in your songs hold little meaning for me; they are but a summary, an incomplete indication which the musical thought practices and develops. I barely listen to them; what I hear, what penetrates to the bottom of my heart is your voice, your accent, your inspiration. Music says everything mysterious and lofty that the soul dreams and predicts.]

This passage presents the most explicit explanation of Sand's ideas to date on the power of music to communicate. And if the goal of language is to communicate, then "le langage divin" must convey the ideas of a higher plane, which would be the task of a poet or musician. Only those with properly developed talents may gain access to the divine language of music and thereby communicate noble thoughts to others. Albert insists on the power of the music to the detriment of the lyrics. The words mean little to him, and in fact he does not listen to them. At a certain point human language loses the power to communicate, and this is where music takes over. Music can express the emotions of exaltation, the thought as well as the emotional manifestation of that thought, in an ineffable language that cannot be replicated in verbal language.[75]

There is in this passage the alarming notion that only the talented and trained can use music to communicate and therefore are the only ones able to share divine thoughts. Sand's socialist ideals cannot allow such an elitist role for music. This is precisely why Consuelo must serve as the mediator, so that the divine language of music can benefit the people. Her move from the stage and professional performance to wandering improviser and interpreter of Albert exhibits the logical development toward this goal.

Consuelo challenges Albert with a desire for a musical exchange: "Puisque la musique est un langage plus complet et plus persuasif que la parole, pourquoi ne le parlez-vous jamais avec moi, vous qui le connaissez peut-être encore mieux?" [Since music is a more complete and more persuasive language than words, why don't you ever speak it with me, you who know it possibly even better?] (*C*, 1:385). Albert admits that he can play beautiful music on his violin only in his grotto, where the religious message reaches its full expression. It is as though he has no control; music comes mysteriously and mystically to his violin without his actually knowing how. Music for Albert is only worthy when it is at the service of God. While his religious discourse remains vague, the ideals he expresses in this passage designate something akin to Deism. The passage ends with the agreement that Consuelo and Albert will soon return to the grotto to pray; it is clear that in this instance "pray" means to play music with a view to religious communication.

The grotto—in this passage Albert calls it his church—contains relics of the Hussite, Taborite, and Lutheran heritage Albert claims. He attempts to explain to Consuelo his refusal to accept a single religious conviction that would be associated with an institution. His explanations demonstrate Sand's research on the history of the Protestant reform, including such issues as the Catholic invention of Satan and the importance of taking the Eucharist in both forms. Consuelo is dazzled by Albert's knowledge of history and his appreciation of theology. As she tries to absorb his wisdom, she notices that he is no longer speaking: "Tout à coup elle s'aperçut qu'Albert ne lui parlait plus, qu'il ne tenait plus sa main, qu'il n'était plus assis à ses côtés, mais qu'il était debout à deux pas d'elle, auprès de l'ossuaire, et qu'il jouait sur son violon l'étrange musique dont elle avait été déjà surprise et charmée" [All of a sudden she realized that Albert was no longer speaking to her, no longer holding her hand, no longer seated by her side, but that he was standing near the ossuary and playing on his violin the strange music that had already surprised and enchanted her] (*C*, 1:413). The mystical and magical connotations of "charmée" are clear, but the important element in this quotation lies in the barely perceptible slippage from verbal language to music. No other expression of music as language could relay so clearly Sand's belief, even though metaphorical, in the communicative powers of music.

Consuelo also communicates with Zdenko through music. Zdenko sings traditional songs that Consuelo tries to replicate. As they volley bits of melody back and forth, they forge a relationship. Still, communication remains superficial and unsatisfactory, at least for Consuelo. She tries to speak to him in Spanish, but the only word he can get out is *consuelo* (consolation): he sounded like "un oiseau parleur [qui] s'essaie à articuler un mot qu'on lui a appris, et qu'il entrecoupe du gazouillement de son chant naturel" [a talking bird who tries to enunciate a word he's been taught that he interrupts with the chirping of his own natural song] (C, 1:274). Here the intermingling of music as language, natural language, music as imitation of natural language, and the attempts, often abortive, at communication, through music and other languages bears witness to the import of the theme as well as the treachery of language. This confusion characterizes the relationship between Consuelo and Zdenko throughout the novel.

On the trip from Bohemia to Vienna, Consuelo and Haydn encounter a variety of people who claim to be musicians or at least to know music. Despite their rudimentary familiarity with music, they represent the dilettante attitude Sand wishes to expose and mock. The scene in this section that explicitly uses music as language finds Consuelo and Haydn, disguised as Bertoni and Beppo, singing and playing the violin to convince a friendly canon's housemaid that they are not thieves:

> "Chanter, dit Consuelo à son compagnon, voilà ce que nous avons à faire. Suis-moi, laisse-moi dire. Mais non, prends ton violon, et fais-moi une ritournelle quelconque, dans le premier ton venu." Joseph ayant obéi, Consuelo se mit à chanter à pleine voix, en improvisant musique et prose, une espèce de discours en allemand, rythmé et coupé en récitatif: "Nous sommes deux pauvres enfants de quinze ans, tout petits, et pas plus forts, pas plus méchants que les rossignols dont nous imitons les doux refrains." (C, 2:119)

> ["What we've got to do is sing," said Consuelo to her partner. "Follow my lead, let me do the talking. On second thought, take your violin and play any old ritornello, in the first key that comes to mind." Joseph obeyed and Consuelo began to sing in full voice, improvising music and prose, a kind of speech in German, rhythmic and broken up into recitatives. "We are two poor children of fifteen, very small and not any stronger or meaner than the nightingales whose gentle refrains we imitate."]

The passage continues with Consuelo explaining in song their innocence and trustworthiness. Consuelo tells Haydn from time to time what key and style of music to play: an A-minor chord, a modulation back to C major, and the like. Their improvisation, both musical and poetic, has a sociological rather than an aesthetic goal. They use improvisation to recall familiar modulations and thereby to reassure the inhabitants of the isolated house. This scene recalls a similar one in *La Chartreuse de Parme* (1839), where Clélia is imprisoned in the Farnese tower and hears the voice of Fabrice.[76]

He communicates his feelings to her in a recitative that he sings before the jailers, who do not suspect his ploy largely because of the reassuring familiarity of the tune. While the communication in these two examples is based on verbal language set to music rather than music alone, the subterfuge music supplies adds a supplemental discourse between Clélia and Fabrice, just as for Bertoni and Beppo, that only the reader appreciates.

This example also demonstrates the difficult task of portraying the performance of music, and ultimately the experience of hearing music, through verbal language. Haydn's instrumental testimony can only be shown by reference to musical elements (key signatures and the like). A similar scene at the end of "Histoire du rêveur" provides an account in words of what the audience feels listening to instrumental music. Diderot experimented with analogous efforts to portray music performance in *Le Neveu de Rameau*, where "Lui" is described as humming, singing, and miming playing the violin and the keyboard. Needless to say, these devices do not bring us very close to the actual experience of hearing music. The device Sand used in "Carl," where actual musical notation intervenes in the narrative, relies first on the musical training of the reader and second on the ability of the reader to interpret the interplay of music and prose. Sand's abandonment of this technique indicates her dissatisfaction with it and the ultimate realization that it restricted her readership.

One of Sand's most eloquent discussions of music as language comes in a passage where Consuelo writes a diary. Imprisoned in Spandau, she decides to record her daily thoughts. It is, she says, the first time in her life she has done so. She compares writing with music:

> Je n'ai jamais écrit que de la musique, et quoique je puisse parler facilement plusieurs langues, j'ignore si je saurais m'exprimer d'un style correct dans aucune. Il ne m'a jamais semblé que je dusse peindre ce qui occuperait mon cœur et ma vie dans une autre langue que celle de l'art divin que je professe. Des mots, des phrases, cela me paraissait si froid au prix de ce que je pouvais exprimer avec le chant! (*CR*, 3:171–72)

> [I've only ever written music, and even though I speak several languages easily, I don't know whether I'd be able to express myself correctly in any one of them. I've never felt I needed to depict what was in my heart and my life in any language other than the one of the divine art that I exercise. Words, phrases, all this seemed so cold to me compared to what I could express in song!]

It is interesting to note that she addresses her diary to Porpora and Haydn. The implication is that she needs the journal to extract herself from her present situation, and thus she prefers to write to loved ones outside prison who will understand her musical allusions. As she writes here, despite knowing several languages, music—therefore one of the various languages she knows—is the one she feels most comfortable in, the one in which she knows she can express her thoughts and feelings. Verbal language palls in comparison.

Still in prison, Consuelo suffers from insomnia; half asleep, she hears a violin "jouant ses vieux airs bohémiens, ses cantiques et ses chants de guerre" [playing his old Bohemian tunes, his hymns and battle songs] (*CR*, 3: 182). The possessive adjective refers to Albert, whose memory haunts her here through his music as she suffers from fevers similar to those she had at Riesenburg. Consuelo imagines the music traveling up and down the prison walls or skipping across the water. It must be some other prisoner who is playing, she thinks. Unsure whether the sound of the violin is real, she must admit that Albert is dead, yet she gathers comfort from the sound of the violin. While the degree of communication here is questionable, music does establish a link between Consuelo and her memory and perception of Albert.[77]

Violin music again serves as a means of communication when Consuelo awaits her interview with "les Invisibles." She resides now in another sort of prison, and although she has music and instruments at her disposal, she does not make music until she demands to see the high Council of the Invisibles. She sings to calm herself before the interview. First she sings some pieces she had composed in Spandau, then she sings the "Libertà" aria from Handel's *Rinaldo*. The allusion to an exhortation of freedom while imprisoned is clear. As Consuelo sings in despair of finding freedom, the sound of a violin exactly repeats Handel's musical phrase with such sadness and suffering that Consuelo is convinced, and rightly so, that it must be Albert's violin. But she again convinces herself it could not be, this time because she had never heard Albert play any modern music.

Oddly, in the long narration of the life of Wanda, Albert's mother, there is no mention of music. Wanda is not a musician. Sand misses here the occasion to portray another female musician, which would have been especially pertinent as a parallel to Consuelo's mother. No other critic has commented on this apparent lack; here Sand could have capitalized on an invaluable opportunity to discuss the maternal transmission of music. But perhaps the length of the manuscript and the need to persevere to the end of an already convoluted plot dissuaded her from further digressions. The only other transmission of music from mother to child Sand does offer, and that only in passing, is in *Le Château des Désertes*, where Lucrezia Floriani passes a love of (and presumably an ability for) music to her son, Célio, and in a nonbiological link to his childhood friend and future wife, Cécilia.

While there is some music in the initiation ceremony of *Consuelo*, it represents more a symbolic sharing of ideals, especially the ideals of the Revolution, than communication between characters. The last important statement in the novel about the ability of music to function as language surfaces in the "Lettre de Philon." This final document of the text describes two adepts, Spartacus (Adam Weishaupt) and Philon, who wander about Europe in search of the meaning of life. They know of Albert's reputation and convince themselves that if they could find him, he would be able to reveal to them the mysteries of the universe. Their first perception of Albert when they do find him is through music. Philon writes that he is struck by "des sons d'un violon d'une force et d'une justesse extraordinaires. . . . Le chant était simple et sublime. Il ne ressemblait à rien de ce que j'ai entendu dans nos concerts et sur nos théâtres. Il portait dans le cœur une émotion pieuse et belliqueuse à la fois" [the forceful and extraordinarily precise sounds of a violin. . . . The song was simple and sublime. It resembled nothing I've heard in concerts or the theater. It carried in the heart an emotion that was at once pious and bellicose] (*CR*, 3:437).

At this point, the listeners have not yet "understood" Albert's music, but they have recognized him thanks to the pureness of his violin playing. The lyrical description of Albert underscores his noble character and posture, his gentleness, and his quiet intelligence. He has become, in his own words, a symbol of humanity: "Mon nom est *homme*" [My name is *man*] (*CR* 3:439). Spartacus tries to communicate with him through Masonic gestures, but Albert refuses that language he once practiced, preferring to express himself in another:

[L]'inconnu, saisissant son violon, se mit à en jouer avec verve. Son vigoureux archet faisait frémir les plantes comme le vent du soir, et résonner les ruines comme la voix humaine. Son chant avait un caractère particulier d'enthousiasme religieux, de simplicité antique et de chaleur entraînante. . . . C'étaient comme des hymnes guerriers, et ils faisaient passer devant nos yeux des armées triomphantes, portant des bannières, des palmes et les signes mystérieux d'une religion nouvelle. Je voyais l'immensité des peuples réunis sous un même étendard; aucun tumulte dans les rangs, une fièvre sans délire, un élan impétueux sans colère, l'activité humaine dans toute sa splendeur, la victoire dans toute sa clémence, et la foi dans toute son expansion sublime. (*CR*, 3:440)

[The stranger grabbed his violin and began to play eloquently. His vigorous bow made the plants quiver like the evening wind and the ruins echo like the human voice. His song had the particular character of religious enthusiasm, of ancient simplicity and of engaging warmth. . . . It was like war hymns that paraded in front of our eyes triumphant armies carrying banners, palms, and mysterious signs of a new religion. I could see the expanse of people united under a single standard; no turmoil in the ranks, feverish but without delirium, an impetuous momentum without anger, human activity in all its splendor, victory in all its compassion, and faith in all its sublime expansion.]

Here Sand displays not only an adoration and a respect for music, particularly for simple and religious music, but also the promise of a new religion (again Pierre Leroux's influence) and a decided courage to persevere. References to military music, quite common since the Revolution, recall the Crusades and the willing acceptance of a struggle for one's ideals. At the same time, this type of music unmistakably identifies the common people as the primary public for Albert's message. In communicating this message wholly through Albert's violin playing, Sand leaves no doubt about her belief that music can and does transmit ideas as well as emotions.

Spartacus attempts an exegesis of the message, asking Albert to be more explicit on certain points. Albert responds, "Que te dirais-je que je ne t'aie dit tout à l'heure dans une langue plus belle? Est-ce ma faute si tu ne m'as pas compris? Tu crois que j'ai voulu parler à tes sens, et c'était mon âme qui te parlait!" [What could I say that I haven't already said in a more beautiful language? Is it my fault that you couldn't understand me? You thought I was trying to speak to your senses, when it was my soul that was speaking to you!] (*CR*, 3:441).

Consuelo, called "la Zingara de la consolation" [the Gypsy of consolation] in this passage, enters the picture once again, communicating with Sparacus and Philon through Masonic symbols, conventionally a language of men. Consuelo acknowledges that Albert, who is called Trismégiste in this section, can and will reveal to them the mysteries they seek, but that he is not always inspired to do so. And when he is, he will communicate through music: "La musique est sa manifestation habituelle. Rarement ses idées métaphysiques sont assez lucides pour s'abstraire des émotions du sentiment exalté" [Music is his accustomed manifestation. Rarely are his metaphysical ideas lucid enough to be separated from the emotions of his impassioned feeling] (*CR*, 3:445). Music serves as a medium of exchange and a means of survival as well as a medium of communication for Consuelo and her family. Such a socialist network of functions expresses Sand's desire to see music and its message of egalitarianism and freedom spread to all peoples of all classes and stations in life. Sand develops the scene along the lines of social progress teeming with religious exuberance so as to combine and at the same time surpass the Saint-Simonian project for a new religion. She overturns the emphasis on industrial strength to reinforce the position of art, renewing a musical commonplace and the social(ist) thesis that underlies it—an idea by now familiar to her readers.

The scene ends with Consuelo and Albert's youngest son performing a ballad, "La bonne déesse de la pauvreté" [the kind goddess of poverty]. The lyrics are by Albert and the music by Consuelo. The beneficent presence of the titular goddess is always manifested by music. She sings throughout the world, she travels while singing. She is the source of all understanding and all explanations of important ideas, and she represents the artistic expression of these ideas: "C'est elle qui inspire le poète et qui rend le violon, la guitare et la flûte éloquents sous les doigts de l'artiste vagabond" [She's the one who inspires the poet and who makes the violin, the guitar, and the flute eloquent in the hands of the wandering artist] (*CR*, 3:450). This goddess is, of course, Consuelo, who embodies Sand's fundamental message of an artistic path to egalitarianism.[78]

It is important to point out the significance of Consuelo's move from musical performance to verbal interpretation. Critics have traditionally seen this change as a weakening of the feminist message of the novel. Such criticism deems that the female musician is demoted to the role of mediator, subordinate to the male creator. Since the publication of Simone Balayé's article, Consuelo's role has been interpreted as one of hope and salvation, still communicated through music despite the different perspective. In the distinction Sand draws between professional performance, whether in an opera house or a recital hall, and the sacerdotal execution of music for religious-social purposes, she at once calls for devoted socialist actions and deplores any tendencies that detract from artistic and aesthetic considerations. Albert, on the other hand, has never been involved in a public display of music. He has now become totally absorbed in musical communication, whereas earlier in the novel he played only on rare occasions and only in his grotto. Consuelo, on the contrary, has experience in several arenas and remains the rational one who actively brings music to all people. She has not abandoned her musical ideals or functions since she continues to compose, conventionally considered a masculine occupation. Consuelo's devotion to musical communication continues to be her principal ideal. As Pierrette Daly says, Consuelo does not forsake music for the word, rather she combines them in an original and strong heroic dimension.[79] Sand does not revert to a patriarchal trope; she allows Consuelo to accede to the world of language and knowledge without repudiating the language she speaks best, the divine language of music.

In *La Filleule* Sand provides music as a voice for Stéphen since he is incapable of expressing his love for Anicée. Returning home from Anicée's house after once again failing to avow his feelings, he knows no other way to express his emotions than to improvise on the piano: "il s'était créé une nouvelle source de jouissances, et tous les soirs, en revenant de la rue Courcelles, il se racontait son propre bonheur dans cette langue de l'imagination et du sentiment que beaucoup de philosophes et de savants croient vague et creuse parce qu'elle est mystérieuse et infinie" [he created for himself a new source of pleasure, and every evening when he returned from the rue Courcelles, he recounted his happiness in that language of the imagination and feelings that many philosophers and erudite people find vague and empty because mysterious and infinite] (*F*, 81). For Stéphen music provides the joy and passion that otherwise remain unattainable.

Music also takes the form of discourse as Stéphen recounts and repeats his happiness through improvisation. In a later scene, still unable to voice his feelings, Stéphen plays at Anicée's house: "Je me suis retrouvé seul dans ma pensée avec *elle*. Je lui ai dit en musique tout ce que l'âme endolorie et inquiète peut dire à Dieu" [I was alone with *her* in my thoughts. I told her in music all that an aching and anxious soul can say to God] (*F*, 84). Sand links intimate, amorous feelings with intimate, religious sentiment, both communicated in music and giving rise to the pain of ecstacy.

From early on in *Les Maîtres Sonneurs*, Joset incarnates the problem of communication. Throughout the novel Joset's principal desire is to be able to express his love for and to Brulette. That he suffers a presumable linguistic retardation and chooses music as a vehicle of communication is central to my argument. From Dauriac's *Essai sur l'esprit musical,* we learn that musical listening precedes verbal listening, requiring less intellectual activity to apprehend and to repeat.[80] Can we then assume that Joset's use of music as language represents a pre-verbal manifestation of arrested development? Certainly that Joset can and does speak when he wants to proves the contrary. His need to communicate, which is different from his ability to communicate and understand, is more easily directed through music than through words. Therefore we are not faced with an example of retardation or underdeveloped abilities, rather an exceptional capacity for nonverbal expression that, combined with general inattention (perhaps attention deficit), allows for more precise and more focused communication through music.

As children he and Brulette always "spoke" to each other in music. Sometimes when Joset was lost in an apparent stupor, the only way to awaken him was through music, "[Brulette] se mettait à chanter, et c'était la manière certaine de le réveiller" [Brulette would begin to sing; that was a sure way to wake him up] (*MS*, 67). Brulette's experience of Joset's flute playing demonstrates total and intimate communication (*MS*, 117–18). Her response brings to the surface several important aspects of Sand's musical aesthetics, but most certainly the ability of music to communicate beyond the capacity of verbal language. Brulette finds it impossible to explain the exact emotions Joset's flute playing has provoked in her, but the memories of their childhood arise spontaneously from the pastoral timbre of the flute and from the simple nature of the melody. For Brulette the music evokes in mostly visual images both nature and domestic scenes and causes dreams that jolt her psyche.

Underscoring the semiotic attributes of music, Joset replies: "C'est bien! Ce que j'ai songé, ce que j'ai vu en flûtant, tu l'as vu aussi! . . . Ça parle, ce méchant bout de roseau; ça dit ce qu'on pense; ça montre comme avec les yeux; ça raconte comme avec les mots; ça aime comme avec le cœur; ça vit, ça existe!" [That's terrific! That's what I was thinking; what I saw while playing, you saw it too! . . . That wretched piece of reed, it tells your thoughts; it displays them so that you can almost see them with your eyes; it tells stories almost like with words; it loves almost like with its heart; it lives; it exists!] (*MS*, 118). He comes alive with the joy of knowing he *can* communicate through music. At first Tiennet does not understand any of what Brulette explains: "je n'avais vu que du feu" [I saw only fire] (*MS*, 119). But as Joset continues to play, Tiennet begins to "see": "il se fit aussi en moi une songerie, et je crus voir Brulette dansant toute seule au clair d'une belle lune, sous des buissons de blanche épine fleurie, et secouant son tablier rose, comme prête à s'envoler" [I also had a sort of dream; I thought I saw Brulette dancing all alone in the moonlight underneath hawthorne bushes with white blossoms, shaking her pink apron like she was ready to fly away] (*MS*, 120). The sexual nature of Tiennet's fantasy stands in stark contrast with Brulette's reverie. Tiennet's jealousy of the attention Brulette has always shown Joset feeds off the flute music and fuels his own desires. We shall see that, although both boys will be disappointed that Brulette does not return their feelings, Tiennet manages to go beyond his regret whereas Joset fails to accept defeat, in love or in music.

One further explicit example of music as language in *Les Maîtres Sonneurs* occurs in the duel between Joset and Huriel for Brulette's heart. Joset throws down the gauntlet, "demandez en paroles, moi je demanderai en musique" [Ask in words, I'll ask in music] (*MS*, 405). Joset's talents in music far surpass Huriel's language, which the latter admits openly, "Je te laisse la musique, où je reconnais que tu es au-dessus de moi. Reprends donc ta musette et *parle* encore en *ton langage*; personne ici ne se lassera de t'entendre" [I'll leave music for you since I admit you're better at it than I am. So take up your bagpipes and *speak your language* again; no one here will get tired of listening to you] (*MS*, 416; my emphasis). No one questions Joset's superiority in music; but Brulette clarifies the distinction between effective discourse on the one hand and sincerity of emotion and worthiness of esteem on the other. Everyone present recognizes that music has functioned as language for Joset; the passage is filled with verbs such as "dire," "parler," "raconter" as metaphors for "singing" or "making music."[81] The strict link between spoken and musical discourse remains not just a thread of the plot, not just the principal characteristic of the protagonist, but the very foundation of the thesis and message of this and other novels.[82]

Malgrétout (1870) takes a similar position in relation to music as language but with different conclusions. Sarah, Abel, and Sarah's father categorize music as a language. Sarah begins a long letter to her friend Mary by saying that while she is no bluestocking, "[j]e n'ai cultivé en moi avec plaisir que le sens musical, et je crois que je me suis habituée *à penser et à souffrir en musique*" [I have fostered only musical meaning and I think I've gotten used to *thinking and suffering in music*].[83] Music for Sarah represents both thought and sorrow, from which we extrapolate the correlation between the two and the similarity of their expression. Verbal language cannot express the depths of reflection and anguish the way music can, as the novel will demonstrate.

To entertain her niece, who is also her goddaughter and namesake, Sarah composes and sings a children's song. Abel overhears her and repeats the melody on his violin. This musical dialogue recalls the one in *La Comtesse de Rudolstadt* where Consuelo sings from Handel and is seconded by a reply on the violin.[84] Sarah is subsequently moved to sing for Abel, which secures a burgeoning relationship. A violinist by trade, Abel affirms that music is his only means of expression. Hearing Sarah sing, he is moved to tears and replies, "j'ai là [in his violin] une voix qui exprime mieux mon émotion que toutes les paroles humaines, et je vais vous répondre comme vous m'avez parlé: en musique" [I have here a voice that expresses my emotion better than any human word, and I shall answer you as you spoke to me: in music] (*M*, 37). He then plays and improvises for an hour and retires completely exhausted. Later Sarah observes Abel making an effort to speak to her nonmusical sister, "et . . . cette note de la 'parole humaine' résonnait parfois à son oreille comme une langue étrangère" [and that note of 'the human word' sometimes resonated in her ear like a foreign language] (*M*, 53). Sarah recognizes Abel's adherence to music as his preferred language of expression. On another occasion, when Abel makes his declaration of love to Sarah, he ends the conversation by stating that he is overcome with emotion and cannot play for her father as planned; in fact he can no longer communicate: "Je vous quitte, il me serait impossible de faire de la musique ce soir et de dire une parole qui eût le sens commun" [I'm leaving you; it would be impossible for me to play this evening and to say a single word that would make any sense] (*M*, 63). Sand consistently replaces language with music for Abel throughout the novel.

Music as language also invokes sarcasm in *Malgrétout*. Sarah's younger sister, Adda de Rémonville, pretends to disdain music and musicians and frequently uses her lack of musical knowledge as an attack on Abel. Her biting rhetoric clearly demonstrates scorn and jealousy for people whose music creates for her a mistrust of music and musicians. However, Adda is not alone is showing sarcasm in matters of music. Abel uses similar causticity to his advantage. At a soirée at the Paris home of M. de Rémonville's mistress, where he was once invited to play and is now a permanent guest, Abel addresses M. de Rémonville in public, referring to an unpleasant conversation of a few weeks earlier in the presence of his wife on the subject of the unstable and subaltern condition of artists: "C'était une de ces théories longuement développées et ardemment soutenues où excelle M. le comte de Rémonville. Je n'ai pas l'esprit aussi prompt que lui, ce n'est pas mon état. Je fais plus facilement une triple gamme que le plus simple raisonnement, j'ai été honteusement battu." [It was one of those theories developed at length and sustained with passion that Count Rémonville excels in. I'm not as quick witted as he; that's out of my class. I can more easily play three scales than make the simplest argument. I was shamefully beaten] (*M*, 79). The comparison of grandiloquence and sincere musicianship characterizes the exchange. But Abel's irony remains remarkable in its clarity, one of the rare instances in the novel where he does show a sharp wit. It is noteworthy that this instance of wit remains outside music, since he and his friend Nouville, a fellow musician, arrive at Rémonville's house without their instruments. Abel leads the conversation so as to gather all those present in his camp in condemning Rémonville's stratification of those who spend money over those who earn it. In response to one guest's estimation that there is money that is shamefully earned and still more shamefully spent, Abel says in quite articulate verbal language:

> Alors, je serais le supérieur d'un homme capable d'exploiter les affections et les dévouements de la famille pour avoir un hôtel comme celui-ci, un mobilier comme celui-ci, le sourire d'une beauté telle que celle-ci, et une société de personnes d'élite telle que je la vois ici? Je vous rends grâce. Je ne savais pas cela, moi, et, quand on tentera de rabaisser mon état, je répondrai que j'en connais un pire; mais je suis trop bien élevé et trop bon garçon pour nommer personne, à moins qu'on ne m'y contraigne en reprenant devant moi la thèse que vous venez de condamner. (*M*, 81)

> [So, I would be superior to a man capable of exploiting the affections and the devotions of a family to have a townhouse like this one, furnishings like these, the smile of a beautiful woman like you, and the company of an elite such as that I see here? I thank you. I didn't know that, and when someone tries to lower my social status, I'll answer that I know of someone worse off; but I'm too polite and too kind to name anyone, unless I'm forced to by someone who adopts before me the premise you've just denounced.]

Abel's ability and conviction in musical language become more poignant in view of his near illiteracy. Sarah discovers he cannot write properly when, after having promised to allow her one year to consider his proposal of marriage, he communicates through his friend Nouville's letters. Nouville becomes their intermediary and writes, "Je ne savais pas qu'il n'a jamais écrit de sa vie ce qu'on appelle une lettre" [I didn't know he'd never in his life written what could be called a letter] (*M*, 88). Abel told him, Nouville reports to Sarah, "Mon expression, c'est le chant; ma plume, c'est mon archet. Quand je parle, il me faut un certain effort pour dire ce que je veux . . . , mais le vide de ce papier blanc qui ne me répond rien glace les paroles que je veux . . . confier" [My expression is music;

my bow is my pen. When I speak, I have to make some effort to
say what I want . . . but the blankness of this white paper that answers nothing to me chills the words that I wish . . . to confide].
And confirming the link between music and language, he adds, "Je
parle sans accent une douzaine de langues, mais je n'ai jamais jeté
les yeux sur une grammaire. J'apprends tout par l'oreille" [I speak
a dozen languages with no accent, but I've never cast an eye on a
grammar book. I learn everything by ear].[85] At the end of the novel,
we see his efforts to fit into Sarah's world by learning to write better. He simultaneously abandons the violin except to play for the
family. Thus for Sarah's love he renounces his profession, but not
his music. Abel's apparent inabilities in verbal language must now
be nuanced to written language. His sharp wit, which he can muster
when necessary, and his effective discourse of love and passion
bear witness to his linguistic capacity. To express himself more precisely, however, he turns not to the written word, but to music.

In 1874 Sand returns to many of her favorite musical themes in
Ma Sœur Jeanne, the story of a relationship that is meant to be despite all odds, including different religions, different education, but
especially since the two protagonists are apparently brother and sister. Throughout the long and sinuous unwinding of the plot where
the narrator realizes the truth more slowly than the reader, music
serves as a sort of language for Jeanne. The eponymous heroine has
long suspected that she is not her brother's sister. She shares her
conjectures with her "brother" Laurent, who quickly puts aside this
hypothesis when "their" mother shows them their birth certificates.
At her brother's urging, Jeanne returns home from the convent and
studies music, "son unique passion désormais [où] elle fait des progrès et révèle des dons surprenants" [her sole passion henceforth,
in which she progresses and reveals a surprising gift].[86] In a characterization that might recall that of Joset, here is how her "mother"
describes Jeanne's musical prowess to Laurent:

> cela est si remarquable, que je n'ose pas lui montrer l'admiration qu'elle
> me cause. Je crains de la voir trop exclusive et que sa santé ne se con-
> sume dans cette extase continuelle où elle semble plongée; cela a rem-
> placé la dévotion, qui paraît oubliée absolument. Tu vois qu'elle est
> toujours ce que tu appelles étrange. Moi, je la vois exceptionnelle, ce
> qui est autre chose. (*SJ*, 55–56)

> [It's so remarkable that I dare not show her the admiration she inspires
> in me. I fear she'll become intractable and that her health will fail in
> this continual bliss in which she seems to immerse herself. It's replaced
> devotion, which seems to be totally forgotten. You see that she's always

what you call strange. As for me, I find her exceptional, which is something else altogether.]

Music has replaced religious devotion. Her piano playing has a great effect on Laurent and his reaction reminds us of the flute scene in *Les Maîtres Sonneurs*: "J'en fus ébloui moi-même, et, quand elle eut fini, je saisis ses deux mains et les baisai avec enthousiasme: «Voilà, lui dis-je, tout ce que j'ai dans le cœur: je suis heureux et je te remercie!»" [I was astounded myself, and when she'd finished, I grasped her hands and kissed them enthusiastically. "This is," I told her, "everything I have in my heart: I'm happy and I thank you!"] (*SJ*, 57). Jeanne's music not only surprises her brother by its exquisiteness, but it also brings to the surface unrecognized and inexpressible emotions.

Jeanne sometimes represses her feelings with music. When Laurent is talking to her about his friend Vianne's interest in her, she promises to consider the possibility, but says that for the present, she sees none: "Quant à moi et à M. Vianne, il n'y a pas de passé, et il ne me semble pas qu'il y ait d'avenir sans cela. J'en suis parfois si effrayée que je ferme les yeux et me *précipite* à mon piano pour oublier qui je suis et ce que l'on veut que je sois" [As for me and Mr. Vianne, there is no past, and I don't think there can be any future without that. Sometimes that frightens me so much that I close my eyes and *throw* myself on my piano to forget who I am and who I'm supposed to be] (*SJ*, 122). Her use of music as a refuge functions at the same time as a repression of her own emotions and desires. Sand has used music as a means of escape before, although Nerval's usage in this domain eclipses hers. Still, Jeanne's capacity to avoid reality in music does make a statement about repression. Here her "mother" shares with Laurent observations he has not made: "Tout le problème à résoudre pour elle, c'est de trouver l'expression des pensées musicales qui l'oppressent. Si elle a encore des jours de rêverie et de silence, c'est que la muse se débat en elle. Quand elle a trouvé sous ses doigts le vrai sens de son rêve enthousiaste, elle renaît, elle s'épanouit, elle est heureuse" [The problem she has to solve is to be able to express the musical thoughts that oppress her. If she still has days of dreaming and silence, it's because the muse is struggling within her. When she finds in her fingers the true meaning of her fervent dream, she is reborn, she blossoms, she's happy] (*SJ*, 268). A dual function of music surfaces: repression and expression. That music is capable of expressing emotions that verbal language fails to formulate, and at the same time serves as an asylum offers a unique paradox in the metaphoric use of music. Jeanne's experience and use of music does not differ so much from Consuelo's or from Laure's, but in this novel the dual function is unique and rich.

Jeanne's devotion to music eclipses other experiences in her life, for instance she cannot imagine herself continuing to play were she to become a mother. Her "mother" asks her, "pourquoi t'imagines-tu que tu cesserais d'être artiste, si tu devenais une bonne mère de famille? —Parce que je suis exclusive. Je ne me sens pas la force d'avoir plusieurs passions à la fois" ["Why do you imagine that you'll cease to be an artist if you became a good mother?" "Because I am intractable. I don't have the force to have more than one passion at a time"] (*SJ*, 62). Although she does love her "mother" and is wholly devoted to her, this is not the passionate love to which she refers. Her terms are clear: "Je n'aime que la musique. . . . [J]e n'ai pas besoin d'épouser personne, moi! Mon amour n'est pas de ce monde" ["I love only music. . . . I don't need to marry anyone! My love is not of this world"] (*SJ*, 61). And when her brother speaks to her about a possible marriage to Vianne, she replies, "je me suis donnée à la musique. Quel rapport pourra donc s'établir entre la musique et le mariage? Je n'en vois pas" [I've given myself to music. What link could possibly exist between music and marriage? I see none] (*SJ*, 121). The analogy of music and passion surfaces again when Manuela, Laurent's would-be inamorata, believes she is being compared to Jeanne: "Une muse divine! c'est-à-dire qu'elle a de grands talents que je n'ai pas" [A divine muse, meaning she has great talents that I do not] (*SJ*, 204).

Laurent's mother bemoans to him Jeanne's decision not to marry and not to experience motherhood: "Écoute! elle joue du piano. Quelle tendresse dans toutes ses idées musicales! Une âme si belle et si aimante serait condamnée à la solitude!" [Listen, she's playing the piano. Such tenderness in all her musical ideas! To think that such a beautiful and loving soul should be condemned to solitude!] (*SJ*, 295). In her "mother's" opinion, Jeanne's music symbolizes not only her originality and artistry, but also her goodness and especially, therefore, her aptitude for being a good mother. This is the same parallel of art and passion, which in turn contrasts the state of artist and wife/mother, that emerges in *Consuelo*. In that novel, the heroine proved Porpora's principle wrong. Here Jeanne will do the same, although continuing to display her musicality less explicitly.

Jeanne's relationship to her biological father, which becomes apparent near the end of the novel, bears testimony to the importance of music as language for the heroine. Laurent asks her to play the piano, and she says she hasn't played since Sir Richard, her real father, visited. "Est-ce qu'il t'a dégoûtée de la musique? —Bien au contraire! mais enfin en musique comme en tout il y a des phases de recueillement." ["Did he put you off music?" "Quite to the contrary! And anyway, in music as in anything else, there are periods of contemplation"] (*SJ*, 261). Laurent only now begins to understand his "sister." After a long conversation on the nature of love, he senses there is much he has not observed in her: "Cette âme muette, qui avait si longtemps trouvé son unique expression dans la musique, semblait avoir pris le courage de se manifester par la parole" [This mute soul that had for so long found its sole expression in music seemed to have found the courage to come forward in words] (*SJ*, 266–67). While her education was interrupted when she returned home from the convent, she now seems to have a clear view and articulate verbal expression of her observations. Jeanne's "mother" explains to Laurent nuances of his "sister's" character he has not managed to apprehend:

Elle a été lente à trouver son chemin, elle redoute le médiocre, en rien elle ne s'accommoderait d'un pis-aller. Cette musique qui l'a enfin passionnée, elle l'a abordée en tremblant. A la fois ambitieuse et modeste, elle craignait de n'y pas saisir son idéal. Timide, elle a bien longtemps douté d'elle-même. Il a fallu que l'admiration des autres la rassurât, et je dois dire que celle de sir Richard a été nécessaire pour lui donner tout à fait conscience d'elle-même. Elle a vu qu'il était un juge compétent; elle a, depuis ce jour, fermé son piano, comme pour savourer sa victoire. Et ne va pas t'imaginer que Jeanne pense à se produire en public. Elle écrit ses compositions, qui ne verront peut-être jamais le jour, car on n'édite avec succès que les noms célèbres, et Jeanne ne voudrait pas devenir célèbre ostensiblement. Elle ne consentira jamais à payer de sa personne. (*SJ*, 268–69)

[She was slow to find her way; she was afraid of being mediocre, and there's no way she would be satisfied with making do. When she finally became excited about music, she approached it with apprehension. At once ambitious and modest, she feared not being able to grasp her ideal. Shy, she doubted herself for a long while. She needed others' admiration to reassure her, and I must say that it was Sir Richard's that made her fully aware of herself. She saw that he was a competent judge; and from that day, she closed her piano as if to savor her victory. And don't go thinking that Jeanne is considering playing in public. She composes pieces that will never see the light of day because only famous names get published, and Jeanne would not want to become overtly famous. She will never agree to such a high price.]

This passionate discourse of music so typical of Sand underscores the lyric nature of the text. Beyond that, however, is also the very rich display of Jeanne's need to find some mode of expression. With idealistic standards that she is not sure of being able to attain, Jeanne hesitates to venture into an expressive language, but soon her fingers find a way to formulate her "musical thoughts." Music, not her sole language but certainly the language of her most intimate ponderings, springs from Jeanne in fits of dreams and silences, but she remains true to herself, uninterested in performing or in publishing her compositions. It is not insignificant that Jeanne composes, one of the rare Sandian female musicians—along with Consuelo—to do so.

What I find especially interesting in this passage is the notion that Jeanne needs a public on whom she can rely to tell her she is good. She has already played for Laurent and for her mother, but it is Sir Richard's opinion that makes the difference. Then, suddenly, she no longer feels a pressing need to play. This is unique for a Sandian musician. At first look, one might be tempted to assume that whereas music replaced language for Jeanne while she was living in turmoil, she no longer needs music after her biological father turns up. In fact, upon closer inspection a more complicated function of the musical language metaphor becomes evident. A convoluted network of duplicity and deception runs through the novel. She can talk to no one about her suspicions. Her only outlet is music. This sole language of intimate expression satisfies her so long as no one shares her thoughts. When Sir Richard comes to visit and reveals that he is, in fact, her father, she no longer needs to suppress her feelings. The revelation of her birth and, more importantly, the ability to talk about it openly now allows her complete candor with those around her. Music is now less necessary as a substitute and can continue solely as an art form.

♫ ♫ ♫

Sand does not fully endorse the Rousseauian model of music as an imitation of human speech, nor does she subscribe to the Pythagorean theory that reduces music to a series of mathematical formulae. Rather, similar to Morellet's notion of music as a metaphoric language based on resemblances or analogies, Sand seems to say that music can suggest ideas and emotions without necessarily being overly precise. And this very imprecision is in fact the beauty of musical expression.[87]

Balzac presents a similar appreciation of music as language in *Gambara* (1837), when the noble visitor criticizes Gambara for composing in an effort to communicate ideas and musical principles rather than emotions. Gambara reacts against the suggestion:

"Quoi! vingt-cinq ans d'études seraient inutiles! Il me faudrait étudier la langue imparfaite des hommes, quand je tiens la clef du *verbe céleste!* Ah! si vous aviez raison, je mourrais." [What! Twenty-five years' study for nothing? Should I have to study the imperfect human language when I hold the key to the *celestial word*? Oh, if you were right, I would die] (467). Later he adjusts his appreciation without totally abandoning it. He admits that the communication of ideas through music is not for everyone: "Ma musique est belle, mais quand la musique passe de la sensation à l'idée, elle ne peut avoir que des gens de génie pour auditeurs, car eux seuls ont la puissance de la développer" [My music is beautiful, but when music moves from feelings to ideas, it can have only geniuses as admirers, because only they have the power to develop it] (472). Sand would not agree with such an elitist segregation of music listeners, even though she does at times refer to *initiés* and *non initiés*. Sand prefers to think and hope that music does communicate to all people, even though perhaps on different levels simultaneously. Among Balzac's musicians, Gambara comes closest to Joset's appreciations.[88]

Sand discusses programme music as early as 1833 in her short essay *La Symphonie pastorale de Beethoven*. Her text begins, "Voici la vision que j'ai eue pendant la grande Symphonie de Beethoven" [Here is the vision I had during Beethoven's great symphony] (*OA*, 2:610), and she continues with a dreamlike reaction to the music. She imagines herself on a mysterious, mystical voyage, flying toward heaven with flocks of white and black birds. The white ones fly higher, closer to heaven, while the black ones remain lower. She is black, while the angels are white. Then a booming voice pronounces that heaven is reserved for the strong. Even though she feels she is falling, she has hope which she gleans from the voice as well as from a bright star she spies. Then trumpets announce the Last Judgment, and she flies upward. Tears falling from above cleanse her of her blackness, and she gradually becomes white. Finally, the voice beckons her and the others to enter. But here her dream ends: "mais je ne vis rien, car la symphonie finissait" [but I saw nothing because the symphony was ending] (*OA*, 2:614).

The emotional reaction and description were inspired, Sand claims, by Beethoven's music. While Sand does not espouse the role of programme music in reproducing or imitating the sounds of nature—she pronounces against such a function in *Les Maîtres Sonneurs, Histoire de ma vie*, and in other texts—she does admit to believing in an emotional vision inspired by music. She does not necessarily endorse the notion that a same or similar reaction will be experienced by all listeners; witness Tiennet's totally different vision when listening to the same music as Brulette (fifth *veillée*). But she strongly insists on a personal, emotional involvement in the musical experience, one which cannot always be expressed in words.

The *Symphonie pastorale* essay repeats the lyrical discourse common in music criticism of the 1830s, a language Sand adopts periodically but that she will alter and personalize over the next fifty years. This is not to say she abandons the notion of an emotional response to music, but rather that she attempts to find another verbal expression that differs from the lyrical, journalistic discourse. This essay precedes her association with Chopin, from whom she adopted a more circumspect attitude toward programme music. Although she will never depart from the position that the music experience remains ineffable, Sand always attempts a sincere and intimate expression of music in words.

Sand rejects the notion that music functions only as entertainment.[89] Emotional response, rather than aligning itself with entertainment, belongs to communication, to the language of music and its ability to transmit ideas, emotional ideas, no matter how imprecise. Nicole Mozet observes that as the fear of God diminishes during the romantic period and along with it the belief in the sincerity of the Word, lying generally increases.[90] In like manner, so does Sand choose music over verbal language as a more sincere form of communication and source of knowledge.

The apparent paradox between the ineffability of music and the communicative function of music requires a brief examination of Curtius's "topoi of inexpressibility."[91] According to Curtius, the rhetoric of adoration in antiquity describes the impossibility of adequately expressing the praise of rulers. Language simply cannot fulfill the infinite veneration necessary in a panegyric or a eulogy. For Sand, music's link to divine communication explains the ostensible incongruity. If the confabulation with a supreme being remains outside the realm of verbal language, then music, serving as the surrogate for divine communication and being equally inexpressible in conventional discourse, can be said to extend beyond the powers of language. There is therefore no contradiction. Music, like appropriately panegyrical discourse, cannot be successfully represented in customary language. Thus it serves as God's *verbum*, the one, true language. For Sand, music expresses the most intimate notions of spirituality and love that conventional language cannot.

3

♫♫ Love, Madness, and Music ♫♫

Le jour où tu te donneras à un mortel,
tu perdras ta divinité.

[The day you give yourself to a mortal,
you'll lose your divinity.]
—*Consuelo*

LOVE AND MADNESS ARE FREQUENTLY LINKED WITH MUSIC IN SAND'S musical novels. As the language of the affect for Sand, music facilitates the transmission of amorous as well as mad thoughts. Music provides a propitious cadre through which the similarly profound feelings of love and madness can be articulated. From a romantic perspective, love and madness not only share symptoms— swooning, loss of memory, disorientation, fever, shortness of breath, inexplicable melancholy—but these symptoms also enjoy expression in music, especially in romantic music. Moreover, the state of madness for Sand, not unlike Nerval, often signifies *une seconde vue* (a sixth sense). In this chapter I study Sand's exploration of music's ability to tap into the profound emotional reaches of the subconscious by associating it with the awakening and the development of love and madness.

MUSIC AND LOVE PLOTS

The coincidence of love and music is a mainstay of the romantic bag of tricks. Many authors of the period called on music to supply a propitious ambience to cultivate a love plot. Balzac frequently played the music-love card, notably in *Modeste Mignon*. Just before he gives us the lyrics and music of "Chant d'une jeune fille" [a girl's song], the heroine and composer's grandmother says, "il n'y a qu'une fille amoureuse qui puisse composer de pareilles mélodies sans connaître la musique" [only a girl in love could compose such melodies without knowing music].[1] Soon thereafter the protagonist

133

herself writes to Monsieur de Canalis that she knows "à quoi sert la divine harmonie de la musique, elle fut inventée par les anges pour exprimer l'amour" [what the purpose of the divine harmony of music is: it was invented by angels to express love] (469). These instances of love and music suggest nothing more than a tidy device. Sand's blend of music with love, on the contrary, far supersedes Balzac's. She develops a network of themes, functions, and symbolisms throughout her œuvre that at once satisfies the reading public's desire for the expected and responds to the need for something more complex.

In all Sand's musical novels, a musical plot parallels the love plot. The concentricity of the two structures suggests equivalence and referentiality. This is to say that any progress or movement in one domain stimulates or effects a parallel change in the other. When an "unexpected" change occurs in the love relationship, a similar and equal modification arises in the musical context and vice versa. Both realms are thus intimately interwoven in a cause-and-effect relationship, substantively as well as structurally.

Sand frequently engineers a meeting of future lovers through music. For example, music is intertwined around Horace's love for Rose in *Rose et Blanche*. He first overhears her singing a ballad and remarks that she has "comme la voix d'un ange; . . . c'était un timbre de voix si suave, si frais, que l'oreille en était caressée et que les nerfs les plus malades eussent repris, en l'écoutant, toute leur élasticité" [a voice like an angel's; . . . the timbre of her voice was so sweet, so fresh, that it caressed my ears, and my most sickly nerves recovered all their elasticity by listening to her] (*RB*, 1:82–83). Rose sings folk love songs. But she remains innocent of the content, thus her singing lacks communicative value. Rose's mother, a stereotypically amoral woman of the theater, will try to use her daughter to extract some money from Horace. Rose does not yet know love, and Horace does not yet see Rose in these terms. But some undefined interest causes Horace to want to rescue Rose from an unseemly situation, and she is drawn to his kindness. Sand reveals her intentions to the reader through musical references before the characters become aware.

Rose's song again links the future lovers in the home of Horace's sister, where Rose has been sent in preparation for entering a convent. At a dinner party when Horace's sister introduces Rose under the alias Mademoiselle de Beaumont, some of the guests want to sing, but they would like some new material. Rose sings the same canzonetta. Her voice especially impresses one of the guests, Lespinasse, who is himself a rather accomplished musician. The same music thus sparks the interests of two different men—and all the while Rose remains unaware of the emotion she inspires. Another dinner guest, an abbot, is also taken by Rose's voice and asks her to allow him to accompany her on the piano. Of these three love interests kindled by music, the last functions in the comic mode, while the one with Horace fulfills the central love plot of the novel. As for Lespinasse, he will return to the house later to ask for Rose's hand in marriage. Although the marriage will not take place, the impetus for love—for it was to be a marriage of love—was aroused in music.

Music continues to provide extra-musical opportunities for the unwitting and inexperienced Rose. She rents a piano in the convent, where the kapellmeister encourages her to develop her voice. Even though she molds her voice into a beautiful instrument, she still lacks "ce feu sacré" [this sacred fire] (*RB*, 2:51). Rose's lack of experience remands the musical symbolism to the realm of incomplete overtures in the first part of the novel, but the musical theme will soon take on a more significant function. Although she has no training or experience in sacred music, Rose steps in to replace a sick nun in a perfect rendition of Bach's *Magnificat*. She is so overwhelmed with her performance experience that she faints and falls into the arms of one of the spectators who has come to congratulate her on her performance. That spectator is the famous singer Giuditta Pasta. Rose's voice touched everyone who heard it, even the most pious, demonstrating the double connotation of religious and sensual ecstasy: "les ames vraiment pieuses tombèrent dans l'extase" [the truly pious souls fell into ecstasy] (*RB*, 2:58). Through a series of plot twists, it is Blanche who marries Horace, while Rose takes the veil. The musical elements that link Rose and Horace do not prove strong enough to bring them together and to help them realize their love for each other.[2]

In *Valentine* it is a bourrée that brings the amorous couple together. The trill of the vielle sparks both a social challenge and an amorous relationship during a local fete. The peasant Bénédict thinks he is in love with his cousin, the bourgeois Athénaïs. She is dancing with someone else and suggests that Bénédict ask Valentine to dance. Partly out of jealousy, partly because he is curious about Valentine's visible interest in dancing with him, he invites her to join him in the bourrée. Because they are aristocrats, Valentine's mother forbids it. But just as she is expressing her class-conscious indignation, the vielle sounds a trill signaling the beginning of the bourrée, which requires the partners to exchange a kiss. Even though Bénédict does not enjoy the bourrée, for he wanted to dance with Athénaïs, the die is cast: he and Valentine kiss and dance.

Later that same evening another musical link strengthens the couple's interaction. All alone, Valentine loses her way home in the dark. She overhears a young man singing;

> Certes, ce n'était pas un villageois qui savait ainsi poser et moduler les sons. Ce n'était pas non plus un chanteur de profession qui s'abandonnait ainsi à la pureté du rythme, sans ornement et sans système. C'était quelqu'un qui sentait la musique et qui ne la savait pas; ou, s'il la savait, c'était le premier chanteur du monde, car il paraissait ne pas la savoir, et sa mélodie, comme une voix des éléments, s'élevait vers les cieux sans autre poésie que celle du sentiment.[3]

> [It was certainly not a villager who could place tones and modulate them so well. Nor was it a professional singer, losing himself in the pleasure of unaltered rhythms, without ornaments or design. It was someone who felt music but didn't know music; or, if he knew it, he was the foremost singer in the world, because he didn't seem to know it. And his melody, like a voice of the elements, rose toward the heavens without any poetry other than feeling.]

Valentine recognizes a mature and experienced voice, surprising for the rural setting, just as Amédée in "Histoire du rêveur" finds it curious for an apparent peasant to sing so beautifully. Both situations position connoisseurs who cannot believe that the beauty of the voice they hear could come from the ignorant and untrained throat of a common peasant. Sand's social commentary is by now familiar, but her ability to communicate it through musical elements continues to be noteworthy.

The singer is, of course, Bénédict. He catches up with Valentine and they discuss music. Valentine says she once played music, but that she gave it up in favor of painting. "Comme profession, la musique ne m'eût pas convenu; elle met une femme trop en évidence; elle la pousse sur le théâtre ou dans les salons; elle en fait une actrice ou une subalterne à qui l'on confie l'éducation d'une demoiselle de province" [As a profession, music would not have suited me; it puts a woman too much in the public eye; it forces her onto the stage or into salons; it makes an actress or a subordinate out of her, someone to whom the instruction of a young provincial lady is entrusted] (V, 57).[4] Aristocrat that she is, Valentine shuns the theater and public professions. Even singing in private salons, which was quite respectable at the time, strikes her as unsuitable for someone of her class. The term "profession" is surprising, as a noblewoman would not usually consider a career. While it is possible that Sand was alluding to the failing economic status of the aristocracy under the Restoration, it is more likely this should be seen as a reference to the place of women in the performing arts. Bénédict wants to contradict her, but he does not dare. Their first conversation both revolves around music and includes an unspoken disagreement, two conditions that will continue to characterize their relationship.

Louise, Valentine's sister who is now living in the area again after being sent away because she was pregnant out of wedlock, provides a profitable complication. Bénédict benefits from the two sisters' secret reunion by relaying messages and thereby seeing more of Valentine. For instance, he comes to the Rambault mansion with some venison as a pretext for bringing Valentine a note from Louise. Valentine's grandmother has asked Valentine to distract her by singing, but Valentine suggests rather that Bénédict sing some rustic songs while she accompanies him. "[D]ès les premières notes, Valentine rougit et pâlit, des larmes vinrent au bord de sa paupière. . . . 'Cet air est celui que ma sœur me chantait de prédilection lorsque j'étais enfant et que je la faisais asseoir sur le haut de la colline pour l'entendre répéter à l'écho.' " [As soon as she heard the first notes, Valentine blushed and grew pale; tears brimmed in her eyes. . . . "This is the tune my sister used to sing to me when I was a child; I made her sit at the top of the hill so I could hear the echo repeat after her"] (V, 74). And Bénédict replies, "Je l'ai chanté à dessein; c'était vous parler au nom de Louise" [I sang it on purpose; I was speaking to you in Louise's name] (V, 74). In addition to establishing the romantic relationship in music, Bénédict serves as the (musical) intermediary to reunite two long-lost sisters just as a piece of musical memory functions as the code understood only by the *initiés*—here meaning those who know that Louise and Valentine are sisters, but also those who know and understand the evocative language of music.

Bénédict's subsequent visits to Valentine's house are made under the pretense of tuning the piano, unexpectedly at the behest of Valentine's mother. As the state of the piano is poor, several visits are assured.[5] Valentine continues to be moved by Bénédict's voice, even after she is married. Her husband's diplomatic demands frequently call him away from home (in fact, it is fairly clear that the marriage is never consummated), allowing more regular visits between Bénédict and Valentine. In one particularly moving scene, Louise and Bénédict play music for Valentine. This is one of Louise's pretexts for bringing the two lovers together, but it is rife with peril as the narrator points out:

> La musique peut paraître un art d'agrément, un futile et innocent plaisir pour les esprits calmes et rassis; pour les âmes passionnées, c'est la source de toute poésie, le langage de toute passion forte. C'est bien ainsi que Bénédict l'entendait; il savait que la voix humaine, modulée avec âme, est la plus rapide, la plus énergique expression des sentiments, qu'elle arrive à l'intelligence d'autrui avec plus de puissance que lorsqu'elle est refroidie par les développements de la parole. Sous la forme de mélodie, la pensée est grande, poétique et belle. (*V,* 153)

> [Music can seem to be an art of diversion, a useless and innocent pleasure for quiet and stale minds. For passionate souls, it's the origin of all poetry, the language of all strong passion. That's just how Bénédict understood it; he knew that the human voice, soulfully adapted, is the fastest, the most energetic expression of feelings, that is reaches others' minds with more power than when it's chilled by wordy digression. In the form of a melody, thought is grand, poetic, and beautiful.]

There is little doubt about the powers of expression Sand ascribes to music, especially melody. Music's communicative superiority over verbal language produces the opposite effect from Louise's well-intentioned plan to allow Valentine and Bénédict to be together innocently.

Valentine feels deeper emotions than is her custom when Bénédict sings, either rustic songs or more mainstream music, which particularly impresses her. Sometimes Valentine is so moved by his singing she cannot remain in the house. She goes into the garden: "La voix de Bénédict lui arrivait ainsi plus suave et plus caressante parmi les feuilles émues, sur la brise odorante du soir. Tout était parfum et mélodie autour d'elle" [Bénédict's voice was sweeter and softer coming to her through the rustling leaves on the perfumed evening breeze. Everything around her was perfume and melody] (*V,* 154). Sand will use the synesthetic comparison of music and perfume in other texts (for example, *Consuelo* and "Ce que disent les fleurs"). Here the mixture of music and scent fills the air during the evening of their first kiss.

While *Valentine* is not a musical novel, its use of music as a link between the protagonists does bear witness to Sand's ability to weave music into her love plots. In similar fashion, "Le Toast," a short story from the same period (1832), uses music to identify the love between the aristocrat Juana and Ramire, both of them sixteen years old and Spanish. Ramire "chantait avec une voix douce et voilée qui allait au cœur" [sang with a sweet and unsteady voice that went straight to her heart] and played "vieilles romances espa-gnoles" [old Spanish ballads] on the guitar for Juana.[6] After Juana's jealous husband, a Dutch governor, sends Ramire away and is feel-ing confident again, they hear outside the window "le son d'une guitare, accompagnée d'une voix triste et voilée, chant[ant] en es-pagnol, sous la fenêtre, le refrain d'une des romances bien-aimées de Juana; cette voix ne pouvait être méconnue un instant des deux personnes qui l'entendirent" [the sound of a guitar under the win-dow accompanied by a sad and unsteady voice singing in Spanish the refrain of one of Juana's beloved ballads; that voice could not be mistaken for an instant by the two people who heard it] (230). Thus the identification and recognition of love is signaled by music, for good and for ill.

In *La Dernière Aldini*, the deception of tuning the piano is again used to ensure the would-be lovers can see each other. Lélio, for-merly a gondolier and now an opera singer, spies a beautiful woman, Alezia, in the audience of the opera house one evening. He is determined to meet her despite her reputation as a cold woman. He encounters her in the country by chance and she feigns not to recognize him. But in the course of the conversation, she manages to let slip that her piano desperately needs tuning. Lélio shows up at her house the next day, and for several days after that, pretending to tune the piano, a technical process about which he knows noth-ing. They discuss tuning the piano a quarter tone lower than usual because she is a contralto. This alteration does not seem unusual to him, as just last season the orchestra at the theater of San-Carlo also lowered their pitch by a quarter tone to accommodate his voice weakened by a cold. Sand displays here not only knowledge of al-terations in concert pitch but also of the accommodations some-times made for particular soloists. Alezia's recognized suitor Nasi, a slow-witted and fatuous aristocrat, finally notices that Lélio is not really a piano tuner at all, and that he keeps casting significant glances at Alezia. The latter laughs off his concerns.

Soon after this scene Alezia and Lélio exchange their first kiss. When she tries to seduce him, she tells him she has loved him since the first night she heard him sing Roméo. But Lélio realizes the union will never work. She makes one more effort, using music as her philter. She visits Lélio's good friend and singing partner, Fran-cesca La Checchina, ostensibly to inquire about music lessons. She has heard that Lélio is coming to town and she would very much like to take lessons from him. The scene is complicated by deliber-ate misunderstandings as Alezia pretends to have been told that

Francesca is Lélio's wife. This is the beginning of the end of any possible relationship between Lélio and Alezia.

Alezia's mother, Bianca, comes from Venice to counsel her in her social obligations. She is confronted not only by her daughter's socially irresponsible infatuation but also by her own dismay at the identity of the object of Alezia's love. Earlier in the novel, when Lélio was a simple gondolier, he heard the sound of a harp, an instrument with which he was not yet familiar. He stole into the house just to see and touch the harp. There he met the aristocratic harpist Bianca, with whom he enjoyed a passionate yet chaste love. Bianca plays the maternal role in a dignified manner, although she is obliged to reveal to her daughter the nature of her relationship with Lélio. In accordance with her duties, as well as Lélio's eventual realization that a mixed marriage would never work, Alezia marries Nasi while Lélio continues singing and delights his friends with the story of his love.

In *Consuelo* three love plots establish the novel's structure, and all three are intertwined with a concomitant musical structure: Consuelo and Anzoleto, Consuelo and Albert, and Consuelo and Liverani. Anzoleto represents a pure, chaste love. Their union, commended by Consuelo's mother, remains nonphysical, which is an important if only partial cause of its dissolution. Theirs is a relationship under the aegis of the Virgin, as we see in the exposition of their first encounters:

> Le hasard lui avait fait rencontrer la petite Espagnole devant les Madonettes, chantant des cantiques par dévotion; et lui, pour le plaisir d'exercer sa voix, il avait chanté avec elle aux étoiles durant des soirées entières. Et puis ils s'étaient rencontrés sur les sables du Lido, ramassant des coquillages, lui pour les manger, elle pour en faire des chapelets et des ornements. Et puis encore ils s'étaient rencontrés à l'église, elle priant le bon Dieu de tout son cœur, lui regardant les belles dames de tous ses yeux. Et dans toutes ces rencontres, Consuelo lui avait semblé si bonne, si douce, si obligeante, si gaie, qu'il s'était fait son ami et son compagnon inséparable, sans trop savoir pourquoi ni comment. (*C*, 1:53–54)

> [By chance he met the young Spanish girl devotedly singing hymns in front of the Madonna statuettes. And for the pleasure of practicing his voice, he had sung to the stars with her for entire evenings. And then they had met on the sands of the Lido, collecting shells—he would eat the shellfish, she would make rosaries and trinkets with the shells. Then they had seen each other again at church, she was praying to God with all her heart and he was staring at the beautiful ladies. And in all these meetings, Consuelo had seemed so good, so sweet, so kind, so happy,

that he made her his inseparable friend and companion without quite knowing why or how.]

Everything in this series of encounters contrasts Consuelo's religious devotion and innocence with Anzoleto's self-interest. It is revealing that Anzoleto gives the account of their first meetings. His point of view suggests that any movement toward a relationship came from him, and typically he does not know what he is doing. Consuelo and Anzoleto thus begin a relationship in music. Anzoleto teaches Consuelo many Venetian folk songs, and Anzoleto needs Consuelo's discipline in order to improve his own singing and advance his burgeoning career. Consuelo continues to devote herself to music in memory of her mother, but mostly "pour s'associer à l'avenir d'Anzoleto" [to tie herself to Anzoleto's future]. Her only interest in continuing her music is the happiness and affection she feels in her relationship with Anzoleto. Already we detect Consuelo's movement away from the Church, since she no longer performs music in the sole service of religion.[7]

The turning point in the relationship between Anzoleto and Consuelo occurs in chapter 8. He wants her to debut on the stage with him. Her audition performance of Marcello's setting of the psalm, "I cieli immensi," transfigures all present. The beauty of her voice crystallizes metonymically so that she appears beautiful in all respects. Zustiniani declares, "Par tout le sang du Christ, cette femme est belle! C'est sainte Cécile, sainte Thérèse, sainte Consuelo! c'est la poésie, c'est la musique, c'est la foi personnifiées!" [Sweet Jesus, that woman is beautiful! She's Saint Cecilia, Saint Theresa, Saint Consuelo! She's poetry, she's music, she's faith incarnate!] (C, 1:101). The saintly allusions—generosity, music, and, of course, Consuelo's own canonization—as well as the invocation of Christ suggest divine intervention in Consuelo's talent and training at the same time they foreshadow the divinity of her role in spreading the news of a new religion at the end of the novel. Music and Church provide a locus for the joining of physical and aesthetic beauty in the canonized personage of Consuelo. That such a judgment comes from the mouth of an inveterate amoretto, however, successfully puts into question this definition of feminine beauty.

Consuelo's entrance and location in the church make it difficult to see her distinctly. In this way the notion of beauty is cast in a different light, since her physical appearance does not precede the auditory impression she makes. In addition, the narrator describes her transformation into a physical beauty from a heterodiegetic point of view that dissimulates the degree to which the other characters in the church can really make out her physical traits. This recalls the discussion of beauty in "Histoire du rêveur." When the female singer sings, it is the beauty of her voice that emerges and pervades all other perceptions of beauty. Sand insists on the beauty of the voice as far superior to any notion of physical beauty. The link is now more erotic than amorous, but music's function remains significant.

Consuelo's success, and especially Zustiniani's attentions to her, begin to concern Anzoleto for purely selfish reasons. Out of jealousy—again an emotion sparked, although indirectly, by music—he urges her to marry him quickly; but when she responds that she is prepared to do so that very day, he recoils, hiding behind their responsibilities to Zustiniani. And when she bends to this reasoning, he rebukes her: "O Consuelo, que tu es calme, que tu es pure, et que tu es froide!" [Oh, Consuelo, how calm you are, how pure, and how cold!] (*C*, 1:122). Marriage is not the object of Anzoleto's desire, rather passion and control. But Consuelo inhibits him in pursuit of the former and Zustiniani holds all the cards in terms of the latter. Thus Anzoleto turns from Consuelo to Corilla, from a simple to an ostentatious musician.

The development of his relationship with Corilla will entirely reshape the direction of both the love and the musical plots. Anzoleto becomes involved with Corilla in part to convince her to form a cabal in Consuelo's favor instead of against her. But Consuelo's overwhelming success at her theatrical debut substantiates Corilla's original misgivings; she then turns against Anzoleto. Not to be outdone, and also not a little jealous of Consuelo's obviously superior debut, Anzoleto sets out to win back Corilla. He is attracted to her not only for her physical beauty and because she uses physical intimacy as a weapon, but also because she is Zustiniani's ex-mistress. With Zustiniani paying court to Consuelo, what better way to extract revenge? Moreover, Anzoleto and Corilla have similar musical tastes. She contradicts Consuelo's advice by encouraging him to use as many fioriture as possible to impress the public. Musical considerations continue to influence the path of love.

Porpora knows about Anzoleto's dalliance with Corilla. Wishing to help Consuelo to concentrate on her own career instead of considering her fiancé's, he reveals Anzoleto's deception to her. She maintains that she has agreed to appear on the stage only in order to help advance Anzoleto's career. Porpora challenges her attitude: "Songe à la musique, à l'art divin, Consuelo; oserais-tu dire que tu ne l'aimes que pour Anzoleto?" [Think about music, the divine art, Consuelo; would you dare say that you love it only for Anzoleto's sake?] (*C*, 1:171). Her response demonstrates the degree to which she has always associated music and her life with Anzoleto: "J'ai aimé l'art pour lui-même aussi; mais je n'avais jamais séparé dans ma pensée ces deux choses indivisibles: ma vie et celle d'Anzoleto" [I loved music for itself too; but I had never separated these two indivisible things in my thoughts: my life and Anzoleto's]. As Consuelo cannot accept Anzoleto's infidelity she leaves Venice, breaking off the relationship with him as well as momentarily halting her career on the stage. Both love and music grind to a halt as she leaves the city that embodies both for her.

Albert and Consuelo's relationship is complex and problematic to say the least. When she first arrives at Riesenburg, Consuelo's contact with Albert is mediated entirely through Amélie, his incorrigibly unmusical cousin and fiancée. Whereas music will function to bring Albert and Consuelo together, it stands as an obstacle between Albert and Amélie. After one of Albert's trancelike attacks, the first Consuelo witnesses, Amélie's uncle suggests some music to calm Albert's nerves and urges his niece to play the harp and sing. Amélie recalls the event: "mais je chantai fort mal, et Albert, comme si je lui eusse écorché les oreilles, eut la grossièreté de sortir au bout de quelques mesures" [but I sang very badly, and as if I had flayed his ears, Albert had the bad taste to leave after a few bars] (*C*, 1:221). The uncle concludes that sometimes music does him good and sometimes it does him ill. The passage suggests plainly that the quality of the musician and the music are of paramount importance in the curative function of music. Music's ability to calm and soothe will become an indelible bond between Consuelo and Albert.

Music evokes the mystical and amorous attachment Albert feels for Consuelo in the scene where she first sings at Riesenberg. Albert's conviction that Consuelo has been sent to him as his partner in life to assuage his suffering—his definition of love—confirms his devotion to and enthusiasm for her. After hearing Consuelo sing, Albert faints and disappears. The fear that music actually causes him suffering first convinces the family she should not sing again. But when they understand that Albert has spoken to Consuelo about consolation, "un mot qu'il a bien souvent sur les lèvres" [a word he often has on his lips] (*C*, 1:258), Albert's aunt encourages Consuelo to sing, hoping her voice might bring him out of hiding. Albert's father seconds the suggestion, comparing her with Farinelli, who was able to cheer up the King of Spain with his singing, just as David had appeased Saul's fury by the sound of his harp (*C*, 1:259).

The musical allusions to David and Farinelli put Consuelo in esteemed company, but of particular interest here is the mention of the curative powers of music and the implicit comparison of Albert and royalty. In the midst of such acclamatory comparisons, Consuelo sings a Spanish hymn in honor of Our Lady of Consolation, "Consuelo de mi alma." As she sings, "un profond soupir exhalé comme d'une poitrine humaine vint répondre aux derniers sons que Consuelo fit entendre" [a deep sigh as if exhaled from a human chest answered the last tones Consuelo sounded]. The sigh, a common indication of melancholy and love, imitates the exhalation of air in singing underscored by the musical expression whereby the sigh answers (read "echoes") Consuelo's last notes. There is no doubt that it is Albert who heaves the sigh from some unknown spot in the room or behind the walls.

The scene where Consuelo descends into the well at Schreckenstein and hears the enchanting sounds of a Stradivarius gives rise to a confused exchange involving music and love. While Albert's emotions are now clear to him and he expresses them openly to Consuelo in words and music, she remains unsure since she still sees love and music, at least a career in music, as antithetical. Back in her room, Consuelo falls into a deep fever. She calls out for Albert, who calms her by speaking in Spanish. She responds only to him and jumps onto the harpsichord, singing from Handel's *Te Deum*. The narrator recounts:

Jamais sa voix n'avait eu plus d'expression et plus d'éclat. Jamais elle n'avait été aussi belle que dans cette attitude extatique, avec ses cheveux flottants, ses joues embrasées du feu de la fièvre, et ses yeux qui semblaient lire dans le ciel entrouvert pour eux seuls. . . . A peine Consuelo eut-elle fini la strophe, qu'elle fit un grand soupir; une joie divine brilla sur son visage. "Je suis sauvée!" (*C*, 1:364–65)

[Never had her voice had more expression or more brilliance. Never had it been so beautiful as in this enraptured pose, with her floating hair, her cheeks aflame with the fire of fever, and her eyes that seemed to be able to read in the sky that was parted for her alone. . . . Consuelo had hardly finished the verse when she heaved a big sigh; a divine joy gleamed on her face. "I've been saved!"]

Consuelo's beauty seems an essential part of her makeup here, whereas in the beginning of the novel she is portrayed as plain, even ugly. The description here depicts an impressive figure, a sculpture-like being consumed with passion. The ecstatic pose she strikes recalls Bernini's *St. Theresa*, joining religious piety and passion. And the significant sigh once again communicates overwhelming emotion. The central role of music throughout this scene attests its strong links to the love theme as well as to the themes of reincarnation and mysticism.

Consuelo's control of the force of music is most evident in the notion of possession, which soon finds a parallel in speech and then song. Further on Albert attributes his feelings of transcendence to Consuelo's singing, sure that if he can reach between humanity and God it is thanks to her singing voice. And in so doing, his soul possesses her, doubtless the source of Consuelo's anxiety and fear. Possession remains an important issue for Consuelo and another manifestation of Sand's feminism.

Consuelo struggles with her emotions, unable to commit and unable to tell Albert. She does not want to repeat the painful experience she had with Anzoleto. Moreover, she fears Albert's love will not satisfy her. The memory of Anzoleto's passion remains just as strong as the memory of his unfaithfulness and his weaknesses. Later she admits to Albert's father that she is devoted to Albert and that she has no other attachments. But she cannot promise herself to him forever since she is committed to her profession: "J'appartiens à l'art auquel je me suis consacrée dès mon enfance" [I belong to the art I've devoted myself to since childhood] (*C*, 1:450). Consuelo's declaration, expressed in the vocabulary of a lover's discourse, demonstrates the hold music has over her, which is much stronger than Albert's love.

Because of her upbringing Consuelo has purposely refused any hint of physical passion and has transferred all her desires to musical passion, religious at first but now more secular. Now, far from the balmy breezes of Venice and the promise of Anzoleto's passion, and removed from a vibrant musical world, Consuelo can no longer define the locus of the passion she needs and seeks. The friction between the two extremes of religious and physical passion is heightened when Anzoleto visits Riesenburg. As Consuelo contemplates the two rivals, she compares their music: Anzoleto's playing and singing revive in her visions of a Venetian summer night with lamps reflected in the waters of the canals. The memory of Albert's music, on the other hand, brings to mind the apparitions of an unknown world of bones and torches reflected in underground waters. The language of music and love has become so confused, so inextricably interwoven, that Consuelo can no longer see clearly and must get away in order to examine her feelings. Thus she must leave Riesenburg.

Sometimes Consuelo transfers her love for music to Porpora,

which occasions further complications of filial obligation. Consuelo effaces herself and suppresses her own desires for those of others. Not only does this represent the stereotypical women's plight of which Sand is quite aware, but it also demonstrates to what degree Consuelo has repressed her own desires. On this subject she states:

> [M]ais je ne suis, en réalité, ni épouse ni fille. La loi n'a rien prononcé pour moi, la société ne s'est pas occupée de mon sort. Il faut que mon cœur choisisse. La passion d'un homme ne le gouverne pas, et, dans l'alternative où je suis, la passion du devoir et du dévouement ne peut pas éclairer mon choix. Albert et le Porpora sont également malheureux, également menacés de perdre la raison ou la vie. Je suis aussi nécessaire à l'un qu'à l'autre . . . Il faut que je sacrifie l'un des deux. (*C*, 2: 193)

> [But in reality I'm neither wife nor daughter. The law has not decreed anything on my behalf, society has not troubled itself about my fate. I must choose with my heart. A man's passion does not govern it, and in my current dilemma, the passion of duty and of dedication cannot clarify my choice. Albert and Porpora are equally unhappy, equally threatened, one by losing his mind and the other by losing his life. One needs me just as much as the other . . . I must sacrifice one of them.]

Deference tinged with sarcasm characterizes the reference to law and society. A Lacanian reading would associate this tendency with an acquiescence to the phallic power of the patriarchy. Consuelo plays her cards wisely in this case since she takes advantage of the lack of social and legal obligations to make her own choice. However, the choice is difficult. Later she still vacillates: "O Porpora! disait-elle dans son cœur, je ferai mon possible pour remonter sur le théâtre. O Albert! j'espère que je n'y parviendrai pas" ["Oh, Porpora!" she said in her heart, "I'll do my best to get back on the stage. Oh, Albert! I hope I won't be able to manage it"] (*C*, 2:214).

Porpora's adamant opposition to her union with Albert—or with anyone—at once complicates Consuelo's situation and supports the antithetical duality of love and music. In Venice he had already told her that she should devote her talents and her energies to her art: "Il te faut la solitude, la liberté absolue. Je ne te veux ni mari, ni amant, ni famille, ni passions, ni liens d'aucune sorte. C'est ainsi que j'ai toujours conçu ton existence et compris ta carrière. Le jour où tu te donneras à un mortel, tu perdras ta divinité" [You need solitude, absolute freedom. I don't want you to have husband, or family, or passions, or ties of any sort. This is how I've always conceived of your existence and understood your career. The day you give yourself to a mortal, you'll lose your divinity] (*C*, 1:171). Now that she has told him of Albert's proposal of marriage and of her own hesitations, he again tries to dissuade her from such thoughts. His machinations include suggesting a marriage of convenience with Haydn and forging a dissuasive letter to Albert over her signature. In this context of jealousy and deceit, he convinces her to sign a contract for the opera season in Berlin. Music, now professional music rather than commitment to the art, functions as the nemesis of love. This distortion of her devotion to music governs the Berlin episode of the novel and explains the misfortunes Consuelo endures there. Sand's coupling of music and love knows its limits. The future of Consuelo's professional practice of music will bear out this correspondence.

After his apparent death, Albert's mysterious appearances at rehearsals and performances in Vienna and in Berlin heighten Consuelo's confusion over the dilemma between a musical profession and a love relationship. She first spies the figure of a man backstage in Vienna during the rehearsal of *Zénobie*, a story about an overly ambitious queen. In the title role, Consuelo finds truth in an aria she sings where she hesitates between the love of two men. She first assumes the mysterious man to be Albert, then decides it must be an hallucination; this hesitation fits nicely into a narrative digression about the illusions of the theater. Here Consuelo begins to confuse illusion and reality along with love and passion, passion and music, and music and herself.

In Berlin, Consuelo's first performance is in Hasse's *Titus*, the story of the Romans' rejection of Titus's new bride, Berenice. Consuelo, who now believes Albert dead, again spies a man in the corner of the house. Thinking she recognizes the "dead" Albert, she faints and is taken away. Consuelo's dramatic role in this opera represents a sequestered woman forced to fulfill a political position in the guise of an amorous one. Consuelo will soon be called upon to fulfill a similar role vis-à-vis Frederick II. This is a role she will refuse, a refusal for which she will be incarcerated.

Liverani, who is Albert in his *Invisible* persona—although neither Consuelo nor the reader will know this for another two hundred pages—whisks Consuelo away from Spandau prison in a most Gothic fashion, complete with mask and cloak, and remaining mute throughout.[8] During the dangerous journey to the palace of the *Invisibles* and the period Consuelo spends there, very little about music is mentioned. Only when Consuelo learns that Liverani's visit and letter to her have been discovered and that he will be punished for these actions does she sing. She has asked for an audience before the high council of the *Invisibles*, and awaiting the appointment she breaks into song from Handel's *Rinaldo*, Almirena's aria "Lascia ch'io piango" [Let me weep], a supplication to be allowed to lament her cruel fate while awaiting freedom.

In Handel's *Rinaldo*, based on Tasso's *Gerusalemma liberata*, Almirena is being held prisoner despite the efforts of her beloved, not unlike Consuelo's situation in the castle of the *Invisibles*. Almirena's lover reassures her in the opera by repeating the melody she has just sung. In similar fashion, immediately after singing the aria, Consuelo hears a violin admirably echoing the melody. Even though she has never heard Albert play any piece of "modern" music, she is sure it is he who mirrors her music and her suffering. She tries in vain to rid herself of this thought as she still believes Albert dead. The play of love and music in the relationship between Consuelo and Liverani remains problematic. They exchange a few unauthorized love letters, but no music enters the transaction. By singing from *Rinaldo*, Consuelo uses music as a source of solace and not as a response to love. However, that her singing is echoed by the sound of a violin, exactly replicating her tone and suffering, proves the love and devotion of the violinist. Music parallels love just as Liverani's violin echoes Consuelo's voice.

As the aria's significance relates directly to the narrative, the plot is advanced by demonstrating Consuelo's emotional progress. At the same time, the direct reference to Handel's aria appeals to the reader's familiarity with baroque opera. Consuelo finds out later that Albert is alive and that he was indeed playing the violin here. Not only does music continue to function as the language of love and freedom, it also guides the protagonist to an understanding of and hope for a new religion and a new social order. Despite all the writings the *Invisibles* have put at Consuelo's disposal, music remains her one true discourse. Writing will always represent the law of the father, while music represents faith and the soul of the people. Using a Kristevan model, Lucienne Frappier-Mazur sees Consuelo's difficulty in this passage as a descent into abjection, wherein she rejects the chastity imposed by her own mother and rediscovers her sexual desire through the mediation of Wanda, Albert's mother and her newly adopted mother figure.[9] I would add here that the absence of music until the moment of imminent liberation indicates Sand's equation of music and freedom, a leitmotif that permeates the novel.

Two reasons explain the absence of music in the relationship between Consuelo and Liverani, one external and practical, the other internal and mystical. Throughout this section of the novel, Sand must explain details of eighteenth-century secret societies and Consuelo's potential role in them. The history of these societies must be linked logically with the history of the Rudolstadt family, the death and rebirth of Wanda and Albert, and the future of society as well as that of the union between Albert and Consuelo. These rather complex data, combined with the confusion of the Liverani-Albert identity already requires sinuous interweaving without adding subtle musical symbolism to the confusion. Moreover, Consuelo's singing career has at this point come to an end and the musical symbolism is being transformed into something more mystical and less practical.

In another perspective, however, the relationship of Liverani and Consuelo is more sensual and less mystical than that between Albert and Consuelo. As such, since music takes on an almost purely mystical role in the novel, musical symbolism has no place in the sensual relationship. Whereas in other love plots Sand would not hesitate to use music to accentuate the play of attraction and sexual tension, she does not do so in this instance since music must retain the untarnished purity of a divine language.

It is evident that the conflict between music and love in this section of the novel not only parallels Consuelo's hesitation about her feelings for Albert, but also signals the unnaturalness of her abandonment of love for a musical career. Music for Sand does not represent a goal in itself; rather, it is a means to an end. The absence of music during the significant passage wherein Albert's mother, Wanda, tells her story also points to Consuelo's abnegation of passion as she tries to resist her attraction to Liverani. If, then, music equals passion, Consuelo's struggle to choose becomes a question of desires and repression. Such an adulterous desire, in her eyes, cannot be sanctioned by the sacred language of music.

The opening scene of the initiation is awash with light, fireworks, and music. A chorus sings from Handel's *Judas Maccabaeus*, "Chantons la gloire / De Juda vainqueur!" and Consuelo spontaneously joins in. When given the chance to sing with Anzoleto, who is present, she says she will do it if it is part of her initiation, but that she would prefer not to. Her self-awareness in this decision strengthens the link between music and love, significantly modified now that she better understands her desires. At the conclusion of the wedding ceremony with Albert, Hubert, a former student of Porpora known as "le Porporino," sings a hymn, accompanied by Benda on the violin,[10] written by Albert in the memory of the martyrs of the cause of the *Invisibles*. Albert takes up the violin and plays a few notes. Overcome with emotion, Consuelo cannot sing.

Contrary to the case of acute laryngitis in Vienna, this instance of not singing results from an emotional state and not a refusal, either conscious or subconscious.

A comment about Consuelo's first loss of voice is useful here. Once Consuelo recognizes Albert and Liverani are the same man, she can accept the two sides of her love. She now enjoys reconciliation between her philosophical and her physical ideals. But the two aspects do not merge easily. Since the lie of Albert's official death must be maintained, Consuelo must tell Maria-Theresa she is married to Liverani, who has been imprisoned in Prague. Liverani's reputation prejudices Maria-Theresa against allowing Consuelo to leave Vienna to go to him. Being too careful and too obedient to overtly challenge the empress, Consuelo subconsciously resolves to find a way to disobey the monarch, and this way comes in the form of her losing her voice. This is no ruse; Consuelo is not capable of such deception, nor would Sand allow her heroine such a duplicitous solution. Reflecting on her fate, Consuelo ponders her future, "ne songeant pas à la perte de sa voix, ne se sentant pas humiliée par l'indignation de ses tyrans, mais résignée et fière comme l'innocent condamné à subir un supplice inique, *et remerciant Dieu de lui envoyer cette infirmité subite* qui allait lui permettre de quitter le théâtre et de rejoindre Albert" [not thinking about her loss of voice and not feeling humiliated by the indignation cast on her by her tyrants, but resigned and proud like an innocent person condemned to endure an evil torture, *and thanking God for having sent her this sudden infirmity*] (*CR*, 3:429; my emphasis).

Sand has given Consuelo a powerful voice to use in contrast to the conventionally silent role of women. Taking away that voice could seem a retrenching into a patriarchal power play. But Consuelo does not lose her voice entirely. At the end of the novel, she maintains the influential position of Albert's interpreter and mediator, for which she uses her speaking voice as well as her musical knowledge and instinct. While some may see the mediator as a subordinate and traditionally female role—indeed often the term "mediatrix" is found—in fact, Sand redefines the strong woman as one able to succeed in a typically man's world, but also the perspicacity to disengage from that world when it no longer offers her freedom. Consuelo's need to go to her husband's aid far outweighs her need to please Maria-Theresa and the Vienna opera-going public; it even transcends her own need to sing. Up to this point in the novel, her musical voice has symbolized her freedom, individuality, and perseverance. Now, her speaking voice will take over, endowing her with the very authority that traditional society denies. In the epilogue, it is Consuelo's speaking voice that commands attention and respect; it is through her voice that the People learn the new direction society must take. Hers is the powerful voice.[11]

But in contrast to this first time, where it was a matter of personal, moral obligation versus professional reputation and responsibility, in the initiation scene Consuelo is so emotionally overwhelmed at the epiphany of music, love, politics, and philosophical ideals that she cannot participate because she lacks the composure to control her instrument. This "failing" also contrasts with the scene of fever and mental crisis where, nursed by Albert, she jumps atop the harpsichord and sings from Handel's *Te Deum*. In this instance she is emotionally drained but controlled by a superhuman power originating in her bond with Albert. In the initiation ceremony, she is in full possession of her wits but at the same time emotionally unable to sing.[12]

Seduction by music plays a doubly important role in *Teverino* (1845). First, the eponymous vagabond's improvisations charm the young noblewoman, Sabina. She is not only dazzled by his manner and his grace, but his voice enchants her. "La facilité et même l'originalité de son improvisation lyrique, l'heureux choix de l'air, la beauté incomparable de sa voix, et ce don musical naturel, qui remplaçait chez lui la méthode par le goût, la puissance et le charme, agirent bientôt sur Sabina d'une manière irrésistible" [The ease and even the originality of his lyrical improvisation, the felicitous choice of the tune, the incomparable beauty of his voice, and the natural musical gift that replaced technique with taste, power, and charm, all soon acted on Sabina in an irresistible way].[13] At the same time, Léonce, the nobleman whose love for Sabina has remained hidden under a veneer of aristocratic *marivaudage* (sophisticated banter), comes to realize his love and the importance of declaring it honestly only when he hears Teverino sing the enchanting name of Amenaïde from Rossini's *Tancredi*: "Il suffirait de t'entendre prononcer ainsi ce nom et chanter ces trois notes pour reconnaître que tu es un grand chanteur, et que tu comprends la musique comme un maître" [It would be enough to hear you pronounce that name and sing those three notes in that way for him to recognize that you are a great singer and that you understand music like a master].[14]

Written only three years after *Consuelo*, although not published until 1851, *Le Château des Désertes* presents many of the same elements of music and musical training: for example, the simplicity of style and sincerity of presentation in musical and theatrical performance. Once again it is the woman, Cécilia, who sees clearly in matters of art and morality and senses how to please the public in a more satisfying and lasting way and at the same time maintain artistic integrity. The love interest in the novel travels a rather confusing route since the expected couple—Adorno, the narrator, and Cécilia— changes quite near the end to Célio and Cécilia. Adorno and Stella, Célio's sister, form a second couple. As in *Les Maîtres Sonneurs*, a double wedding closes the novel.

How, then, does music support and abet the love theme in this novel when the love interest does not remain constant? Sand attaches the significance of the love-music coupling to relationships that brave changes, similar to the modification Célio's musical and moral *Bildung* undergoes. Two men fall in love with Cécilia. A series of parallel structures links the rivals for Cécilia's hand. Neither Adorno nor Célio have experienced love at the beginning of the novel. Both men are artists, Adorno a painter and Célio a singer; and both are the product of an illegitimate union where the name of one natural parent—Adorno's mother, Célio's father—has been kept secret. The lives of these three characters come together in the opening scene of the text at a performance of *Don Giovanni* in Vienna, where Célio is making his debut as Leporello[15] and Cécilia is singing the role of Zerlina. Adorno has gone to the performance to accompany the duchess of ***, who is most interested in Célio's success. The duchess is the supposed object of their rivalry.

The musical performance provides the opportunity for Adorno to meet the two singers, thus occasioning Adorno and Célio's friendship and the unfolding of Adorno's attraction to Cécilia. He announces his admiration of her musicianship and artistry to the duchess: "son organe manque d'éclat, mais son chant ne manque jamais d'ampleur" [her instrument lacks brilliance, but her song never lacks fullness] (*CD*, 46). He goes on to say that her voice is not only good but that she brings life to the opera. Music thus defines the context in which Adorno first sees Cécilia. Her musical performance is what attracts him to her, and music reminds him of his attraction and provides the hope of success. The duchess leaves him to his pursuit of the "second-rate" singer while she pursues Célio. Adorno's attraction to Cécilia is clear and he fears that Célio might be a potential rival, but Célio assures him, apparently sincerely, that he is no obstacle.

Cécilia and Célio have to leave Vienna quickly and mysteriously just after the performance. In desperation, Adorno tries to follow them. He goes to Turin, where the duchess follows him. He is about to succumb to her seduction when outside his window he hears a voice he recognizes singing "Vedrai carino" from Mozart's opera.

This determines him to resist the duchess, and he departs Turin without a plan. He ends up in the small town of Les Désertes (a name evocative of the isolation in this passage of the novel), just outside of Briançon. Here he finds Cécilia, Célio, and other members of the family.

Throughout this section of the novel, Adorno grows closer to Cécilia. Célio tells him that he was with Cécilia in Turin when she sang "Vedrai carino" under his window. He was jealous and angry on her behalf, since he thought Adorno might love the duchess. Later Cécilia tells him about singing under his window. She was unaware he had heard her. Adorno explains to her that it was hearing her song that prevented him from making the mistake of succumbing to the duchess. The lyrics of this aria are significant: "If you are a good boy, you will see what a wonderful cure I have to give you" (*CD*, 80). The aria is usually played as a demonstration of flirtation, which could not be further from Cécilia's nature. Sand's application suggests that both male characters, Adorno and Célio, are in desperate need of experiencing love before they can develop emotionally. Cécilia possesses the "cure" both men require and she alone will make the decision to whom the gift should be proffered.

Music also creates a bond for the merry band at Les Désertes, who busy themselves with rehearsals of *Don Juan*, a commedia dell'arte mixture of the influences of Molière, Mozart, and Hoffmann. Adorno finds himself surreptitiously drafted into the role of the Commandatore. Cécilia sings the trouser role of Ottavio. Boccaferri, her father, declares that his daughter, never before able to develop musically and dramatically in front of an ignorant public, is progressing here admirably. Her Ottavio, a character who appears only in the Mozart/da Ponte version, is marvelous, he says. She brilliantly manages to create a subtle personage solely by virtue of Mozart's music: "elle traduisit la pensée du maître dans un langage aussi élevé que sa musique" [she translated the master's thought into a language as lofty as his music] (*CD*, 116). Sand's use of "language" here remains ambiguous: is this an instance of words as opposed to music, or words and music, or music as language? At any rate, the resolute parallel between music and language is constant.

A few pages later Boccaferri explains how she gives meaning to a line in Mozart he has always found insipid: "Respiro." Ottavio's line in act 1, scene 13, reads "Ohimé! respiro" [Thank God! I can breathe again]. After Donna Anna's impassioned account of Don Giovanni's attack, Ottavio breathes a sigh of relief when he learns that his fiancee's honor has been preserved. Amid Donna Anna's grief for her father's murder and anger at Don Giovanni's violation, Ottavio thinks about himself, his honor, his reputation. This is the moment, according to Sand's interpretation, that we discover just how self-interested he is. For the rest of the opera, although he valiantly attempts to avenge his fiancée's honor, his principal concern is when they will at last be married. Donna Anna is hard pressed to convince him that they must delay their original plans for a wedding until a year after her father's death. Sand points to "Respiro," a short line wherein the interpreter can display the whole moral makeup of the character, to show how expressive a singer Cécilia is. An otherwise conventional part, Ottavio in this one line provides the essence of his character. Before and after, Donna Anna's words and music are aflame with the passion of anger (and perhaps also of lust), while Ottavio remains egocentrically concerned about reputation and "honor," both masculine and feminine. Sand's statement about the importance of this line and about Cécilia's expert interpretation suggests as much about her position on women's issues as about the contralto's musicianship. That such an important theme should be expressed and made explicit to the reader through a musical exchange demonstrates once again Sand's ability to weave musical symbolism into her narrative. Here the link between love and music adopts a more cynical disposition, underlining Sand's interpretation of the insincerity of Ottavio's goal.

Cécilia's love for Célio prevails. Her attachment to him arises simultaneously from her respect for art as professed by Célio's mother Lucrezia, and from an attraction to Célio himself. This musical and sensitive link is based on shared experience and shared attraction, creating a bond between Cécilia and Célio with which Adorno cannot compete. To a degree this relationship resembles that of Joset and Brulette insofar as a common accumulation of childhood memories—many of them musical memories—brings them together.[16] However, Cécilia's musical talent as well as her patience and willingness to help Célio overcome his impudence distinguish her from Brulette. In like manner, Célio's ability to recognize both his flaws and his overly proud performance techniques sets him apart from Joset, as well as from Anzoleto. And Célio's musical and moral progress makes him more attractive to Cécilia, as Adorno notes: "Je comprends ce qui s'est passé en vous depuis ce jour-là [à Vienne], parce que je sais ce qui s'est passé en lui" [I understand what has happened inside you since that day because I know what has happened inside him] (CD, 146). Adorno's resignation at Célio's having won Cécilia's heart also bears witness to his own maturation. His statement that he knows what has happened inside Célio clearly shows that the same change was effected inside him. In fact, Adorno's growth is doubly impressive in that he learns to accept the reality of unrequited love as well as the meaning of love.

In *La Filleule* (1853) a ten-year age gap separates the would-be lovers. Restrained by societal conventions, by their own hesitations—his because of inexperience and hers because of a failed marriage—and by the firm yet kind stance of the heroine's mother, Stéphen and Anicée are slow to express their emotions to each other. In an important scene at Anicée's home in Paris, Stéphen plays the piano. It is the first time he plays for her and her mother. "Je lui ai dit en musique tout ce que l'âme endolorie et inquiète peut dire à Dieu. . . . Anicée, . . . ne disait rien et me dérobait son visage. . . . [Elle] s'est penchée vers moi et m'a dit tout bas, avec des yeux pleins de larmes: —Stéphen, vous m'avez fait bien du mal; vous souffrez donc?" [I told her in music all that an aching and anxious soul can say to God. . . . Anicée said nothing and hid her face from me. . . . She leaned toward me and said quietly, her eyes full of tears, "Stéphen, you've really hurt me. Are you suffering then?"] (*F*, 84–85) The declaration of love is communicated through music: Stéphen expresses his love by playing the piano, and Anicée comprehends his suffering through his music and understands his not being able to speak it. Her own feelings remain somewhat vague, however. Could she be sensitive to his suffering without returning his love? Although his doubt about her feelings pervades many pages yet, she will eventually display her love for him.

Stéphen and Anicée share the responsibility of raising an adoptive daughter. Moréna, the eponymous goddaughter, is the child of a gypsy woman and a Spanish aristocrat. When Moréna reaches puberty, she develops an infatuation for Stéphen. The parallels with Chopin and Sand's daughter Solange cannot be ignored. More interesting, however, are the Freudian resonances in the family structure. Moréna's "love" is mediated through music. Eager to hear her godfather play the piano, Moréna finally experiences feelings of fulfillment and understanding:

Il a enfin joué et improvisé ce soir. Oh! quel talent, quelle âme, quel charme! Voilà la seule de ses grandes facultés que je sois un peu capable de comprendre, moi! Pour le reste, j'admire sur parole. Mais la musique, c'est une chose que je sens, que je possède dans mon cœur, comme lui, quoi qu'il en dise, et quoique je ne la possède pas encore dans ma tête. (*F*, 139)

[Finally this evening he played and improvised. Oh, what talent, what charm, what a soul! That's the only one of his great gifts I can understand! The rest, I admire them on faith. But music is something I feel, that I possess in my heart, like he does, no matter what he says, even though I don't possess it in my head.]

Moréna's commentary here is twofold. On the one hand she demonstrates her gratefulness for finally being able to hear her godfather play and for the exquisite emotions she experiences through his music. On the other hand, she acknowledges her own powers to understand music. It is the beginning of a new phase for her musical education, and hereafter she will become more serious and more dedicated. She perspicaciously observes the musical link that binds her to her godfather and realizes, perhaps with a sensitivity beyond her years, that she feels and possesses music even though she might not yet understand it intellectually.

Another love plot, suggesting incest in a typically Sandian way, puts Moréna together with her long-lost brother. Algénib enters the novel significantly at the same time as Moréna's musico-cultural awakening occurs. Algénib has been spying on his sister and her protector for some time. Aware of this, Stéphen tries to stump the boy, but to no avail. Here we see an instance of Sand's nod to the stereotype of gypsy cunning. When he finally does manage to see Moréna alone, a spark of seduction colors his discourse as he tells her who he is, who she is, and introduces gypsy music and dance to her. The dovetailing of culture and identity, made all the more attractive through the promise of love, is filtered through music.

Algénib and Moréna are, of course, not at all sister and brother. Indeed they share no biological connection. Moréna's mother was married to Algénib's father; she is not Algénib's mother. Moréna's father is a Spanish nobleman currently living in Paris who had known Algénib's father in earlier times. Thus they can and do marry and live out their lives as professional musicians. Sand will again explore the pseudo-incestuous relations of brother and sister in a later novel, *Ma Sœur Jeanne* (1874), where music also plays an important role in the characterization of the female protagonist. Music actually replaces love in this novel. Jeanne does not abandon music entirely, since she does play the piano in the final pages; but it no longer serves as a substitute.

I have already shown how love and music overlap in *Les Maîtres Sonneurs*, published the same year as *La Filleule*. Tiennet, Joset, and Huriel vie for Brulette's heart. Two of the three love plots revolve around music and form a triangle, for both Joset and Huriel are in love with Brulette, both are musicians, and both demonstrate their love for her through music. Joset's first overt sign of attachment to Brulette comes through music. The reed flute scene remains a central moment for the definition of Joset's character, of his devotion to Brulette, and of his quest for pure music. These concepts and ideals fuse in this scene, demonstrating to what degree Joset is incapable of separating his aesthetic from his personal goals. This weakness will prove his downfall. Joset's response to Brulette's reaction to his flute music is an overwhelming feeling of happiness. His happiness is twofold: he is pleased to have been able to communicate through his music, and he equates the senses since he says seeing and hearing (read also: "understanding" [entendre]) can transmit information. This notion will surface on other occasions in the novel. He is also overjoyed that he could communicate these thoughts through music to Brulette, whose opinion and appreciation he prizes over all others'. What is especially clear is the depth of feeling and understanding Brulette receives and which Tiennet does not.[17]

The relationship between Brulette and Huriel, Joset's rival, also begins in a musical context. At the feast of St. John, Huriel offers to replace Carnat's son on the bagpipes. Huriel's playing far surpasses that of the young Carnat in both quality and endurance. Brulette dances the whole night. While Brulette entertains thoughts of Huriel, and he of her, Joset goes to Bourbonnais to improve his bagpiping with Huriel's father, a master piper. His goal is not, however, purely musical; he wants to be able to declare his love for Brulette in music: "J'ai voulu me donner à la musique, autant par amour de la chose que par amour de ma mie Brulette" [I wanted to give myself to music, as much for the love of it as for the love of my beloved Brulette] (*MS*, 181).

To compare Brulette's three would-be lovers, Sand puts a traditional song in the mouth of Père Bastien, "The Song of Three Woodsmen" (*MS*, 295–96). The song tells the story of three *fendeux* (woodcutters) who make their pitch for a young girl, each one with an attribute—respectively a rose, a wood-splitting wedge, and an almond blossom—and each one announcing his desire in his own way: "Le plus jeune disait: J'aime bien, mais je n'ose" [The youngest said "I love but dare not"]; "Le plus vieux s'écriait: Quand j'aime je commande" [The oldest declared "When I love, I command]; "Le troisième chantait: Moi, j'aime et je demande" [The third sang, "I love and I ask"]. While the rose would normally indicate the love-kissed suitor, the verb he appends to his declaration shows a blandness, and his inability to declare himself underscores his lack of imagination. The second man is aggressive, wielding an axe and crying out his request, or rather his order. Only the third woodsman approaches the girl with respect, and in song. The girl, then, takes up the song and refuses the first two woodsmen and accepts the third: "On donne à qui demande" [He who asks shall receive].[18]

This short scene provides an institutionalization of the three suitors. Transforming the love situation into verse and setting it to music is a concrete example of Sand's musical manipulations in matters of love. Traditional song represents a strong sign of folk culture in Sand's Bourbonnais and Berry,[19] and this specimen provides a source of lyricism and humor to illustrate the triangle. The song is referred to several times later in the novel to remind the reader of the situation and its lesson. Tiennet learns the lesson, assimilates it, and moves on. Joset, on the other hand, understands the lesson but cannot accept it.

The decisive moment leading to decisions and conclusions comes, as one might suspect, in a musical experience. I have already discussed the challenge between Huriel and Joset in terms of musical language. Brulette makes her choice on the day of the May ritual, when Bourbonnais tradition allows a suitor to attach a bouquet of flowers to his intended's door. When Huriel arrives at Brulette's house, a bouquet is already on her door handle. Just as he is attaching his flowers, Brulette opens the door and finds the two bouquets. She asks what it means, and Huriel answers simply and honestly: "Je ne peux rien dire, sinon que voilà le mien" [I can say nothing except that here is mine] (*MS*, 414). These are the words she hoped to hear, and accordingly she accepts his bouquet. At this moment, from the wooded hillock just across the clearing come the sounds of a bagpipe playing "The Song of Three Woodsmen." The piper manipulates the tune in various ways according to his abilities, as I have already discussed. Notwithstanding Joset's talents in musical expression, Brulette chooses Huriel.

Music and love again intermingle at the culmination of the love plots and the novel. The penultimate scene of the novel represents two weddings: Brulette and Huriel's, and Thérence and Tiennet's. Joset adds to the joy of the occasion with his music. Tiennet recounts:

[I]l prit la musette des mains de mon beau-père et joua une marche de noces qu'il avait composée, la nuit même, à notre intention. C'était une si belle chose de musique, et il y fut donné tant d'acclamation, que son chagrin se dissipa, qu'il sonna triomphalement ses plus beaux airs de danse et se perdit dans son délice tout le temps que dura la fête. (*MS*, 491)

[He took the bagpipes from my father-in-law's hands and played a wedding march he'd written the night before just for us. It was such a beautiful piece of music, and there was such acclaim given it that his sorrow dissipated and he triumphantly played the most beautiful dance tunes and lost himself in his delight for the rest of the festivities.]

This last musical sign of love in the novel thus represents Joset's most generous gesture. For a few moments he is capable of putting aside his own disappointment and demonstrating in the way he knows best that he wishes Brulette happiness. Music and disillusionment will soon turn inward as he wanders off, already contemplating his suicide. The effect of this final, generous musical gesture is a poignant moment of compassion. Sand does not wish to paint an entirely negative portrait of Joset, and the wedding march and dance music give the reader one last, positive image of the "hero" of *Les Maîtres Sonneurs*.

Sand now turns her attention to a more sensitive musician. Adriani is an opera soloist who has left his position and gone to Ardèche to reflect on his disillusionment with his profession. He is first attracted to Laure by her voice. He hears her singing the gondolier's aria from Rossini's *Otello* (*A*, 24–25) and is tempted to rush and meet the person who expresses "avec un charme infini la plainte d'une âme brisée" [the lament of a broken heart with infinite charm]. "Nessun maggior dolor" is an aria that claims there is no greater suffering than to remember happiness in a moment of misery.[20] He is moved by the beauty of her voice and by the choice of the piece, but he is repulsed by her reputation of being mad. He then sings the aria himself, thus establishing the melody and the sentiment of the lyrics as a link between the two characters, who have yet to meet. Once again the gondolier's melody serves Cupid's purpose when Adriani plays and sings it, causing Laure to weep. Both characters experience an emotional response to hearing the other sing the melody, establishing a musical link between the future lovers.

Adriani and Laure are both suffering, the former from disappointment and disillusionment with his profession, and the latter from the recent loss of her husband. Neither has truly known love. Repelled by Laure's reputation yet attracted by her voice, Adriani explores the neighbor's garden, where Toinette, her nursemaid and companion, spots him and bids him to enter the parlor. There he spies a beautiful Pleyel. The servant invites him to play: "Ah! vous regardez la jolie musique à Madame! On n'avait jamais rien vu de si beau ici, et Madame musique que c'est un plaisir de l'entendre! . . . Si vous voulez musiquer, faut pas vous gêner, c'est fait pour ça" [Oh, you're lookin' at Ma'am's pretty music-maker! We'd never seen anything so beautiful, and Ma'am makes music so's it's a pleasure to hear! . . . If you want to make music, you just go right ahead; that's what it's there for] (A, 59). The farm girl's language also deserves a brief commentary. The metonymy that identifies Laure's piano with the music she produces on it allows us to associate music as an identifying characteristic of the heroine. The use of the verb "musiquer," as well as adding a peasant flavor, brings extra life to the concept of making music. Moreover, applying the verb to both Adriani and Laure underscores music as a foundation for the future relationship.

Adriani takes a seat and sings the Rossini aria several times, accompanying himself on the piano. At the fourth time through, his performance shows such mastery that he himself believes he is hearing the gondolier on the canals of Venice below Desdemona's window.

> Je ne sais pas comment je chantai pour la quatrième fois, ce couplet. Je dus le chanter très bien, car ce n'était plus moi que j'écoutais, mais le gondolier mélancolique des lagunes sous le balcon de la pâle Desdemona. Je voyais un ciel d'orage, des eaux phosphorescentes, des colonnades mystérieuses, et, sous la tendine de pourpre, une ombre blanche penchée sur une harpe que la brise effleurait d'insaisissables harmonies. (A, 61)

> [I don't know how I sang this verse for the fourth time. I must have sung it very well because it was no longer myself I heard but the melancholy gondolier of the laguna underneath pale Desdemona's balcony. I could see a stormy sky, phosphorescent waters, mysterious colonnades, and underneath the crimson canopy a white shadow bent over a harp that the wind touched lightly with elusive harmonies.]

His ability to step outside himself and to listen to his singing shows less the critical distance one hopes to find in any artist than an eerie, fantastic vision wherein his own voice captivates him. The sight he pictures resonates with synesthesia as Sand mixes colors, sounds, the tense atmosphere of an impending storm, and the vision of a white figure bent over an Aeolian harp from which emanates unspeakable music. Sand paints a scene of typically romantic ecstasy in a musical context that surrounds the moment. And the aria is heard from the perspective of Adriani himself—Laure, and also the reader, multiplying the effect of the musical experience.

As he contemplates the beauty of the aria, he notices that Laure is sitting at the other end of the room, her head in her hands and her companion at her knees. She flees, and Toinette tells Adriani that these are her first tears since her illness. It is she who identifies both Laure and Adriani as musicians (*A*, 62). When Toinette originally asked Adriani if he is a musician, he replied, "Eh bien, oui, je sais la musique; je l'aime avec passion. J'ai entendu chanter votre maîtresse hier au soir, en passant derrière cette vigne. Elle chante admirablement. On m'a dit qu'elle n'avait pas sa raison. Cela m'a fait peur; j'en ai rêvé. Je suis venu ici sans trop savoir pourquoi" [Well, yes, I know music; I love it passionately. I heard your mistress singing last evening as I strolled past this vine. She sings superbly. I was told she'd lost her reason. That scared me; I've dreamed about it. I've come here without knowing quite why] (*A*, 45). Three important elements of the text are combined in this citation: the importance of music to the hero, the quick transition in his thought from music to his attraction to Laure, and a similarly quick transition to his fears faced with her possible madness. These three themes intertwine throughout the novel to form a complicated construct of emotions linked by music.

While the piano constitutes one of the strongest material links between them, it serves later to introduce a change in the relationship. One day while Adriani is practicing, a workman comes to pack up the instrument since Laure has gone to her mother-in-law's in the Vaucluse. Adriani determines to follow her. But his status as a musician is complete anathema to the aristocratic matriarch. While Sand has used the device of cross-class relationship involving an artist before, here she exploits the situation a bit differently. Laure clearly feels threatened by the emotions Adriani's music evokes in her and could easily use her mother-in-law's class-conscious objections as a safeguard. However, she revolts against those aristocratic conventions, like the good Sandian heroine she is, and returns to Ardèche, where Adriani has already had the piano unpacked. Laure now feels she can risk singing along with him, whereas beforehand she did not dare. And her voice produces in him an overwhelming sense of beauty and intimacy. Their relationship is now sealed in music.

The happy couple have not yet declared their love for one another when a sudden financial disaster demands that Adriani return to Paris to seek employment. Not pleased with having to return to the profession he has left behind with disdain, he does recognize the necessity of a three-year contract to relieve him of his debts. He goes back to Paris with a heavy heart, thinking he has lost Laure

forever. Back in the Capital, he sings beautifully, with a full understanding of the suffering of love for the first time in his life. Adriani's performance enthralls the audience. He has never before felt
so close to his public. For the first time he could sing of love having
had firsthand experience of that emotion. The thematic structure has
come full circle: music forms the cornerstone of his relationship
with Laure, and his love for Laure allows him to experience greater
aesthetic satisfaction in his musical performance.[21]

Balzac also uses music to define a love relationship in *La Duchesse de Langeais*, but instead of making music an essential element in the initial meeting between lovers, his device here is for
music to spark the reunion of two long-lost lovers. As Armand de
Montriveau listens to a nun playing the organ in a Spanish convent,
he is convinced he is hearing his beloved. Music links his love—
both the emotion and the woman—to this religious place and thus
to religion itself: "La Religion, l'Amour et la Musique ne sont-ils
pas la triple expression d'un même fait . . . ? Ces trois poésies vont
toutes à Dieu, qui dénoue toutes les émotions terrestres. Aussi cette
sainte Trinité humaine participe-t-elle des grandeurs infinies de
Dieu, que nous ne configurons jamais sans l'entourer des feux de
l'amour" [Religion, Love, and Music, are these not the triple expression of a single fact . . . ? These three types of poetry all tend
toward God, who resolves all earthly emotions. Thus this holy Trinity participates in the infinite grandeurs of God, which we can never
conceive of without engulfing it in the fires of love].[22] Music thus
serves as a medium for love, both of which, along with religion, are
a human construct for the author of *La Comédie humaine*. We cannot ignore Balzac's equation of music and text. Here the analogy
remains simple; in *Gambara* Balzac provides more developed discussion of the phenomenon of a musical language.[23] Nowhere,
however, does he enter into the kind of disquisition Sand offers in
many of her novels.

Adriani appeared one year after *Les Maîtres Sonneurs*. Some thematic and structural similarities connect the two novels. Both Joset
and Adriani represent the selfish musician, although the reasons and
circumstances of their selfishness differ significantly, which partly
explains the divergent outcomes. Adriani's renewed devotion to his
art constitutes a counterbalance to Joset's resignation to failure in
music, symbolized by the destruction of his bagpipes. And just as
Salomon and Mallion, in their edition of *Les Maîtres Sonneurs*, saw
countless references to Chopin in the character of Joset, so are there
many in Adriani. In contrast with Consuelo, Adriani offers a more
human, less mythical musician. Accordingly the social(ist) element

does not compare. What Adriani learns about himself surfaces outside the musical profession but still within the realm of music. And just as there is growth in Adriani's emotional makeup, the personal *Bildung* is paralleled by a musical one since he learns to express love in music as never before. Again Sand attacks the "professionalism" of the performing world, partly answering Pauline Viardot's experiences and partly responding to her own aesthetic views of the purity of art, which is often sullied by the profession.

Music in *Le Dernier Amour* (1866) defines and symbolizes both love and jealousy, which are inextricably intertwined in this novel. Félicie and her cousin, Tonino, have both inherited musical talents from their grandfather. Félicie plays the violin superbly though she has had no formal training. The narrator, Monsieur Sylvestre (see Sand's novel of that name), regards his fifty years as an impediment to any relationship with Félicie, twenty years his junior. He first realizes his love for her when he hears her playing the Cremona violin she inherited from her grandfather.[24] She takes the violin away from Tonino, who is playing it admirably, and dazzles the narrator with her simplicity of style: "Elle ne savait faire sans doute aucune difficulté, mais elle avait le chant large et pur des vrais musiciens. L'ampleur de son geste et la simplicité majestueuse de son attitude répondaient à cette saine intuition musicale" [Certainly she could handle nothing difficult, but she played broadly and purely like a true musician. The breadth of her gestures and the majestic simplicity of her bearing corresponded to a healthy musical intuition] (*DA*, 56). Of importance here are two details. First, the narrator is never Félicie's explicit public; he listens as a third party, with the violin often being the second. Yet, he is always the implicit narratee and bears the effects of her music. Second, the musical rivalry with Tonino Félicie shows in this scene bespeaks the underlying love she feels she cannot express for him. As this expression of love surfaces, so does the narrator's jealousy. This brings us to the next important musical scene, where he understands the voice of the violin speaking to him, "il [le violon de Crémone] répétait sans se lasser sa phrase monotone et sublime: *l'amour, rien que l'amour!*" [it repeated without weakening its monotonous and sublime phrase: *love, nothing but love*] (*DA*, 94). The irony of this clear musical communication unfolds as the narrator continues to realize the depth of his love as commensurate with the awareness of his jealousy of Tonino. The narrator again hears music at the moment when he realizes once and for all that his relationship with Félicie is over. She plays the same tune he heard when he first realized he was in love with her, but this time it is only the memory of love that the music evokes (*DA*, 293). Félicie changes the tune in many ways, improvising a fury of variations and demonstrating her anger. This musical outburst recalls Joset. She finishes her enraged playing by throwing the violin down and breaking it (*DA*, 303). This is the end of the music and the end of any hope for Félicie and Sylvestre's relationship.

In *Malgrétout* (1869) Sand offers yet another example of love through music. The intervention of the children's song "La Demoi-selle" ["The Damsel"], composed and sung by the heroine Sarah Owen and overheard by the violinist Abel, creates an auditory and musical link for the two protagonists. Abel repeats the melody on the violin, much the way Albert repeated Consuelo's rendition of Handel's aria from *Rinaldo* at the chateau of the *Invisibles* in *La Comtesse de Rudolstadt*. Sand characteristically personifies the in-strument: "Tout à coup nous entendîmes tout près de nous un admi-rable violon qui *chantait* admirablement mon petit air" [All of a sudden we heard nearby a remarkable violin that was admirably *singing* my little tune] (*M*, 30). And adjoining personification to the imitation of nature, "Sarah [the heroine's goddaughter and name-sake] fut . . . charmée de cet écho mysterieux. Elle crut que c'était la rivière ou les arbres qui chantaient" [Sarah was . . . enchanted by the mysterious echo. She thought it was the stream or the trees sing-ing]. Abel calls the song "un *bijou*, un *chef-d'œuvre*" [a *jewel*, a *masterpiece*], which Sarah takes as a great compliment, as "[i]l était musicien par passion et viruose de son état" [he was a passion-ate musician and a virtuoso by profession].

Sarah reacts first with alarm, then with amusement. She is con-vinced, however, that Abel is a wandering musician who only wants to displays his exaggerated skills in search of something else. Then he plays a dance tune with frenzy. His performance at once im-presses and frightens Sarah: "Il avait joué l'air de danse si folle-ment, qu'on ne pouvait dire si son exécution était celle d'un maître en gaieté ou celle d'un saltimbanque adroit; mais les phrases de ma chanson qu'il avait *interprétées* auparavant étaient comme une *tra-duction* idéalisée par un véritable artiste" [He had played the dance tune so brilliantly that the execution could be said to be either that of a master of cheerfulness or one of a clever acrobat. But the phrases of my song that he'd *interpreted* before were like a *transla-tion* idealized by a true artist] (*M*, 31; my emphasis). The metaphor of translation from one musical expression to another recalls the notion of musical language as well as the author's constant struggle to translate the musical experience into words. Only later, when her father shows up at the house with Abel, declaring him "un incomparable artiste," does she realize who he is, a well-known and currently sought-after violinist. Sarah's sister, Adda, adds with irony, "le célèbre Abel, le violoniste incomparable, si recherché, si riche, . . . et c'est à lui que ma sœur a donné cent sous?" [the famous Abel, the incomparable violinist, so sought after, so rich, . . . and he's the one my sister gave some change to] (*M*, 32).

It is only later in the evening, when Adda urges Sarah to sing, that the music-love connection becomes obvious. A parallel scene in the beginning of the novel, when Adda meets her future husband, shows Adda's attitude toward the power of Sarah's voice. M. de Rémonville comes to the house, presumably to pay court to Sarah. She is not inspired and refuses his proposal, but Adda is ready to take her place. M. de Rémonville returns to the Owen house to try his luck a second time, and Adda wants to succeed. She forbids her sister to sing for fear it will charm the young suitor and draw his attention away from Adda. The significance of the later scene becomes clear when, faced with the visit of Abel, Adda says to Sarah, "Va donc chanter! M. Abel, à qui mon père a vanté ton talent, meurt d'envie de t'entendre" [Go ahead and sing! Mr. Abel, to whom father has boasted of your talent, is dying to hear you] (*M*, 34). Sarah sings and Abel is reduced to tears of joy. He replies by playing his violin for an hour, which exhausts him. The connection is established; love has sprung from a mutual appreciation and capacity for music.

Sarah's song "La Demoiselle" continues as a thoroughbass to the plot. Abel sings the song throughout France and Belgium on his recital tour, and in the manner common in France in the mid- to late nineteenth century, this composed folk song becomes popular and passes into folk culture as though it were an authentic folk song. Sarah hears about Abel's successes in particular in reference to the performance of her song. The lyrics of the song, which Sand gives *in texto*, seem innocent in the child's interactivity they are meant to spur. But when taken as a dialogue between Sarah and Abel, they seem to point to Sarah's fear of intimacy:

Demoiselle,	—Non, dit-elle,
Arrête un peu!	Je ne peux.
Sur ton aile	Si mon aile
De Dentelle	Etincelle,
Je vois du feu.	Ferme tes yeux. (*M*, 29)
[Damsel,	—No, says she,
Stop a while!	I cannot.
On your lacy wing	If my wing
I see	Catches a spark,
Some fire.	Close your eyes.]

Sarah's emotional state does not allow her to "perform" comfortably. Unaccustomed as she is to receiving the attentions of a gentleman she admires, she feels shame that she supposes is deserved because of her overly confident ease in composition. "Je voulais bien faire de la musique pour paraître n'attacher aucune importance à l'exagération de l'artiste, mais je ne pouvais pas. Ma voix ne voulait pas sortir de mon gosier, et je sentais un vertige comme si j'eusse respiré un parfum trop fort pour moi" [I wanted to make music to appear not to attach any importance to the artist's exaggeration, but I couldn't. My voice wouldn't come out of my throat, and I felt a sort of dizziness as if I'd breathed in some perfume too strong for me] (*M*, 37). In this additional example of the synaesthesia of music and scent, Sand effects a turn-around of the musical impetus to love. Sarah wants to feign tranquility, but the opposite occurs, and her emotion is so strong she cannot sing. Transposing her conventional use of music in a potential love situation to the opposite effect permits Sand to demonstrate just how much in tune Sarah's emotions are with her music.

In all these instances one is taunted by the question of the sufficiency of music. While music serves as an impetus, sometimes an inspiration for the advancement of the love plots, once love has been recognized and declared, music is not always so important. Consuelo loses her voice after her marriage and leaves the profession when it proves an impediment to the higher cause. Joset commits suicide when he realizes that the perfection of his musical talents did not attain the desired results in love. Cécilia's musical aspirations never overshadow her more idealistic goals, and she manages to show Célio the value of honesty and sincerity over that of success in the musical world. Adriani provides little praise for the world of professional music, which he has left and to which he returns only under financial exigencies.

Yet, it is through a renewed capacity in musical expression that Adriani understands his new outlook on life. He loves, and this emotion—which has been the subject of countless operas he has sung—has only now become a reality for him. The pain and suffering he now feels cause him to process a realization that he translates into his singing in a way neither he nor his public had ever before anticipated. In like fashion, Consuelo does not forsake music; rather, it is only the professional stage she abandons. Music remains for her and Albert the purest form of communication. Célio, from all accounts, will continue in the profession, but his recognition of his failings and his willingness to improve demonstrate the usefulness of his lessons through music. Cécilia participates in these lessons, but she does not represent the professional threat to Célio that Consuelo does to Anzoleto. Célio's progress represents a maturity that Anzoleto cannot experience. In all these cases, music serves as a tool but not as a goal in itself. This very important aspect of Sand's aesthetics surfaces again and again as she puts her heroes into situations where music provides sometimes a solution and sometimes a temptation. But the solution always comes from working out problems *through* music and not a solution *in* music itself. *Malgrétout* also presents the inverse of the trope. While Abel's love for Sarah is first sparked and fueled by music, he eventually leaves the profession to remain with her and her father. He continues to play the violin but only for the simple pleasure of making music. The purity of the art form and its relation to the love it inspired continues beyond the thrill of pleasing the public.

In *Massimilla Doni* (1839) Balzac tells the story of the conflict between ideal and real love. Emilio Memmi loves the duchesse de Cataneo (Massimilla Doni), who has taken the game of social flirtation farther than she anticipated, making their union impossible since the game now overpowers and obscures her true emotion. At the same time, the famous singer Tinti is appearing at la Fenice, and Emilio becomes captivated by her, and she by him. A long scene at la Fenice puts la Tinti on stage singing in Rossini's opera *Mosè*,[25] while Massimilla Doni explains the function of the music and the lyrics to a French doctor visiting Venice. Emilio, a witness to the musicological explanation, slowly realizes that his attraction to and pleasure with la Tinti represents only an approximation of his love and admiration for Massimilla: "Aux yeux d'Emilio, il y avait comme une joute entre l'amour saint de cette âme blanche, et l'amour de la nerveuse et colère Sicilienne" [In Emilio's eyes, there was a kind of spar between the blessed love of this white soul and the love of the excitable and hotheaded Sicilian]. The expression of love through music, although less subtle than Sand's, provides a clear notion of the power of music to express—indeed, to replace—emotions:

Pour toute volupté, pour extrême plaisir, Massimilla tenait la tête d'Emilio sur son sein et se hasardait par moments à imprimer ses lèvres sur les siennes, mais comme un oiseau trempe son bec dans l'eau pure d'une source, en regardant avec timidité s'il est vu. Leur pensée développpait ce baiser comme un musicien développe un thème par les modes infinis de la musique, et il produisait en eux des retentissements tumultueux, ondoyants, qui les enfiévraient. Certes, l'idée sera toujours plus violente que le fait.[26]

[For total voluptuousness and extreme pleasure, Massimilla held Emilio's head on her bosom and chanced from time to time pressing her lips to his, but as a bird dips his beak in pure spring water while watching to see if he's been seen. Their thought developed this kiss just as a musician develops a theme through the infinite modes of music, and it produced in them tumultuous waves of echoes that gave them a fever. Of course the idea will always be more violent than reality.]

In this passage the author explains human emotions in quasi-musical terms. The elements of music that Balzac assigns to passion concern principally rhythm and movement, although one cannot ignore the musical and sexual inventiveness in the use of "développer." The result is somewhat trite despite the passion being described, especially evident in the final sentence of the passage. Later, as Massimilla describes to the French doctor the depth of devotion portrayed in the opera, the degree of her appreciation of Rossini's music and the degree of emotion she feels as she listens to it become evident: "L'analogue d'une pareille conception ne pourrait se trouver que dans les psaumes divins du divin Marcello, un noble Vénitien qui est à la musique ce que Giotto est à la peinture" [The analogy of such a conception could only be found in the divine psalms of the divine Marcello, a noble Venetian who is to music what Giotto is to painting] (*Doni*, 375). Her comparisons to painting and to musical colors raise a question from the doctor; she explains: "Dans la langue musicale, c'est réveiller par des sons certains souvenirs dans notre cœur, ou certaines images dans notre intelligence, et ces souvenirs, ces images ont leur couleur, elles sont tristes ou gaies. Vous nous faites une querelle de mots, voilà tout" [In musical language it's a matter of awakening particular memories of our hearts or particular images of our minds with sounds, and these memories, these images have their colors, they are sad or cheerful. You're making an argument about words, nothing more] (*Doni*, 376). The synaesthesia inherent in this conventional argument is not absent from Sand's discourse, though she manages to downplay the topos in favor of the correspondence between music and scent.[27]

On several occasions Massimilla talks about the necessity of the composer to include set pieces for the pleasure of the singers even though they disrupt the flow of the music and the coherence of the piece. But these are the exigencies of the theater, well understood by the public and often more important than the unity of the narrative. Throughout this long passage, Balzac provides many insightful comments about Rossini and his oratorio, but his commentary remains outside the narrative structure. The exaggerated use of musical terminology and instrumentation adds nothing to the narrative and indeed detracts from the story and the characters.

> A force de l'entendre allant d'*ut* mineur en *sol* mineur, rentrant en *ut* pour revenir à la dominante *sol*, et reprendre en *fortissime* [*sic*] sur la tonique *mi* bémol, arriver en *fa* majeur et retourner en *ut* mineur, toujours de plus en plus chargée de terreur, de froid et de ténèbres, l'âme du spectateur finit par s'associer aux impressions exprimées par le musicien. (*Doni*, 358)

> [By dint of hearing him going from C minor to G minor, back to C and then to the dominant G, just to go back again to the tonic E♭ in fortissimo, and to end up at F major and then back at C minor, always more and more filled with terror, cold, and shadows, the spectator's soul ends up feeling the same impressions the musician expressed.]

It is impossible to tell whether the harmonic modulations Balzac points out are meant to communicate a loss of stability, a deepening of emotional expression, or simply virtuosic prowess. Sand's use of musical indicators is more subtle, provides more information about the character and the narrative, and better satisfies the musical reader because it is more musical. The music in Sand forms part of the narrative structure and the characterization. It is not an embellishment intended to display an amateur's knowledge of musical terminology.[28]

The evidence of Sand's integration of music into the love plots proves her dedication to the musical underpinning in many of her novels and not just the musical novels. Rambeau calls Sand's use of music a "fil conducteur entre deux sensibilités qui s'ignorent et découvrent leurs affinités puis leur sympathie essentielle par son truchement" [thread between two sensibilities that are unaware of each other and that discover first their affinities then their essential sympathy by its intervention.][29] In all these amorous instances— Adriani and Laure, Anicée and Stéphen, Morénita and Algénib, Consuelo and Albert, Célio and Cécilia, Joset and Brulette—love is discovered and enhanced by music, surrounded by music, expressed through music, and grows along with musical sensitivity. The symbolism could not be more evident: music and love function together in Sand's universe.

MADNESS AND MUSIC

Madness is often seen as an outgrowth of love. Many critics have treated madness in literature, and music often enters the formula. A

vestige of the Dionysian myth of unbridled revelry, which incorporates drink, dance, and music in a frenzy of wild activity, no doubt
informs almost any exploration of madness and music. Music's association with madness, therefore, originates in notions of instability and unchecked freedom. A mad character, Lillian Feder
suggests, is usually confused and fragmented.[30] She or he seeks a
hidden unity never to be found, and yet an essential unity results
from this dissolution of the self. To be sure, rhythmics, dynamics,
and the harmony of music go hand in hand with madness. Music,
when added to the state of a mad character, helps to convey the
ethereal nature of hallucinations, dreams, unreason, and the fluidity
of exploration.

Shoshana Felman states that it is music that influences madness
in Stendhal in the most direct and immediate manner. She distinguishes instances where music soothes a violent effect from those
where music provokes madness. She pays particular attention to the
influence of music and madness on the state of the artist. For Stendhal, says Felman, " 'mad' souls are artists' souls; and reciprocally
artists' souls are often riddled with madness."[31] We shall see that,
for Sand, the madness of a musician covers the gamut of possibilities, from a complete separation from reason to the state of a seer
whose madness speaks the truth through music.

Michel Foucault posits that "[m]adness is the purest, most total
form of *quid pro quo*; it takes the false for the true, death for life,
man for woman."[32] This can only be true if we who are observing
a manifestation of madness are convinced of our own reason or of
the narrator's. Characters who show moments of madness may or
may not be turning the world on its head. The context will tell
whether they are to taken seriously or rather discounted as crazy.
The participation of the reader is of paramount importance in the
interpretation of this element. And in cases of musical madness, the
reader must read the musical cues appropriately.

The first case of musical madness in Sand's works occurs in "La
Prima donna." The singer Gina marries an aristocrat and subsequently disappears from the stage. She accepts her fate, but the absence of music in her life causes her to weaken and fade. "La tête
de l'infortunée Gina s'était égarée. Malheureuse, son mari l'avait
accusée de folie. Folle, il l'accusa d'ingratitude" [The ill-fated Gina
had lost her head. As she was unhappy, her husband had accused
her of madness. And as she was mad, he accused her of ingratitude"].[33] The perception of madness on the husband's part could be
faulty or prejudiced, especially the perceived move from madness
to ingratitude. But we soon see evidence to the contrary:

[S]e croyant sur la scène, pensant avoir un public à remuer, des couron- nes à recevoir, elle était tour à tour Anna, Julienne, Aménaïde. . . . On dit que parfois, lorsque ses chants avaient cessé, ses yeux inquiets et hagards semblaient interroger la foule; qu'elle répondait par un long cri au silence de mort qui régnait autour d'elle, et qu'elle tombait alors, froide comme la pierre qu'allait frapper sa tête échevelée. ("Prima," 43)

[Thinking she was on stage with a public to arouse and bouquets to re- ceive, she was in turn Anna, Julienne, or Aménaïde. . . . It's said that sometimes, when her songs had stopped, her anxious and haggard eyes seemed to question the crowd, and that she cried out into the deadly silence around her, and then she fell, as cold as the stone that her tousled head was about to strike.]

Clearly Gina's mental distraction is not just an invention of her husband. She lives in a past world that is now forever forbidden to her. To compensate, she refuses the present world and takes refuge in the absent one. Yet she is not totally unaware of her actions, for she suffers from the knowledge of no longer belonging to the musi- cal realm. The mixture of nature and music, again characteristic of Sand's musical metaphors, offers more confusion than not since it suggests that Gina's mental straying may be quite natural given the circumstances. And as if in response to Gina's madness, the narra- tor identifies with her derangement: "On assure qu'à cette époque ma raison se troubla. Il est certain qu'une étrange rêverie s'empara de mon cerveau; je ne sais par quelle fatalité je vins à croire que Gina m'aimait. . . . J'étais fou, fou de malheur" [I'm told that my reason was disturbed at that time. Surely a strange dream took con- trol of my brain. I don't know by what accident I came to believe that Gina loved me. . . . I was mad, mad with misfortune] ("Prima," 43).

The narrator has a compulsive fixation with Gina. He thinks he loves her and that his love is returned. In his delirium he imagines that she sees and recognizes him. If he is truly struck by such a distraction, he can no longer be considered a reliable narrator. Yet, the story he tells continues a logical line that we are tempted to believe, even though he hallucinates that Gina comes to visit him. The hallucination begins with music: "Une voix s'éleva dans le si- lence solennel de la nuit" [A voice arose from the solemn silence of the night] ("Prima," 43). He sees Gina before him, singing the "Willow Song" from Rossini's *Otello*, significant here since Des- demona sings this aria in the last act just before she is killed. Gina doubtless feels she has been killed by her husband's social con- ventions, or in this context it would be more accurate to say that

Valterna, the narrator, feels his idol has been assassinated: "tout à coup elle poussa un cri *délirant*, et je frissonnai. Elle avait vu dans l'ombre surgir une figure froidement atroce: elle venait d'apprendre qu'il fallait mourir!" [all of a sudden she screamed hysterically, and I shuddered. In the shadows she had seen a coolly atrocious face: she'd just learned that she must die!] ("Prima," 43; my emphasis). While the story is told from the narrator's point of view, this and other instances of free indirect discourse give insight into the heroine's thoughts. This narrative device is paralleled in the musical commentary Valterna gives, where often the singer's sensations while singing join the narrator's reactions.

Valterna attends a performance of *Don Giovanni*, in which the yet unmarried Gina sings the role of Donna Anna. She is, as always, well received. She also recognizes Valterna, he reports, and mumbles his name.

> Ce n'était donc pas un songe, une vision de mes nuits agitées. Gina savait mon nom, mon amour; peut-être aussi se rappelait-elle confusément m'avoir parlé dans une de ses nuits de fièvre et d'égarement. Une rapide espérance me rendit la raison: je fis des projets comme eût pu les faire un homme dans son bons [*sic*] sens, je prêtai intérêt aux choses extérieures, je compris ce qui se passait autour de moi. Gina se mourait. ("Prima," 44)

> [So it wasn't a dream, a vision of my disturbed nights. Gina knew my name, my love; perhaps she also remembered self-consciously having spoken to me in one of her feverish and deranged nights. A quick hope returned my reason to me: I made plans as someone with all his senses might have done, I paid attention to external things, I understood what was happening around me. Gina was dying.]

Interesting in this passage is the discourse of madness: Valterna believes he has found reason in the midst of his derangement. The sound of Gina's voice, beautifully executing a favorite role—favorite to both Gina and Valterna—brings back all his dreams. It should not go unnoted that the role she sings is one of unrequited love resulting in emotional and mental turmoil and condemnation for the perpetrator of the deception. He is not totally unaware of his state of madness, since he declares that he begins to make plans "as someone with all his senses," suggesting that his own state remains ambiguous even in his own perception.

Gina's husband finally permits her to reappear on the stage in *Giulietta e Romeo*. She is ardently applauded; "Elle chanta comme jamais elle n'avait chanté en ses plus beaux jours" [She sang as she'd never sung in her most exquisite days] ("Prima," 45). She whispers to her former female pupil who is singing the role of Romeo, "qu'il lui semblait qu'une autre voix que la sienne, une voix magique, s'exhalait, mâle et pleine, de ses poumons élargis" [that it seemed that a voice not her own, a magical voice was floating masculine and full from her expanded lungs] ("Prima," 45). That her voice should seem to be the product of magic is not surprising. Again Sand uses the adjective "mâle" in the sense of forceful, strong, powerful. The qualifier is particularly significant insofar as it is Gina's voice that gives her freedom—traditionally a man's right, which she is about to lose, and which Gina acquired by means of a traditionally man's activity, using her voice, which she is also about to lose.[34] In the final scene, as Romeo drinks poison and bends over Juliet to give a final adieu, at the moment when Juliet is meant to awaken, the contralto singing Romeo sees that Gina is dead: "Gina était morte aux accords suaves et religieux de Zingarelli, au milieu du dernier et du plus beau de ses triomphes" [Gina had died with Zingarelli's lofty and religious chords in the midst of the last and most beautiful of her triumphs] ("Prima," 45). The music provides the context and perhaps the impetus for Gina's final performance and death. To finish his tale of woe, Valterna rushes to the stage to hold his beloved and dies a sympathetic death. Valterna's madness perhaps more than Gina's combines with music to present a cautionary tale to opera aficionados.

In "Histoire du rêveur" the question is, who is mad? Amédée seems the obvious choice since he imagines fantastic scenes of an irrational nature incited by the sound of an ethereal voice. A discourse of madness abounds. Amédée clearly responds to the unknown singer's voice, which seems to mesmerize and charm him. The singer, fully aware of the power her/his music has over Amédée, encourages his derangement, leading to the fantastic scene where they leap into the volcano together. When all is said and done, Amédée returns to reason, unsure of what has happened: "Il regarda autour de lui avec cette sorte d'égarement qui suit un profond sommeil, et les souvenirs tumultueux de la nuit s'agitant dans son cerveau" [He looked about himself with that distraction that follows a deep sleep, and turbulent memories of the night churned in his brain] ("Rêveur," 28). It is the resurgence of repressed memories that often sparks hallucinations. Is it therefore not also possible that the memory of a hallucination can be experienced as a moment of unreason? In the majority of the text, Amédée vacillates on the brink of madness, yet only the reader witnesses this vacillation.

One wonders whether the singer might not also be mad. While at first she seems to be the product of Amédée's imagination, she maintains her own personality and directs the actions of the couple. More important, she surfaces later in the story as the famous Portia, a renowned opera singer, and then once more in masculine garb, then finally performing on stage again as Protia. In this final scene of the tale, she too seems distracted and separated from reality: "Elle semblait plus occupée de recevoir les inspirations de son génie musical que de travailler à conquérir des applaudissements. Elle resta quelque tems immobile et comme absorbée dans *un rêve de mélodie*" [She seemed more worried about receiving inspiration from her musical genies than about working on garnering applause. She stood still for some time as though enthralled by *a dream of melody*] ("Rêveur," 33; my emphasis). A performing artist can seem to receive inspiration at the moment of execution, but the extent to which Portia is consumed by the process lends just enough doubt to question her sense of reality. Is she inspired, or is she under a spell? Or is she disingenuously appealing to the public's desire for spectacle? Her accompanist suffers from similar unreason in his confusion at the keyboard and his belief that a demon inhabits the harpsichord. In all cases, madness is tightly linked with music as the conveyor of uncontrolled and uncontrollable reactions.[35]

Les Sept Cordes de la lyre is the first text where Sand represents the discourse of musical madness as possibly saner than the supposed reason of others. The theme of reason versus intuition gives Sand leave to introduce her thoughts on madness. It soon becomes evident that she does not consider Hélène's condition to be an illness, but rather a state of enlightenment that departs from the standard conception of reason. Hélène's "madness" resembles more a divine inspiration than a mental derangement. From the beginning of the text, she is said to have been ill and may still suffer from her mental crisis: "elle a recouvré la raison" [she recovered her reason] (*SC*, 48); "vous avez été folle" [you've been mad], "monsieur votre père était fou" [your esteemed father was mad] (79); "[la lyre,] c'est mon héritage. On appelle cela *la folie*" [it's my inheritance. They call it madness] (100); "Je crains bien que la pauvre Hélène ne soit ensorcelée" [I fear that poor Hélène might be bewitched] (105); "le bruit de sa folie miraculeuse [est] répandu dans la ville" [the rumors of her miraculous madness are spread all over town] (124); "tout son délire vient de cet instrument" [all her delirium comes from this instrument](166). Hanz, one of Albertus's philosophy students, states that sometimes when one is mad "in a certain way" (*SC*, 63), one does not really wish to be cured. Wilhelm, the young poet who loves Hélène, can also see through the veneer of madness: "Hélène n'est pas folle, elle est inspirée" [Hélène isn't mad, she's inspired] (*SC*, 132). Albertus agrees that she incarnates a sort of "folie sublime" ["sublime madness"].

Hélène's so-called madness is the focus of Méphistophélès's strategy. In the beginning Hélène alone can hear the music of the lyre. When Albertus finally hears sounds from the lyre, they are an awful noise that is painful to his ears. This is proof of his inability to appreciate music, or in other words, his inability to understand love. This, according to Sand, is true madness. Sand mocks a blind devotion to positivist education that, according to her, masks the ability to see life clearly.

Freud tells us that hallucinations and the like often spring from the memory, providing a vehicle for forgotten material to force its way into consciousness. Frequent mention of distant memories punctuate *Les Sept Cordes de la lyre*. So that the Spirit of the Lyre can speak/sing to Hélène, he beseeches his cohorts to bring Hélène to him, "instruisez-la, ou rendez-moi la mémoire. Montrez-lui Dieu, ou rendez-moi le prisme qui me servait à le contempler" [teach her or give me back my memory. Show her God, or give me the prism that I used to look on him with] (*SC*, 137). The prism, a metaphor for the lyre, indicates that music is the language of communication with God. The key to music symbolically resides in the lyre, and thus with Hélène. Only she can help the Spirit to recall his memory. Amnesia, or the absence of memory, is often confused with a moment of madness. Albertus and others frequently find that Hélène's wandering (physical and mental) indicates a loss of memory. Late in the play Albertus says, "Peut-être, si je lui montrais la lyre, retrouverait-elle la mémoire" [Maybe if I showed her the lyre she would get back her memory] (*SC*, 180). And when the gesture has no effect, he sighs, "Allons! sa raison est entièrement perdue, il faut un miracle pour la ressusciter" [All right, her reason is completely gone, we'd need a miracle to bring it back] (*SC*, 180). Hélène's musical rambling may well be a form of memory searching. She does seem to know that music is the divine language and that she should understand it. As the text progresses, she becomes increasingly more confident about her ability to hear and understand the music of the lyre, as though her memory were becoming clearer. It remains evident that madness in *Les Sept Cordes de la lyre* belongs to the realm of music, beauty, and poetry, but it is also linked to musical memory.

One of Sand's best-drawn mad characters is Albert. Chapter 28 of *Consuelo* gives details of the Rudolstadt family history, a history

Albert's aunt prefers to deny since it reveals their Protestant origins and the militant ancestors they forsook when they pledged allegiance to Catholicism in order to maintain citizenship under Maria-Theresa. Albert, on the contrary, is proud of his anarchistic forebears and often imagines he is in fact the reincarnation of one of them. His mental and physical wandering is a matter of great concern to his family, especially since when he returns he seems to have no memory of having been gone. The chaplain believes the devil gave Albert these hallucinations.

Oddly, Consuelo's thoughts turn to Anzoleto upon hearing of Albert's ravings. She wonders whether her Venetian lover's strayings may not have been the result of similar madness, in which case she would be happy to rush to his side: "S'il fût tombé dans le délire au milieu des enivrements et des déceptions de son début . . ." [if only he'd fallen into delirium in the midst of the intoxication and the deception of his debut . . .] (C, 1:255), a speculation that brings us back to the world of music as yet another example of Consuelo's belief in its power, even its power to induce madness.

Two scenes I have already discussed demonstrate Albert's madness as it is linked with music. The first time he hears Consuelo sing, he inexplicably succumbs to the beauty of her voice, speaking to her in Spanish and calling her Consuelo. A second scene shows how Consuelo's singing when Albert slips into lethargy can infallibly bring him out of his trance. These scenes demonstrate both the curative power of music and the association with madness.

Like Hélène's madness, Albert's unreason links him to a past, although Albert's is a historical past that for him remains quite present. Again like Hélène, Albert seems to drift away from reality when hearing and playing music. Often these ramblings are not entirely undesired by the subjects. Both Albert and Hélène use their musical mysticism to influence those around them and direct them toward God. But where Hélène and Albert differ is in the religious application of their gift. While Hélène certainly believes in God, hers is a new religion, one that recalls Saint-Simonian and Leroucian principles. Albert remains Catholic, but in a Hussitic vein, ever remembering his ancestry and the blood shed in defense of the principle of the celebration of the Eucharist in both forms and similar reforms of the late Middle Ages. If Albert's religion reflects the past while Hélène's points to a future state, it is important to remember that both originate in a period of Sand's personal history when the influence of Lamennais and Leroux was strong. Music, mysticism, and madness converge in *Les Sept Cordes de la lyre* and *Consuelo*.

The other character in *Consuelo* who suffers from madness is Zdenko. This idiot savant, a peasant like Patience in Sand's *Mauprat*, represents the Bohemian past of Albert, or Albert's imagined memory, and the history of the Taborite rebellion. His knowledge of Bohemian folk songs symbolizes his vast familiarity with regional history, both cultural and political, and with Albert's personal, albeit revisionist, history. In this realm, he is superior to Albert, who has great respect for Zdenko's talent and knowledge.

However, there is no doubt that Zdenko suffers from mental derangement. The most flagrant instances of his madness surface when he comes into contact with Consuelo, suggesting that his jealousy of her invokes an irrational reaction rooted deep in his psyche. His jealous rage frequently manifests itself in the form of music. On one occasion, Zdenko instantly becomes angry when Consuelo displays through Bohemian folk songs that she knows too much about Albert. Zdenko agrees to sing but asks that Consuelo provide the first words of the song. She suggests an incipit, but he declares that that was yesterday's song, which he no longer knows today. He wants another beginning, and she offers, "Le comte Albert est là-bas, là-bas dans la grotte de Schrenkenstein" [Count Albert is down there in Schrenkenstein grotto]. Indignant, Zdenko calls her "fille du mal, menteuse, Autrichienne" [daughter of evil, liar, Austrian], and picks up a huge rock and tells her never to speak to him again or he will crush her. Consuelo flees and runs into a peasant, who reassures her that while Zdenko laughs, sings, and tells pretty stories no one understands, he never gets angry and she must not be afraid of him. Consuelo calms down and realizes she has just pushed him too far too fast: "j'ai éveillé, dans l'âme paisible de cet homme privé de ce qu'on appelle fièrement la raison, une souffrance qu'il ne connaissait pas encore. . . . Il n'était que maniaque, je l'ai peut-être rendu *fou*" [I've awoken in the peaceful soul of this private man what's proudly called reason, a suffering he didn't yet know. . . . He was only a maniac; I may have driven him *mad*] (*C*, 1:311). But Consuelo wonders whether she has misjudged the peasant: "Zdenko, qui lui avait paru si intelligent et si empressé jusque-là à seconder les desseins d'Albert, était-il lui-même plus tristement et plus sérieusement fou que Consuelo n'avait voulu le supposer?" [Was Zdenko, who had seemed to her so intelligent and so eager till then to assist Albert in his plans, more sadly and more seriously mad than Consuelo had dared imagine?] (*C*, 1:312). Interesting in this question is the hesitation between already knowing Zdenko is deranged and the various degrees of his madness. Even though she calls him intelligent, it is an intelligence of madness. On what basis

178 WHILE THE MUSIC LASTS

does Consuelo make this assessment? The only sources of information she has so far are Amélie, not always so reliable, and her own observations, based mostly on Zdenko's musical abilities and musical memory. Thus music remains the essential source of information of Consuelo's conclusions about Zdenko's mental capacities.

Laure de Monteluz, in *Adriani*, has the reputation in the Ardèche of being mad. The people of the area call her house "la Désolade" ["the House of Desolation"]:

> C'est un nom qu'on lui a laissé comme ça dans le pays, à cause de la pauvre dame qui y reste. C'est une jeune femme très jolie, ma foi, qui a perdu son mari après six mois de mariage et qui ne peut pas se consoler. Elle est malade et comme égarée par moments. On a même peur qu'elle ne devienne folle tout à fait. (*A*, 24)

> [It's the name it goes by in the area because of the poor lady who lives there. She's a young and very pretty lady, I dare say, who lost her husband after six years of marriage and now she can't console herself. She's ill and sort of deranged at times. Peoples even 'fraid she'll go completely mad.]

Thus Laure's near madness seems to originate in the shock of the premature loss of her husband. We will learn later that the real cause of her despair and unhappiness is that she never really loved her husband but imposed on herself the duty to love him. Now that he is gone, she suffers from the guilt associated with a lack of regret. Laure's despondency has made her listless and lethargic, hence the reputation of possible madness. When Adriani first hears her voice, he is drawn to her and wishes to meet her, yet he fears her reputation of madness: "Un moment il faillit laisser là son guide et courir vers cette maison, vers cette plainte, vers cette femme; mais il fut retenu par la crainte de voir une folle. Il avait, pour le spectacle de l'aliénation, cette peur douloureuse qu'éprouvent les imaginations vives" [For a moment he almost left his guide behind and ran toward that house, toward that plaintive cry, toward that woman; but he was stopped by the fear of seeing a madwoman. He was painfully afraid, as only vivid imaginations can be, of the curiosity of madness] (*A*, 25).

Madness in *Adriani* surfaces not just in the supposed madness of the heroine and in the expression of that madness through music, but also in the fear of madness on the part of the hero. His hesitation is symptomatic of the apprehension of going mad himself. Otherwise a stable character, in these instances he weakens and displays a real dread of encountering madness in any form.

Je veux tâcher de savoir, se disait-il, si c'est vraiment une folle qui chantait si bien. Dans ce cas, je m'éloignerai toujours de cet endroit, je ne passerai plus par ce sentier. Je me suis toujours figuré que la folie était contagieuse pour moi, et ce que j'ai éprouvé cette nuit me fait croire que j'ai une prédisposition. (*A*, 26–27)

["I want to try to find out," he said to himself, "if it was really a mad woman who was singing so well. In that case, I shall always keep clear of this place, I shall no longer take this path. I always imagined that I was susceptible to madness and what I felt last night makes me believe that I have a predisposition."]

The event to which he refers is a dream in which he hears Rossini's gondolier aria performed beautifully and at the same time sees before him the image of a *desolate* woman, consecutively taking the form of an angel, a genie, a fairy, and a monster. No explanation for his fear is ever provided, but the connection between music and progressively frightening specters strongly suggests a subconscious realization that music has a hold on him equalled only by his growing love for Laure.

Laure's housekeeper, Toinette, offers Adriani an explanation of Laure's condition:

Oui, je sais qu'on [la croit folle], parce que les *âmes vulgaires* ne comprennent pas la vraie douleur. Plût au ciel qu'elle le fût un peu, folle! Ce serait une crise, les médecins y pourraient quelque chose, et j'espérerais une révolution dans ses idées; mais ma pauvre maîtresse a autant de force pour regretter qu'elle en a eu pour espérer. Oui, monsieur, elle regrette comme elle a su attendre. Elle est calme à faire peur. Elle marche, elle dort, elle vit à peu près comme tout le monde, sauf qu'elle paraît un peu préoccupée; vous ne diriez jamais, à la voir, qu'elle a la mort dans l'âme. (*A*, 42)

[Yes, I know she's supposed to be mad, because *common souls* don't understand true pain. May it please the heavens that she was, a bit mad, I mean! If it was a fit, the doctors would be able to do something, and I hoped for a turn-about in her ideas; but my poor mistress is just as capable of being sorry as she was able to hope. Yes, sir, she's sorry just like she was able to wait. She's calm enough to scare a body. She walks, she sleeps, she lives just about like everyone else, except she seems a bit preoccupied. You'd never say it to look at her, that she's got death in her soul.]

The notion that madness would be preferable to the hopeless state in which Laure currently exists again suggests that Sand sometimes views madness with a generous eye. Toinette speaks of a curable madness, one doctors would at least be able to palliate. Laure's actions, according to Toinette, do not seem those of a deranged mind, but rather arise from the lethargy of despondency.

The very idea of madness has its place in music. As Adriani recounts his activities and his fears to a friend in a letter, he writes how much he is attracted to Laure but that the reputation of her madness holds him back. His imagination uncontrollably attributes to Laure actions that are not corroborated by anything he has witnessed. Still, the musical side of the supposed madness remains. Adriani begins to doubt the rumors of her madness and to contemplate the possibility of a different explanation for her languor. Later the narrator gives another interpretation of the burgeoning relationship:

> L'espèce de maladie ou plutôt de courbature morale qui pesait sur cette femme amena entre elle et d'Argères [Adriani] une manière d'être assez inusitée, et l'espèce d'abîme creusé entre eux par sa douleur fut précisément la cause d'une sorte d'intimité étrange et soudaine. Il est très certain qu'à cette époque, sans avoir jamais eu aucun symptôme d'aliénation, la veuve d'Octave [Laure] ne jouissait pourtant pas d'une lucidité complète. (A, 78)

> [The kind of sickness or rather moral aching that weighed on this woman led to her and Argères (Adriani) acting in a rather uncommon way, and the sort of abyss hollowed out between them by her pain was the precise cause of a kind of strange and sudden intimacy. It was quite certain at this time, without any kind of symptom of madness; Octave's widow, however, did not possess complete lucidity.]

Adriani and the narrator vacillate between believing her mad and allowing that she might have reason to be despondent. Referring to her as Octave's widow also functions to distance her from the reader, thus making her madness more acceptable because less threatening. In the meantime, music remains the sole successful means of communication between the two.

> Sa répugnance pour les fous lui faisait croire que la belle Laure ne pourrait jamais être à ses yeux qu'un objet de pitié; mais par un phénomène bien connu des imaginations vives, cette pitié et cet effroi le fascinaient et s'emparaient de sa contemplation, de sa rêverie, de sa pensée continuelle. Il croyait l'oublier en faisant de la musique. (A, 80–81)

> [His aversion to mad people led him to believe that the beautiful Laure could never be anything other than an object of pity in his eyes. But through a phenomenon that is well known to vivid imaginations, this pity and this dread fascinated him and took control of his reflection, his

daydreaming, his every thought. He thought he could forget her by making music.]

Adriani's attitude vacillates as he hesitates, wonders, and hopes. At the same time, the narrator reminds us of Adriani's own problems. This is not the first time the expression "vivid imaginations" has been used to describe Adriani and his faculty for exaggeration. Might not he, too, suffer from a mild form of madness that at once allows and prevents him from seeing beyond the musical veneer of Laure's torpor? Toinette attempts to divert Adriani's fears at the same time as she tries to assist the relationship between the tenor and her mistress: "Elle n'est pas folle, comme il plaît à votre valet de chambre de le dire: elle n'a jamais eu l'idée du suicide. . . . Votre musique lui faisait tant de bien!" [She's not mad, as your valet likes to say. She's never entertained suicide. . . . Your music does her so much good] (A, 83). For Toinette suicide is a necessary component of madness. While Adriani has never mentioned suicide, it is not an inconceivable source of his fear.

On the brink of declaring his love, Adriani senses complicated causes for Laure's disquietude and asks her to speak frankly. She warns him she's mad and takes her hands from his. Adriani urges her to confess her problems to him. When she inquires why, he answers, "Pour que je sache si je dois vous aimer" [So I can know whether I should love you] (A, 89). He has finally moved beyond his fear of madness, or at least he is willing to understand the causes of Laure's behavior because of his love for her.

Toward the end of the novel, it is Adriani who acquires a reputation for madness. When Adriani returns to the stage and is preparing to go on in *Lucia di Lammermoor*, he shuts himself up in his dressing room and imagines Laure before him, "puis il cacha son visage dans ses mains et s'enfuit comme un fou" [then he hid his face in his hands and fled like a madman] (A, 200). And during the performance, he thinks he sees Laure in the audience: "Je suis fou; je la vois partout!" [I'm mad; I see her everywhere!] (A, 216). In actual fact, he does see her since she has come to Paris to hear him sing and to declare her love for him.

His first return performance in *Lucia di Lammermoor* proves doubly symbolic because of the famous mad scene. An interesting gender reversal enhances the use of the final scene of *Lucia*. One would expect a reference to an opera known for Lucia's mad scene to focus on the insanity of a woman. Instead, Sand concentrates on Adriani's madness. She seems to have insisted on this reversal as a way to link the intense emotions of both characters, and perhaps also to hint that men as well as women sometimes "go mad" from love. And as Adriani gets ready to go on stage, he appears to be in a trance, but happy and smiling mechanically (*A*, 213).

Madness in *Adriani* is always expressed through music, around music, after music, or somehow connected with music. The admixture of music and madness in this novel, albeit a bit heavy-handed, attests to Sand's dedication to the notion that music not only communicates but can also be the key to the realization of an emotional state, love in this case, which is perhaps but another form of madness. There is no doubt about the power of music, and as Sand presents it, music has the power to promote or delay emotional reactions; it can aid or hamper personal expression according to the use the musician makes of it. Once again, music is a powerful tool in the hands of those who know how to manipulate it.

♫ ♫ ♫

Sand uses music to enhance the themes of love and madness, especially where love and madness coexist. Not only does music occur as an essential component of the love plots, Sand emphasizes its frequent place in the origin, development, and comprehension of love. But music is not an idle gadget within anyone's grasp; it must be revered and respected and applied in the appropriate circumstances and in an appropriate way. Madness, a danger for those who become too absorbed in music, is also a possible path to truth. Sand's musical characters who suffer from love or madness or both most often experience these states through music.

Lith. de Thierry Frères.

Mme G. SAND

George Sand, Thierry frères. Courtesy of the Bibliothèque Nationale de France. Thierry frères, d'après J. Boilly.

George Sand, Charpentier. Courtesy of the Musée Carnavalet. Photothèque des Musées de la Ville de Paris. Charpentier, oil.

Franz Liszt at the piano, surrounded by Alexandre Dumas père, George Sand, Countess Marie d'Agoult; standing: Hector Berlioz, Niccolò Paganini, Giacomo Rossini. Bust of Beethoven on piano and painting of Lord Byron on wall. Josef Danhauser. Courtesy of the Bildarchiv Preußischer Kulturbesitz, Berlin. Danhauser, 1840. (Photo: Jürgen Liepe)

Liszt at the piano, caricature by Maurice Sand. Courtesy of the Bibliothèque Nationale de France. Maurice Sand, ink drawing.

Pauline Viardot and Frédéric Chopin, drawing by Maurice Sand. Courtesy of the Bibliothèque Nationale de France. Maurice Sand, ink drawing, 1844. Chopin says, "Ça, c'est le jeu de Listz [*sic*]! Il n'en faut pas pour accompagner la voix." [That's Liszt's music. You can't use that to accompany a vocal part.]

Sand and Chopin, lead drawing by Delacroix. Courtesy of the Musée du Louvre. Eugène Delacroix.

"L'Assemblée de Nohant," Maurice Sand. Courtesy of the Musée de Montluçon. Maurice Sand, watercolor. Collection: "Les Gars du Berry."

G.SAND

George Sand, photo by Nadar. Courtesy of the Bibliothèque Nationale de France. Nadar. 1864.

4

♫♫ The Musical Fantastic ♫♫

... comme absorbée dans un rêve de mélodie ...

[. . . as if lost in a dream of melody . . .]
—"Histoire du rêveur"

CRITICAL LITERATURE ON THE FANTASTIC HAS NOT ADEQUATELY EX-
ploited the frequent use of music and its structural relation to the
genre. However, when looking for a model of the fantastic tale,
most critics are quick to refer to E. T. A. Hoffmann, a master of the
musical fantastic. It is evident from even a cursory study of Hoffmann's writings that many elements of music enhance and embellish the elements of the fantastic. Despite Walter Scott's
disapproval of the German author, Hoffmann's enormous popularity in France—greater than in Germany, according to Gautier—is
largely responsible for the presence of music in the fantastic writing
of nineteenth-century French authors.[1] A detailed analysis of the
structural and technical functions of music in several of Sand's fantastic texts will further the understanding of the romantic tendency
for polyvalent expression in general and of the musical text in particular.

Excellent work has already been published on the fantastic. My
purpose here is not to retool a well-articulated description of the
romantic fantastic genre. A brief overview of criticism on the genre
will suffice as a groundwork for my discussion. Pierre-Georges
Castex states that the fantastic is fueled by dreams, superstition,
fear, remorse, nervous or mental excitement, drunkenness, and
morbid states. Whereas readers of the marvelous must accept the
premise that the laws of the universe are controlled by higher powers out of the purview of the "normal" human, readers of the fantastic, on the contrary, have no such assurance and must become
more involved with the fictional universe presented to them and de-
cide for themselves, if possible, what is real and what is not. Marcel
Schneider singles out personal experience as an important element
of reading the fantastic. Citing Nodier's 1830 essay, "Du fantas-

190

tique en littérature," he extols the influence of Hoffmann and declares the fantastic the antidote to the materialist, positivistic world. Nodier attaches the persistence of the fantastic to a religious and spiritual need for superstitious beliefs without rational explanation.

For Tzvetan Todorov, the principal element of the fantastic is hesitation, a vacillation the narrator and the reader share between illusion and reality, between a supernatural and a rational explanation of narrative events. Bellemin-Noël refers to the same phenomenon as "irresolution," while Freud calls it "intellectual uncertainty," which heightens considerably the desired effect of the *Unheimliche*.[2] Franc Schuerewegen says we hesitate only because the narrator asks us to willingly suspend, albeit partially, our belief. Tobin Siebers focuses rather on superstition and the relation between violence and superstition. He affirms that superstition expresses the romantic need for a belief, a lost faith, by way of a subversive retrenchment in lies and doubts.[3] Few studies discuss Sand's fantastic and none delves into the interaction of fantastic and music.

The link between music and the fantastic, according to Sand, is especially fertile in Berrichon culture. She capitalizes on the current nationalist movement in her determination to contribute to a French fantastic corpus. Sand remarks in "Les Visions de la nuit dans les campagnes" [Nocturnal Rural Visions] that Germans and Slavs have recorded their share of fantastic tales, much maligned by French critics. Yet, she continues, the fantastic is alive and well and living in the French provinces, which are replete with vibrant examples. Recently Brittany has been the subject of research in this domain, she points out, but the other provinces of France remain to be discovered. As for her homeland, she says, evoking the relationship of music to literature, "Le Berry a sa musique, mais il n'a pas sa littérature, ou bien elle s'est perdue comme aurait pu se perdre la poésie bretonne si M. de la Villemarqué ne l'eût recueillie à temps" [Berry has its own music, but not its own literature, rather it's gotten lost just as Breton poetry might have done if M. de la Villemarqué hadn't saved it in time].[4] Sand discovers in the fantastic another petri dish in which to conduct her experiments on the relationship between music and literature.

Like the fantastic, music, especially as it functions in the romantic ethos, sits astride the real and ethereal worlds. Music speaks to our illusions, our fears, and our dreams. It helps us to remove ourselves from the weighty existence of the real world. Yet the physical, sensuous nature of music, the fact that there is a physical effect on the hearing organs that somehow translates into emotional reactions and sometimes intellectual thoughts, precludes its complete separation from the material world. It would be foolhardy to try to attach specific musical figures to various elements of the fantastic, as such a methodology compromises the uniqueness of the two art forms.[5] I prefer to consider how the various components of the fantastic genre are enhanced and intensified by musical references, quasi-musical functions, and representations of music.

According to Todorov the elements of the fantastic in fiction come directly from language, thus one cannot impose a musical interpretation on them. Siebers disagrees with Todorov on this point, suggesting rather that the supernatural remains the basis of language and not the inverse. The supernatural, he says, creates the necessary environment for language to emerge. In this view, the supernatural would generate language, and therefore music. But neither of these interpretations satisfactorily explains how writers of the fantastic frequently exploit music. Moreover, as Bellemin-Noël states, the main purpose of the fantastic is to produce signifiers whose signifieds would only be the signifiers themselves.[6] This appreciation closely resembles many modern musicologists' definition of music, where the signified and the signifier are one and the same: that is, music refers only to itself, not to music in general but to the elements that constitute any particular piece.

My goal is not to suggest that the musical fantastic attempts to view musical phenomena through a fantastic lens. Rather I wish to explore a subgroup of Sand's fantastic tales that use music and musical elements thematically and especially structurally.[7] Thinkers and aestheticians had already in the mid-nineteenth century begun to reject the neoclassical insistence on imitation and mimesis. In 1854 Eduard Hanslick, while not a formalist per se, set up a polemic against the notion of feeling as representing music.[8] At the same time, thinkers of the period generally agreed that, apart from certain types of programme music, musical structure was highly codified and bore little resemblance to structures found in nature.[9] Thus music, especially for the nineteenth-century listener but perhaps also for us today, falls somewhere between the real and the abstract world. The world of feelings occupies a similarly unstable locus. Music fades in and out of reality, alternately between recalling sounds heard in the outside world and eliciting internal affective responses, which may or may not be new. It then recombines these motifs in an artistic way recognizable on a formal, more abstract level. The hesitation between the musically familiar and the unfamiliar parallels the hesitation that defines, in part, the fantastic. Combining music with the fantastic in literature accentuates the unstable, the ambiguous, the unearthly, the supernatural, without relinquishing the attachment to the real world.

Music easily infiltrates and enhances the fantastic in several ways. For example, if the protagonist is a musician, he or she can escape from the real world into another realm of existence through music, taking the reader along at the same time. Moreover, to the nonmusician the production of music often remains a matter of wonder, even magic or supernatural. Therefore, whenever a fantastic tale refers to the production of music, this music can be perceived as unworldly or superhuman. The tendency to associate music with the supernatural is further heightened when the represented music seems to come out of nowhere, a common device in musical fantastic texts. In addition, music as a language of communication in a fantastic text enhances the standard rhetorical figures of the genre, exaggerating them and sometimes moving them closer to the supernatural. There is often a hesitation on both the hero's and the narrator's part as to whether the reported music is recognized as supernatural or real. If it is supernatural, we have moved into the marvelous, but if it is perceived as possibly real, we search for further proof of stability and in the interim remain in the fantastic.

In the case of the musical fantastic, the narrator-hero's perception of the music remains vague and unsure, partly because the music is produced by someone not always identified or identifiable. The subject often seeks anyone who could corroborate the existence of the music, but the perception usually remains ambiguous, leaving it to the reader to make a choice. Music mediates the sense of hesitation and instability, much the same as the reader is distanced from the action by a double narrator, another common technique of the fantastic. Finally, the representation of music in a fantastic text, as in any text, grapples with the difficult issue of the representation of music in the written word. The effort to represent music to readers requires a certain discourse, one that the reader recognizes. In the case of a fantastic text, the attempt to represent music in writing parallels the narrator's challenge to portray a believable divergence from reality.

The close relationship of the narrator and the reader both enhances and impedes the problem of illusion and reality. Nicole Mozet posits that narrators are not mystics themselves, they merely relay mystics' stories, maintaining a rationalist approach.[10] And I would add that the musical element in the fantastic works in similar fashion. The narrator who knows or feigns knowing about music tampers with the reader's comfort zone in this domain by inducing a false sense of security. In this manner the reader follows the narrator's commentary and judgment of the characters from a desire to be knowledgeable about music while at the same time remaining distant from the narrator just as the narrator stands back from the often mystical characters of the tale.

E. T. A. Hoffmann exploited many of the nuances of music in his fantastic writings. Unsatisfied in his professional and personal life, he sought an outlet for his artistic expression that touched both his dream and his real world. As he says in "Princess Brambilla," these are not nocturnal dreams, but the dreams of our whole lives, where the painful weight of daily life is relieved of its suffering. Baudelaire, who admired Hoffmann's imagination, lauds his unique use of humor, which we should read as "ironic humor," as stronger than that of any of his French imitators. Baudelaire exalts Hoffmann's art of creating humor so as to have it seem to spring spontaneously from the reader's mind.[11] This pseudo-Socratic technique, in which the writer creates a situation that the reader and only the reader can unfold, requires reader participation, in the text as well as in music, all the while without allowing the reader a free hand in the (re)solution of the fantastic hesitation. Thus the functional instability of the receiver heightens emotional and cognitive instability. Music serves as a doubling agent in Hoffmann's tales insofar as it allows the reader to shift automatically from the real world to the world of auditory dreams and illusions.

One of Hoffmann's stories that bears comparison with Sand's work is "Rat Krespel" (1816). Similar to *Les Sept Cordes de la lyre*, the principal medium of communication here is a musical instrument. Hoffmann's tale centers around the magical qualities of a violin made in Cremona, home of several famous violin makers including the Stradavarius family. Krespel's violin represents the superb workmanship of a gifted craftsman, but also the magical qualities of a fine instrument. Sand adroitly portrays the mystical and almost superstitious belief on the part of many musicians that their instruments carry special powers. In the night Krespel hears, or thinks he hears the sound of his fantastic violin and the voice of his daughter, Antonie. As Antonie is consumptive—like her dead mother, a famous opera singer—her health risks being compromised if she sings any passionate music. He is awakened by a blinding flash of light and thunderous crash of music to find his daughter dead.

Several similarities link Hoffmann's tale to Sand's closet play. Sand's story focuses on the mysterious and mystical lyre inherited by a woman and the message it has to share with her and humanity. Both Krespel and Albertus try to disassemble the instruments, seeking the secret of their magic. Both tales assign anthropomorphic traits to the instruments. Both narrators describe music as coming from nowhere. And both stories present madness as caused by music. Once again the message transmitted through music reaches only the ears of those trained to understand it, indicating the listener must earn the ability and thus the right to understand the divine message. Musical training comes from humans, but music, inspiration, and talent originate with God. A commentary on progress in contemporary society, Sand's musical message presents a far more intellectual content than Hoffmann's. The power of passion, Hoffmann's principal theme, is not neglected in Sand's text, as might be expected in a piece inspired by Goethe's *Faust*.[12]

Sand comments on Hoffmann's "poésie musicale" [musical poetry] in her *Entretiens journaliers*.[13] She points out that he expertly combines "merveillosité et . . . idéalité" [marvelosity and ideality], showing that all poetic and musical compositions have a meaning that can be understood in human thought since they are both inspired by human feeling. Hoffmann, she says, "popularized the 'exquisiteness' of poetic impressions in painting and music." She thus identifies the German master of the fantastic as her model for the literary representation of musical communication.

More than any other romantic writer in France, Sand takes Hoffmann's notions of the magical power of music and exploits them in her own writing. Balzac had little respect for Hoffmann; he testifies in an 1833 letter to Madame Hanska that Hoffmann is inferior to his reputation. "Sarrasine," Balzac's only musical fantastic text (1830), offers an interesting foray into the world of performance, but it deals more with identity and artistry than with music per se. Apart from a few stories by Erckmann-Chatrian ("Le Violon du pendu," 1866; "Arria Marcella," 1852), Gautier ("Jettatura," 1856; "Avatar," 1856; and "Spirite," 1866), and perhaps Villiers de l'Isle-Adam ("Le Secret de l'ancienne musique," 1878; "Claire Lenoir," 1867; and *L'Eve future*, 1880–81), very few musical fantastic tales of French romanticism reap the same results in meshing music with the fantastic as do Sand's. She exploits the Hoffmannesque notions of the musical fantastic in a variety of texts, in a variety of ways.[14]

The Tales

"Histoire du rêveur"

From the beginning of Sand's career, she delved into the musical fantastic. Her first venture into the genre was "Histoire du rêveur"

(1830), a highly imaginative yet poorly constructed tale of an aristocratic Frenchman—the use of a foreign narrator enhances his status as an outsider[15]—who hikes up Mt. Etna, presumably to find the meaning of life. He states, "je veux enfin abandonner mon âme au désordre de ces élémens fougueux, qui règnent en maîtres absolus sur une terre déchirée et bouleversée chaque jour au gré de leur caprice" [I finally want to leave my soul behind to the chaos of these wild elements that reign as absolute masters of a world that's torn apart and upside down each day at their every whim] ("Rêveur," 10). During his quest, he encounters a curious being, unidentifiable as to age or gender, who sings with a most remarkable voice. The tones of this voice mesmerize the narrator and seduce him into performing dangerous acts. Later in the story we learn that the voice is that of the venerated Italian soprano Portia. The music in the story is described as ethereal and releases the narrator from his earthly bounds. The narrator's expectation of finding a higher level of understanding adds another dimension to the story. The narrator is not disappointed with his encounter, though his inability to identify and categorize the singer proves an endless source of frustration for him until the end of the tale when he, and the reader with him, discovers the identity of the soprano.

There is no doubt that "Histoire du rêveur" is a fantastic story. A vocabulary of the fantastic abounds: "fantastique," "fantasque," "fantasmagorie," "rêve," "délire," "surnaturel," "diabolique," and "fée" [fantastic; unpredictable; phantasmagoria; dream; delirium; supernatural; diabolical; fairy]. Bellemin-Noël calls the presence of such vocabulary a proof of the "fantasticité" of the tale. There is also an abundance of auditory vocabulary; sounds of all sorts from nature as well as the human voice join together in this tale to produce what Sand refers to generically as music. This technique parallels that of using a fantastic vocabulary to help define the genre. The traveler, alone at night on the side of Mt. Etna, hears "des voix humaines [qui] se mêlaient aux plaintes du vent dans les vieux chênes de la forêt [human voices that mingle with the groaning of the wind in the old oak trees in the forest"] ("Rêveur," 12). This is the first indication of what is to come, where the sounds of nature and the sounds of a human voice—although it is almost too beautiful to be human—intertwine to produce a hypnotic effect on the traveler. While "plaintes" is not an uncommon term to use for the sound of the wind in the trees, it nonetheless personifies the sound, strengthening the bond between humanity and nature in this scene. The traveler joins in and sings in response to the voices he hears.

The narrator next hears a single voice, probably a shepherd, he surmises. But the voice displays traits and abilities uncommon for a peasant. Sand never allows her musicians to succeed with only natural musical talent. A musical gift must always have the support of disciplined training, a constant mixture of nature and culture. A few lines later she will use the words "artist" and "improvisation," which add connotations of human involvement to the development and the production of music.

The traveler finally comes face to face with the singer. As the narrator tries to categorize her/him, she/he resists definition and proclaims, "Je suis organisé pour chanter comme vous pour parler et c'est en chantant que je me repose" [I am built for singing just as you are for speaking, and that's how I rest, by singing] ("Rê-veur," 14). It is thus in musical terms that she/he expresses her/himself.[16] The reader experiences this character as playful and possibly mean, but certainly other-worldly. The musical character sings to the Spirit of Mt. Etna, who responds in song communicating some urgent message to the singer. Amédée, the traveler whose name we learn only now, to hear the celestial music the voice of the Spirit, showing once again his inferior position vis-à-vis the singer. The singer chides him: "ton oreille est fermée aux sons ravissans de sa voix et aux accords aériens de la harpe éolienne!" [your ear is shut to the delightful sounds of his voice and the ethereal chords of the aeolian harp!] ("Rêveur," 16). In the rest of the passage it remains unclear whether Amédée eventually hears the Spirit's voice or simply acknowledges its existence because of the singer's enthusiastic response to it. But by the end of the story, he seems to have surpassed the other idle music lovers and is not just entranced but also engaged by Portia's singing.

Pezzanini, the harpsichordist and accompanist in "Histoire du rêveur," undergoes a similar progression. He will lose his self-assuredness when he experiences, in a wildly supernatural scene, the mysterious humiliation of not being able to read the music while accompanying Portia. Once he gets back on track thanks to Portia's encouragement, he is rightly humbled and thanks her for the experience: "[V]ous avez fait de moi, un musicien, d'un barbare que j'étais" [From the barbarian I once was, you made a musician of me] ("Rêveur", 35). The romantic belief in the necessary suffering that makes for a fully developed artist is present in many of Sand's works.[17]

Another aspect of this musical scene elucidates both a fantastic device and Sand's powers of musical representation. Witness this description of the accompanist's music as it becomes the central musical interest and then recombines with Portia's singing:

> Pezzanini avait suivi les inspirations de Portia, il semblait qu'un génie les lui communiquat par une révélation antérieure à des tableaux avec des sons. Il peignit Venise, le ciel bleu, la mer calme, la gondole légère. Il ne fut personne qui ne vit tout cela dans l'accompagnement de Pezzanini. Quand la chanteuse eut fini les strophes, elle vocalisa un refrain de sa composition à la manière des gondoliers, et, s'égarant sur les flots on entendit la barcarolle s'éloigner, se rapprocher et s'éloigner encore. Pezzanini imitait les ondulations de la mer, l'haleine du vent et le choc de la rame. ("Rêveur," 35)

> [Pezzanini had followed Portia's inspirations. It seemed that a genie had communicated them to her by a previous revelation to tableaux with sound. He described Venice, the blue sky, the calm sea, the nimble gondola. There was no one who hadn't seen all this in Pezzanini's accompaniment. When the singer had finished the verses, she vocalized a refrain of her own composition in the style of gondoliers, and drifting off on the waves one could hear the barcarolle growing fainter, then stronger, then fainter again. Pezzanini imitated the swaying of the sea, the sigh of the wind, and the jolt of the oars.]

At once fantastic and mystical, this description mixes narrative present with an unspecified past. It combines painting with music, as well as the synesthetic confusion of sight and sound. Such oscillation, an essential characteristic of the fantastic, shakes the stability of the reader as well as that of the text. In addition, the spontaneity of Portia's improvisation indicates a fleeting instant of musical invention that contributes to the other-worldliness of the scene for both Pezzanini and the fictive audience as well as for the reader. It is important to note that it is purely music, whether the harpsichord or the soprano, and not the text that communicates the notion of the gondola, of movement, of sky. It is, in fact, a musical painting of Venice. One recalls the beautiful pages from the second letter of the *Lettres d'un voyageur* on the evocative powers of gondoliers' music. Sand will exploit the power of lyrics in other texts, but here she lays the groundwork for her devotion to the communicative powers of music, be it instrumental or vocal.

A brief commentary on Sand's use of musical vocabulary will distinguish her techniques from other novelists'. In "Histoire du rêveur" on several occasions she uses the word *bémol* (flat). Even though this term is surely not unfamiliar to the lay reader, it can have a moderately alienating effect on the nonmusician. Moreover, she uses the symbol "#" in almost each instance instead of the word *dièze* ("sharp"), which may further alienate the reader, even one quite familiar with musical notation, who would be surprised to see such a symbol appear in a literary text. It jars the mind and causes one to wonder which mode is functioning, literature or music, and which code should be used to interpret here. The mixture of languages, fantastic discourse, commentary on music, and actual musical symbols not only invites a musico-literary analysis, but indeed suggests a reevaluation of the genre.[18]

The reader's alienation through music in "Histoire du rêveur" parallels the problems of identity. The singer is commonly referred to as "l'inconnu" ["the unknown one" or "the stranger"].[19] It is a constant source of intrigue and frustration for Amédée not to know the age and gender of the singer, even less her/his name and reputation. As Amédée tries to discern the identity of the singer, he remarks that the voice is too sweet, caressing, and resplendent to be a man's and too full, deep, and sonorous to be a woman's. And when he attempts to characterize the singer's vocal range, he is uncertain as to whether he hears a bass, a contralto, or a tenor voice. The absence of soprano in this list is not only surprising, but it is particularly interesting as Portia is a soprano. Amédée's own voice, says the narrator, while more masculine ["plus mâle"] than that of the singer, cannot fill the same space. Whether boy or girl, she/he must be a professional singer, he says, to have such a voice. The singer takes offense: "Voulez-vous dire que je sois une fille déguisée?" [Do you mean to say that I'm a girl in disguise?] ("Rêveur," 14) . Not wishing to insult the singer further, Amédée attempts to retreat by assuring the singer he believes in his masculinity since a woman could not have run and jumped over such rough terrain. Ambiguity, the earmark of the fantastic, serves Sand well in the dichotomy of illusion and reality, but also in the identity of the fantastic being, in the status of the narrator, and most importantly in the vacillation of discursive codes.

Amédée falls victim to the singer's charms, and during the seduction scene, replete with a vocabulary of fire and passion, the singer "devint une femme" [became a woman] ("Rêveur," 18). As they jump into the lava-spewing crater of Mt. Etna (and one cannot mistake the sexual symbolism of the image), Amédée, nestled in the snowy arms of the fairy, reaches up to kiss her. Instead of a passionate embrace, he receives an electric shock and falls unconscious to the "magic life intoxicating him." Just when the singer's gender is defined, Amédée is thrown into another confusion. The apparent misogyny of this transformation, reminiscent of the female spider topos, is contradicted later in the text by various elements. This is yet another fantastic trick designed to unsettle the reader.

By keeping the singer unidentified, Sand increases the mystery and thus the fantastic aspect of the story. Amédée does not want to know the singer any better than he already does despite his protests to the contrary. An unwelcome discovery would too abruptly and too crudely remove him from the shadows of his unconscious. He much prefers remaining in the dark and being subjected to the unexpected actions of the *inconnu*. In addition, as Bellemin-Noël tells us, "the referential falseness of the 'thing' dedicates it as a *verbal object*; its status is entirely metaphorical."[20] Thus, the most fantastic character and consequently the most fantastic element of the story remains a literary construct, a pure signifier.

Androgyny holds an important place in Sand's fantastic universe, and this androgyny is clearly not unrelated to Sand's childhood deity, Corambé. Amédée's ambiguous sexuality is certainly intriguing, but it is Portia's that interests me here. Endowing the singer in "Histoire du rêveur" with an androgynous nature necessarily removes the discussion of the artist from the realm of an all-male profession, despite the all-male group that discusses Portia and other female singers, actors, and performing artists. A long discussion on beauty, specifically the beauty of a female performing artist, is debunked by the statement of the kapellmeister, who says that,

> Dans le sexe féminin, il n'y a qu'une espèce de femmes à qui appartienne exclusivement la beauté, car celles-là peuvent la remplacer, l'imiter, l'acquérir par le talent en dépit des dispositions aveugles de la nature à leur égard. La femme artiste, la tragédienne, la cantatrice sont toujours belles en dépit du cours des ans, tant que subsiste le génie qui les embellit et les élève. ("Rêveur," 29)

> [In the feminine sex, there is only one type of woman to whom beauty belongs exclusively, because she can replace it, imitate it, acquire it with her talent despite the blind tendencies of nature in her regard. The female artist, the tragic actress, the female singer are always beautiful in spite of the flow of time, so long as the genius that adorns and exalts them subsists.]

In this, the only contribution by the kapellmeister, Sand removes the discussion of beauty from one of physical gifts to one of perception and appreciation of other attributes. Portia's musical talent alone makes her beautiful and irresistible. Thus it is music that creates beauty, not the singer's physical attributes and not nature. The performer does belong to the group of superhumans that comprises all artists, despite Portia's fantastic manifestation in the beginning of the story. Amédée's perception changes during the course of the narrative from seeing the singer as a mysterious being to an entity of beauty and talent for whom he has the utmost awe and respect, regardless of sex or age.

In the same year that "Histoire du rêveur" appears, Balzac publishes "Sarrasine." The narrator of the frame story recounts the tale of Sarrasine to a woman he hopes to seduce, the marquise de Rochefide. Balzac's singer, Zambinella, is a castrato who bemoans the impossibility of love for someone in his circumstance. Zambinella, whose voice captivates all Rome, knows that Sarrasine has fallen in love with him, thinking he is a woman. He tries to discourage him, but the would-be suitor can see only his ideal. An artist in his own right, Sarrasine has sculpted his perception of Zambinella, a statue imbued with the cold perfection of his ideal that crystalizes Zambinella's hopelessness. The message clearly debunks the romantic notion of the Ideal as possible or even desirable at the same time as it ridicules Parnassian ideals. Balzac conducts the aesthetic discussion mostly in visual terms, capitalizing on Sarrasine's métier as sculptor. Evidence of the power of music is evoked throughout but the aesthetics of the plastic arts prevails.

The androgynous nature of the object of desire in Balzac's text provides a satisfying focus for fantastic hesitation, as Sarrasine and the reader are manipulated despite a number of clues. "Fantastique" and "fantasmagorique" describe Zambinella, and the twittering of the other characters hints at an unknown and beguiling anomaly. Only Sarrasine, the naive and lovesick Frenchman, remains blind to Zambinella's true gender. In the frame story, the narratee, like the hero of the embedded story, is duped by her vision of an Ideal. The portrait of a beautiful creature "trop beau pour un homme" [too beautiful to be a man][21] has captivated her in an illusion of beauty just as it represented the illusion that tormented the sculptor. An old man who is cherished and protected by the hosts of the soiree turns out to be Zambinella and the inspiration for the statue, which has now been represented in a portrait, effectively multiplying the layers of illusion, deception, and blindness. The marquise expresses contentment that Paris is a safe haven for the unfortunate people of the world. But she also expresses relief at not belonging to such a needy group. The interaction of the frame story and the embedded story, with the figure of Zambinella functioning as the connecting hinge, emphasizes the classic link in the fantastic between illusion and reality. Further, the interplay of music, sculpture, and painting serves to enjoin the reader to accept all art as illusion. As usual, Balzac employs a cynicism Sand will rarely express. Illusion links Balzac's text to Sand's, but the authors' respective use of artistic illusion, one doubly communicated through art—first to the narrator or protagonist, second to the reader—differs in their focus. Balzac multiplies art forms to emphasize the idea of illusion in art, whereas Sand concentrates on one art form, furthering her point of the elusiveness and the etherealness of music.

"Histoire du rêveur" proliferates in dreams. Amédée dreams of leaving behind his earthly existence to enter the realm of superior understanding and wisdom. His first stop on the way up Mt. Etna introduces a dream scene. Whether the "music" of the wind wakens him from his sleep or rather induces deeper sleep, what remains clear is that the resulting images come to him in a dream. The musical dream, with a mixture of romantic musical metaphors and some specific musical vocabulary, will sustain Amédée throughout this and subsequent scenes, demonstrating to the reader the acutely evocative function of music in this story.

Amédée is not the only character in the story to rely on a dream world. Portia, too, performs in a hypnotic or dream state and produces the same effect on her public:

> Quand elle se tut, un profond silence régna dans la salle. Personne ne songeait à l'applaudir, on craignait de détruire par le moindre bruit l'impression délicieuse qu'elle avait fait naître. . . . Elle semblait plus occupée de recevoir les inspirations de son génie musical que de travailler à conquérir des applaudissements. Elle resta quelque tems immobile et comme absorbée dans *un rêve de mélodie*. ("Rêveur," 33; my emphasis)

> [When she finished, total silence reigned in the hall. No one thought to applaud; they were afraid of destroying the delightful impression she had produced with the slightest noise. . . . She seemed more concerned about receiving the inspirations of her musical genius than by working to command applause. She remained silent some time as though she were lost in a *dream of melody*.]

This "dream of melody" that characterizes Portia's state both during and after the performance answers the romantic call for inspiration and the eagerness to escape to a higher plane of existence, while at the same time inspiring a dreamlike effect on her public. Sand offers her reader a reliable comparison between performer and spectator, demonstrating that through the dream of music both can participate in an experience of the beyond. Such a transgression is therefore not limited to the trained musician or artist but is equally open to the common individual who knows how to listen to and appreciate music. Sand's portrayal of the power of music comes across as at once forceful and ethereal. Musical communication with a superior being—the singer's exchange with the Spirit of Mt. Etna as well as Portia's performance—emanates from and creates a state of nervous tension that is sensual and sexual in nature. And the tension of such a state amplifies the hesitation inherent in the fantastic. A "dream of melody" also evokes the idealistic state that Sand identifies with "pure" music.

The dream state is a quintessentially fantastic element. It signals a position somewhere between the real and the imaginary, leaving the dreamer and the reader wondering, somewhat embarrassedly, about the nature of the dream. Just as when one wakes up in the middle of a vivid dream and wonders for a moment if it were real, so does Amédée observe on the slopes of Mt. Etna, "C'est donc un rêve que j'ai fait" [So, then, I was dreaming] ("Rêveur," 16).[22] But the illusion continues. Amédée first hears voices singing. He juggles the sounds in his mind, showing his ability and desire to use his imagination to savor the (imaginary) sounds of nature: "Il écoutait [les voix humaines] avec un plaisir mélancolique et puis son imagination leur prêtant des modulations qu'elles n'avaient pas il les répétait intérieurement jusqu'à ce qu'il fût excédé de leur monotonie" [He listened to the human voices with a melancholy pleasure, and then, his imagination contributing modulations to them that they didn't have, he repeated them in his head until he was infuriated by their monotony] ("Rêveur," 12). The separation between reality and illusion is all but erased here. The play of the imagination in matters of music provides an essential element of the dream and thus of the musical fantastic.

The female narrator of the frame story also dreams. She states quite explicitly that she will settle in while Tricket tells his story: " 'So tell me slowly, my good spirit.' I hung my hammock on hooks destined to rock my golden dreams. . . . I didn't lose a word since no one possesses better than I do the sweetness of magnetic sleep that's known as somnambulism" ("Rêveur," 9). Again ten pages later she mentions sleeping, and once again when Tricket resumes the story of the traveler, she indicates he could "charm my sleep by continuing his tale" ("Rêveur," 28). It is clear that the protagonist dreams this fantastic story while she is sleeping.

There remains only the matter of the dreamer of the title. On the first level of significance it refers to Amédée. He is the dreamer of the story who innocently strives to better himself by seeking a higher level of experience, whether it be in the real or the illusory world. His escape, typical in the romantic ethos, originates in travel and in dream and is mediated through music. Despite the narrator's mocking tone, we are to understand Amédée as a model, and like him, we also can endeavor to discover another plane of understanding. Portia is also a dreamer. Her experiences move us in the direction of the Ideal. The female narrator of the frame story, too, is a dreamer, who perhaps dreams up her relationship with Tricket, reminiscent of Sand's imaginary Corambé.[23] Finally, the reader is a dreamer. From the moment we pick up a piece of literature and read it openly and frankly, we willingly fall into the abyss of fiction where time stands still. The reader of fantastic fiction is all the more a dreamer, thanks to the tendency to falter between reality and illusion.

Only Tricket is not a dreamer. And yet, even that is not so clear. We do not have the first chapter of "Histoire du rêveur." The text begins with the "2de Nuit" [second night]. But the first sentence gives a clear identification of the two narrators: "Tricket comme vous voyez est sérieux quand je veux. Il est gai aussi quand je suis disposée à l'être" [As you can see, Tricket is serious when I want him to be. He's also happy when I'm inclined to be so] ("Rêveur," 9). The identification of the two narrators remains problematic. And while the female narrator takes a nap, her male component takes over and the dream world evolves. Tricket may not be a dreamer himself, but he may be a dream. The frame narrator continues to point out that Tricket cannot abide humans' desire to "rêver quelque bien au delà" [dream of something beyond what they already possess] ("Rêveur," 9). She tells him that if he cannot dream of something or somewhere better, some future that will exceed the present, he must be inferior to humans. Yet, she retrenches when Tricket laughs at her: "Arrête, arrête Tricket, et ne foudroye pas la pauvre humanité. Tu sais comme je l'estime peu au fond du cœur, et j'ai plutot besoin que tu la défendes pour m'empêcher de la haïr" [Stop! Stop, Tricket, and don't strike down poor humanity. You know how little esteem I have for it already, and I need you to defend it to keep me from hating it] ("Rêveur," 9). Here again Sand separates the narrator's conflicting reactions to the world around her into two narrators, one dreamy-eyed and the other rational. Only music allows the conflicts to reconcile, to conciliate discord among the male spectators of Portia as well as the dissenting attitudes of the original narrator(s). Through music the characters present at Portia's recital leave aside their pompous arguments about beauty and art. The harpsichordist puts aside his professional pride

4: THE MUSICAL FANTASTIC

to join the musical experience that Portia offers him. Even the lack of a return to the frame story suggests that the musical experience suffices—even though the possibility of a lost ending, just like the "lost" beginning, persists. Finally, the dreamer of the title is potentially everyone including the reader. Sand uses the definite article, with a general connotation, as opposed to an indefinite article, which would have restricted the reference to a single dreamer.

Music functions doubly in "Histoire du rêveur." On the one hand, it serves to encourage the flight of the imagination heavenward, away from the confines of an earthly existence, which is encouraging for the common reader. On the other hand, it provides a reasonable, technical structure that is alienating for the non-initiated, witness the use of musical terminology as well as of musical symbols. Herein lies the fantastic quality of Sand's story, in the hesitation between the soothing and alienating qualities of music. That the notion of confused identity is throughout associated with music demonstrates an essential aspect of Sand's musical fantastic in this story. Moreover, the element of illusion inherent in the performances of la Portia and in the way Amédée, and thus the reader, receives them affirms the disquieting and yet attractive nature of music when associated with the fantastic.[24]

"Carl"

Sand goes further still in her use of music to advance the fantastic narrative in "Carl" (1843). Sand wrote this short story at the same time she was writing *La Comtesse de Rudolstadt*. The influence of her masterpiece on the tale can be detected in several details, from the name Carl to the setting of Vienna for the opening and closing scenes and even the implicit commentary on folk music. Once again Sand sets the stage carefully and clearly for a fantastic tale, beginning with a well-nourished fantastic vocabulary as well as a setting designed to alienate the narrator and reader, disasters and circumstances that solicit sympathy and terror (death, fever, illness, physical and mental abuse, disorientation, an avalanche), and a clear message of reincarnation.[25]

One detail of "Carl" that distinguishes it from Sand's other fantastic tales is the presence of musical notation within the text.[26] There are seven instances of a musical staff with a melody, supposedly drawn from Halévy according to a note by the author,[27] some with lyrics, some in a high register, some in D major and others in D-flat. The degree of the narrator's musical knowledge is never made explicit, but he seems to have at least an amateur's appreciation. At any rate, he remembers the melody, sings it, and plays it on his flute. Throughout the story, he uses it as a link with his past, with his dead friend, and with his new friend—also named Carl. The melody is the unifying element of the story in several ways, namely its relation to the themes of dream, reincarnation, and the memory of music.

The narrator in "Carl," whose name we never know—Sand's narrators in her short stories often remain anonymous—has just recently lost a close friend, Carl, a composer. On his deathbed, Carl sang a religious melody of his own invention that the narrator associates not only with his friend, but also with Carl's death. The eight-bar melody sums up the essence of Carl's simplicity and eloquence in music. Now on a long trip with the clear intention of trying to cope with his friend's death, the anonymous narrator meets a young boy also named Carl, the slow-witted son of an innkeeper. The homonym irritates him at first as it seems to him that the memory of his friend is compromised. These two are also linked by their musical gifts, again an annoyance to the narrator. It is important to note the stark contrast between the nameless narrator and the double name Carl. The narrator is solely a mediator even though he does locate the fantastic. This coincides with many examples of the genre, where the narrator symbolizes the reader's potential experience of disorientation, and does so all the better by remaining anonymous.

The narrator is ill and feverish, and each time he hears the innkeeper call his son's name, he shivers and the ghost of his dead friend appears before him. In one such apparition, Carl-the-friend asks the narrator whether the reason he is happy to let him disappear into eternal oblivion is that he himself might be afraid of death. The manifestation of the fear of death surfaces frequently in fantastic tales. Sand associates that fear with music, or more precisely with the memory of music. And insomuch as memory can be a strong tie to death, death, memory, and music are inextricably intertwined. She thus demonstrates music's pervasive effect on our emotions and our willingness to abandon ourselves to the powers of music.

The innkeeper treats his son cruelly. Consequently, young Carl often reacts like a down-trodden, even a mentally deficient child. The narrator, grateful for the attention and care the boy has shown him during his illness, offers to employ him as his personal servant, thereby removing him from the damaging dominion of his father. Once the narrator feels better, they leave the inn and start on their trek toward Innsbruck. He begins to suspect that Carl-the-friend has brought him together with Carl-the-boy. Lying in a field thinking about his friend Carl, the narrator feels a tear bathe his eyelid, and he takes up his flute and plays the tune he heard Carl singing at the moment of his death. This is the first time the musical notation of the melody appears in the text, without words, in a high register (in the octave above the staff), and in D major. The nature of the tune recalls liturgical melodies and inspires calm and melancholy.

("Carl," 242)[28]

The sound of the melody awakens Carl, sleeping in the field beside his newly acquired master. He comes alive with a color and a vivacity different from his ordinary countenance, but he quickly falls back into his characteristic listlessness. The narrator thinks he has allowed "un instant d'exaltation musicale et sentimentale" [a moment of musical and sentimental elation] ("Carl," 243) to cloud his own perceptions. The conclusion he draws from this experience is that his friend Carl has sent him Carl-the-boy for some reason. He tells the boy that if ever he mistreats him the boy is to remind him to respect the name of Carl.

This is the first of several scenes where the narrator confuses the two Carls under the influence of his dead friend's music. A similar disorientation occurs in a church where they are forced to take refuge as there is no other room for them in the village.[29] In uncomfortable accommodations and with a renewed fever, the narrator falls asleep and dreams about Carl's death scene. He thinks he hears Carl singing the melody, which drifts upward in the church, disappearing in the sky along with the specter of Carl. The narrator sleeps fitfully, imagining he hears Carl's music each time he closes his eyes. When his eyes are open, he imagines he hears the same melody being played on the church organ. As the church itself becomes personified with the mysterious manifestation of the melody, the narrator wanders through the structure until his hand comes to rest on the organ, which is indeed vibrating with the music. Carl-the-boy, who is sleeping in a nearby confessional, has heard nothing.

Once again the fantastic music heard by the narrator does not seem to exist in the fictional reality of the narrative. A common device in the fantastic genre, the discrepancy as to whether the music exists adds to the general sense of hesitation. It emerges from our appreciation of the ethereal nature of music, a sense that it cannot be captured and examined to the point where we wonder whether we have actually heard it. Sand capitalizes on the transience of auditory perception by exploiting music, which results in a dual effect: a representation of the vanishing quality of sound(s) as well as the time-bound nature of music.

Sand again combines music and nature when the travelers cannot determine whether they are hearing an avalanche, a waterfall, or music. Here nature could be destructive or pleasant, but later when the narrator goes in search of Carl, he sees—or thinks he sees—Carl, and interprets every sound as music, which allows for the transition to the next manifestation of Carl's music: "Je ne sais par quelle liaison d'idées la phrase musicale de Carl me revint à la mémoire. Mon rêve, un instant oublié, me revint aussi, et la fièvre qui venait de m'envahir embrouilla tellement mes idées, que je perdis de nouveau l'empire de ma volonté" [I don't know what train of thought brought Carl's melody back to my mind. My dream, forgotten a moment earlier, also came back to me, and the fever that had just assailed me jumbled my thoughts so much that I once again lost control of my will] ("Carl," 249). He remembers vividly the scene in the church and begins to sing the melody, first quietly and then out loud. Then, just as he sings the words "O Dieu, que ta puissance est grande" [O God, how great is your power]—and here the music is again written, although this time in D-flat and in the octave on the G-clef staff—a voice answers him, repeating the same lyrics but with the music of the second period of the melody, again written out in the text in the same register and key.

("Carl," 250)

Then the sky seems to be filled with voices, all singing the words "est grande," the final two bars of the melody. As these voices fade away, the narrator imagines he hears the final, musical breath of his friend Carl similar to the sounds of the air dancing on the strings of a harp in summer. The narrator believes he has seen the angelic form of Carl-the-friend flying off into the heavens. Such a musical apotheosis illustrates not only Sand's belief in the hereafter and in some form of reincarnation, but also in the ability of music to evoke dreamlike and timeless memories that offer hope.

Now concerned at Carl-the-boy's absence, the narrator sets off into the rugged terrain. Once again he hears the melody (first period, D major, on the staff, p. 252) sung by what he thinks is the voice of Carl-the-friend. He spies Carl-the-boy, who at first seems to be a ghost. The narrator then prays, but his prayer is interrupted by a "voix fantastique" [fantastic voice] singing the "phrase fatale" [fateful phrase]. He recognizes that he is confusing the two Carls: "Par quelle magique combinaison vois-je le spectre du nouveau Carl, en même temps que j'entends la voix de Carl, l'ami qui n'est plus?" [By what magical association do I see the ghost of the new Carl at the same time as I hear the voice of Carl, the friend who is no more?] ("Carl," 254). The reference to the "new" Carl is further indication of the underlying message of reincarnation or metempsychosis. Here is an example of why Todorov stipulates that the fantastic is not a genre unto itself, since it constantly shifts back and forth. But it is that very shifting, teasing the reader with a marvelous "explanation" only to jolt back into a fictional reality with a plausibly rational explanation, that constitutes the "hésitation," the "irrésolution," the "intellectual uncertainty" that is the fantastic.

Wandering all night through the dangerous terrain of the snow-covered mountain, the narrator continues to hear the voice and to see the specter of Carl-the-boy. The next morning at dawn, he finds Carl and hugs him, just as Carl sings: "Tu fais ma force et mon espoir" [You create my power and my hope] ("Carl," 255). This is the penultimate musical citation. That the music here differs from all the other musical passages in the story and that this music is more ponderous than the other quotations demonstrates the importance of the musical message. While in the same key and register, the melody is monotone and chantlike, though ending with the same cadence as the original version. The style of this coda recalls the religious nature of the music. It is at this moment that the narrator realizes the significance of Carl-the-boy's presence. It is also the first time the narrator is absolutely certain that the boy is singing, a fact of the narrative that is conveyed by the verb "dire" and that remains vague if the music is not printed in the text: "Je le saisis au moment où il *disait* . . . " [I grabbed him at the moment when he was *saying* . . .], and here follows the musical notation. The verb underscores Sand's insistent message that music can and does communicate as language. While some editions have reprinted Sand's story without the musical notation, we see here that the force and significance of the music are lost without it.[30]

Tu   fais   ma   for - ce   et   mon es - poir,   tu

You give   me   strength___   and   hope,___   you

fais   ma   for - ce   et   mon   es - poir.

give   me   strength___   and   hope.___

("Carl," 255)

Carl tells the narrator of his love for music, which his father did everything to squelch as he saw it as a sign of weakness. His sickly nature and near madness date from this period. The boy also recalls the brief visit of a traveler five years earlier, a musician who stayed in his room writing music. He often hummed a certain tune that Carl-the-boy retained. He sings it for the narrator, and this is the last musical quotation in the story, this time the original melody in D-flat in the middle register complete with lyrics. Carl remembers, too, that the traveler had the same name and encouraged him to develop his voice. He had forgotten the melody until he heard the narrator playing it on the flute.

Carl assumed the tune to be well known in the region. This aspect of folk music resurfaces in *Consuelo* and again in *Les Maîtres Sonneurs*. But a more compelling reason for his not talking to the narrator about the tune is the repression he had undergone because of his father's ridicule: "On m'a habitué à regarder ce goût comme une folie dont je devais rougir, ou comme une désobéissance que je devais expier sous le bâton" [I was led to consider my taste in music as a madness that I should be ashamed of, or as a disobedience that should be punished with the rod] ("Carl," 258). Here lies the fantastic element of Sand's story, where she removes the hints of magic and supernatural, diabolical and grotesque, to return to the realm of reality. The assertion of a "rational" explanation suppresses the hesitation and thus the fantastic, according to Todorov. Carl's supposed mental deficiencies and unsubstantiated claims of madness clearly stem from his father's chastisement. Hearing the familiar melody played by the narrator on the flute awakens his repressed memory and desire for music. Here also lies the psychological force of Sand's tale, as she not only links child abuse with repression but also expounds on her notions on the curative powers of music. In this sense, Carl resembles Gottlieb from Hoffmann's *Kreisleriana* in his modest background, his backward ways, and his "cure" thanks to music. Sand will use this character, also with the name Gottlieb, in *La Comtesse de Rudolstadt*.[31]

The narrator now sees Carl as an individual in his own right, even though the final sentence of the story reaffirms the possibility of his being the reincarnation of the composer Carl: "quant à son cœur, il est toujours le plus pur, le plus généreux et le plus fidèle que j'aie connu depuis la mort de Carl le maestro" [As for his heart, he's still the purest, the most generous, and the most faithful person I've ever known since the death of Carl the maestro] ("Carl," 260). Having determined that Carl-the-boy suffers from somnambulism, in a scene that may have inspired Maupassant's "Le Horla," the narrator takes him to a doctor in Vienna, who diagnoses the problem as the repression of a passion: he must develop his passion or he will surely die. Accordingly, Carl successfully studies organ and composition and promises to become an accomplished composer. Reminiscences of Gina ("La Prima donna") are obvious.

The issue of identity, although different from that in "Histoire du rêveur," remains an interesting problem in "Carl." The narrator constantly relives his friend's death scene and then, through the curative influence of the musical phrase, finds a renewed sense of calm with Carl-the-boy. Throughout the story, the reader recognizes the pretense of the two Carls' identity. Only the narrator fails to see the overlap until the end of the scene on the mountain. And yet the identification remains less than complete since Carl-the-boy's musical development is only just beginning at the end of the story. His ontogeny will perhaps replicate the development of Carl-the-friend, thus not replacing him but rather continuing his work on earth. Glasgow posits that the relationship between the narrator and the boy Carl resembles that of Pygmalion and Galatea.[32] I would disagree with this analysis since there is no suggestion that the narrator molds or shapes the young Carl other than to arrange for his musical and psychological development at the end of the tale. Rather, it is the narrator who grows from exposure to the rejuvenating powers of music in the reincarnation of his friend.

Sand's association of music and double identity goes back to the famous echo scene in Madrid, which she recounts in *Histoire de ma vie*: "C'est que j'étais double, et qu'il y avait autour de moi un autre *moi*" [So then, I was double, and there was somewhere around me another *me*] (*HV*, 1: 573). She recalls playing the game repeatedly and comparing, with her characteristic use of synesthesia, the sound of the echo of her own voice to the spots that came in front of her eyes from staring at an object, "les orblutes" [circles in front of her eyes] (*HV*, 1:572–73).[33]

Memory functions in "Carl" much the way dream does in "Histoire du rêveur." Both use memory as a construct of the subconscious that takes us away from a conscious state into an unreal or other-than-real place where time and space are altered and where we have the leisure to contemplate our thoughts without having to obey the laws of physics. Music, like memory, is the key to this world, for it removes us from the real world. It can also bring us back thanks to its sensuous attributes that reinforce our attachment to the real world.

Memory acts as vehicle for keeping the past alive and for allowing for the development of the future. Music stimulates memory in this story. Time and again the narrator's auditory memory becomes alert thanks to a musical stimulus; or sometimes the memory causes him to repeat the music. In all cases, the music comes from the narrator's memory, just as the echo in Madrid comes from Aurore's own voice. For the narrator's memory is the origin of all the music in the story until Carl's contribution, which is not the identical musical phrase. Music symbolizes Carl's death for the narrator, but for Carl-the-boy music represents his passion and his future, thus his rebirth. Sand proposes in this story that while memories of dead friends can give us a certain melancholy pleasure, they are much more useful if we use them to point to the future. The involuntary memory evoked by music, half a century before Proust, will remain one of Sand's contributions in the realm of music's function in literature. She uses this device often, not only in fantastic tales but in many of her musical texts.

"L'Orgue du titan"

In the 1870s, now a grandmother, Sand wrote two series of short stories for the amusement and edification of her granddaughters, published under the title *Contes d'une grand'mère.*[34] Generally they are cautionary tales with a moral. "L'Orgue du titan" (1873) focuses on the moral and psychological development of a young musician. The story takes place in Auvergne and takes full advantage of the rugged mountain terrain of that region. Angelin takes music lessons from the church organist, Maître Jean, who treats him more like a servant than a pupil.[35] The organist takes a trip to visit his brother, a curé in a remote mountain village, Chanturgue, and the young music student tags along. On the last day of their visit the curé indulges them in a goodly dose of the regional wine, which he calls Chant*orgue* ("*orgue*" = "organ"). This phonetic titillation is not only a delight to the children who are the intended readers, but it also lays the groundwork for the musical symbolism of the tale. They begin their trek home inebriated. As they pass through the most mountainous section of their path, Angelin remembers what Maître Jean told him about the spectacular rock formations, that they were the titans' attempt to reach Jupiter. The organist made up this explanation to mask his ignorance in geology and was quite proud of his witicism. With night falling, the memory of this story, and the drowsiness induced by the wine, Angelin begins to imagine the formations as something more than just rocks.[36]

In Auvergne the pattern of erosion on certain rock formations have caused them to resemble the vertical tubes of a pipe organ, and consequently they are known as "des orgues" or "des jeux d'orgue" ["organ stops," although the literal maning of "games" is also significant]. His judgment diminished from the excessive wine, Maître Jean decides to combine the story of the titans and the metaphor of the organ. He sits down at a flat rock, which he dubs the keyboard, and tells Angelin to man the bellows. Angelin, less drunk than Jean, does not see the humor and does not wish to participate in the game. Frustrated at the insubordination of his ward, Jean sets Angelin at the keyboard and takes up the position at the bellows himself. He commands Angelin to play the "Introit" to his mass. Angelin pretends to play as Jean cries out "Et toi, orgue, chante! chante, *orgue!* chante *urgue!* . . . " ["And you, organ, sing! Sing, organ, sing *urgan!* . . ."]—and we appreciate the homophony of the name of the town and its wine, Chanturgue, and the exhortation, "Sing, organ!"[37]

Suddenly the air is filled with music as Angelin moves his fingers across the fantastic and stony keyboard. But it is not Jean's "Introit" but a beautiful piece of music that spontaneously springs from Angelin's imagination. As he plays, Angelin's fingers begin to swell and hurt, becoming "the hands of a titan." At the same instant, the sky fills with thunder and the rocks crumble around them. Angelin and Jean fall unconscious. When they wake up, now sober, the organist wants to know where Angelin learned the melody he was singing at the time of the rock fall, but the young musician has no answer.

That Sunday as Maître Jean begins to play the organ for mass, he forgets the music several times and is unable to continue. Angelin again replaces him at the keyboard, this time a real organ keyboard. Instead of the traditional mass Jean usually plays, Angelin plays the music he invented in the mountains. The priest who is present at the mass asks to see Angelin later to examine him with a view to making a church musician out of him. Pleased with the talent he notes, he orders that Angelin should be given proper musical instruction and no longer serve as Maître Jean's servant. Angelin goes to Paris and eventually becomes a famous organist. But for the rest of his life when he improvises on the tune of the mass in the mountains, he again feels the pain and swelling in his hands and he imagines he hears the sound of falling rocks.

Sand joins music and nature, not only to present the possibility of divine inspiration but also, and perhaps more importantly, to warn against the powerful force of nature, and thus the powerful force of music. Music comes out of the rock in this story, but at the same time the rock crumbles at the sound of the music.[38] Angelin's musical talent, still fairly dormant at this point in the story, comes to life in the midst of a natural phenomenon, springing from unknown sources and with unexpected strength. His pain will ever serve as a reminder of his humble origins and of the natural source of his musical talent.

Sand introduces a linguistic game with Maître Jean's and his brother's manipulation of vocabulary. The geological use of the term "les orgues" comes as no surprise, but the context in which Sand places it here adds a humorous dimension, setting the stage for the irony to come. The village of Chanturgue, which our hero can find on no map in his adult life—does it, in fact, exist even in the narrative?[39]—lends its name to the local wine, but the curé easily changes it to "Chantorgue" in honor of his brother's profession and of the basalt formations. The shift of one vowel pleases Jean, who claims the wine must have been conceived for him. Similarly, Jean transforms the name of the mountain peak where the dramatic musical scene takes place, called Sanadoire, into "Sonatoire" ["soundatarium"], suggesting a place especially conceived for the production of music. This alteration follows a similar phonetic shift, this time shifting from one nasal vowel to another and the vocalization of one consonant.

Like many of Sand's young musicians, Angelin begins the story in a subordinate position and must make his way, despite his own insecurities and the domination of others, toward a satisfying development of his talent and of his self. Angelin's music lessons with Maître Jean are few. While no indications suggest that Jean is jealous of Angelin's talents before the invention of the music in the mountains, we can safely assume that an underlying uneasiness, along with laziness, rules Jean's actions. Beginning with a seemingly insignificant detail, the musical scene in the mountains exemplifies Jean's need to control Angelin and Angelin's reaction to this oppression. Maître Jean is still quite drunk and has been taunting Angelin with his riding crop. Angelin fears for his master's safety and takes his crop away, throwing it down a ravine. The crop,

Jean's means of control over the mule and thus over the present situation, can also be seen as his control over Angelin and, indeed, himself. He has clearly used the crop to discipline Angelin in the past, and the boy rushes to gain control over this symbol of power. Having dropped the crop, Jean has relinquished control; and by throwing it away, Angelin assures he will never again come under his master's domination. The act depicts a typical coming of age fantasy where the young man, struggling to become an adult, replaces the older man, thus removing himself from the subordinate position. Angelin again replaces Jean at the keyboard once back in church—thus the young man supplants the older one, moving into the profession despite the organist's misgivings and, in fact, with his invitation.

The riding crop resembles in form and in function a conductor's baton: both are long and rigid and serve to direct or control. Disposing of this symbol of power, especially significant thanks to its phallic nature, symbolizes the boy's desire to usurp his master's power, or to effect the castration of the father. Sand uses the phallic symbolism to further the fantastic interest of the story by repeating it with the swelling of Angelin's fingers when he plays the rock organ. The uncanny recurrence of the same painful sensation gives life to Sand's story. Herein lies the *Unheimliche*, bound up in repetition as Freud describes it. Symbolically castrating his master, music teacher, and adoptive father, Angelin does accede to a position of musical power. But success only serves to intensify his feelings of guilt. Thus, the memory of the act, resuscitating each time he plays this melody, results in pain.

Angelin begins the story among friends whom he is entertaining with some improvisations, always the sign of an accomplished musician in a mid-nineteenth-century context of salon music. When one of the piano strings breaks, he tells them the story of Chantorgue, relating the pain that comes about each time he improvises on this particular melody. Angelin offers an explanation: there must have been briars and nettles on the rock keyboard he played. Here is the locus of the fantastic insofar as Sand provides, in the last sentence of the story, a rational explanation for the pain that otherwise seems quite supernatural. And yet, the explanation does not entirely convince us. The romantic notion of the suffering of the artist can be seen clearly in this tale, and the renewed suffering throughout Angelin's life serves to remind him of his humble origins, an idea important to Sand. The repetition of the pain, mirrored in the repetition of the melody—not just repetition because he plays it many times in his life despite the painful result, but also repetition because it is now called improvisation, which implies a repetition of the same melody in different forms—satisfies Freud's generic definition of the uncanny as being characterized by repetition.

Improvisation is the public proof of musical prowess that demonstrates a virtuoso's worth. In this way a performer becomes a musical titan, like Liszt and Thalberg and Paganini. But who is the titan in the title of Sand's tale? Maître Jean speaks of the titans who built the formations in an irreverent attempt to reach Jupiter. The several references he and his brother make are to titans in the plural, as are Angelin's several questions. And yet the title clearly proclaims the possessor of the organ as a singular titan, who must therefore be Angelin. So, the story of many titans trying to reach and thereby conquer Jupiter is replaced by the story of a single boy who conquers in his own world, who conquers his "master," his low self-image, and his profession. The conflict between Christianity and mythology surfaces briefly as the explanation of the titans is invented in the absence of any real knowledge. That the story is shared by the curé, even though as a joke, furthers the combination of Christian culture and mythology. The mythological explanation feeds into Angelin's native fears and superstition. Sand often points out the survival of such superstitions in the practice of Christianity, practices encouraged if not by the Vatican at least by the local clergy. In a subtle undercurrent, Sand advances her notion of the usefulness of combining pagan superstition and Christianity. We must not, she says, forget our origins. In another vein, "titan" also refers to "le peuple" in Sand's lexicon, as Michelle Perrot reveals.[40] Thus Angelin is again the titan, but this time he represents the people struggling to free themselves from the oppression and domination of the ruling classes through music.

On a social level, "L'Orgue du titan" resembles the other fantastic stories I have studied insofar as the musician always belongs to a lower social class. Angelin is an orphan who performs duties for Maître Jean, and for his pains he receives food and shelter and a music lesson from time to time. The developing character of "Carl" is an innkeeper's son whose father despises him; he is taken on by the narrator as a manservant and only accedes to a position of independence after many months of music lessons that the narrator provides for him. In "Histoire du rêveur" the musician is described as "un ragazzo" [a boy] dressed in the poor garb of a local peasant; nothing further is said of Portia's social status. Sand is perhaps reacting against the aristocratic dominion of the Parisian musical world. She wishes to demonstrate that worthy musicians can and do come from the modest classes and can and do become successes.

Consuelo is a similar character who rises from the lowest social class to enjoy, through the merits of her talent and hard work, a professional life equal to any other. Joset, in *Les Maîtres Sonneurs*, is another musician that originates, and remains, in the peasantry, which does not in any way prevent him from acceding through musical training to a higher plane.[41]

Finally, Sand's fantastic musicians also seem to discover significant aspects of their lives while traveling. Carl and Angelin both travel, in many senses, toward a new life, one that they neither fully expect nor understand. As we have already seen, Sand uses the conventional metaphor of travel for development and growth; here the young musicians discover aspects of themselves they may not have seen without the benefit of travel. In the case of "Histoire du rêveur" the situation is slightly different since it is Amédée who is traveling, and he is not the musician of the tale. Still, his travels take him along a path of growth, not of the music performer but of the music consumer. We have already seen the importance of travel in Sand's conception of the musician's development for Joset and Consuelo; Carl and Angelin also need to displace themselves physically as well as emotionally and socially in order to advance.

THEATER

Maître Favilla

Maître Favilla premiered at the Odéon in September 1855. The play is a well-constructed, three-act, Marivaudesque comedy ending with a wedding. Very little of Hoffmann's fantastic style characterizes the text, contrary to the opinion of a contemporary critic.[42] A certain hesitation does, however, keep the spectator guessing from the beginning to the end of the play. Music is an integral part of the play; although never made explicit, the eponymous character's title of "master" must surely indicate his status as a retired master musician. It is precisely the music Favilla plays and remembers playing that bridges the gap between illusion and reality— rather, between the standard illusion of drama and the further illusion within this drama.[43]

At the opening of the play, Maître Favilla has just lost his oldest and dearest friend, Wolf, and becomes disoriented. The musicians were playing a Handel piece at the moment the old friend died. The reenactment of that scene one month later will demonstrate the sanity of the title character. Wolf's nephew, Keller, assumes he has inherited the château and all his uncle's property. On first inspection of the house, he bemoans all the money wasted on the music that fills the library. And when he meets Favilla, whose grief has unsettled him to an alarming degree, Keller remarks, "grâce à la musique, il était devenu un peu fou, lui aussi!" [thanks to music, he had also gone somewhat mad!].[44] Placing both his uncle and Favilla in the category of madmen and claiming music as the source of their madness, Keller declares his disapproval of the arts and is thus clearly Sand's antagonist. It is interesting to note, however, Sand's use of "thanks to" instead of "because of," which suggests either her own (unintentional) intervention or an ironic subtlety in Keller's character; in fact, both obtain. Any attempt to mollify his criticism only reinforces his condescension: "Je ne la déteste pas, la musique; ça me chatouille agréablement l'oreille comme à tout le monde" [I don't hate music; it pleasantly tickles my ear like anyone else's] (*MF*, 191). Later Keller will lament that his son, Hermann, shows too much compassion for Favilla and his family, "mon fils a lu des romans! et puis cette musique! . . . ça ne vaut rien pour la jeunesse" [My son has read novels! And then this music . . . that's no good for young people] (*MF*, 202). The analogy of novels and music is not lost on the reader, nor is Sand's irony of the uncultured attitude of the economically driven nephew.

Favilla's character provides the locus of hesitation.[45] He and his family are Italians, living in Germany at the home of his close friend, Wolf. We note that, as in "Carl," Sand focuses the story around an absent character, whose death relegates all details about him to the memory of his survivors. When Wolf dies, Favilla seems to lose his reason (although we know little of his state beforehand) and veers off into a dream world where the spectators/readers cannot determine whether he imagines things or actually knows more than they do. He thinks his friend has bequeathed all his worldly possessions to him, and he further thinks he is generous to allow Keller and his son to stay at the château. Other than Keller, everyone is content to allow Favilla his illusions. Music, or rather memories and promises of music, shroud Favilla's transitory state during the period between Wolf's death and the resolution of his inheritance, and thus that of the drama. Herein lies the dramatic conflict, which succeeds in leading the spectator to wonder about Favilla's insight.

Italian and living in Germany, thus doubly foreign for the reader since he inhabits a French text written for French readers, Favilla continues Sand's customary use of the foreigner, the outsider who stands apart and who speaks, perhaps, the truth. He makes a cogent speech praising Mozart as neither German nor Italian, thus validating his status as doubly foreign. He vacillates between obscurity and lucidity until the third act, when music helps him to see clearly. The reenactment of the rehearsal that marked the friend's death takes place on the feast of Saint Cecilia, the patron saint of musicians. Favilla cannot at first remember the melody of the Handel piece and puts down his violin, even though his daughter tries to help him by playing the tune on the harp.[46] But he soon recalls the entire scene of a month earlier. Wolf, sensing death near, took out a piece of paper, Favilla recalls, on which he had designated Favilla as his legal heir. Not wanting to be "rewarded" for his friendship, Favilla threw the paper into the fire. Frantz, the old baron's secretary, testifies that while there had originally been no fire in the room, when he returned to find his master dead, a bright fire was indeed burning in the fireplace.

The scene lacks realist, or for that matter fantastic, conviction, but it does bring the plot to a neat end, allowing Keller to recognize that he has perhaps been too harsh. He will return to his business in the city and leave his son and the Favilla family to live in the château. He also asks for Favilla's daughter's hand in marriage for his son, Hermann, which allows for a traditional comedic ending. The role of music in the play is clear even if not so pervasive as in other texts. The fantastic aspect also remains subtly regulated through music's effect on the vacillations of Favilla'a character. The spectator wants to believe him, and the Handel piece functions to demarcate the blurry line between illusion and reality.

One aspect of the play that stands out, and that earned Sand a severe review from Jules Janin, is the criticism of the bourgeoisie. The character of Keller is a merchant who shows no understanding of culture and often considers humanistic pursuits to be injurious to financial ones. Sand continually pits him against the other characters of the play, including his son. She ridicules his desires to revamp the running of the farms attached to his uncle's château when it means letting go long-standing employees and changing outmoded traditions.[47] Favilla represents the counterpoint (if you will), spending most of the play in a fog and longing after musical communion with his friend. As Bessière points out, he plays a passive role that serves to obscure the events around him. This allows him, and the reader/spectator, the time to discover how things work.[48]

La Nuit de Noël

In Sand's theater in her home at Nohant, she and her family and friends often filled the long winter hours with fantastic and marvelous plays, sketches, and improvisations. Once again Hoffmann serves as an inspiration for Sand's play *La Nuit de Noël*, written and performed at Nohant in December 1862. She states in the foreword that she manipulated the characters and some of the themes of Hoffmann's *Master Flea* [*Meister Floh*], "une des plus bizarres créations d'Hoffmann" [one of Hoffmann's strangest creations].[49] Indeed, this is one of Hoffmann's oddest and least coherent tales. Written and published just before his death and the subject of a legal penalty for libelous material, *Master Flea* tells the complicated story of a dreamer caught in the positivistic world of pretentious scientific advancement. Hoffmann offers a man whose ideological makeup is held up to ridicule by his contemporaries and must be examined from all sides before the happy ending.

Sand's *La Nuit de Noël* is much simpler than Hoffmann's tale, partly because of the exigencies of her theater at Nohant and partly because of the nature of the story she wished to tell. She uses only four characters, as opposed to Hoffmann's panoply of friends, neighbors, acquaintances, relatives, and the like. She keeps the scene in Frankfurt and maintains a classical unity of time, the entire story taking place within twelve hours on Christmas Eve, as indicated by the title.[50] The main character, Pérégrinus Tyss, is an orphan of thirty-some years. He delights in giving presents to disadvantaged children on Christmas Eve. However, before surprising the children with toys, he plays a game with himself, pretending that these toys were left for him by his own parents. He opens the parcels, plays with the toys, and then gathers them up for the children. On this particular Christmas Eve, a longtime friend, Max, has come to the house unannounced. He suspects Tyss's activities and wishes to expose and discourage them. One at first supposes he simply wants to help Tyss out of a fantasy world, especially since it prevents him from maturing and satisfying his bourgeois dream of meeting a woman and getting married. But Max's methods are selfish and he remains an unpleasant character. The Hoffmann character on which Max is based is far meaner and more deceitful. Sand modified him considerably to make him fit into her atmosphere of love and concern.

The fantastic element first comes into Sand's play during Max's encounters with a ghost. In order to observe Tyss's actions throughout the evening, Max hides in the former bedroom of Tyss's master and teacher of mechanical engineering. The master has been dead for some time and the room has not been opened since his burial. In the bedroom stands an old clock that has stopped working, a symbol of resisting progress. Max tries to adjust the clock, when he hears a voice warning him, "Touchez pas, touchez pas!" [Don't touch. Don't touch!] (*NN*, 245). He persists. The window opens and an owl appears, saying "Touchez donc pas! touchez donc pas!" [Don't touch, will you? Don't touch!]. But he does not heed the warning and makes the adjustment. The golden cock on the clock then crows three times, and the owl declares, "Cassée, cassée! vous l'avez cassée!" [Broken, broken! You've broken it!]. The ominous augur of the cockcrow gives Max pause but does not deter him in his mission.

The ghost appears to Max and asks whether he has found what he has been looking for. This is the spectator's first indication that Max has not come to Tyss's house solely for altruistic purposes. Max wants a secret formula that Tyss's master has undoubtedly left behind, the secret of perpetual motion—in other words, the promise of progress without moral reflection. The ghost's questions are pointed and accusatory. And when Max does not run off, the ghost tells him he has left the secret formula with Nanni the housekeeper, but that she will give it to him only if she loves him. And in order to convince her to give him the formula, he must actually love her.

Max tries to convince Nanni that he loves her, but he is awkward and aggressive. She thinks it is a cruel joke, and Tyss walks in just as Max attempts to force himself on Nanni. Tyss throws Max out of the house to protect Nanni from what he perceives as attempted rape, when in fact Max was actually attacking her just to get at the formula, which she had in her apron pocket. Now Nanni shows the paper to Tyss, who sets it aside until after his Christmas Eve ritual.

The musical aspect of Sand's story, surprisingly absent in Hoffmann's version, comes from a violin that hangs on the wall of the master's bedroom. When Max is hiding in the bedroom, he takes the violin off the wall. On its own it makes discordant sounds, so he replaces it on the wall and goes about his business. Later, with Max out of the house and Tyss about to enjoy Christmas Eve, Nanni is ready to leave him alone, as is their custom. But the doors swing shut by themselves and the violin begins to play, the bow moving by itself. The marionette theater, Tyss's oldest toy, which fascinates him Christmas after Christmas, now comes alive. And here we note the influence of Hoffmann's story, *The Nutcracker and the Mouseking,* as well as Maurice Sand's marionette theater. The puppets, representing Tyss and the old master, his godfather, begin to act out the traditional scene wherein the godfather chides him for never defending himself. Just then, the puppet Tyss stands his ground and declares his love for Nanni. Nanni, still present and observing the wonderful scene, responds positively to the puppet's declaration, and the doors symbolically swing open. The wonder of this scene is due to the unexplained powers of music that allowed the marionettes to come to life and to speak the truth.

The play ends with Tyss discovering a mistake in the master's formula. Max tries to steal the formula from him but is stopped by the ghost's warning, "Touchez pas!" Tyss and Nanni go off to get married. There is an interesting metaphor of a *bûche de Noël*, a traditional Christmas cake, which has been in the oven during the entire play. In the final scene, the *bûche* makes a loud noise, which is a sign of good luck according to Tyss. It is at this moment he discovers the mathematical error in the formula. The yule log symbolizes wholesomeness and goodness, the pastry embodiment of the Christmas spirit.[51]

The musical fantastic in *La Nuit de Noël* does not provide much material for discussion in terms of the genre, the structure, the metaphoric function of music, and says nothing of the role of the musician. In fact, the musical elements may actually assign the tale to the marvelous rather than the fantastic. The other texts I have examined are far richer in their musically fabulous fabric. Still, it is interesting to see that Sand incorporated into her theater her taste for the magical powers of music. She felt strongly about the dangers of the positivistic world she lived in, and the escape to a fantasy world that music could provide represented a sense of security. The fantastic approach to these texts does not totally reject reason or logically thinking in the ways Nerval's does, but it does curb the runaway progressive tendency of positivistic thinking and retains a balance between reason and fantasy.

MUSIC, FANTASTIC, AND THE DIABOLICAL OR OTHER-WORLDLY

As Sand and all writers of the fantastic learned from Hoffmann, the devil can provide rich material for a genre that essentially encourages the reader to vacillate between good and evil. Max Milner suggests that the romantic devotion to the devil originates in the Revolution.[52] While this may be true for the political and psychological fantastic texts, Sand's use of the fantastic as an exploration of the aesthetic recalls rather an eighteenth-century apostasy, an emptiness due to the unexplained and misunderstood loss of religion. The tradition of selling one's soul to the devil in exchange for immortality, eternal youth, or superhuman talent is hardly original with Sand or any of the romantic writers of the fantastic. But the presence of Satan in some of Sand's texts, and principally the musical texts, insists on the notion of the mysterious origins of music and art. While Sand offers no clear answer to her query, she nonetheless acknowledges a superhuman influence that must be respected and revered if not understood.

The equation of music and magic, most often devilish magic, can be found in texts of antiquity in a marvelous and superhuman setting. Yet romantic sensibility is particularly apt at locating the supernatural in a pseudo-realistic context. Not only does the fantastic mode lend itself expertly to the desires of dabbling in the occult and the supernatural, the fashion of magnetism in the 1830s made the subject captivating for most contemporary readers. Music adds a reasonably elusive dimension to this formula thanks to its intangibility and etherealness. Sand mocks the tendency to equate music with the supernatural, with the devil, with magic. At the same time she explores the rich possibilities of such an association. Taking her cue from Hoffmann, she examines the role of the devil in the origins of music and in the nature of the musician. But unlike her German predecessor, Sand is not content to suggest the fantastic, supernatural, or marvelous possibilities of the correlation. Rather, she pushes past the psychological traits of her literary inheritance to advance the inquiry into the social realm. For her, music opens avenues to an unknown and unknowable world, paths that take us beyond the here and now, ever closer to a level we can never attain but that we can partially experience. A Saint-Simonian application of religion, the arts, and social progress pervades these texts. Herein lies the magic, where the connection between religion and music occupies a locus not unrelated to the supernatural and yet relevant to society. Indeed, the question of magic and music surfaces continually in Sand's works, more often than not in a context of religious and spiritual searching. But it is the origin of music— its purpose, if there be one—that fascinates Sand, and this fascination leads to wonderment and awe.

One of the essential questions Sand asks in her pursuit of an understanding of music is that of origin: where does music come from? If music removes us from the earth, from reality, from the human experience, then it must come from some extrahuman or superhuman source, perhaps God or Satan. Representing the devil as the source of music reflects peasant superstition—not to mention fundamentalist Christian thought in today's American society—but it also indicates the fear that comes of ignorance. Sand thus attacks the general public's fear of music, the mistrust and uncertainty of the non-initiated; and on a social level, she tries to allay the general fear of social change.

On the other hand, Sand frequently refers to music as "le lana-gage divin" [the divine language] and alludes to its heavenly ori-gins. The romantic ethos of the fallen angel inhabits Sand's aesthetic and spiritual world, where it is perhaps just as much Luci-fer's knowledge as god's that informs her concept of art. Her focus is clear and simple: Sand speaks of supernatural origins and pur-pose to music in a serious tone, no matter how her conception of religion changes throughout her career. In the instances where she invokes the devil, her humor and irony shine through. Satan re-mains, however, a real possibility in Sand's Christian world, and that ever-present possibility makes it a perfect element for the fan-tastic. Sand links the devil to folklore and superstition, however, and allows an ambiguity to envelop the question of his existence and his involvement in the origins of music.

The fantastic presents a game wherein narrator and reader con-stantly shift between reality and illusion, outside and inside influ-ences, evil and good. Satan fits into such a construct naturally, along with the possible role of the devil in a musician's virtuosity. Sand does not ignore the romantic penchant for the occult and often exploits it in commentary on superstition and religious fervor. Mil-ner points out that the French writers of the fantastic did not make much use of the devil.[53] Even though Sand's devil never attains the complexity of Milton's or even Hoffmann's Satan, he is on a par with the deviltry in some of the works of Nerval, Berlioz, and Hugo.

Most occurrences of the devil in Sand's musical works are im-plicit, references to the diabolical nature of a particular character, but the devil himself is rarely a character.[54] The notable exception is, of course, *Les Sept Cordes de la lyre*, where all the characters are allegorical, including Méphistophélès. He represents the nega-tive power of the lyre and thus of music and art. He cannot touch the lyre, but he wants to possess it and understand its power. This typical device of horror stories, which facilitates the relationship between the devil and the human characters, provides a way to demonstrate Hélène's virtue in contrast with Méphistophélès' jeal-ousy and egoism. At the insistence of Méphistophélès, Hélène at-tempts to play the lyre, consecutively breaking the seven strings, which represent the seven stages of the development of Western civilization. This allegorical struggle between good and evil, housed in a musical context, combines music, ethics, progress, and the devil in a text that shares some characteristics with the fantastic.

In "Histoire du rêveur," it is the voice of the unknown singer that is diabolical, or at least such is the perception of Amédée when he hears the mysterious and other-worldly voice. From the beginning of the story, references to Greek mythology, where the gods are good and/or evil, allow the reader to associate the powers and talents of the unknown singer with the gods. The hero resists any non-rational explanation as long as he can. However, when the singer responds to a voice coming from Mt. Etna that Amédée cannot hear, the protagonist is forced to accept a higher power and a nonrational realm. Now completely engulfed in the mysteries of the fantastic music, Amédée totally abandons himself to the ecstasy: "[A]nge ou démon, entraîne-moi dans ce tourbillon que je vois déjà t'envelopper" [Angel or demon, drag me into this cyclone that I can already see engulfing you] ("Rêveur," 17). The following scene, filled with fire and smoke, establishes a diabolical setting without any doubt as to the power of the devil over the singer and Amédée. "[R]ire diabolique . . . éclat diabolique" [diabolical laugh . . . diabolical radiance] ("Rêveur," 18); such is the vocabulary of the passage, to which Tricket responds with irony: "[Ç]a ne vaudra pas le diable" [It won't be worth the devil] ("Rêveur," 19).

Portia is not an agent of the devil, but Amédée's confusion and fear conjure up suspicions of diabolical influences. Sand posits that music is not a tool of the devil but that our perception of the magic of music is tinged with diabolical beliefs. While Portia is "comme absorbée dans un rêve de mélodie" [all but preoccupied by a dream of melody], Pezzanini, the accompanist, struggles with the score, which seems to change key signatures at every blink of the eye. His frustration turns to anger: "Il y a là de la magie . . . un démon caché dans les entrailles du clavecin. . . . Il diavolo! è il diavolo!" [There was magic in it . . . a devil hidden in the harpsichord's entrails. . . . The devil! It's the devil!] ("Rêveur," 34). The personified—not to say deified—harpsichord evokes the convention of the devil's presence in inanimate objects and his power to make them act on humans. Sand exploits the French stereotypical perception of Italian superstition by quoting the musician in Italian. Even when calm is restored, the accompanist is convinced that the mysterious transformation in the music originated in some extrahuman source ("Rêveur," 35). But as that inspiration, be it divine or diabolical, comes to Pezzanini through Portia, she represents for him a tangible source of all art: "le génie des beaux arts réside en vous" [the genius of the fine arts resides in you] ("Rêveur," 35). Here a shift operates in the connotation of "génie," from evildoer and minion of the devil to the late eighteenth- and early nineteenth-century notion of genius. In addition, the female artist as mediator will find another incarnation in the character of Consuelo. Rambeau also

points out the link between magic and the relationship between female and male characters in Sand's works, where the terms "mystérieux, magique, miraculeux" [mysterious, magic, miraculous] recur
regularly in passages dealing with a woman nursing a man back to
health.[55] The identity of the diva—human, devil, or goddess—adds
to the fantastic aspect of "Histoire du rêveur." We will never know
exactly where her inspiration comes from or how she learned to use
it. Nor will we ever know whether the visit to Mt. Etna, the source
of art and eternal life, should be considered as kindled by heaven
or hell.

In "Carl" the presence of the devil is less explicit. Many of the
odd occurrences in this story can be attributed to the hero's state of
grieving. His fever-induced visions of specters and of organs playing in the middle of the night might easily be explained as psychological manifestations of his grief. And yet, the element of
metempsychosis suggests an unconventional aspect of unclear origins, diabolical or providential. Matters of reincarnation and the
like are conventionally seen to evolve from a superior or heavenly
source, but here the manifestations of the narrator's friend as ghost
and as possibly the young Carl are wrought with danger and malev-
olence. Each time the narrator hears the music he associates with
his dead friend, a vision of that friend appears. While ghosts are not
the exclusive domain of the devil, we can assume that the narrator
is haunted by the recurring vision of his friend. For my purposes,
the coincidence of music and spectral vision communicates the importance of the music for the memory of the dead friend transmitted
by some other-worldly manifestations.

The nature of the young Carl's musical history and training adds
a flavor of coincidence, which renders the story less sophisticated
than some by Nodier or Maupassant. However, there is once again
a confusion of good and evil, an unknown and misunderstood
power that has yet to be harnessed and developed. Carl's sleepwalk-
ing as well as the hints at magnetism recall the romantic penchant
for the occult as well as the fantastic delight in sleep and dream
manifestations of unknown powers.

"Mouny-Robin" (1841) evokes only a passing musical element
in that it is patterned after Weber's *Der Freyschütz*.[56] The story
deals with selling one's soul to the devil and the consequences of
this act. In the end it is a story about the impossibility of communication.[57] Two aristocrats are attending a performance of Weber's
opera, during which the narrator relates a story he heard about a
miller, Mouny-Robin, who possesses uncanny success in hunting.
The narrator's brother, keen to become an excellent hunter, re-

quests that Mouny-Robin instruct him. But the more they go hunting the more Mouny-Robin's talent seems to be a combination of luck and supernatural power. The narrator and his brother spy on Mouny-Robin, who is writhing on the ground in an inexplicable fit. He then utters predictions about their success in hunting that came true. After many tribulations and turns in the story, Mouny-Robin dies after a mysterious fall into the wheel of his mill. Some say he was pushed by the devil, unhappy that Mouny-Robin was not evil enough to be his servant. In an effort to find a logical explanation for his death in typical fantastic style, the narrator recounts that the miller's wife was young and pretty and enamored of the miller's young, brutish assistant. But Mouny-Robin treated his wife well, not wanting to waste energy jealousy or love that would be better spent on hunting. Local rumor concluded that the devil was the assassin: "il n'est aucun de nos paysans qui ne l'attribue encore aujourd'hui à une lutte avec l'esprit malin, le diable chasseur, le terrible Georgeon de la Vallée Noire [Not a single one of our folk does not to this day attribute it to a struggle with the evil spirit, the diabolical hunter, the horrible georgeon the Dark Valley]."[58]

An interesting narratological aspect of "Mouny-Robin" sees the restoration of the frame structure at the end. The narrator has been telling this parallel story during the performance of *Der Freyschütz*; meanwhile the interlocutor has fallen asleep. He awakens just in time to hear the finale of the opera, whereupon he asks for the end of the story. The narrator has begun rambling about other encounters, which has led him to believe in a secret divinity that endows some people with special gifts; he does not tell of the miller's demise. Sand shows us by this interruption in the embedded story that the myriad theories about "seconde vue" [sixth sense] become tiresome and the only recourse is to believe in them without all the while becoming superstitious. The return to music as the only "real" context adds a note of irony since it is thus in music that the narrator and his interlocutor find the stability of reality as opposed to the illusion of divinity or deviltry of Mouny-Robin's story.

In her *Légendes rustiques*, an essay on Berrichon culture, Sand offers the possible explanation that the devil felt Mouny-Robin was sharing too much of his knowledge with the narrator's brother, a *non-initié*, and sought revenge for that reason. The narrator prefers to believe that Mouny-Robin had another of his fits, lost his balance, and fell into the mill wheel.[59] This hesitation between a reasonable and a supernatural explanation characterizes the fantastic nature of the story. The musical side of the story relies on the reader's familiarity with *Der Freyschütz*, where similar events involving the devil (Samiel) and a shooting contest end in disaster. However, Max, the hero of Weber's opera, is spared thanks to the pleas of an old hermit. While there is no musical symbolism in Sand's story per se, the Weber reference reflects the musical culture of her readers, and the narrative parallels provide an intertextuality not unlike that in Balzac's *Gambara*. The opera-going, reading public is thus flattered, and a musical world external to the narrative is evoked.

"L'Orgue du titan" begins with a scene that suggests the intervention of the devil. When the piano string breaks, Angelin's hands pain him and he mutters, "Diable de titan, va!" [Infernal titan, be gone!] ("Orgue," 107). It is interesting that not music, but the malfunctioning of a musical instrument should serve as the catalyst for the pain as well as for the narration. In the rest of the story, music is the source of the action, from the avalanche to Angelin's pain, and even to Maître Jean's jealousy. But the devil is associated with the titan of the title and thus with music. The central event of the story, the thunderstorm and avalanche in the mountains of Auvergne, suggests the anger of Jupiter and symbolizes in a Judeo-Christian world the anger of God toward a human's attempt to wrest power in the guise of creating music. While not explicitly inspired by the devil, this act places Jean at odds with all that is good. Maître Jean compares himself to Jupiter when he declares, "Mais ne suis-je pas un titan, moi? Oui, j'en suis un, et, si un autre géant me dispute le droit de faire ici de la musique, qu'il se montre!" [But am I not a titan? Yes, I am, and if another giant wants to quarrel with me over the right to make music here, let him show his face!] ("Orgue," 119). As this challenge demonstrates, Jean's presumptuousness and lack of humility distinguish him from Angelin. But the association with God, the gods, or the devil remains unclear. Jean charges Angelin with diabolical association, "Vous souffliez l'orgue comme un beau diable!" [You were going at the organ like the devil!] ("Orgue," 122), which gives added significance to the off-handed exclamation, "Que diable chantes-tu là" [What the devil are you singing?] ("Orgue," 121). Paradoxically, Angelin's name recalls a heavenly protector rather than a devilish one.

Sand's apparent refusal to conclude that music finds its origins in a godly or a devilish source is another device of her musical fantastic. The hero and his music are clearly protected and inspired by the forces of good. If Jean's imprecations take on the name of the devil, they represent an old trick of Satan himself, knowing that the one thing that will wound his adversary is to call him a devil. Sand's musicians are still human beings, with human emotions and feelings. Angelin ends the tale by providing a rational explanation for his pain, stating that briars on the rocks were responsible for the initial pain. Yet, "Vous voyez, mes amis, que tout est symbolique dans mon histoire" [You see, friends, that everything in my story is symbolic] ("Orgue," 125). The pain of music symbolizes the artist's suffering, but what does the angry intervention of nature symbolize? Clearly, a powerful energy invoking the forces of nature intercedes in the relationship between Angelin and Maître Jean. In this disturbance, as much natural as supernatural, the triumph of good over evil surfaces in the form of Angelin's "divine" inspiration, his own music in the place of Jean's. Does not his very name suggest an angelic identification? It is his music that encourages the parish priest to promote Angelin to the status of apprentice organist and subsequently to send him to Paris for further instruction. Music is then both the means and the end of Sand's symbolic universe here.

Consuelo and Les Maîtres Sonneurs offer the most explicit references to the devil in relation to music. As these are not fantastic texts, I shall mention them here only briefly. Consuelo's first opera buffa is Galuppi's La Diavolessa, where the primary role is a crazed woman whose talent seems to be a gift of the devil. Porpora responds with amazement that displays both admiration and fear: "C'est toi qui es le diable en personne" [You're the one who's the devil incarnate] (C, 1:112). In Consuelo the devil's participation is most notable in the social and aesthetic discussions of the Bohemian section of the novel. While a Rosecrucian-type glorification of Satan permeates this portion of the novel, Sand is careful to point out the beneficial results of this relation with the devil. This part of Consuelo displays the eighteenth-century interest in superstition and illuminism. As in her approach to the fantastic, Sand does not miss a chance to inject a bit of humor.

Musical manifestations of the devil surround Albert's talent. The relationship between madness and genius, which Sand inherits from Pierre Leroux, can be seen again in "Carl" and in Adriani, as it was in Les Sept Cordes de la lyre.[60] In all cases, the real possibility of Satan's existence is felt through music, beautifully demonstrated in Consuelo in a scene in the grotto when Albert plays the violin. The devil speaks to Albert in this passage and in the following passage when he recites Church history to Consuelo, at which time she realizes he is not speaking at all but rather playing the violin.

The Orphic references in Consuelo beg a brief examination. While the multiple descents into Albert's grotto already suggest the allusion to the mythical musician, many other hints of Orphic influence or likeness exist. The narrator comments on Consuelo's state after one such descent with an explicit nod in this direction:

> Comme le héros fabuleux, Consuelo était descendue dans le Tartare pour en tirer son ami, et elle en avait rapporté l'épouvante et l'égarement. A son tour il s'efforça de la délivrer des sinistres hôtes qui l'avaient suivie, et il y parvint à force de soins délicats et de respect passionné. Ils recommençaient ensemble une vie nouvelle, appuyés l'un sur l'autre, n'osant guère regarder en arrière, et ne se sentant pas la force de se replonger par la pensée dans cet abîme, non moins mystérieux et terrible, qu'ils n'osaient pas interroger non plus. Mais le présent, comme un temps de grâce que le ciel leur accordait, se laissait doucement savourer. (*C*, 1:373)

> [Like the fabled hero, Consuelo had gone down into Tartar in an effort to summon her friend out of there, and she brought out horror and disorientation. In turn he endeavored to free her from the sinister occupants who had followed her, and he managed to do so by dint of his sensitive care and passionate respect. They started a new life together, leaning on each other, hardly daring to look back, and not feeling up to thinking of jumping back into this no less mysterious and terrible abyss, and neither daring to ask it any questions. But the present, like a moment of grace that heaven allowed them, suffered to be sweety savored.]

The signs of Orpheus and Eurydice are unmistakable, although the gender shifts are in flux. What is certain is the descent into hell and the resurfacing to a new life—not without concerns but with the firm determination not to look back. Music cannot be ignored in this reference to Orpheus, and the role of music in Consuelo's and Albert's recovery in these moments bears witness to the importance and the completeness of the allusion.

The diabolical nature of "cette musique curieuse" [this peculiar music] that emanates from Albert's violin as if speaking confirms the Orphic reference. Naturally mysterious, Albert and his music work their charms on Consuelo. When she hears his violin, she cannot resist the urge to dream and escape:

> et bientôt le son admirable de l'instrument lui chanta le psaume ancien qu'elle avait tant désiré écouter une seconde fois. La musique en était originale, et Albert l'exprimait avec un sentiment si pur et si large, qu'elle oublia toutes ses angoisses pour approcher doucement du lieu où il se trouvait, attirée et comme charmée par une puissance magnétique. (*C*, 1:402)

> [and soon the admirable sound of the instrument sang the ancient psalm that she'd so wanted to hear again. The music was inventive and Albert

expressed it with such a pure and open feeling that she forgot all her anxieties in coming here, drawn and almost enchanted by a magnetic force.]

Not only is this music original and not a Bohemian tune, it produces the effect of magnetism in the nineteenth-century sense evoked elsewhere in the novel. The devil's role in such matters, although indistinct, occupies an important place in the context of the other-worldly nature of music and of the human constitution and the meaning and functioning of the universe. I would liken Sand's use of the violin to what Brian Juden points out as the symbolism of the lyre as lyric idealism.[61]

Albert's explanation of the creation of Satan by priests and organized religion (chapter 54) brings us to a more explicit level of the discussion of deviltry and music. He tells Consuelo that good could not have created evil, God could not have created Satan. The Manichaean division of spirit and body into good and evil became the basis for allowing faith and superstition to coexist. Thus God and Satan remain rivals in the teachings of the Church instead of being integrated into a complete conception of the human condition. It is this speech that, Consuelo finally realizes, modulates from verbal language into music, thus establishing the link between Satan and music, between Orpheus and music. Music, like Satan, has long been wrongly associated with evil, and Albert's musical sermon brings Consuelo to a new level of understanding: of God, the universe, humanity, and music.

While it is true that Sand's use in *Jehan Cauvin* (1831) of the doctrine that idolizes Lucifer amalgamates Lollard, Hussite, and Taborite beliefs, she remains true to the concept of the rehabilitation of Satan/Lucifer in *Consuelo*, as seen throughout the novel in the phrase: "que celui à qui on a fait tort te salue" [may he who was done wrong hail you]. Her attempt to reconcile political and social revolt with religious aspirations, already evident in *Lélia*, resurfaces in *Consuelo* with the Rosicrucian principle, seen through Leroux's reading, of the rehabilitation of the material side of humanity. While Albert plays his violin in religious and metaphysical explanation of Satan, Consuelo imagines him "comme une belle figure pâle et douloureuse, sœur de celle du Christ, et doucement penchée vers elle, la fille du peuple et l'enfant proscrit de la famille universelle" [like a beautiful, pale, and painful face, akin to Christ's and gently bent toward her, the daughter of the people and the banished child of the universal family] (*C*, 1:413). Satan's rehabilitation, expressed here in music, thus becomes part of Sand's message to society.

Diabolical vocabulary abounds in *Les Maîtres Sonneurs*. Tiennet calls Joset's music "endiablée" [bedeviled] (*MS*, 99), "un sabbat de musique folle" [a sabbath of mad music] (*MS*, 100), "un sabbat de fous" [a sabbath of madmen] (*MS*, 116), and "une musique enragée" [fanatical music] (*MS*, 116). And the ending of the novel overtly evokes the possibility of Joset's having sold his soul to the devil in exchange for superior musical talent. Only Tiennet and other unnamed characters give any credence to these associations with the devil. But how else can one explain Joset's "uncanny" talent. The first manifestation of a devil figure occurs when Joset's bagpipes are delivered to him. The description of the man who brings them is ominous, "un homme bien vilain à voir, car il était noir de la tête aux pieds, mêmement sa figure et ses mains, et il avait derrière lui deux grands chiens noirs comme lui" [a man quite nasty to look at, because he was black from head to toe, even his face and hands, and behind him there were two big dogs as black as he] (*MS*, 122). The black that covers the man, as we will discover, comes from the soot and dirt of the woodsmen's hard work, also from a tradition of blackening their faces so as not to be distinguishable and thus to hide their identity. But black is clearly associated with the devil. In addition, Sand's fictional people of Berry despise the Bourbonnais woodsmen and mistrust their motives. Therefore, be he Satan or a Bourbonnais woodsman, he is to be feared. Despite Joset's insistence on having received the pipes from "le bon Dieu" [the good Lord] (*MS*, 123), the sight of the soot-covered man will permeate the story. It is not coincidental that Huriel's dog's name is Satan. The entire initiation episode is replete with references to the devil, wherein the "musique d'enragés" [music of fanatics] (*MS*, 473) clearly represents the devil's influence. The initiation then introduces a costumed "devil" who demands Joset's soul, but Joset refuses: "Qu'est-ce qu'un diable aussi sot que vous ferait de l'âme d'un musicien?" [What would a devil as silly as you do with a musician's soul?] (*MS*, 476). A fight ensues wherein Joset defends himself with only his fists against the "devil," who is armed with blades. Huriel and Bastien now step out of hiding and put a stop to the bloody ceremony. The ceremony is ended.

One other important scene evokes the role of the devil, Joset's death. Le Grand-Bûcheux finds Joset's body in the frozen water without any sign of violence, his bagpipes broken and lying around him. It was not a dangerous area; peasants here fear only the devil (*MS*, 495–96): "Ils croient fermement en ce pays, ce que l'on croit un peu dans celui-ci, à savoir: qu'on ne peut devenir musicien sans vendre son âme à l'enfer, et qu'un jour ou l'autre, Satan arrache la musette des mains du sonneur et la lui brise sur le dos, ce qui l'égare, le rend fou et le pousse à se détruire" [In that area they firmly believe what folks here also kind of believe, that you can't become a musician without selling your soul to the devil, and that one day or another, Satan will wrench your bagpipes from your hands and break them over your back, making you dazed, mad, and pushing you to kill yourself]. The rough-and-tumble bagpipers, who often get into scuffles, regularly blame the devil for their ills and wounds. But the lack of bruises and the like on Joset's body suggests rather a solitary mishap. Suicide is indeed the cause of death, but the devil is never far off.

This scene has been adumbrated throughout the novel. The multiple references to music as the devil's tool prepare the reader for this equivocal ending. One last time we contemplate Sand's position on music and the devil. Clearly she is mocking the superstition of the devil's role in music making. Still, the myriad recurrences of the devil in association with music give pause. The uncharacteristically whimsical nature of this ruse, which asks the reader to reject superstition but not to dismiss readily the possibility of a superior power, does not differ significantly from Sand's inclusion of superstition in commentary on religion in *Jeanne* and other rustic novels and in essays on Berrichon life. The import of such tolerance and open-mindedness to music remains general: we must be nonrestrictive in matters of music no matter what the origin, all the while recognizing that the mysteries of this "langage divin" belong to a superior order.

In *Malgrétout*, the devil's influence in the violinist's talent is frequently evoked. "Je crois bien que le démon s'en mêla, car je fus tout à coup prise du besoin de bien exprimer ma pensée musicale. . . . Je chantai comme je crois n'avoir jamais su chanter avant ce jour-là" [I truly believe that the devil was mixed up in this, because all of a sudden I was seized by the need to express my thoughts in music. . . . I sang as I'd never sung before] (*M*, 37). The role of the devil in music is explained further on by the insistence on Sarah's devotion to reason as opposed to the hold passion has on Abel.

The devil thus provides Sand with an ambiguous construct in which to hide the unknown origins of music. Good or evil, God or Satan, music has a power that we assign to a superhuman potency, of one dimension or another and often both at once. Not an antithesis, this entity represents rather a willful concatenation of powers beyond our domain, which touch us from time to time and to which we must remain responsive. Can the question of origin be answered for music and the arts? Sand says no, but that we must always be sure to trust in the power of music and to receive and to produce it when we are called upon to do so. This calling is lost if it falls on deaf ears; our task as humans is to be open and receptive to the call of music, no matter where it comes from.

♫ ♫ ♫

Sand's purpose in using the fantastic genre is largely to create an atmosphere of doubt and ambiguity, wherein music guides us through the maze of confusion. The melding together of illusion and reality parallels that of good and evil as well as music and non-music. Thanks to music, Sand's fantastic characters are often lost and cannot distinguish between dream and reality. Yet at the same time, through music they find their way to accepting if not explaining a power beyond human understanding. Paradoxically, the fantastic does not advance a definition of music nor an understanding of the origins or purpose of music. Sand is little troubled by these problems, which is to say she introduces them and discusses them, but she eschews serving up facile conclusions. The nebulous nature of the fantastic represents for Sand the intangibility of music.

If Sand was drawn to the fantastic genre, some device must link the uncanny to music in her mind. While not all of her writings on music fall into the fantastic, all her fantastic tales, save two from *Les Contes d'une grand'mère*, deal with music. More than just an emulation of Hoffmann, Sand's fantastic is sensitive and humanistic. The Berrichon author focuses on the marginalization of the artist. What better genre in which to portray an outcast than the fantastic?

5

♫♫ Folk Music ♫♫

Le Berry a sa musique, mais il n'a pas sa littérature.

[Berry has its own music, but not its own literature.]
—*Les Visions de la nuit dans les campagnes*

THAT FOLK CULTURE OCCUPIES AN IMPORTANT PLACE IN GEORGE Sand's work surprises no one. Anecdotal material as well as autobiographical testimony exist to highlight Sand's participation in regional fetes and her lively defense of the people of Nohant, La Châtre, and "la vallée noire" [the dark valley]. She determined to acquaint her readers with her region through setting, dialect, and authentic Berrichon music in her novels and stories as well as for the Paris production of her rustic stage plays. Most persuasive are the uses of folk music to define social roles and relationships of characters. In this chapter I shall examine the function of folk music insofar as it shapes the reader's opinions about the provinces and Berry in particular, about traditional music, and about egalitarianism.

Music and poetry always intermingled in the Greek tradition as well as in the tradition of the troubadours and *trouvères* of France in the Middle Ages.[1] As interest in troubadour poetry and music grew during the romantic age, even though research remained naive; attention also turned to regional poetry and music within contemporary France. Sand joins this tradition in the spirit of a troubadour, with the important difference that her mission is to inform and enlighten the general public about the nature and value of folk culture. In the aftermath of the 1789 Revolution, attempts on the part of academics, artists, and politicians to preserve and encourage regional art display at once the nationalist tendencies of the early to mid-nineteenth century and the socialist efforts to valorize the common people. It is hardly surprising that Sand's readers found her use of folk music provocative and revealing.

235

There were several ventures in nineteenth- and early twentieth-century France to record and preserve folk music. Frederick Chopin failed to complete his notations of Berrichon folk tunes, but others, including Pauline Viardot, were able to preserve some of these melodies. Of note are Charles Nisard's *Des chansons populaires chez les anciens et chez les français* (1867); Julien Tiersot's *La Chanson populaire et les écrivains romantiques* (1931); André Cœuroy's *La Musique et le peuple en France* (1941); Joseph Canteloube's *Anthologie des chants populaires français, groupés et presentés par pays ou provinces* (1951); and Léon Guichard's *La Musique et les lettres au temps du romantisme* (1955). We should include in this list the resourceful work of Marie-Louise Vincent, *Le Berry dans l'œuvre de George Sand* (1919), especially volume two, *George Sand et le Berry*. These studies not only make valuable information available but they also demonstrate the conservation efforts of folklorists over a considerable period.

Nisard traces the folk song by genre: love songs, drinking songs, historical songs, trade songs, war songs. He draws conclusions based on vocabulary and subject matter rather than merely listing titles or incipits. His conclusions remain rather general and often self-evident. Tiersot searches in nineteenth-century literature for evidence of folk music. In his section on Sand he refers to the authenticity of the songs and their notation by Pauline Viardot. Cœuroy presents a more sensitive commentary on the nature of folk music, both vocal and instrumental. He also makes several references to Sand's familiarity with Berrichon music although he restricts himself to the commonplaces of a primitive relationship to nature and the expression of such an essence in music. Canteloube has amassed a rich collection of folk tunes with interesting and pertinent commentary valuable to any ethnomusicological study. Guichard provides an in-depth survey of the artistic scene in early nineteenth-century France, singling out Sand's rustic novels as exemplary in blending folk music and narrative. Vincent's collection and commentary focus on Sand and provide a wealth of information. Of further interest is Max Milner's more general study, *Le Romantisme, 1820–1843* (1973), where he counts Sand among the writers who have contributed extensively to folk culture. Another important source of information and methodology is to be found in Paul Bénichou's *Nerval et la chanson folklorique* (1970). Bénichou discusses the folk song in the works of several romantic authors. Sadly, his comments on Sand amount to a listing of titles plus some poetical and musical variants.

Sand considerably advanced the notion of preserving folk culture by bringing it to the attention of Parisian readers. Sand notes in "Les Visions de la nuit dans les campagnes" that France's provinces are replete with fantastic tales that no one has noted. Only Brittany has been the subject of study, the famous *Baraz-Breiz* by M. de la Villemarqué (1839). She recognizes several of the ballads cited by Villemarqué as existing also in Berry. She reflects on the manner of the songs' transmission, underscoring the tendency of illiterate minstrels to "corrupt" a text and change it as they pass it on to others. Sand thus witnesses the blossoming of ethnography and ethnomusicology and its application to the culture of the French provinces.[2]

Of particular interest in the realm of Sand and folk music is the generation of the myth of the "sonneurs" [bagpipers] after the publication of *Les Maîtres Sonneurs*. Gérard Guillaume affirms that the spirit of Sand as well as that of her fictional characters lives on in current-day traditional music circles in Berry. Since its founding in 1888, the "Gars du Berry" has been organized by ranking candidates following public admission tests, similar to the process portrayed in Sand's novel. Similarly the "Réunions internationales des luthiers et maîtres sonneurs de St. Chartier" (founded in 1976) always gather before the Aimé Millet statue of Sand in the center of La Châtre before their annual meeting. Deliberations on the contests are held at a local café, the "café Langlois" since the "Bœuf couronné" from Sand's novel no longer exists.[3]

Sand's contribution to the understanding of the social and ethnological functions of folk music are at best fictionalized versions of reality. But Sand was writing fiction. She never claimed otherwise, and her works must be understood as such. Far more important than a historical account of the state of bagpipers in Berry and Bourbonnais in the late eighteenth century are the themes of social intercourse among factions of a community, no matter how small. Among others, Sand explores the interplay between producers and consumers of music, whether folk or academic; the question of the individual musician versus the culture of traditional folk music; and the intertwining of all these themes in a complex network of love plots that is nourished by the musical backdrop.

THE RUSTIC NOVELS

The assignment of the term "rustic" to the novels Sand wrote in the 1840s, all of which take place in Berry and represent the Berrichon peasantry,[4] presents an easy categorization and can be found

in most treatments of Sand's work, from school manuals to schol-
arly studies. However, Sandists do not always agree which novels
should be classed under the rubric. A core of three novels whose
rustic nature cannot be and is never disputed firmly establishes at
least a preliminary corpus: *La Mare au diable* (1846), *François le
champi* (1847), and *La Petite Fadette* (1848). To this trio, which at
one point Sand intended to group under the umbrella title "Veillées
du chanvreur" [the hemp worker's evening tales], critics often add
Jeanne (1844) and *Les Maîtres Sonneurs* (1853). Marie-Claire
Brancquart also includes *Mauprat* (1837) as well as Sand's theatrical rewrite of that novel in 1853, which constitutes a neat circle.[5]
For my purposes, I shall focus on the three kernel texts and *Les
Maîtres Sonneurs,* with some brief comments on other texts.

During the last years of the July Monarchy, Sand spends increasingly more time at Nohant. Proud of her attachment to the soil and
fond of the locus and people of her childhood, Sand undertakes to
introduce her beloved province to the French literary world. It is
significant that she chooses this route to express her thoughts at a
time when the state of the French nation seems to be in flux. Critics
have recently begun to uncover some of the political subterfuge in
the rustic novels, which had heretofore been considered to represent
merely Sand's refuge and retirement from political thought. Nothing could be further from the truth, as attested by the heavy undercurrent of social commentary in these novels.[6]

Self-conscious transmission of folklore—not exactly "transmission" in the sense that folklorists use it, but the representation of
regional culture to Parisian readers—defines Sand's overt goal for
her rustic novels. From the nostalgic style of Chateaubriand's,
Hugo's, and Balzac's provincial settings, intended to evoke scenes
of their youth, Sand modulates the genre into the apotheosis of the
fin laboureur (excellent farm worker) and the courageous women
who indefatigably perform innumerable tasks and perpetuate the
soul of the peasant. Sand carefully presents all aspects of rural life:
setting, artefacts, clothing, work, leisure, dialect, dance, and song.
For her, folk culture defines Berry much as Berry defines the people
of France. Sand refers to Berry as "le centre de la France," by
which she signals not only its geographic location but also the sociological and demographic representativeness of the French people. Her intention is to share an understanding of the multiplicity of
the French people with those planning for the restructuring of
France. The peasants who populate these novels lead simple lives
and have little contact with the upper classes. They exist happily
among themselves, far from the political concerns of Paris. The

economic and social matters that concern Sand's Berrichon characters affect their lives directly, but on a local scale. Sand's treatment
of these issues, however, reflects her position concerning French society as a whole.

Language naturally plays an important role in transmitting folk
culture to Sand's readers. However, local Berrichon dialect, with its
indigenous vocabulary, grammar, and syntax, would be incomprehensible to the Parisian reader. In the preface to *François le champi*
Sand explains the problem of legibility versus authenticity. Sand's
friend François Rollinat offers a way to achieve communication,
"Raconte-moi [l'histoire du champi] comme si tu avais à ta droite
un Parisien parlant la langue moderne, et à ta gauche un paysan
devant lequel tu ne voudrais pas dire une phrase, un mot où il ne
pourrait pas pénétrer. Ainsi tu dois parler clairement pour le Parisien, naïvement pour le paysan" [Tell me the waif's story as though
you had a Parisian who speaks modern French on your right and on
your left a peasant to whom you wouldn't want to say a single sentence, a single word that he couldn't understand. That way, you'll
speak clearly for the Parisian and plainly for the peasant,"] (*FC*,
217). In so doing, Sand manages to combine standard French with
a rich sprinkling of Berrichon vocabulary and syntax without confusion or pretension. This is her most successful use of dialectal
language. Several critics have investigated the dialectal innovations
of Sand, although much remains to be said.[7]

In contemporary nineteenth-century literature seeking to represent provincial or rural life, the narrator would ordinarily be a Parisian who befriends a "local" to serve as a source of information
about important sociological phenomena. We observe this narratological device for Balzac's Touraine, Flaubert's Normandy, and
Zola's Provence. Sand's version, with provincials discussing differences among themselves, demonstrates not only that provincials are
different from Parisians, but that there are also differences among
provincials. The absence of any mention of Paris in these texts emphasizes Sand's innovation in this device, removing it entirely from
the realm, that is, the control, of the Parisian to that of provincials
and holding it up for Parisians to observe and not to judge. Music
provides the medium for this comparison in *Les Maîtres Sonneurs*.

Sand insists that language, in the conventional, Parisian—read
"artificial"—sense, remains inadequate for relating folk culture,
which is instinctual and natural. In the dialogue with Rollinat, she
specifies that "[l]es chansons, les récits, les contes rustiques, peignent en peu de mots ce que notre littérature ne sait qu'amplifier et
déguiser" [songs, stories, country tales paint in a few words what

our literature only knows how to elaborate and disguise] (*FC*, 211). Rollinat replies, "Et la musique donc! N'avons-nous pas dans notre pays des mélodies admirables?" [And what about music? Don't we have delightful melodies in our region?] (*FC*, 211–12). He refers to traditional tunes folklorists call *briolages*.

Music has a linguistic as well as a sociological and historical function in the rustic novels. Sand uses it to depict a slice of peasant life. For example, in *Jeanne* the druidic stones seem to sing. The parish priest explains that when the wind blows just right, the "pierres jaumâtres," so precariously positioned atop each other, tremble and emit a grating sound that is not without a certain charm. It is attributed by local legend to the mysterious voice of the idol of Memnon at sun break.[8] The stones of the druidic rituals are called *jo-mathr*, meaning "to cut, to mutilate, to cause to bleed and suffer." One stone, however, known as the *Ep-Nell*, a Gallic word meaning "headless," represents the ancient and free cult of the region, as opposed to the reigning and despotic druids. The pleasant and harmonious sounds of the Ep-Nell are continuous, and legend has it that a spirit residing within tells the past and predicts the future, all the while bemoaning the present (*J*, 87). The sociopolitical commentary is clear.

Two aspects of musical communication emerge from this passage that can be found in other Sand texts: first, the pleasant and calming effect of the music that the democratic stone emits as opposed to the harsh sounds of the despotic stones. Music in this perspective conveys an essential notion of antithesis—good and evil, society and individual, democracy and monarchy. Not merely a quaint rendition of the superstitious realm of the peasantry, Sand's message is to be understood as a general reflection of mid-nineteenth-century French society and its politico-religious vacillations.

The second aspect of the singing stones that warrants consideration pertains to the mystical ability of an inanimate body to produce music that can at once recount history and predict the future. One cannot forget that the rustic novels originate during the period just before and just after the events of 1848. Sand used another inanimate object to communicate through music the power of love and a critique of the coming industrial age, the lyre in *Les Sept Cordes de la lyre* (1839). That the Ep-Nell can not only generate sounds construed as music but also impart mystical knowledge clearly announces Sand's notion that nature has a message for us and that we must listen closely in order to apprehend it. This is the most important form of communication, yet one that remains difficult to perceive and therefore difficult to describe and relate. Peasants are typically more gifted at hearing and understanding (*entendre* in both senses) than Parisians, a notion Sand exploits fully in the rustic novels.

Musical stones that move and sing, and a lyre suggest references to mythology. Amphion is said to have used his musical talents to move stones into place to build the city walls of Thebes. And the allusion to the enchanting powers of Orpheus's lyre does not escape the attention of the reader of Sand's 1839 *roman dialogué*. Sand does not often use explicit mythological references, but when she does, the effects are usually strikingly transparent.[9]

From a sociological perspective, Sand uses music to depict the daily lives of her peasants. In *La Mare au diable* we see a typical use of folk music, the song of the farmer working the fields. The farmer's song, *le chant du laboureur*, fits into one of the classic categories of folk songs, *les chants de métier* (trade songs), and clearly portrays Berrichon daily life and struggles.[10] Using a Holbein engraving as her point of departure, Sand announces in the opening chapter, entitled "L'Auteur au lecteur" [From the author to the reader], that contrary to a trend in contemporary fiction, she intends to depict a hopeful, optimistic view of the life of simple folk. Enough portrayals already exist of the misery of the working people and their supposed welcoming of death as a relief from their burdens. She prefers to advance a sanguine and cheerful view of life: "L'art n'est pas une étude de la réalité positive; c'est une recherche de la vérité idéale" [Art is not a study of positive reality; it's an inquiry into ideal truth] (*MD*, 12). And music as it echoes the rhythm of the farmer working his fields displays, for Sand, the joy and calm of peasant life.

One cannot ignore Sand's article on realism, published fewer than ten years later as a favorable review of *Madame Bovary*. She comments on Champfleury's attitudes toward realism, calling him insincere and hypocritical. The goals declared by the realist school to which Sand did subscribe, namely naturalism and honest ugliness, have already been exploited and attained, she says, by the romantics. She regrets the realists' attempts to force a certain "realist" vocabulary and ethos, positing that each author is free to write in the manner she or he deems appropriate as long as she or he is capable of doing it well.[11] Needless to say, Sand and Flaubert did not agree on the goals and practice of realism.

Thus Sand develops her own style of realism mixed with idealism. In *La Mare au diable* she extols the art of the singing farmer: "la voix mâle de ce jeune père de famille entonnait le chant solennel et mélancolique que l'antique tradition du pays transmet, non à tous les laboureurs indistinctement, mais aux plus consommés dans l'art d'exciter et de soutenir l'ardeur des bœufs de travail" [the masculine voice of this young father launches into the solemn and melancholy song the age-old tradition of the region transmits not indiscriminately to all farmers but to those who are the most consummate in the art of stimulating and maintaining the oxen's zeal] (*MD*, 20). Not only is the artistic beauty of the song and the voice a subject of admiration, but the qualities of a good singer are associated with those of a good farmer: "on n'est point un parfait laboureur si on ne sait chanter aux bœufs, et c'est là une science à part qui exige un goût et des moyens particuliers" [you can't be a good farmer if you can't sing for the oxen; that's a science in itself that requires taste and specific resources] (*MD*, 21).

Notwithstanding the difficulties of describing music in general and folk music in particular, Sand undertakes to detail the farmer's song. She calls it a sort of recitative that the farmer interrupts and continues freely. Tiersot remarks that from a formal perspective, the *briolage* is less a song than an improvisation, with certain definable formulae that are never twice the same.[12] Sand points out this "irregularity" as mirroring the farmer's work, the oxen's awkward gait, and the calm of the countryside's rolling but uneven topography. Further privileging the singing farmer, she continues to say that none other than a *fin laboureur* from this region could possibly replicate the musical aspect of the process.

Sand discerns a strange tonality in the peasant's song, one that conventional musical tastes of her time would deem not only dissonant but erroneous. She suggests that the singer uses quarter tones, which makes it impossible to notate using traditional Western methods of musical notation. But while these sounds may at first surprise the non-initiated listener (read non-provincial or non-Berrichon), she continues, one soon becomes accustomed to them, and they define this music to a degree where their absence would disturb the harmony (*MD*, 22). By "harmony" Sand surely refers to the balanced beauty of nature, but the allusion to music is indisputable. Such use of musical metaphors is not uncommon for romantic authors, but Sand manages to weave musical figures into her prose so naturally that the mixture of expressions is seamless.

Various references to the mysteries and beauty of folk music can be found in Sand's works. In *Jeanne* a deceased friend is remembered by the song he used to sing, which old lady Guite reproduces: "La vieille se mit à chanter d'une voix chevrotante en mineur, et sur une mélodie très remarquable, une de ces chansons bourbonnaises dont la musique mériterait bien d'être recueillie, s'il était

possible de le faire sans en altérer la grâce et l'originalité" [In a
shaky voice, the old woman began to sing in a minor key a very
exceptional melody, one of those Bourbonnais songs whose music
should be compiled if it were possible to do it without changing the
grace and originality] (*J*, 54). Reference to Chopin's inability to
note down Berrichon music as well as the general denunciation of
standard music notation systems is again evident as well as the distinction between Berry and Bourbonnais, which a Parisian reader
would, according to Sand, tend to lump together as provincial. She
will pursue this distinction in *Les Maîtres Sonneurs*.

A similar reference is found in *La Daniella* when a washer
woman is observed working and singing. An allusion to the Berrichon legend of *lavandière de nuit* (nocturnal washer women) is
made explicit. Here she sings

> quelque chose d'inouï, avec une voix haute, nasillarde et plaintive, dans
> un patois. . . . J'aurais été désolé que Tartaglia me traduisît le reste ou
> qu'il m'apprît quel était ce dialecte. On sent en soi le besoin de respecter
> les mystères de certaines sensations. . . . J'aurais bien défié le plus
> habile musicien de noter ce que chantait la sibylle. Cela n'avait aucun
> rythyme, aucune tonalité appréciables d'après nos règles musicales. Et
> cependant elle ne chantait pas au hasard, elle ne chantait pas faux selon
> sa méthode. (*LD*, 1:106)

> [something never before heard, in a high, nasal, and plaintive voice, and
> in some dialect. . . . I would have been disillusioned if Tartaglia had
> translated it or had told me what dialect it was. You can feel the need to
> respect the mysteries of particular feelings. . . . I would have challenged
> the most skilled musician to note down what the sybil was singing.
> There was no perceptible rhythm or key, at least in terms of our musical
> rules. And yet she did not sing randomly, nor did she sing out of tune
> according to her technique.]

Again Sand underscores the importance of admitting the difference
between folk music and academic music, the impossibility of standard notation systems to represent the former adequately, and the
inestimable gift of the folk musician that cannot be likened to the
"artists" of the Paris stage.

Sand returns to the farmer's song in the preface to *La Petite Fadette*, discussing in particular the inspiration that emerges from the
act of listening to music. Calling the song a recitative and an improvisation, Sand likens it to a reverie about nature where the union of
farmer and earth produces a mysterious formula in musical form.
The music causes the author to muse on a concept of poetry that
supersedes the conventional one of originating in the human voice,

"une harmonie bienfaisante qui pénétrera vos âmes d'un religieux soulagement" [a beneficial harmony that will permeate your souls with reglious comfort].[13] Sand again marries music with nature, positing a union that assuredly creates a "langage furtif" [a transient language] that can lift one's soul away the cruel yoke of humanity. This natural language is the common possession of all people, and the simple often appreciate it more than the cultured. Not surprisingly, Sand's frequent admixture of music and nature provides a plethora of metaphors. In her 1848 essay "À propos de *la Petite Fadette*," Sand states, "J'écoutai le récitatif du laboureur, entrecoupé de longs silences, j'admirai la variété infinie que le grave caprice de son improvisation imposait au vieux thème sacramental. C'était comme une rêverie de la nature elle-même, ou comme une mystérieuse formule par laquelle la terre proclamait chaque phrase de l'union de sa force avec le travail de l'homme" [I listened to the farmer's recitative, disrupted by long moments of silence; I admired the infinite variety that the serious whim of his improvisation imposed on the old, ritual theme. It was like a daydream of nature itself or like a mysterious formula by which the earth announced each phrase of the union of its power with the man's work].[14] Sand demonstrates not only her fascination with the farmer's work song but also her firm belief that music from the "peuple" remains closer to nature, which in turn speaks to us through that music.[15]

The end of *La Mare au diable* offers another glimpse of the sociological function of music in the rustic novels. Sand describes a typical Berrichon wedding ceremony, which the reader may or may not take to be that of the protagonists, Germain and Marie. Fiction and documentary combine in this appended text to provide an incomparable example of Sand's determination to bring a worthy, albeit romanticized, view of rural life to the urban reader. As one might expect, music abounds in the depiction of the festivities, which begin with a march the day before the ceremony:

[V]ers deux heures de l'après-midi, la musique arriva, c'est-à-dire le *cornemuseux* et le *vielleux*, avec leurs instruments ornés de longs rubans flottants, et jouant une marche de circonstance, sur un rythme un peu lent pour des pieds qui ne seraient pas indigènes, mais parfaitement combiné avec la nature du terrain gras et des chemins ondulés de la contrée. (*MD*, 135)

[About two o'clock in the afternoon the the music arrived, which is to say the bagpiper and the vielle player, with their instruments decorated with long, flowing ribbons, playing a march befitting the occasion on a rhythm that would be a little slow for the feet of strangers to the area, but perfectly suited to the nature of the lush terrain of the uneven paths of the region.]

The personification of music evokes an active and lively image of the musical component of the ceremony, made more vivid by a description of the adorned instruments. Of particular interest is Sand's commentary on rhythm, which she judges rather slow for outsiders (no doubt the Parisian reader) but in perfect accord with the area's hilly terrain and thus well suited to Berrichon peasants.[16]

The ritual of the *livrées,* or wedding gifts, enjoys an acutely musical description. As the groom's envoys approach the bride's house, they are accompanied by "des chants, des rires et le son des instruments rustiques" [songs, laughter, and the sound of rustic instruments] (*MD*, 142). Sand insists not only on the central role of music, but also on the uniqueness of regional instruments less familiar in Parisian concert halls. The bride's party imposes a trial on the groom's: they must sing a local song, "mais chantez une chanson que nous ne connaissons pas, et à laquelle nous ne puissions pas répondre par une meilleure" [but sing a song that we don't know so that we won't be able to come back with a better one] (*MD*, 150). Thereupon follows a series of songs, of which Sand provides only the first line or two. While it is her habit in similar contexts to give only the incipit, this technique is heightened here by the challengers' constant interruptions as they are keen to prove they already know each example. As both sides possess an impressive familiarity with the repertory of local songs, the contest lasts over an hour and shows no sign of concluding. The bride's party agrees to a truce on the condition that the groom offer her a worthy gift; "alors commença le chant des livrées sur un air solennel comme un chant d'église" [then the wedding gift song started with a tune as solemn as a church song] (*MD*, 152). Again a series of offers and refusals extends the ritual, ending with "un beau mari qui vient vous chercher" [a handsome husband is coming for you] (*MD*, 153).

This last song marks an important point of the ceremony and provokes two comments. The solemn nature of the song recalls a church hymn, thus the religious nature of the ceremony is underscored by the ritual and regional music. In addition, the anticipation and hesitation that characterize both this song and the game of the previous musical challenge point to the long preparation of marriage ceremonies in the provinces and the importance of these events in the lives of a whole village. This aspect of the ritual clearly parallels the anticipation of the wedding night, also a matter of interest to the entire community.

After several more challenges, the ceremony proper finally begins with a cortege of minstrels playing a wedding march. Then on the third day of the marriage celebrations, the ritual of the cabbage, a Gallic symbol of fertility, answers the need to retain certain aspects of paganism. The newlyweds are impersonated by two of the wedding party, dressed as *jardinier et jardinière* (male and female gardners) and accompanied by music, barking dogs, laughing children, and pistol shots. The pantomime consists of hiding and seeking the cabbage, symbolizing an active effort in the hope of progeny. The celebration ends in music and dancing: "On entendait au loin les chants des jeunes garçons des paroisses voisines, qui . . . redisaient d'une voix un peu enrouée les refrains joyeux de la vielle" [In the distance we heard young boys from the neighboring parishes singing, and with hoarse voices they restated the vielle's joyous refrains] (*MD,* 175). Thus song not only announces and accompanies the ceremony, it also serves afterwards to recall the joys of the celebrations, fixing them in the villagers' collective memory. One notes the now-common Sandian use of the verb *(re)dire* (to restate) for singing, underscoring her notion of music as language. The presence of music at a wedding celebration is not unique to the Berrichon tradition. What makes the musical aspect of Sand's description noteworthy is that she accentuates the insistence on music at each turn of the festivities and incorporates it into the narrative rather than leaving it as an accompaniment.

Sand appeals to contemporary readers by invoking general knowledge about popular music. In the prologue to *Jeanne,* she introduces the name of Béranger along with that of Chateaubriand in a comparison to the druidess Velléda. Léon Marsillat, the bourgeois attorney in the novel, prefers the Parisian street poet to both the Breton writer and the Berrichon mystic, whereas the aristocrat Guillaume de Boussac finds that Béranger keeps questionable company. He asks for the opinion of the Englishman Sir Arthur, who pronounces both Chateaubriand and Béranger to be of equal stature and assures his friends that the two will one day shake hands. It is noteworthy that it is the outsider who sees the equal value of the two widely different poets. When Marsillat sings the well-known Béranger tune, "Quoi, Lisette, est-ce vous?", he is at once extolling Béranger's art and appealing to the Parisian's sense of contemporary culture.[17] At the same time he announces his own predilection for stories of easy love. It is significant that he interrupts himself singing this glorification of a courtesan as he discovers the sleeping, virginal eponymous heroine.

Guillaume Boussac compares folk music with Chateaubriand again when he reminisces about his upbringing by Jeanne's grandmother. His memories are echoed by those of an elderly peasant couple, who also sing familiar Berrichon folk songs. Boussac remembers that his nursemaid, his mother for all practical purposes, sang thousands of songs and told thousands of stories, all of which activated his dreams. This is, in fact, his first language. Thus Guillaume Boussac, the aristocrat who is destined to fall in love with the heroine, recognizes his links to her mostly through peasant song.

Dance, being dependent on music, introduces a tangential category of interest to my topic. The bourrée is the traditional dance in the mid-nineteenth century in the regions of central France, specifically in Auvergne and Berry. In the eighteenth and nineteenth centuries, music for the bourrée is usually provided by bagpipes, but in its absence the music can be sung. Jeanne sings so that the other girls at the manor may dance. While Jeanne sings, Claudie, a chambermaid, teaches Elvire de Boussac and Marie de Charmois to dance the bourrée. With this characteristic mixing of classes Sand makes a familiar social statement through music and dance.

In *La Petite Fadette* the role of the bourrée is central to the turning point of the plot. After Fadette has twice helped Landry out of a difficult situation, he is grateful and promises to repay her in any manner she should prescribe. Fadette extracts from him the pledge to dance with her at the feast of Sainte Andoche, the patron saint of Berry: "Vous me ferez danser trois bourrées après la messe, deux bourrées après vêpres, et encore deux bourrées après l'Angélus, ce qui fera sept" [You'll dance three bourrées with me after mass, two after vespers, and two more after angelus, which makes seven] (*PF*, 115). One notes in this oath not only the close attachment to religious rites that also serve as times of the day, but also the magical and biblical number seven. In an addendum to the oath Fadette makes Landry promise to dance with no one else. This double commitment yields a dual effect. Not only is Landry ridiculed for dancing with the ugliest and most ill-kempt girl of the village (she is often referred to as a cricket because she is dirty and awkward), but he is also forbidden to dance with Madelon, the girl he fancies. He learns from the experience that the mockery of the village adolescents is largely unwarranted. Fadette is an excellent dancer, and in a certain way she is not so ugly, especially as she made an effort to clean up and dress more appropriately for the festival. He learns further that the attentions of Madelon are not so estimable since her reaction to his dancing with Fadette proves her to be a jealous and ungenerous flirt.

A talented dancer, Fadette demonstrates her heretofore hidden abilities in a social situation: "le grelet commença à sautiller avec tant d'orgueil et de prestesse, que jamais bourrée ne fut mieux marquée ni mieux enlevée; . . . elle dansait par merveille" [the cricket started to hop with such pride and nimbleness, never had a bourrée been more vigorous or more lively; . . . she danced marvelously] (*PF* 119). As if the taunting of the other adolescents were not enough, Landry must also bear the remonstrances of his twin brother, Sylvinet: "J'ai toujours dit que tu aimais trop la danse, et que cela te ferait faire des choses sans raison" [I've always said you liked dancing too much and that it would make you do unreasonable things] (*PF,* 129). Sylvinet's remark shows not only his disapproval of Landry's dancing with Fadette, but of his dancing at all. Sylvinet does not dance well, certainly a lack of practice but also a sign of his paucity in matters of the artistic soul. But the principal reason he admonishes Landry about his dancing is that it is an activity he cannot share with him. The fear that Fadette will take his twin away from him characterizes Sylvinet's actions throughout the novel.

Once Landry and Fadette have come to an agreement about their relationship, wherein they love each other but have agreed not to let it generally be known, Landry regrets not being able to dance with her more. In a scene where Sylvinet eavesdrops,[18] Landry tries to urge Fadette to dance with him. She refuses because she wants to avoid gossip. The playful argument continues until Landry brings up the subject of the traditional kiss that begins the bourrée. Landry rebuts Fadette's sincere encouragement that he go ahead and dance since he seems to miss it so much:

> —[J]'aimerais mieux me faire couper les deux jambes que de danser avec des filles que je n'aime point, et que je n'embrasserais pas pour cent francs.
> —Eh bien! si je dansais, reprit la Fadette, il me faudrait danser avec d'autres qu'avec toi, et me laisser embrasser aussi.
> —Va-t'en, va-t'en bien vitement, dit Landry; je ne veux point qu'on t'embrasse. (*PF,* 195)

> ["I'd rather cut off both my legs than dance with girls I don't like and that I wouldn't kiss for a hundred francs." "Well, if I did dance," retorted Fadette, "I'd have to dance with others besides you and let them kiss me too." "Get going then, go on, right now," said Landry; "I don't want anyone to kiss you."]

From a lighthearted discussion about dancing, the conversation devolves into an argument about possessiveness. The innocent and ritualistic kiss that traditionally marks the beginning of the bourrée now takes on a more important significance, one that will require Landry and Fadette to better define their relationship, especially insofar as how they will approach public disclosure. Sand thus uses a cultural-artistic convention as a pivotal point in a private conversation that at the same time has wide-reaching social repercussions.[19]

From bourrée kisses it is a short leap to the sexual resonances of music. Once Landry agrees to Fadette's command of seven bourrées, he begins to reflect on the possible reactions of others to such an action. The promise of dancing with her does not bother him since he knows Fadette to be a good dancer. Rather it is her appearance that causes him to flinch. He perceives her as ugly because this is the received opinion. He is also intimidated by her because, though a girl, she is superior to him in several ways traditionally the domain of boys; this is especially evident in the scene where he gets lost in the woods. He is embarrassed to admit that he is afraid of seeing the "feu follet" [will-o'-the-wisp] and has to accept that Fadette guide him out of the forest. He has trouble sleeping and dreams:

> [I]l vit la petite Fadette à califourchon sur le fadet, qui était fait comme un grand coq rouge et qui tenait, dans une de ses pattes, sa lanterne de corne avec une chandelle dedans, dont les rayons s'étendaient sur toute la jonchère. Et alors la petite Fadette se changeait en un grelet gros comme une chèvre, et elle lui criait, en voix de grelet, *une chanson qu'il ne pouvait comprendre*, mais où il entendait toujours des mots sur la même rime: grelet, fadet, cornet, capet, follet, bessonnet, Sylvinet. (*PF,* 117; my emphasis)

> [He saw little Fadette astride the sprite, who looked like a big red rooster and who was holding in one of its claws a horn lantern; inside there was a candle whose light illuminated the whole place. And then little Fadette changed into a cricket as big as a goat, and with a cricket's voice she was hollering at him *a song that he couldn't understand* but in which he could still hear rhyming words: cricket, sprite, cone, cloak, spirit, twin, Sylvinet.]

This is doubtless the most explicitly sexual dream in all of Sand's corpus. The dream marks the beginning of Landry's desire for Fadette. Her position atop the country pixie, not ignoring the similarity between the masculine form of this Berrichon term (*fadet*) and the feminine form (*fadette*), which is the heroine's nickname and the title of the novel, nor the simile of the red rooster and the phallic shape of the candle in the lantern, points unmistakably to Landry's desire. That Fadette changes into a giant cricket in his dream only underscores his fear faced with her reputed ugliness. The song she sings in a cricket's voice creates an atmosphere of mystery, especially since the language of the song is incomprehensible to Landry. Fadette has always represented for him mystery and deviltry, as demonstrated by the bizarre nature of her manifestation and actions in his dream. Music is often coupled with magic or the work of the devil; witness the many references in *Les Maîtres Sonneurs* to this effect. Music's deviltry enjoys an especially sexual nature in Landry's dream, quite rare for Sand and thus all the more interesting.

The cricket's song will appear again near the end of the novel. On the night of her grandmother's funeral, Fadette sits in front of the smoldering fire and listens to the cricket singing: "Grelet, grelet, petit grelet / Toute Fadette a son Fadet" [Cricket, cricket, little cricket / Every girl sprite has her boy sprite] (*PF,* 228). Not only does this song have the same rhyme as in Landry's dream song but the gender play between *fadet* and *fadette* reinforces the ambiguity of Fadette's identity and the confusion in Landry's desire. *Fadet* often refers to Fadette, which makes her an androgynous character, all the more so since the village children frequently find her clothing and actions to be those of a boy. The second line of the song thus could indicate a union of her two selves. We might also assume *fadet* to be a reference to Landry as the passionate beloved of Fadette. In this case, we return to Landry's dream *fadet,* which can now be reinterpreted as Landry whom Fadette is straddling.[20]

As well as evoking passion and excitement in the rustic novels, music can also summon a sense of calm. In *La Petite Fadette* in particular several references point to music's ability to "calm the savage breast," and in these cases it is evil spirits that music calms. When Landry first sees the *feux follets* he is frightened and sits down paralyzed. Fadette happens by and stops at the ford in the stream. Before proceeding she sings the following song:

> Fadet, fadet, petit fadet,
> Prends ta chandelle et ton cornet;
> J'ai pris ma cape et mon capet;
> Toute follette a son follet. (*PF,* 107)

> [Sprite, sprite, little sprite,
> Take your candle and your cone;
> I've taken my cloak and my cape;
> Each "spiritess" has her spirit.]

Not only does the song have the same vocabulary as Landry's dream, but the gender play in the last line adds new meaning to Fadette's song at the end of the novel. Here the song has a soothing effect on evil spirits, or so Landry thinks. In any event, Fadette performs it as though she is accustomed to conjuring up calm before crossing the stream.

One of the most interesting narrative uses of music in the rustic novels introduces the discussion of music as language. At the beginning of the "Noces de campagne" ["Country Wedding"] appended to *La Mare au diable*, the notion of translation arises naturally: "Je te demande pardon, lecteur ami, de n'avoir pas su te traduire mieux [l'histoire]; car c'est une véritable traduction qu'il faut au langage antique et naïf des paysans de la contrée que *je chante* (comme on disait jadis)" [Friendly reader, I beg your pardon for not having been better able to translate this story, because what we really need is a translation of the ancient and modest language of the peasants of this region; that's what I'm *singing* (as we used to say in days of yore] (*MD*, 131). The narrator plans to describe and laud a region with the idea that it will be musical. Thus "sing" is synonymous with "tell" or "describe."

In the preface to *La Petite Fadette*, Sand writes about art as a means of escape. Again she proclaims her anti-realist notions, especially strong in this post-1848 era.

Les allusions directes aux malheurs présents, l'appel aux passions qui fermentent, ce n'est point là le chemin du salut: mieux vaut une douce chanson, un son de pipeau rustique, un conte pour endormir les petits enfants sans frayeur et sans souffrance, que le spectacle des maux réels renforcés et rembrunis encore par les couleurs et la fiction. (*PF*, 16)

[Direct allusions to current misfortunes, the call to passions that sour, that's not the path to salvation: much better are a gentle song, the sound of a rustic reed pipe, a story to put little children to sleep without fear or suffering, rather than the display of real troubles bolstered and obscured even more by the tints of fiction.]

Music is synonymous with idealistic storytelling in the fictional representations that Sand prefers to fictionalized realism. With the negative connotation the term "fiction" carries here, Sand advances a concept of natural communication as opposed to fictional communication. Music and stories, according to Sand, convey more truth than do realist fictions. Her argument is weakened by the fact that the musical stories she prefers are also fictions.

No other novel in Sand's corpus makes as strong a statement for the preservation and appreciation of folk music as does *Les Maîtres Sonneurs*, written four years after the third work of the rustic trilogy. Sand's exploration and description of folk music in the bagpiping novel concentrates on three essential aspects of her musical aesthetics: communication, improvisation, and individuality. I have already examined the communicative role of folk music as well as the role of improvisation in this novel. However, the problem of individuality cannot be separated from the phenomenon of improvisation in folk music.

The part that individuality plays in improvisation accounts for an apparent contradiction that Sand subtly exploits in *Les Maîtres Sonneurs*. While improvisation is a musical device that belongs to both academic and folk music, it is nonetheless a mainstay of folk music. Most early commentators on folk music, for example, Cœuroy, Tiersot, and Vincent, observe the multitude of versions for a given tune or lyrics, remarking that this very orality distinguishes it from academic music. Improvisation is the most important aspect of bagpiping in *Les Maîtres Sonneurs*. And while improvisation is important for all pipers, the style and extent of improvisation offered by the run-of-the-mill piper differs drastically from that of Joset. The more he develops his talent to compose and improvise—that is, to be an individual—the more he alienates the other pipers. Jealousy certainly plays an important role here, as Sand comments on the place of competition in the musical world. On another level, her commentary on competition applies equally to the Paris Conservatoire.

Sand conveys a mixed message in *Les Maîtres Sonneurs* concerning individuality. On the one hand, Joset garners the praise of Huriel and Bastien for his inventiveness and individuality of creation. Bastien commends him and compares him positively to his own son, also a master piper, for just that reason. Huriel's unmistakable talent relies on memory and technique, whereas Joset's artistry includes originality and inventiveness. On the other hand, it is this very effort to be different from and better than others that causes Joset to be despised by the other pipers. The circle of jealousy and arrogance soon becomes the focal point of the novel.

Sand states in *Consuelo*, in the rustic novels, but especially in *Les Maîtres Sonneurs* that the folk musician is gifted with a good memory and a talent for sizing up the public and giving it what it wants. In the first instance where Joset demonstrates a critical perspective of bagpiping and bagpipers, namely his critique of Carnat, he states his underlying principle for a good folk musician: "Il y en a qui sont dans la vérité de la chose" [There are those who deal directly with the truth of the matter] (*MS,* 107). Brulette will repeat Joset's words soon afterward, whereupon she introduces the notion of original composition: "La vérité de la chose, c'est que Joset prétend inventer lui-même sa musique, et qu'il l'invente, de vrai" [The truth of the matter is that Joset claims to invent his own music, and he truly does invent it] (*MS,* 110). This remark connotes a strong belief of truth in art. Music, says Sand, original and artful music, brings us closer to truth, to God, to the possibility of humankind living in harmony under a new social order. Saint-Simonian and Leroucian influence on Sand's concept of the role of art in social progress remains evident.

Sand's allusions in *Les Maîtres Sonneurs* to actual Berrichon and Bourbonnais music are less specific and less explicit than in the other rustic novels. The wedding music Joset composes for the multiple ceremony that closes the novel recalls the wedding music Sand described in "Les Noces de campagne," even though Joset's music is original. One of the few direct references to a folk song is the story of the three woodsmen (eighteenth *veillée*). This song, as Tiersot tells us, is Sand's invention.[21] She took as her model a folk song known to many in the region, "Joli tambour" [Pretty Drum], which she rearranged to fit her plot. From the original she borrowed only the incipit and the refrain, "Trois fendeux y avait" and "J'entends le rossignolet" ["There were three woodsmen" and "I can hear the little nightingale"].[22] What can we conclude from this inauthentic use of folk music? Simply that the fictionalization of popular culture undergoes the same modification as does historical fiction. Sand freely uses this narrative device in *Les Maîtres Sonneurs* and *Consuelo*.[23]

Perhaps the most detailed aspect of Sand's ethnomusical discussion in *Les Maîtres Sonneurs* lies in her comparison of Berrichon and Bourbonnais folk music. The first to articulate the differences, Huriel states to Tiennet that, "ni toi, ni les tiens ne savez ce que c'est que chanter. Vos airs sont fades et votre souffle écourté, comme vos idées et vos plaisirs" [neither you nor your friends know what it is to sing. Your tunes are dull and your breath is short, like your ideas and your pleasures] (*MS,* 140). It is in the forests, he says, that music truly comes to life. Later he characterizes music thus:

La musique est une herbe sauvage qui ne pousse pas dans vos terres. Elle se plaît mieux dans nos bruyères, je ne saurais vous dire pourquoi, mais c'est dans nos bois et dans nos ravines qu'elle s'entretient et se renouvelle comme les fleurs de chaque printemps; c'est là qu'elle s'in-

vente et fait foisonner des idées pour les pays qui en manquent; c'est de
là que vous viennent les meilleures choses que vous entendez dire à vos
sonneux; mais comme ils sont paresseux ou avares, et que vous vous
contentez toujours du même régal, ils viennent chez nous une fois en
leur vie, et se nourrissent là-dessus tout le restant. (*MS*, 176–77)

[Music is a weed that doesn't grow in your domain. It's happier in our
heather fields. I can't say why, but it's in our woods and our ravines that
it preserves and renews itself like the flowers of each springtime. That's
where it invents itself and makes ideas abound for districts that don't
have any of their own. That's where the best things come from that you
hear your pipers speak of; but as they're lazy or greedy and as you're
happy enough with the same fare all the time, they come to our area
once in their lifetimes and feed off of that for the rest of their days.]

One last question on Sand's presentation of traditional music in
Les Maîtres Sonneurs is the importance of training. Sand's Berrichon and Bourbonnais pipers do not undergo such a rigorous and
formal musical education as do the musicians at the Paris Conservatoire, but they are not without some training. The official atmosphere of the piping examination at "le Bœuf couronné" tavern
suggests at the very least a formal approach to the training and approbation of master pipers. Despite the ahistoricity of this account,
the notion of belonging to a group of professional musicians permeates the novel and provides a paradox since Joset at once desires
and shuns membership in this official group.

The great detail with which Sand describes Joset's training seems
to attenuate the distinction between folk and academic musicians.
The nature of traditional music as Sand presents it, where orality
and unwritten transmission of melodies serve as the basis of folk
music, is, however, not harmed by this attention to training. Dauriac's insistence that an imaginative composer learn first the rules of
the game before attempting to change them does not have to apply
only to academic musicians. *Les Maîtres Sonneurs* presents a clear
notion of superior, adequate, and inadequate training as well as inspiration as the source of differences among pipers. These formal
differences notwithstanding, the nature of folk music is not altered.
What does remain constant is Sand's insistence on training, on the
rejection of the notion of a "natural" musician who plays or sings
artistically without training. In this domain, there is no contradiction.

Sand implicitly introduces in *Les Maîtres Sonneurs* the notion of
social progress in matters of music. That Joset, or others like him,
might be able to affect or encourage social progress is a hope Sand

shares with Liszt, Leroux, and some disciples of Saint-Simon. However, Sand sacrifices this symbolic possibility in her hero, unlike the socialistic development of Pierre Huguenin in *Le Compagnon du tour de France*. If Sand opted for a civically irresponsible hero in *Les Maîtres Sonneurs*, she was guided in this direction by her disappointment in the 1848 fiasco, by her disappointment in Chopin, and by her desire to contrast an ineffectual male musician with an ideal female musician in *Consuelo*.

And yet Joset is not an entirely negative character. The reader sympathizes with him, pities him, and empathizes with his plight. Sand has drawn in Joseph Depardieu a musician who embodies at once romantic passion and rebellious nature. He recalls both Musset and Chopin in this way. At the same time, Sand imbues him with the sense, albeit belated, to acknowledge his limits. The tragic ending she chooses satisfies several functions, including a latterly romantic desire for sacrifice and an ending conventionally assigned to a female character. In so doing, Sand continues her quest for combining idealism and realism, a struggle made all the more difficult in this post-1848 climate.

Music in the rustic novels does more, then, than add local color. It creates an atmosphere of peasant life that would remain incomplete without it. Moreover, Sand uses folk music to further her notions of the values of peasant life and the importance of peasant culture in the understanding of the nation. Micro- and macropolitics enjoy a common bond in the music of Sand's *romans champêtres*. As she became more aware of the political and social commentary possible in the use of music in narrative, Sand exploits it in a variety of other novels. We shall now examine some of the instances of folk music as introduced by Sand in novels other than the rustic works.

CONSUELO AND LES LETTRES D'UN VOYAGEUR

Although not a rustic novel, *Consuelo* repeatedly contrasts folk music with academic music. It is through Venetian folk songs that the heroine first meets Anzoleto, and she often returns to those songs in times of turmoil and confusion. Her encounters with Zdenko bring her back to her origins with renewed respect for the music of the people. The novel ends not with the apotheosis of opera or the art song, but with the glorification of God and humanity through a hybrid type of music that shares more traits with folk music than with any other.[24]

Sand inserts a Venetian musical scene into the middle of the Bo-

hemian section of the novel when Anzoleto arrives to claim his former lover. As he sings for the Rudolstadt family, Consuelo finds
herself transported back to Venice largely thanks to Venetian folk
songs, which Albert's uncle requests. Anzoleto knows them all, but
as they require two voices, he would need Consuelo's help. Consuelo resists making music so close to Anzoleto, but finally she is
obliged to sing.

> Enfin, cédant aux instances de ce bon Christian [Albert's uncle], . . . elle
> s'assit auprès d'Anzoleto, et commença en tremblant un de ces longs
> cantiques à deux parties, divisés en strophes de trois vers, que l'on en-
> tend à Venise, dans les temps de dévotion, durant des nuits entières, au-
> tour de toutes les madones des carrefours. Leur rythme est plutôt animé
> que triste; mais dans la monotonie de leur refrain et dans la poésie de
> leurs paroles, empreintes d'une piété un peu païenne, il y a une mélanco-
> lie suave qui vous gagne peu à peu et finit par vous envahir. (*C,* 1:
> 461–62)

> [Finally yielding to kind Christian's insisting, she sat down next to An-
> zoleto and trembling, began one of those long hymns for two voices,
> divided into three-line stanzas that you hear in Venice at devotions the
> whole night long around all the street corner madonnas. Their rhythm
> is more lively than sad, but in the monotony of their refrain and in the
> poetry of the words that are branded with a somewhat pagan piety there
> is a sweet melancholy that gradually wins you over and ends up pene-
> trating you.]

Consuelo's emotional reaction to these songs returns her to an
intensity of musical passion she thought she had left behind. As
beautiful as Albert's music is, it cannot match the passion of Anzoleto's. One notes the care with which Sand describes the Venetian
songs, not only their formal construction but also the sociological
aspect of their performance, including the recognition of street
music and of the mixture of Christian and pagan passion.

Sand also describes the passionate nature of Venetian folk music
in the first three of *Les Lettres d'un voyageur* (1834). She cites several songs, in particular barcarolles, that give the flavor of Venetian
gondolier music. One lyrical passage describes particularly well the
beautiful music of the Venetian night and combines nightingale and
gondolier music:

> La nuit, [les rossignols] s'appellent et se répondent de chaque côté des
> canaux. Si une sérénade passe, ils se taisent tous pour écouter, et, quand
> elle est partie, ils recommencent leurs chants, et semblent jaloux de sur-
> passer la mélodie qu'ils viennent d'entendre. (*LV,* 2:695)

[At night the nightengales call to each other and answer each other from opposite sides of the canals. If a serenade passes by, they get quiet so they can listen, and when it's over, they start up their singing again, appearing to be vigilant so as to do better than the melody they've just heard.]

Sand's use of bird imagery is well known, a trait often linked to her maternal grandfather's profession as a Parisian bird seller. But it is more likely a reflection of her love of nature. In this passage the personification of the nightingales raises their song to the level of folk music commensurate to that of the gondoliers, with whom they feel themselves to be in competition. In addition, the spatial and temporal materiality of the serenade, which physically passes along the canal and stops the birds' singing for the duration of its melody, lends it an undeniable presence as both art and artefact.

Venetian street music also left an indelible impression on Sand. She depicts the combination of voices that make up the street choruses and the nature of their songs. A long passage, of which I offer here only a truncated version, describes the mixture of classical and folk styles that Sand characterizes as typically Venetian, a technique analogous to that of folk music:

Les chants qui retentissent, le soir, dans tous les carrefours de cette ville sont tirés de tous les opéras anciens et modernes de l'Italie, mais tellement corrompus, arrangés, adaptés aux facultés vocales de ceux qui s'en emparent, qu'ils sont devenus tout *indigènes*. . . . [L]'*instinct* musical de ce peuple sait tirer parti de tant de monstruosités, le plus heureusement possible, et lier les fragments de cette mutilation avec une adresse qui rend souvent la transition difficile à apercevoir. Toute musique est *simplifiée et dépouillée d'ornements* par leur procédé, ce qui ne la rend pas plus mauvaise. *Ignorants de la musique écrite*, ces dilettanti passionnés vont recueillant *dans leur mémoire* les bribes d'harmonie qu'ils peuvent saisir à la porte des théâtres ou sous le balcon des palais. (*LV*, 2:697; my emphasis)

[All the songs that echo in the evenings at every corner of this town are drawn from Italian operas old and new, but they're so adulterated, arranged, adapted to the vocal abilities of those who take them over, that they have become quite *indigenous*. . . . The musical *instinct* of this folk is able to make something out of monstrosities in the most agreeable ways and to link together fragments of this mutilation with a skill that often makes the transition difficult to sense. All music is *simplified and pruned of ornamentation* in this process, which doesn't make it any worse. *Uninstructed as to written music*, these ardent dilettanti will collect *in their memories* bits of harmony they've managed to snatch up at theater doors or palace balconies.]

The passage distinctly paints the nocturnal and open-air atmosphere of Venice. Sand's observations of music display her usual aplomb in reducing the potentially complex to the simple and approachable. Clearly the well-known tunes of the masters remain recognizable but are so profoundly altered by the singers, either because of their vocal abilities or the social exigencies of the moment, that they have become a product of the people. I have highlighted the terms in this passage that suggest a similarity with folk music, particularly labels of technique and performance. Far from being a patronizing portrayal of folk music, the modification of a somewhat severe judgment on the part of cultured society perfectly reflects Sand's attitude toward and appreciation of folk music in general and the street music of Venice in particular.[25]

In contrast, traditional music in *Un Hiver à Majorque* communicates quite a different message. As outcasts, Sand and Chopin are subject to the most vile treatment by the inhabitants, and her bitterness is transparent in her travel diary. She writes surprisingly little about folk music in Mallorca and only in negative terms, judging the song of the natives to be "l'expression de cette morne mélancolie qui l'accable à son insu, et dont la poésie nous frappe sans se révéler à lui" [the expression of a gloomy melancholy that unknowingly devastates the music and whose poetry strikes us without making its mark on the song].[26] During a mardi gras celebration, she observes music and dance that intrigue her by their strangeness. The constant rhythm of castanets that remind her of battle drums stun the author by the dry and harsh tones that make them difficult to endure for a quarter of an hour (*OA*, 2:1129). Then they sing in unison a stanza to a musical phrase that seems to start again and again endlessly. Sand compares this music to what she imagines Arabic music to be like, clearly a biased judgment.

Only in a footnote (*OA*, 2:1129) does she write of a pleasant experience listening to the song of the helmsman during their passage from Barcelona to Palma. His voice was gentle and toned down; his strange song was more like a reverie, "une sorte de divagation nonchalante de la voix, où la pensée avait peu de part, mais qui suivait le balancement du navire, le faible bruit du remous, et ressemblait à une improvisation vague, renfermée pourtant dans des formes douces et monotones. Cette voix de la contemplation avait un grand charme" [a kind of nonchalant vocal rambling, where thought had little to do with it, that matched the ship's rocking and the weak sound of the eddy, and vaguely resembled an improvisation though contained in gentle and monotone forms. This voice of contemplation was quite charming]. Reminiscent of her description of music on the canals of Venice, this observation expresses Sand's notion that music is closely linked to nature. The helmsman's song no doubt struck her as closer to nature than the other folk music she heard in Mallorca.[27]

Another aspect of conventional folk music in *Consuelo* is the tradition that Zdenko represents. Most often in his exchanges with Consuelo he speaks through music. Albert's relationship with Zdenko illustrates Sand's egalitarian views in that he respects the peasant sage for the history he represents and for his memory of that history. Folk songs constitute the bulk of Zdenko's memory of Bohemian history, and Albert has learned much from these songs. Albert frequently refers to this history and its music, giving constant recognition to Zdenko. The preservation of history, an important theme in the novel and Albert's raison d'être, is accomplished largely through this music. Consuelo, too, admires Zdenko's memory, especially as it evokes memories of her childhood and the folk songs that inhabit them. The remembrance of folk songs represents not only a return to one's origins but also notions of equality and democracy. Sand's socialist ideals, like those of many of her contemporaries, were often to be found in the people. And the expression of the people, for Sand, was primarily experienced through music.

Albert has learned some of the Bohemian tunes so well that he can now improvise on them. Sand calls this music natural, "une musique qu'on pourrait appeler naturelle" [music one could call natural] (*C*, 1:415), music of the people that is free from restrictive conventions.[28]Sand then embarks on a discussion of folk music that lays the groundwork for *Les Maîtres Sonneurs*.

L'artiste inconnu qui *improvise* sa rustique ballade en gardant ses troupeaux, ou en poussant le soc de sa charrue . . . s'astreindra difficilement à fixer ses fugitves idées. Il communique cette ballade aux autres musiciens, enfants comme lui de la nature, et ceux-là la colportent de hameau en hameau, de chaumière en chaumière, chacun la modifiant au gré de son génie individuel. (*C*, 1:416)

[*The unknown artist* who *improvises* his rustic ballad while tending to his flock or while pushing the plow . . . will force himself only with difficulty to focus his evanescent ideas. He communicates this ballad to other musicians, children of nature like himself, each one modifying it according to his own individual genius.]

The references to links between music and the farmer will reappear five years later in the rustic novels, as we have seen. All the traditional terms to define folk music appear in these few pages. One notices in particular the anonymous and innocent nature of peasant artisans of music, whose music is transitory and therefore all the more valuable because fleeting.

Even more interesting is the footnote Sand appends to this section. Footnotes are not unknown in Sand's texts, especially in the rustic novels where she explains a certain number of dialectal words or phrases. Here, however, the note constitutes the germ of the musical theme for *Les Maîtres Sonneurs*. Doubtless Sand was not at this time consciously thinking of the novel in these terms. We know that the 1853 text on bagpipers started out as a short story about a motherless child being raised by a local, coquettish young woman whose reputation suffered from the circumstances. "La Mère et l'enfant," as she entitled the original story, quickly grew into a long novel where the problem of individuality within the notion of folk music eclipsed the feminist theme. In the footnote (*C*, 1:416–17) Sand recounts a conversation she had with a minstrel bagpiper who assured her that while he knew music perfectly, he had no concept of notation or theory. Further, almost all the pipers he knew were in fact woodsmen, whence the local saying that music grows in the woods. All master bagpipers go annually to the woods to renew their art, she says. The superiority of Bourbonnais pipers permeates this piper's discourse. Like Joset, he hails from the plains of Berry, and he affirms the need to travel to Bourbonnais to acquire the true piping technique. But as for composing, one has to be born in the woods: "pour inventer, nous [les Berrichons] n'y entendons rien, et nous faisons mieux de ne pas nous en mêler" [as for inventing, we Berrichons don't understand it at all, and we do better not to get involved]. Sand was unable to satisfy herself as to the piper's definition of *accent*, but she did find a probable etymology for bourrée, since the word in Berry is synonymous with fagot.[29]

The footnote amplifies the narrator's statement in the body of the text that the genius of the people knows no limits. Sand will restate this notion, as we have seen, in the prefaces and forewords of the rustic novels. This is also the period of her essay on "Sur les poètes populaires" (1841). To be sure, the people, in this instance the peasantry, and the proletariat do not represent the same population, but Sand's democratic socialism embraces all classes of people who in the July Monarchy rank below the aristocracy and the bourgeoisie. Sand always defended what Leroux called the people's "sacerdoce poétique" [poetic vocation].[30]

The power of folk music is revealed as Albert recounts to Con-

suelo a dream Zdenko had about her, wherein she sang "nos vieux
hymnes bohémiens d'une voix éclatante qui fit trembler toute
l'église. Et pendant que vous chantiez, il me voyait pâlir et m'en-
foncer dans le pavé de l'église, jusqu'à ce que je me trouvasse en-
seveli et couché mort dans le sépulcre de mes aïeux" ["our old
Bohemian hymns with a brilliant voice that made the whole church
shake. And while you were singing, he saw me growing pale and
sinking into the floor of the church until I was buried and lying dead
in the tomb of my ancestors"] (*C*, 1:427). Zdenko thus imagines
that Consuelo's mastery of Bohemian folk music represents her
power over Albert, much as he must consider his own folk musical
abilities to constitute his principal bond with Albert. Zdenko at
once thinks he must protect Albert from ruination and at the same
time preserve his own relationship with him. Thus folk music represents both Zdenko and Consuelo's commonality and their division.

FOLK MUSIC IN OTHER PROSE FICTION WORKS

Le Meunier d'Angibault (1845), written just after *Jeanne*, presents a focused view of *la vallée noire* and Berrichon customs, character traits, and dialect. Music serves as an illustration of the
characters' emotional state. In the beginning of the novel, Marcelle
de Blanchemont and her son, Edouard, are stranded in the forest
with their servant, Suzanne. From a distance they hear the sound of
a peasant singing. Suzanne thinks it is a wolf howling. Marcelle,
whose ear and composure make her superior to the servant, reassures her: "quant au loup qui hurle, c'est un homme qui chante"
[as for the howling wolf, it's a man singing]. And the narrator adds,
"En effet, une voix pleine, et d'une mâle harmonie, quoique rude
et sans art, planait sur les champs silencieux, accompagnée comme
en mesure par le pas lent et régulier d'un cheval" [In truth, a full
voice of a masculine harmony, although crude and artless, wafted
over the silent fields, accompanied by the slow and measured pace
of a horse].[31] A few minutes later, after Marcelle's horseman has
gone off for help and the women and child are alone, they again
hear the song: "la chanson rustique qui s'était fait déjà entendre
reprit un second couplet, et cette fois à une distance fort rap-
prochée" [the rustic song that they'd already heard came back with
a second verse and this time at a much closer distance] (*MA*, 41).
The song and the voice reassure Marcelle that help is close by and
that they will not be victims of their plight. The singing peasant is
none other than the titular miller. Marcelle recognizes, perhaps not

the voice, but a sense of security in the voice: "c'est la voix d'un brave paysan" [it's a kind peasant's voice], to which the narrator adds, "En effet, cette voix était pleine de sécurité, et ce chant calme et pur annonçait la paix d'une bonne conscience." [Indeed, his voice was full of confidence, and the composed and simple song predicted the serenity of a good conscience] (*MA*, 41).

The miller's voice and song communicate peacefulness and safety. What is it about the "chanson rustique" that Marcelle finds so reassuring? Louis's voice conveys confidence, perhaps because it is without artifice or training. Perhaps it is the "maleness," the stable, frank, and honest nature of the voice that imparts a feeling of safety. However, Sand's notion of the value of the peasant musician, equal to the academically trained singer, suggests a more far-reaching interpretation. The "folkness" of the song and the voice impart calm and trust. Hecquet describes the "socialist" novels as a corpus where Sand seeks to exhibit people with limited education and culture in an effort to valorize their thoughts and language by inventing new modes of expression.[32] In like manner, Sand explores the musical gifts of this group in the rustic and other novels in order to suggest a different web of symbols coexistent with those of the larger society. Sand's peasants continue to surprise the Parisian reader by displaying emotional and psychological depth at the same time as artistic and aesthetic sophistication.

In anticipation of a wedding feast, the characters enjoy an evening of dancing. They invite musicians, a bagpiper and a vielle player, and dance the bourrée for hours. "Aucun peuple ne danse avec plus de gravité et de passion en même temps" [no community dances with more seriousness and more passion at the same time] (*MA*, 267). Sand will often refer to an odd mixture of tones that tends to confuse Parisian observers. Sand's description clearly transmits her respect and admiration for the dances. She is also convinced that a Parisian audience will have difficulty at first understanding the elegance of the dance but with some attention will not fail to appreciate it.

A les voir avancer et reculer à la bourrée, si mollement et si régulièrement, que leurs quadrilles serrés ressemblent au balancier d'une horloge, on ne devinerait guère le plaisir que leur procure cet exercice monotone, et on soupçonnerait encore moins la difficulté de saisir ce rythme élémentaire que chaque pas et chaque attitude du corps doivent marquer avec une précision rigoureuse, tandis qu'une grande sobriété de mouvements et une langueur apparente doivent, pour atteindre à la perfection, en dissimuler entièrement le travail. Mais quand on a passé quelque temps à les examiner, on s'étonne de leur infatigable ténacité, on apprécie l'espèce de grâce molle et naïve qui les préserve de la lassitude, et, pour peu qu'on observe les mêmes personnages dansant dix ou douze heures de suite sans courbature, on peut croire qu'ils ont été piqués de la tarentule, ou constater qu'ils aiment la danse avec fureur. Le caractère berrichon est tout entier dans cette danse. (*MA*, 276–68)

[To see them moving forward and back in the bourrée so half-heartedly and invariably that their tight square formations resemble a clock's pendulum, you would hardly be able to guess the pleasure this monotonous exercise brings them. You would suspect even less how difficult it is to understand the elementary rhythm that each step and each position of the body must exhibit with rigorous exactness, while a great seriousness of movment and an apparent sluggishness must completely hide the toil in order to reach perfection. But when you've spent some time watching them, you're surprised at their persistent determination, you appreciate the kind of listless and naive grace that saves them from collapse; and, just watching the same people dancing ten or twelve hours in a row without cramping, you might think they'd been bitten by a tarantula, or else you notice that they love dancing intensely.]

At one point, the piper trips over the keg he is using as a pedestal, and the air left in his pipes seeps out with a strange and plaintive sound, causing the dancers to stop and look.

Au même moment, la vielle, brusquement arrachée des mains de l'autre ménétrier, alla rouler sous les pieds de Rose, et la folle sautant de l'orchestre champêtre où elle s'était élancée d'un bond semblable à celui d'un chat sauvage, se jeta au milieu de la bourrée en criant: "Malheur, malheur aux assassins! malheur aux bourreaux!" (*MA*, 268)

[At the same instant, the vielle was suddenly ripped form the other minstrel's hands and rolled under Rose's feet. The mad girl, jumping from the country orchestra where she'd bounded like a wild cat, threw herself into the center of the bourrée and screamed, "Get them! Get the killers! Get the butchers!"]

Rose's reaction is one of horror and doom. She is convinced this is a sign of disaster and that her life will be a failure. Throughout the novel her madness serves as an implicit metaphor for the ills of the bourgeoisie. This scene is one of several where her inappropriate reactions portend disaster for her family, a Balzacian manifestation of their greed. That music should herald such an outburst only supports the notion of the force it has in evoking emotional reactions.

At the wedding celebration proper, the dancing goes better and everyone enjoys themselves. In fact, several groups of musicians play at the same time, creating general disorder:

> [L]a foule des jolies filles se pressait autour des ménétriers placés deux à deux sur leurs tréteaux à peu de distance les uns des autres, faisant assaut de bras et de poumons, se livrant à la concurrence la plus jalouse, jouant chacun dans son ton et selon son prix, sans aucun souci de l'épouvantable cacophonie produite par cette réunion d'instruments braillards qui s'évertuaient tous à la fois à qui contrarierait l'air et la mesure de son voisin. Au milieu de ce chaos musical, chaque quadrille restait inflexible à son poste, ne confondant jamais la musique qu'il avait payée avec celle qui hurlait à deux pas de lui, et ne frappant jamais du pied à faux pour marquer le rythme, tour de force de l'oreille et de l'habitude. Les ramées retentissaient de bruits non moins hétérogènes. (*MA*, 276)

> [The mass of girls crowded around the minstrels placed near each other two by two on their platforms and attacking with arms and lungs and giving themselves up to the most envious competition, each one playing in his own key and according to his own fee with no worry as to the horrible cacophony produced by this assembly of shrieking instruments that were jointly devoted to thwarting their neighbors' tunes and beats. In the midst of this musical chaos, each square formation unfailingly remained in place, never confusing the music they had paid for with the music that was wailing next to them, never missing a step in tapping the beat, a veritable tour de force of hearing and habit. The branches resounded with no less heterogeneous noises.]

This scene's apparent disarray, paradoxically accompanied by an underlying discipline, offers Sand's most lively and complete representation of a folk celebration. The sounds, movements, and humors of all the participants come alive in this passage, from the musical chaos to the steadfastness of the dancers, all reflected in the equally disparate sounds of the trees. Sand singles out the role of money in the musicians' function as well as their individual playing styles and the rigor and earnestness of the dancers.

Playing on the critical perception of rustic music and instruments she imagines Parisian readers will have, Sand points out the so-called unpleasant sound of the bagpipes while at the same time drawing attention to their uniqueness in evoking sincere emotions. Witness the juxtaposition in the following passage where Marcelle needs to get away from the group of revelers and wanders out for a walk. Sand evokes the derogatory terms she anticipates, then interjects positive judgments and explains the advantages of rustic originality and sincerity of expression.

Le son de la cornemuse, uni à celui de la vielle, écorche un peu les oreilles, de près; mais, de loin, cette voix rustique qui chante parfois de si gracieux motifs rendus plus originaux par une harmonie barbare, a un charme qui pénètre les âmes simples et qui fait battre le cœur de quiconque en a été bercé dans les beaux jours de son enfance. Cette forte vibration de la musette, quoique rauque et nasillarde, ce grincement aigu et ce *staccato* nerveux de la vielle sont faits l'un pour l'autre et se corrigent mutuellement. (*MA*, 265)

[The sound of the bagpipes taken with that of the vielle does grate on the ears close up. But from afar, this rustic voice that sometimes sings such gracious motifs made even more original by a primitive harmony has a charm that penetrates simple souls and sets the heart of anybody who was rocked in the lovable days of his childhood to beating. This strong vibration of the bagpipes, even though harsh and nasal, this sharp scraping and this nervous *staccato* of the vielle are made for each other and amend each other.]

La Filleule (1853) presents a hero from Berry whose mother taught him regional songs. Stéphen plays these songs on the piano, an interesting shift from rustic music and instruments to a Parisian salon instrument. The music reminds him of his mother, who died when he was sixteen. Stéphen's friends in Paris grow weary of these Berrichon tunes, but the German neighbor, a former professional musician starving in Paris, is quite moved by them: "Ces airs champêtres que vous répétez tous les soirs me sont agréables pour m'endormir" [These country tunes that you rehash each evening pleasantly lull me to sleep] (*F*, 79). The effect on Schwartz is calming and melancholic. But the same songs will display a sincerity and a depth of emotion when Stéphen plays them for Anicée, for whom he has an undeclared adoration. Moréna, the eponymous goddaughter, will also admire his clarity of expression when he plays these melodies.

Schwartz encourages Stéphen to play and to play often, but not to take lessons. He continues, "Vous faites des fautes d'orthographe musicale qui sont d'un grand artiste et que vous auriez le droit d'imposer comme du purisme si vous étiez auteur célèbre" [You make musical spelling errors that are those of a great artist, and that you would have the right to dictate as purism if you were a famous author] (*F*, 80). We are reminded of the comments Sand makes in the preface to *François le champi* about the quarter tones she claims to hear in Berrichon music that Western music cannot accommodate. Stéphen defends these "mistakes," picking up on Schwartz's encouragement:

Mes fautes d'orthographe, les voici, dit Stéphen en reproduisant sur le piano certains passages de ses airs du Berry. N'est-ce pas, c'est là ce qui vous étonne et vous charme? Moi, cela me charme sans m'étonner, parce que mon·oreille y est habituée et que mon sentiment en a besoin. Je ne saurais vous dire le nom de ces accords; je ne le connais pas. Ils me plaisent parce que je les ai entendus faire aux ménétriers de mon pays. Quant à ces transitions, je sais bien qu'elles ne se rencontrent pas dans la musique officielle; mais elles sont dans la nature, et comme la nature ne peut pas ne pas avoir raison, c'est la musique officielle, la musique légale, si vous voulez, qui a tort. (*F*, 80)

["Here are my spelling mistakes," said Stéphen, reproducing on the piano some passages of his Berrichon tunes. "Isn't that what surprises and enchants you? As for me, it enchants me without surprising me, because my ear is used to it and my sensibility needs it. I wouldn't be able to tell you the name of these chords; I don't know it. I like them because I've heard minstrels back home play them. As for these transitions, I know very well you can't find them in official music; but they are in nature, and as nature can't not be right, it's official music, legal music if you like, that is wrong."]

The expression "spelling mistakes" underscores Schwartz's humor. But more than that, it returns to the constant comparison Sand draws between music and language, in this case written language.[33] The burlesque continues with the terms "surprise" and "enchant," both of which fall into the realm of the indefinable effect that music produces. Proud of his regional music, Stéphen does not know how to describe it in the terms of the Conservatoire, nor does he care to. His light-hearted dismissal of "la musique officielle" (Schwartz's term) underscores a difference and not a hierarchy. It is not without some irony that Sand's experienced musician suggests that if Stéphen were a famous author, he could prescribe his spelling errors as accepted purism.[34] The allusion to criticism levied against Sand for incorporating Berrichon vocabulary into her prose does not go unnoticed.

Another aspect of folk music in *La Filleule* that Sand introduces though without much detail is the gypsy music of the *gitano* Algénib, or Rosario as he is known in the first part of the novel. He sings his songs, some traditional and some of his own composition, at a *soirée musicale* held at the home of la duchesse de Florès, the wife of Moréna's biological father. The effect on the gathering is curious, since the strange music at once offends and intrigues the ears of the aristocrats. They vacillate between mocking the unsophisticated nature of the music and praising the young musician's voice and expression. "C'est du gitano si l'on veut, mais c'est de l'art, chanté ainsi" [It's gypsy if you like, but it's art sung that way] (*F*, 185). From a sociological point of view, the reception of the gypsy singer presents an interesting commentary on European society. Algénib tells Moréna that he had sung in public before, and the reaction of the French listeners had always been one of interest and curiosity. Spanish listeners, on the contrary, found his music lacking in taste and distinction, obviously harboring a prejudice against the race of Bohemians whom the Spanish aristocracy looked down on. Later Algénib will ask Moréna to learn these songs as part of her heritage. He wants to acculturate her through music and language (*F*, 197).

Sand focuses on gypsy music and culture in this novel to an extent that befits the interests of her time. Gypsy commentary also appears in *Consuelo* but only in passing. First, Consuelo's "gypsiness" is seen negatively by the other girls in the Mendicanti music school in Venice, but otherwise it is a source of exoticism and a positive exposure to folk music. The term "bohémienne" occurs numerous times, always in a positive light. Sand's treatment of gypsy music and culture in *La Filleule* is more stereotypical, perhaps partly due to the recent publication of Mérimée's *Carmen*. Still, the theme of identification through one's language and music remains the important element.[35]

FOLK MUSIC IN SAND'S THEATER

François le champi and *Claudie*

Sand wrote and produced several plays with rustic settings and peasant issues, including *François le champi, Claudie, Le Pressoir,* and *Mauprat*. Other plays also take place in Berry but they concern urban provincial mores rather than peasant ones and thus cannot be considered rustic. For my purposes, only the first two have pertinence for the essential place music holds in them. Sand's insistence on authenticity and appropriateness in matters of music, as well as in those of costume, dance, and language, render her rustic stage productions a tour de force for the romantic stage.

François le champi (1849) and *Claudie* (1850) were both directed by Pierre Bocage, Sand's friend and manager of the Odéon theater since 1841. He encouraged her to put *François* on the stage and promised to maintain its rustic atmosphere. When the play reaped financial and critical success, Bocage urged Sand to write another rustic play for the Parisian stage. Sand had great reserva-

tions about bringing a Berrichon play to Paris, fearing that sophisticated audiences would not accept a piece about simple ideals
recounted in simple language. She was pleasantly surprised, however, for these plays enjoyed successful runs and several revivals.
Sand was nonetheless disappointed at subsequent revivals not under
the direction of Bocage, in which some aspects of the costuming
and decor were dressed up to appeal to the urban public. But on the
whole, taking Berry to the Paris stage proved a positive experience.

Music plays an important role in both *François le champi* and
Claudie. Sand took great pains to ensure that the music as well as
the dancing and costumes were authentic and well executed. She
gathered Berrichon folk music herself, wrote it down, and sent it to
Joseph Ancessy, the orchestra conductor at the Odéon. He arranged
and orchestrated the melodies for the production of *François*. In the
preface, written in 1860, Sand acknowledges Ancessy's contribution. "La musique est indispensable. Elle se compose de vieux airs
berrichons recueillis par l'auteur, ordonnés et mis en rapport avec
les scènes qu'ils accompagnent par M. Ancessy" [The music is cru-
cial. It comprises old Berrichon tunes gathered by the author, put in
order and with regard to the scenes they accompany by Mr. An-
cessy].[36] No particular scene in the play has any narrative requirement for specific music, which is to say that, as with the novel,
music does not hold a symbolic or thematic place in the narrative.
Berrichon tunes are used to create a rustic atmosphere in keeping
with the characters and their context. Sand insists on the pastoral
aspect of the play in the preface, referring to the foreword of the
novel wherein she exposed the taste of the aristocracy and the bourgeoisie for indulging in the pastoral.

Claudie also takes place in a Berrichon village. As the play treats
the way in which society accepts or rejects an unwed mother, it is
fitting that social gatherings should hold an important place in the
action. And music of course plays an important role in these social
events. In a letter to Adolphe Vaillard, orchestra conductor at the
Porte-St-Martin theater (11 December 1850), Sand discusses the
importance of authenticity in matters of music. She gives two examples of Berrichon tunes in musical notation in this letter to illustrate her points.

Si vous aviez pu venir passer 24 h chez moi, je pense que vous auriez
pu comprendre par vous-même, ce que je ne peux pas rendre en écri-
vant, cette musique, qui n'a souvent ni règle ni mesure dans la bouche
des paysans. . . . J'ai marqué les mouvements. Il n'y en a guère que deux
pour les paysans, un *andante* très lent pour les romances, complaintes et

ballades, un *allegro* un peu lâche pour les danses et bourrées. . . . Dans une fête de village, tout est calme ici, et presque triste, la musique et la danse; et les chanteurs de cabaret ont l'air de chanter les vêpres. Puis il vient un accès de folie, où les ménétriers, les danseurs et les ivrognes prennent un allegro furibond. Cela dure un instant et tout reprend son sang-froid, comme si de rien n'était. . . . [D]ans *la bourrée de Marsillat*, il y a un trille affreusement faux. Oserez-*vous* le risquer? Ce fa naturel est produit par l'insuffisance de l'instrument du ménétrier, la cornemuse ne va pas jusqu'au dièse, les oreilles s'y habituent si bien que la bourrée demeure ainsi dans la tradition. . . . Il y a aussi dans cet envoi la ballade des *trois petits fendeurs*, que Chopin et Mme Viardot regardaient comme un chef-d'œuvre, et qui, si je ne [me] trompe, n'a pas été em- ployée dans le *Champi*. Elle mérite attention.[37] . . . Je n'ai pas besoin de vous dire que l'harmonie la plus élémentaire, les moyens les plus sim- ples, les *sutures* les moins sensibles, enfin l'instrumentation la moins chargée seront ce qu'il y aura de meilleur. (*Corr*, 9:837–41)

[If you could come spend twenty-four hours with me, I think you'd un- derstand for yourself what I cannot explain in writing about this music that often has neither rules nor beat in a peasant's mouth. . . . I've marked the tempi. There's really only two for peasants, a very slow *an- dante* for the ballads and laments, and a rather loose *allegro* for dances and bourrées. . . . In a village festival, everything is calm and almost dismal, music and dance. The cabaret singers seem to be singing ves- pers. Then there's a rush of madness, where minstrels, dancers, and drunks take on a incensed allegro. That lasts a moment and then every- thing goes back into a sort of composure as though nothing had hap- pened. . . . In *Marsillat's bourrée,* there's a horribly out of tune trill. Will *you* dare risk it? This F natural comes from the inability of the minstrel's instrument; bagpipes don't go up to the sharp. The ears get so used to it that the bourrée has stayed that way in the tradition. . . .I've also included here the ballad of *The Three Little Woodsmen* that Chopin and Mme Viardot deem a masterpiece and that, if I'm not mistaken, was not used in *Champi*. It's worth your attention. . . . I don't need to tell you that the most elementary harmony, the simplest means, the least visible *seams,* finally the least ornate instrumentation will work best.]

We notice Sand's characteristic deference before musicians, be they academic or folk; she insists she is no musician herself. Still, she knows what she wants and details it to the orchestra conductor in no uncertain terms. Also evident in this letter is Sand's equivocal attitude concerning Berrichon music, which she lays bare in *Les Maîtres Sonneurs*. At the same time, however, she is quick to point out that these deprecating attributes define what she assumes will be the reaction of Parisian theatergoers, but that in reality the music of her province has a unique charm. Sand at once recognizes the anticipated complaints of the sophisticated Parisian public and gently warns them of the error of such an evaluation. Sand's marketing acumen helps her seduce her public into opening their minds without insulting them. Here she entreats the orchestra conductor to represent her seduction musically vis-à-vis the audience.

At the end of the first act of *Claudie*, the village comes together to celebrate the harvest, the festival of the *gerbaude*. Denis hears bagpipes, which announce the opening of the festival, "J'ai entendu la musette, et je crois que la gerbaude n'est pas loin" [I've heard the bagpipes, and I think the *gerbaude* must not be far off].[38] In scene 11 we see the bagpiper arrive on stage and the entertainment begins. Rémy sings a short piece that is provided *in texto* in the script. When it came time to finalize music for the production of *Claudie*, Sand wrote to Bocage (26 November 1850),

> *La musique.*—Je ne me souviens pas de tous les airs qu'on a pris pour le *Champi*. J'ai l'ouverture, mais non les mélodies qui accompagnaient les scènes. Ce sera un point à vérifier, pour que ce que je vous envoie ne fasse pas double emploi. Mon répertoire commence à s'user. Il y a des milliers de chansons et de bourrées. Mais toutes ne sont pas caractérisées et ne sont pas d'une mélodie distinguée ou originale. Je vais peut-être regretter Ancessy qui avait du sentiment et de la naïveté musicale sous sa perruque. Tâchez qu'on soit simple, *sobre d'effets d'harmonie*. Ça irait comme des cheveux sur de la soupe. (*Corr*, 9:813–14)

> [Music.—I don't remember all the tunes we took for *Champi*. I have the overture, but not the melodies that go with the scenes. You should check to see that what I'm sending you doesn't repeat what's already been used. My repertory is beginning to wear thin. There are thousands of songs and bourrées, but all of them are not characterized by a distinguished or original melody. Perhaps I'll miss Ancessy, who had musical feeling and naivete underneath his wig. Take pains to be simple, *sober in matters of harmony*. Otherwise, it would be distasteful.]

Again on 6 December she writes to Bocage to suggest he use what had been played for *Champi*; her appreciation of Ancessy's work is now less complimentary. "Qu'avez-vous fait de ce que je vous ai envoyé pour le *Champi*? vous l'avez abandonné à Ancessy qui en a pris quelques motifs bien choisis pour la pièce, mais qui a gâché le reste, des motifs superbes, pour d'atroces contredanses où cela allait tout défiguré de sens et de rythme comme des cheveux sur la soupe" [What have you done with what I sent you for *Champi*? You've left it to Ancessy, who took a few motifs for the play but butchered the rest, some splendid motifs, for abominable contredances where they'll all be disfigured in meaning and in rhythm, completed out of place] (*Corr,* 9:829). Sand's pivoting esteem of Ancessy's contribution to the music notwithstanding, we notice her unceasing efforts to verify the authenticity of the musical aspect of the production. One also notes the reference to endless traditional tunes with the proviso that not all are of interest to outsiders, that is, Parisians. Sand also writes to her son Maurice that she has sent Bocage some Berrichon tunes that she noted from a mason, Jean Chauvet, who sang them while piercing her kitchen wall for a stove: "Pour charmer ses ennuis, il chantait sans s'apercevoir que je l'écoutais. Il chante juste et avec le vrai chic berrichon, je l'ai emmené au salon et j'ai noté trois airs dont un fort joli, après quoi je l'ai fait bien boire et manger, là, *tout son saoul*" [To take his mind off his worries he sang, unaware that I was listening. He sings on key and with a real Berrichon aptitude. I took him into the drawing room and wrote down three tunes, one of which is very pretty, after which I gave him his fill of food and drink] (*Corr,* 9:835). Although not an ethnomusicological collector of tunes, Sand is always listening with the ear of an appreciative outsider in order to insure the authenticity of her sources.

Sand's desire to bring cultural knowledge of the provinces to Parisian audiences is especially evident in her rigorous concerns for authenticity. However, her goal partly attempts to put peasants on a par with the rest of French society. In the preface to *François* she makes "paysan" the equivalent of "peuple." In Sand's mind, the people of the soil or of the countryside equal those of urban centers without property or title. As widely differing as they may be, both groups represent for her the soul of the nation and the population that must be targeted in any sociopolitical reform. Keeping in mind that these texts come after the debacle of 1848, it is interesting to note the lingering hope Sand still harbors despite her and many people's profound disappointment.

La Petite Fadette

Like *François le champi, La Petite Fadette* underwent drastic transformations for its stage production.[39] The musical version of the rustic novel opened at the Opéra-Comique in September 1869, an *opéra comique* in three acts, words by Michel Carré and music by Théophile Semet.[40] Typical of French comic opera, the tone of the music and lyrics is lighthearted and engaging. The music consists largely of simple melodies with uncomplicated harmony, the interest coming mostly from key changes and the occasional rhythmic variation. Only one melody could be interpreted as having originated in a folk tune, Fadet's song, which is repeated near the end of the opera.

The most interesting music comes in the second act, where key and tempo changes mark the vacillations in Landry's and Fadette's moods and inclinations. In a trio where Sylvinet spies on the amorous couple—which repeats a scene from the novel, but communicates less convincingly Sylvinet's suspicion—Landry tries to convince Fadette to give him a kiss as a sign of forgiveness for his having treated her so badly. She refuses and he plays hurt. Then the melody changes from A-flat major to A major, giving a brighter sound in which Fadette declares she is not a flirt, otherwise she could charm him. The double inference of female charm and sorcery are not lost. Another key change, to C major, provides a still cleaner, simpler tone for Fadette to ask that Landry simply give her his hand in recognition of friendship and the promise that he will show her the same respect the following day. In this scene the musical modulations underscore the characters' mood changes, thus guiding the listener along the rapidly moving emotional turmoil that underlies the focus of the opera's plot.

Fadet's song, an important element in the novel, also appears twice in the opera. In act 1, scene 1, Fadette sings it off stage. This is her first intervention in the opera, much earlier than in the novel. Later, in act 3, Fadette again sings the song to identify herself to Landry, who has become distracted and nearly mad in her absence. Even when he hears Fadette singing, he still believes he is dreaming. No change from *fadet* to *fadette* underscores the gender game so apparent in the novel. Interesting also is the unusual use of Fadet's song to identify Sylvinet, who sings it while Landry searches for him (act 1, scene 2). No explanation as to why Landry is looking for his brother or why Sylvinet is hiding is given, but the fact that he sings Fadet's song surprises, as it falsely connotes a relationship between Sylvinet and Fadette.

In the famous scene of the bourrée (act 1, finale), Madelon feels slighted. The traditional signal for the start of the dance is given by oboes and trombones. While the harmony of this signal could imitate the drone of bagpipes, the effect is quite different. On a few other occasions harmonies in the bass line also seem to imitate bagpipes. Even though irregular, the use of actual bagpipes would have been obvious; this option must not, however, have occurred to Semet. All in all, the folk flavor of the opera is minimal and passes as a mere suggestion. One cannot imagine that Sand would have been pleased with the result. According to the correspondence, her satisfaction seems to be mostly fiduciary.

(*La Petite Fadette* [II, 8], 136–37)

One song in the opera (act 1, scene 3) carries the name "chanson berrichonne." The melody is simple and the lyrics describe the pretty wood, in which there is a tree, in which there is a nest, in which there is god, who is the god of love. Madelon and Cadet, joined by the chorus, perform this scene, which seems to have little to do with Berrichon folk music and casts the two characters in roles much more important than in the novel. Here another pragmatic change from novel to opera requires the composer to provide adequate parts for principal singers, and as the roles Madelon and

(*La Petite Fadette* [I, 1d], "Chant du Fadet," 21)

Cadet play in ridiculing Fadette and Landry are greater in the opera, this would explain the scene.

Several changes radically distance the opera from the novel. Disappointing is the loss of Fadette's darker side. She dances and sings well, in keeping with the portrayal in the novel, but she plays no tricks, does not counter meanness with quips and threats of sorcery, nor does she display any of the "devilish" antics of the novelistic Fadette. One important omission in the opera is troubling: the details of Fadette's help when Landry is searching for his brother. Similar details are also missing in the subsequent scene where Landry is lost near Fadette's house. These scenes are collapsed into one in the opera (act 1, scene 2), with only a hint of Fadette's encouragement to follow the will-o'-the-wisp, but without any of the suspicion of witchcraft or evil. Without these two scenes, the reason for Landry's promise is obscured; no justification for it is offered in the opera. On the other hand, Fadette does retain her strength of character. It is she who insists she should go away from La Cosse for a while until the rumors of her having cast a spell on Landry die away.

Equally troubling is the generous nature of Mère Fadet. She is kind, likes Landry and approves of their marriage, gives her savings to Fadette as a dowry, and bestows her blessings on them. That the grandmother does not die weakens Fadette's motive to return to La Cosse; and giving Fadette her cache of money as a dowry simplifies the novel's well-constructed financial theme, indicating at least for some scholars Fadette's attempt to attain middle-class status.[41]

The twins' mother, an important and sympathetic character in the novel, does not appear in the opera. And Père Barbeau undergoes severe changes. While concerned for his son's future, he gives little indication of what is actually bothering him. Since the money issue is not a concern in the opera as it is in the novel, the only matter of distress is Landry's apparent though temporary madness. An entire scene is devoted to Madelon and Cadet trying to convince Barbeau, now drunk as a result of his distress, of the truth in the rumors of Landry's madness, an innovation in the opera. In the end Barbeau recovers when he sees Landry happy and sane. The money issue has been resolved by this time, although the suggestion that money influences Barbeau's shift to acceptance of his son's marriage remains much too subtle, if not nonexistent.

Folk customs such as the Saint Andoche and Saint Jean festivals enjoy a privileged place in the opera as well as in the novel. The feast of Saint John the Baptist incorporates an additional celebration at the end, as Landry and Fadette as well as Cadet and Madelon—another innovation—announce their betrothals. Dancing and singing accompany the festivals, which provides an opportunity to include the chorus. Little detail is offered in the piano score about costumes or decor, except Fadette's ridiculous outfit for the Saint Andoche festival.

Most disappointing is the complete transformation of the character of Sylvinet. Gone is his jealousy, gone is his fever and Fadette's cure, gone too are his devious machinations to persuade Landry to relent and return home. All that remains of Sylvinet's suspicious nature is some surprise at seeing Landry take Fadette's hand (act 2, scene 8). The tension between the brothers—it is never mentioned that they are twins—and the movement from Fadette's being an obstacle to her being a somewhat uncomfortable link in the relationship of the brothers has been omitted.[42]

In the final analysis, the comic opera concentrates on the love story, typical of *opéra comique* tradition. While the love plot certainly occupies an important place in the novel, the part of superstition in peasant culture and that of money, an extremely integral element of the novel, are lost or minimized. It is not surprising that the opera had few performances and was never revived.

La Mare au diable was also to have been set to music. Pauline Viardot wrote to Sand over many years of her intention to compose a musical piece, basing the music on Berrichon tunes she had come to know and love at Nohant. Problems in her personal life and career caused continued delays. Most of all, however, Viardot felt the action of the text inspired little musically. The project was never completed.[43]

FOLK MUSIC IN NONFICTION TEXTS

In *Promenades autour d'un village* (1857) Sand's references to music are few. The one scene that inspires her to think about a specific piece of music brings classical, not folk, music to her mind. During a nocturnal walk around Châteaubrun, she pauses to think how the scene reminds her of Gounod's symphony *La Nonne sanglante* or Weber's *La Chasse infernale*. In the course of these promenades, Sand makes frequent remarks about artists, about how the scenery and surroundings would provide ample inspiration for artists.

One entry, written during a village festival in honor of Saint Anne to honor the beginning of the harvest, does privilege folk music. As in any Berrichon festival there is dancing. Sand describes the traditional bourrée, while noting that she fears the dance is fading out. She has noticed bourgeois people from neighboring towns trying to adopt the Berrichon dance, but they look awkward and clumsy doing it, just as the peasants look silly dancing the contradance they learned from townspeople. She even goes so far as to say that the bourrée is a boring, monotonous dance, though of solid character.[44] Yet on the next page she praises its simplicity, "Leur danse [celle des paysans berrichons] est souple, bien rythmée et très gracieuse dans sa simplicité" [Their dance is graceful, moderate, and very gracious in its simplicity].

Naturally where there is a bourrée there are bagpipers. Sand describes two pipers who were employed for the festivities, an older one, Doré, and a younger one, Blanchet. While there was a practical need for two pipers given the number of dancers, the real reason soon emerges. Doré, she explains, had once been good, but his success and his talent had waned of late. Blanchet is better trained and more talented. He knows the traditions and can play religious music as well as dance music. Doré complains to the author that formerly she had always sought him out, but when the famous Pauline Viardot came to the area to transcribe some regional tunes, she asked Marcillat du Bourbonnais to play instead of him. The thrust of this section focuses on both Sand's predicament in having to justify her choice to the older piper and on the notion that folk musicians whose artistic prowess abates suffer financially but also emotionally.

In *Légendes rustiques* (1857) Sand details information about Berrichon beliefs and customs, providing regional vocabulary and comparing it with the language and traditions of other provinces that had been recently studied, namely Normandy and Brittany.

Along with commentary on "le trou aux Fades" [sprites' hole], "les pierres-caillasses" [stones], "les demoiselles du Berry" [young ladies of Berry], "les lavandières, les broyeuses de nuit" [washerwomen, nighttime wringers], "le follet d'Ep-Nell" [the mad man of the Ep-Nell stone momument], and similar creatures of local reputation, she also discusses the place of music in the tradition of the "meneux de loups." Werewolves who devour children can be charmed and tamed only by wise men who know the secrets of their power. These "meneux de loups" are often minstrels, who have learned music only by devoting themselves to the devil, who frequently beats them and breaks their instruments on their backs when they disobey him.[45]

Sand recounts the old story of a master bagpiper, Julien, who was so talented and led his life in such a Christian way that the parish priest asked him to play in church during the Eucharist. Because of the bagpipers' reputation for secret dealings with the devil, they were rarely allowed to play in church. But Julien played marvelously and the parish was only too happy to have him perform during mass. One night on the heath, Julien came across a set of bagpipes playing by themselves. Others said the wind that was playing them. Julien was so captivated by and jealous of the quality of the performance that he followed the bagpipes and tried to capture them but without success. The next day he was sad and despondent, saying that the night air played better than he. He began to study a different music that resembled nothing he had played before. He would go out on to the heath all night and come back playing better and better, but playing a tune no one could understand. The priest approached him and told him he must be under the devil's influence and that he should be content with the talent and knowledge he possessed and not try to learn how to lead the wolves.

The next day the sexton told the priest he had seen Julien on the heath playing "d'une manière qui n'était pas chrétienne et menant derrière lui plus de trois cents loups qui s'étaient sauvés à son approche" [in an unchristian way and leading behind him more than three hundred wolves who had scattered as he got near] ("Meneu," 190). Julien denied the accusation and reminded the priest that the sexton was wont to drink. He went to the church and was ready to play, but at the moment of the Elevation, he found he could not play the usual music, but instead played the song the devil had taught him. The priest tried to catch his attention and make him stop. When he lifted the host to bless it, Julien's bagpipes deflated in his hands with a sound that could have been the devil's soul leaving it. Julien felt a blow to the stomach and fainted. He was taken home and was ill for some time. When he recovered, he admitted his association with the enchanted bagpipes and promised to renounce his evil practices. Thereafter he played "chrétiennement" ["in a Christian way"] and let the wolves parade around him. He taught his children the bagpipes and instilled in them the satisfaction of their talent without seeking to learn more than they should.

Many elements of *Les Maîtres Sonneurs*, written four years earlier, resurface in this tale. The musician's temptation to play better and better, to outdo himself and thus everyone around him, is a prideful desire that deserves to· be punished. Such a lure can only be inspired by the devil, and must be chased out of an overly willing host. Joset represents just such a prideful musician. Joset does not reveal the secret of his talent, as had Julien, and thus has no reason to incur the wrath of Satan. Sand's message is clear: one's unhappiness is of one's own doing, and any consequence of disappointment or chagrin can only be blamed on oneself. Joset is his own devil. When he finally realizes his music is not the key to his desires, he reneges and abandons his desire, his music, and his life.

♫ ♫ ♫

Folk music carries a heavy weight of communication in Sand's work. Not only does she exploit musical symbolism and narrativity as in other musical texts, but she also capitalizes on the value of Berrichon music to define and valorize the peasantry in a time when French society was searching for redefinition. In addition to the sociological function of folk music, Sand also capitalizes on its musical nature. The differences between regional music and music of the Conservatoire are reduced to differences of simplicity and sophistication, which is perhaps somewhat reductive. And Sand's commentary on the classical music taste of Paris concertgoers in these works is not generous, especially considering the merit she gives it in her other musical works. Still, Sand's need to change societal attitudes toward the French people through music displays at once a socialist and an aesthetic goal that knows no peer in French literature of this or any time.

6

♫♫ Musician, Public, and Society ♫♫

L'artisan expédie sa besogne pour augmenter ses produits: l'artiste pâlit dix ans, au fond d'un grenier, sur une œuvre qui aurait fait sa fortune, mais qu'il ne livrera pas, tant qu'elle ne sera pas terminée selon sa conscience.

[The craftsman expedites his job to increase output: the artist grows pale for ten years holed up in an attic for the sake of a single work that would have made his fortune, but which he'll not relinquish so long as it does not satisfy his conscience.]
—*Lettres d'un voyageur*

SAND HABITUALLY ENGAGES IN DEFINING THE GOALS, FUNCTION, AND position of the artist in a progressive society. Sand's musicians, who often represent an ideal artist, serve to demonstrate not only musical aesthetics but also the moral and spiritual responsibility of performing artists toward society. In all her musical texts, an important aspect of musicianship is the ability to understand the symbiotic relationship between musician and public. As Sand's musicians spiritually mature toward a recognition of and the value of performance and its role in society, the quality of the music they produce improves. As they struggle to comprehend the extent of the public's role in performance and their duty to it, they acquire a keen awareness of the value of the exchange between artist and audience. Although Sand's portrayal of her artists' successes and failures necessarily contributes to her definition of the artist, I am less concerned with success in an aesthetic or commercial sense. Rather I am interested in Sand's portrayal of musicians' relationships to the public and generally their role in society. Examining this aspect of the musician allows a privileged insight into Sand's views on artistic responsibility and social structure, Saint-Simonism, religion, and finally the female musician—all through music.

279

Musicians and the Public

Sand considers an open, bilateral relationship between musician and public not only as an essential element of the interpreter's profession but also as a metaphor for the proper functioning of society. Discussing the protagonists of Sand's socialist novels, Michèle Hecquet affirms that Sand imagines a dialectic of solitude and communication for her heroes; she draws the steps toward integrating and emancipating society.[1] The same could be said of her musicians. The musician seeks quiet introspection for the maturation process but at the same time must commune with others, with other artists and with the public. The constant vacillation between private and public self, between individual and society constitutes a psychological dilemma for Sand's musicians that translates into an aesthetic and socialist paradox. The musicians that people Sand's universe must recognize this quandary and find a solution. For most of Sand's musicians, the solution entails an internal and external maturation commensurate with the two-pronged goal Hecquet discloses.

Sand's first musician, Gina in "La Prima donna," provides a preview of the author's attitudes toward the artist in relationship with her public. The tale focuses less on Gina and more on the narrator, possibly a function of Sandeau's influence. It is the story of the narrator's perception of the relationship between Gina and him. But Valterna presents his perceptions and desires as though he represented the general public, and in a way he does. But through the murky confusion of expectations, the reader must distinguish between the narrator's obsession and the public's demands.[2]

Gina's reputation pervades the narration. She is called "diva" and "benedetta" by those who admire her. The sacred connotations of these appellations demonstrates the degree of adulation Valterna and her public bestow on her. The French extradiegetic narrator, who is the reader's source of information, exhorts Valterna, the intradiegetic narrator, to share his knowledge of Gina's past. The effect of her singing on Valterna constitutes the focus of the story.[3]

Valterna's account of Gina's fame, talent, and subsequent demise is colored by his own adoration. He explains that while others admired her, he worshiped her: "[les autres] avaient pour elle de l'enthousiasme, pour elle mon ame avait un culte" [others felt enthusiasm for her; my soul worshipped her] ("Prima," 41). Nothing could equal his joy at hearing Gina perform, nothing could constrain his ecstasy, unless Gina failed to keep her end of the bargain by not performing. This is what happens when she marries a French

aristocrat and abandons the stage. Leaving behind her theatrical career demonstrates an adherence to social convention; no mention of
a disagreement between Gina and her husband, the duke of R***,
makes him out to be the ogre in the story, suggesting Gina did not
have the strength of character to resist the social code. On the contrary, Valterna clearly accuses Gina of forsaking her public, or
rather of abandoning him: "Eut-elle la faiblesse de se croire au-dessous de ces femmes qui l'applaudissaient tout haut, et qui l'envi-
aient en secret? Hélas! Elle était plus qu'elles toutes; elle préféra
devenir la dernière d'entre elles" [Was she weak enough to consider
herself less than those women who applauded her loudly and who
envied her secretly? Alas, she was more than all of them; she preferred to become the last among them] ("Prima," 42). The force
of the negative vocabulary in this quotation underscores the hero's
disdain and confusion at the turn of events.

When Gina subsequently falls ill, Valterna perceives this development as proof of the error of her decision. But soon he becomes
more sympathetic to her situation, which he sees as detrimental to
her health and her instrument: "Dès le premier jour elle se sentit à
l'étroit dans cette destinée nouvelle. . . . Pauvre femme! le luxe et
l'opulence ne lui allaient pas; il fallait à ses larges poumons un air
et plus âpre et plus libre" [From the first day she felt stifled in her
new destiny. Poor woman! Luxury and opulence weren't for her;
her ample lungs needed more biting and freer air] ("Prima," 42).
His evaluation is defined by musical considerations and therefore
by musical symbols, hence the metaphor of the weakened state of a
singer who cannot breathe adequately and the paradox of liberation
and constriction that characterizes a performing artist's life—part
of the romantic ethos, certainly, but also a firm belief of Sand's.
The specter of dejection and abandonment haunts Valterna as he
fantasizes about meeting Gina. As Gina's absence from the stage
drives her mad, Valterna also falls (sympathetically?) victim to
madness. The vacillation between illusion and reality is paralleled
by a linguistic antithesis, since Valterna's madness leads to words
and Gina's to silence.

Valterna's and the extradiegetical French narrator's positions on
Gina's abandonment of the theater demonstrate a belief in her
breach of contract. She did not sustain her promise to perform and
satisfy the desires of her public. For this renunciation of her duty
she is punished with madness. Only partial reparation is permitted
when Gina's husband accepts her doctor's (and Valterna's) advice
that she should once again sing on the stage, for this would be her
last performance and the exacting of the ultimate penalty: her ironic

death while singing the role of Juliet. Sandeau's hand is unmistakable in the tragic end of a heroine who must die for her transgression. While different from many nineteenth-century stories where the female artist who succumbs to physical passion loses her divinity, there is no mention of Eros in Gina's case. Rather her perceived abandonment of the public is her true failing.

In *Consuelo*, ten years after "La Prima donna," Sand redeems her heroine and allows her a more individual and reasonable relationship with her public. Throughout her development, Consuelo contemplates the role of the public and her duty toward it. By and large she despises the public's penchant for fioriture and determines to maintain the standards of purity and simplicity she learned from Porpora. She shares her concern for integrity in music with Anzoleto. He concedes to the will of the audience, which he at first disdains but finally admits: "Nous nous étions trompés, Consuelo. Le public s'y connaît. Son cœur lui apprend ce que son ignorance lui voile. C'est un grand enfant qui a besoin d'amusement et d'émotion. Il se contente de ce qu'on lui donne; mais qu'on lui montre quelque chose de mieux, et le voilà qui compare et qui comprend" [We were wrong, Consuelo. The public knows about these things. Their heart teaches them what their ignorance hides. They're big children who need entertainment and emotion. They're happy with what we give them, but when someone gives them something better, they compare and understand] (*C*, 1:160–61). Sand has artfully led the reader through a critique of taste and the issue of the artist's responsibility. The true artist cannot acquiesce to the whims of the public, nor can she or he ignore its cultural needs. Moreover, even a relatively uncultivated public recognizes and appreciates sincere artistry and will not be fooled. Thus the challenge for the honorable and successful artist lies in understanding and replying to the expectations of the audience while bringing them up to a standard worthy of art.[4]

In *Teverino*, Sand allows herself to mock the public's fickle attitude, but she uses the device to expose the suggestibility of Sabina, the noblewoman who is falling in love with the title character. Fooled by his aristocratic costume and grace, she assumes he is a nobleman and observes with mockery the mercurial reception the townspeople give him. Teverino first appears in ragged costume and sings badly, and he is hissed. He then changes into a refined outfit and appears from the balcony as a different person. This time he sings expertly and the public showers him with accolades. Sabina mocks the public's naivete, and at the same time the reader appreci-

ates the narrator's commentary on the noblewoman's own prejudices of appearance.

Simplicity and integrity in art often contrast with the public's
taste, a constant concern for Sand. While recognizing the need to
appeal to the public to a certain extent, she never approves of pan-
dering to mediocre sensitivities. Pauline Viardot disdained a common performance practice of the day that required the performer to
stop the dramatic action to acknowledge applause and reprise an
aria for the public's amusement. Viardot refused to comply under
the principle that it would break the dramatic continuity.[5] Such
strength of character to refuse and therefore mock the public for the
sake of artistic integrity found its way to Consuelo's characterization, although perhaps in a modified version. Anzoleto's vacillation
in this matter highlights the delicate balance an artist must strike in
order to become a success while maintaining integrity.

The relationship between Consuelo and Haydn revolves around
music, performance, composition, and relations with the public. In
one of their first conversations, they debate the goals of music.
Their discussion links music, art, and wealth with social structure.
Haydn comes to the conclusion that all poor people should be artists (*C*, 2:42). Consuelo agrees, pointing out that the rich then
would no longer despise the poor, since artists are always respected.
Haydn seems to have an epiphany: "L'art peut donc avoir un but
bien sérieux, bien utile pour les hommes?" [So then, art can have a
very serious goal? It can be quite useful for people?] With a nod to
Saint-Simon's teachings and Pierre Leroux's writings, Sand helps
Consuelo to bring Haydn to another level of philosophy: "Avez-
vous donc pensé jusqu'ici que ce n'était qu'un amusement? —Non,
mais une maladie, une passion, un orage qui gronde dans le cœur,
une fièvre qui s'allume en nous et que nous communiquons aux autres" [Did you think until now that it was just for entertainment?"
"No, but I thought it was an illness, a passion, a storm that rumbles
in our hearts, a fever that lights up in us and that we communicate
to others"]. Clearly the passion of music must be bridled and used,
at least in part, for a socialist cause.

Struggling to choose between music and Albert, Consuelo tries
out her opinion of the public and its dominion over the artist on
Porpora:

[I]l y a dans la vie quelque autre chose que l'argent et la vanité, et ce
quelque chose est assez précieux pour contrebalancer les enivrements
de la gloire et les joies de la vie d'artiste. C'est l'amour d'un homme
comme Albert, c'est le bonheur domestique, ce sont les joies de la fa-

284 WHILE THE MUSIC LASTS

mille. Le public est un maître capricieux, ingrat et tyrannique. Un noble époux est un ami, un soutien, un autre soi-même. (*C*, 2:160)

[In life there's something other than money and vanity, and this other thing is rather precious for offsetting the intoxication of glory and the joys of an artist's life. It's the love of a man like Albert, it's domestic tranquility, the joys of a family. The public is a capricious, ungrateful, and tyrannical master. A noble spouse is a friend, a support, another self.]

Consuelo does not forsake her respect for the public. However, she does recognize the dangers of devoting oneself wholly to a public that could at a moment's notice topple one artist in favor of another. More than glory and ambition, she values the stability and support of a loving partner. Here her goals differ considerably from those of her mentor, who affirms that "la liberté, le seul bien, la seule condition de développement de l'artiste" [freedom, the only good thing, the only condition for the development of the artist] (*C*, 2:161), cannot be replaced with the love of a human being.

Trying to find work in Vienna, Consuelo learns that she needs to please, and not always musically. Empress Maria-Theresa does not present the only obstacle; there are also the internal politics of the court. The Venetian ambassador's mistress is also a soprano and not about to allow Consuelo to take over her roles at the opera. In addition, the theater director's wife is the prima donna of the Viennese opera. Only when Consuelo sings with Caffariello, a former student of Porpora who has recently had much success in London, do people recognize her great talent. These problems represent politics more than aesthetic concerns, which Sand paints as external factors that partially define society's dominion over artists. These difficulties contribute to Consuelo's emerging rejection of a commercial career. Clearly inspired by Pauline Viardot's difficulties and no doubt her own to some degree, Sand expresses through Consuelo her frustration at an unjust and unproductive influence of politics over art.

No further mention is made of an artist's relation to the public in *Consuelo* until the epilogue, and here the commentary remains implicit. Consuelo, now in the role of interpreter, explains to Spartacus and Philon that Albert's music is the fruit of his inspiration. He answers to no public demand nor to any convention. He simply plays what he feels he must "say" and hopes those listening will "understand." The notion of a conventional, commercial public is absent from the end of the novel. Sand has gone beyond respectfully and responsibly satisfying an audience to eliminating the paying public. Albert and Consuelo no longer consider public taste of any importance. Only the word of God is important. Spartacus and Philon represent the new public, one that seeks the truth in a new religion, in a new (French) society. Accordingly, Consuelo asks the pilgrims to leave them at the end of the novel, as they continue their musical crusade.

The predictions of the French Revolution at the end of *La Comtesse de Rudolstadt* coincide with Sand's purging of the public, or more exactly, with her refusal of a social hierarchy based on economics. If music has become, as Albert and Consuelo claim, a pure language of communication with God, the struggle to understand must inevitably lead to revolution and total social reform. The role of the artist as messenger and guide takes shape in this text. Consuelo's discoveries in music have led her to this conclusion, partly through her relationship with Albert and partly through her own experiences. She has traveled from gypsy to opera singer, to postulant, to social reformer—all through music. And her perception of the public and her responsibility to it has changed from financial dependence to aesthetic reference, to religious association, to relative indifference, to devoted initiator. At the end of *La Comtesse de Rudolstadt* it is no longer the public that is important, but society: society in the socialistic sense in which Sand uses it represents a population who work and play together and for which the lessons of egalitarianism and freedom are paramount. Béatrice Didier posits that Sand cannot write after *Consuelo* as she did before, since now the relationship between professional and amateur musicians is blurred.[6] In like manner I would say that the relationship between musician and public has also been altered. The role of the public in *Le Château des Désertes* is a thoroughly revised one since it is now the actors themselves who serve as the sole public for each other. They strive for aesthetic success, with only Boccaferri to serve as their critic. This venerable but choleric old man represents not the public, not society, but the artistic ideal.

The position of the musician vis-à-vis society poses a constant problem for Sand. Her fictional musicians in a Parisian setting invariably face a class-conscious society in which their function as entertainers eclipses their consideration as artists. Consuelo embodies the ideal of an artist who crosses class lines, as do so many Sandian heroines, and restores the performer's dignity. *Malgrétout* tirelessly places the violinist Abel in a situation of judgment. Abel is a professional violinist with a European reputation. Sarah and her father admire him because of his renown but more because of his musicianship. Adda, the heroine's sister, finds him inferior because an artist, calling him a *"râcleur de crincrin"* [fiddle scratcher] (*M*, 144). M. de Rémonville, Adda's husband, also denigrates him and artists in general, though his position is complicated by the fact that Abel has performed at his Parisian mistress's home.

Carmen d'Ortosa, the character supposedly based on the Empress Eugénie, plays both sides of the question.[7] On the one hand, she is attracted to Abel because of the passion he displays in his playing. On the other hand, she disdains him because she could never marry him; she is a social climber and Abel can not help her reach the privileged place in society she seeks. There is also a lingering suspicion about the public that adores him, since he pleases the masses as well as the elite. This gift is at once troubling to Carmen and pleasing to the narrator.[8]

An interesting discussion and extended metaphor between Sarah and Carmen springs from Mr. Owen's analogy of artist to attorney. Sarah's father is a retired attorney, and he likens his experience in the courtroom to that of a performing artist. Sand's memories of Michel de Bourges, whose passion in legal and socialist matters earned him a great reputation, can be detected in this passage. The syllogism is precious and worth quoting in full.[9]

> Je pourrais vous dire aussi que, dans ma carrière d'avocat, j'ai ressenti des émotions analogues, et que je n'ai jamais pu me trouver en contact avec l'émotion du public sans être en proie à la fièvre. On eût pu alors taxer d'exagération ma parole, mon attendrissement, mon indignation, mes affirmations passionnées. Pourtant, je vous le jure, jamais je n'ai été plus sincère et plus convaincu que dans ces moments-là, et, comme je suis un honnête homme, je vous jure aussi que, sans conviction intime et profonde, je n'eusse pu trouver en moi la puissance de convaincre mon auditoire. Les avocats sont des artistes, et voilà pourquoi je comprends les artistes comme si je vivais en eux. (*M*, 38)

> [I could also tell you that in my career as a lawyer, I felt similar emotions, and that I was never able to be in contact with the public's emotion without falling victim to fever. My speech, my tenderness, my indignation, my impassioned affirmations could then have been charged with exaggeration. However, I swear to you that I was never more sincere or more reassured than at those moments, and as I am an honest man, I also swear to you that without innermost and profound conviction, I would never have been able to find the force to persuade my audience. Lawyers are like artists, and that's why I understand artists as if I were living within them.]

The representation of public in *Les Maîtres Sonneurs* proves slightly more complex than in other texts. That this novel takes place wholly in the Berrichon and Bourbonnais countryside and that the music is folk music played for village festivals adds a different perspective. Joset and his fellow master pipers do play for money, fulfilling a contract according to established rules of trade. Joset never actually plays in a formal venue as his right to do so comes at the end of the novel—followed quickly by his demise. Others, notably Huriel, do play for formal functions—however, Huriel does not accept payment for his piping—and the response of the peasant public determines the musician's success.

Joset hardly represents an ideal musician in respect to his attitude toward the public. His first and primary public is Brulette. She "sees" the very images of her childhood that Joset reflects on as he plays in the scene of the reed flute. Even though Tiennet is also present at this scene, his reaction is of no concern to Joset. From this point of view, the scene is doubly important since it divulges his desires in the realms of both communication and performance, the dual role of music in the novel.

Sand does not, however, avoid the question of the musician's ability to communicate to a larger public in this novel, since the model master piper must be able to meet the expectations of the village. Such is the situation when Carnat the younger plays for the festivities of the feast of Saint John the Baptist (the seventh *veillée*). The young people who have assembled to dance are not happy with his playing, saying he is too much of a novice and that his playing takes away their dancing legs (*MS*, 153). At this point enters Huriel, "un grand beau sujet. . . . 'Voilà un cornemuseux de rencontre, qui vous en baillera tant que vous en voudrez, et qui, mêmement, ne vous prendra rien pour sa peine' [a fine specimen. . . . "Here's a bagpiper of reckoning who will give you as much as you want, and what's more, he won't take anything for his efforts"] (*MS*, 154). And he plays at length to the group's great contentment.

Sand emphasizes here several elements of the relationship between musician and public. First is the matter of compensation. Huriel agrees to play without pay, which demonstrates his joy in making music, but also his choice not to play professionally despite his earned rank of master piper. This decision, made mostly for reasons of stability of employment and income, suggests at the same time a tendency among professional musicians—folk musicians, yes, but also musicians in general—to lose sight of the joy of making music and to allow financial exigencies to dominate. Later we will encounter other master pipers who wish to keep Joset out of their brotherhood because his talent will surely garner him gigs that the others would normally get, resulting in a loss of income.[10]

Sand also represents here the right of the public to judge and its power in determining a performer's career. Dissatisfied with Carnat's playing, the people would rather stop dancing than to endure a poor performance. While Carnat is only somewhat disturbed by the turn of events, his father disrupts the festivities and demands an explanation. When he learns that Huriel has agreed to play without pay, he becomes even more upset and asks whether Huriel has a license to play. Huriel points out that artists do not pay for a license in France, but Carnat stipulates that in this region one must prove one's abilities before a jury. In a rapid exchange between the two that no one else can comprehend, by which we understand that they recognize each other by means of the gestures and formulae of a secret society, Huriel is able to quell any reasonable objection to his playing. Notable in Carnat senior's objection is the predominance of money over music.

Another important element of this discussion focuses on the term "artist," which Huriel uses and which Carnat and the others do not recognize, understand, or appreciate. Sand demonstrates not only that the peasants of the region are not familiar with the habits, conventions, and discourse of Parisian society, but also that such distinctions belong to an artificial society and ultimately hold little significance. Sand again emphasizes that peasant musicians are just as much artists as Parisian concert musicians. That Huriel uses the term remains surprising, but he has traveled more than Carnat and the other Berrichon pipers of the novel.

It is interesting to note that Joset actually plays the bagpipes only three times in the narrative: to show his disappointment at having lost Brulette's heart; for the master piper's exam; and finally at Brulette's wedding, all occurring in the last seven chapters of the novel. Even though playing appears to be important to Joset, Sand minimizes its occurrence in the narrative, but the reactions of his public are significant. While in two of these occasions Joset plays for friends, which skews the value of their judgment, it is the competition to become master piper that best demonstrates the public's appreciation. The exam is an open event where other master pipers are joined by townspeople. Joset's instrument dazzles all present. He takes on a confident and healthy countenance, which surprises the general public. These details of setting suggest the atmosphere of public performance. The people present at the exam, all of whom knew about music, appreciated his playing:

> Mais comme il ne manquait pas là de monde qui s'y connaissait, et surtout les chantres de la paroisse, et puis les chanvreurs qui sont grands

experts en idées de chansons, et mêmement des femmes âgées qui étaient bonnes gardiennes des meilleures choses du temps passé, Joseph fut vitement goûté, tant pour la manière de faire sonner son instrument sans y prendre aucune fatigue, et de donner le son juste, que pour le goût qu'il montrait en jouant des airs nouveaux d'une beauté sans pareille. (*MS*, 446)

[But as there were a lot of people there who knew music, especially the parish cantors and the hemp workers, who are great experts in matters of song, and also elderly women, the fair guardians of the best of times past, Joseph was savored as much for the way he played his instrument without tiring and with a suitable sound as for the taste he displayed in playing new tunes of uncommon beauty.]

The qualified and exacting nature of the listeners, all nonprofessionals, defines Joset's public. The "official" public for this event are the other master pipers, the judges of the exam. Clear also is the importance of women in transferring traditions from one generation to the next. This detail gives importance to the role of women in society as well as to their role as judges of aesthetics. The difference between the professional and the general public emerges from the reactions: "Les juges ne firent rien connaître de leur opinion, mais les autres assistants, trépignant de joie et faisant grande acclamation, décidèrent que rien de si beau n'avait été ouï au pays de chez nous" [The judges revealed nothing of their opinion, but the others in attendance, jumping up and down with joy and cheering loudly, decided that nothing so beautiful had ever been heard in these parts] (*MS*, 446).

That the public accepts him, however, only emphasizes the poignancy of Brulette's nonacceptance, at least as her lover. This brings us full circle in the purpose of Joset's music, which is to express his love to Brulette and thereby to win hers. For him the importance of the general publics esteem, much more important for him than that of the other pipers, is eclipsed by that of his beloved. The role of the public for Joset is equivocal and stands as a midpoint between his respect for Brulette and his disdain of the master pipers, Huriel and Bastien excepted. This trait again distinguishes Joset from Sand's other musicians, who in one way or another pay close attention to the needs and desires of their public.

For Sand the troubling relationship between performer and public, between music maker and music listener, centers around the delicate balance between self and other. Musicians exist in a world where they are venerated and adored. Their serious and arduous training as well as a talent of mysterious origin encourage them to believe in their superiority. Yet, they learn all too quickly in Sand's universe the power of the public in their professional lives and must determine how to juggle superiority with duty. Consuelo discovers the formula, as do Adriani and (eventually) Célio. Joset does not, or rather perhaps he does and is unable to accept what he sees as a compromise unworthy of his goal. Abel does not suffer from the same obstacle as Joset, but he, too, discovers that his obligations to the public are a detriment to his personal relationship, so he abandons them for Sarah. In the end, all Sand's musicians discover the problem and elaborate one solution or another.

Sand writes on this subject to Charles Poncy, a young Berrichon poet who solicits Sand's advice and support, telling him of his obligations to the public. At the same time as she points out grammatical errors in his manuscript, she alerts him to pitfalls of the role she encourages him to assume: "La vanité est l'ennemi intérieur que les poètes portent en eux. . . . [I]l faut être bon enfant. Le génie ne grandit qu'à condition d'être modeste. . . . Soyez sévère envers vous-même, et faites la guerre à votre amour-propre. . . . [V]ous verrez le respect qu'on doit [aux poètes illustres], mais le respect plus grand encore qu'on doit à ce qui est au-dessus d'eux: *la vérité*" [Vanity is the inner enemy that poets carry inside. . . . You must be a good sport. Genius grows only in direct proportion to modesty. . . . Be strict with yourself, and wage war against your pride. . . . You'll see the respect you owe great poets, but a still greater respect you owe to what is above them is *truth*] (*Corr*, 6:405–13). Sand's essential word of advice to her protégé focuses on sincerity and candor, which ultimately can come only from the respect an artist owes her or his public. Her approach to a fledgling worker poet does not differ from her presentation of fictional artists. She is just as severe with Anzoleto and Joset as she is with Poncy. Her insistence on honesty and respect does not wane or waver.[11]

In a letter to Alexandre Saint-Jean, an obscure writer whom she advises in matters of literary style, Sand has recourse to a musical analogy when counseling the young author on the delicate issue of dealing with the public. At some length she demonstrates for him the care he must take to observe the public's tastes while remaining true to his artistic ideals.

> Il y a deux écoles, je dirais volontiers deux religions dans les arts. La première dédaigne la médiocrité, le nombre, le public. Elle dit, avec raison, que peu de personnes peuvent comprendre les choses élevées et qu'il faut travailler pour le peu d'esprits délicats sans s'occuper des autres; elle appelle *vulgarité* tout ce qui est une concession à la lente et lourde intelligence des masses, c'est l'école de Beethoven.

L'autre école nous dit qu'il faut être compris de tous, parce que, dès que l'on se met en rapport avec la foule, il faut se mettre en communication avec les cœurs et les consciences; ne veut-on être compris que de soi, qu'on chante tout seul au fond des bois! Mais, si un auditoire accourt, fût-il composé de faunes, et que l'on continue à chanter, il faut se résigner à parler à ces génies[12] incultes de façon à les éclairer et à les élever au-dessus d'eux-mêmes par des paraboles claires ou tout au moins pénétrables.

J'ai longtemps hésité entre ces deux écoles. Je me suis rangée à celle de Mozart, en me disant que si j'avais dans l'âme un bon ou un beau sentiment, je devais lui trouver une expression qui le fît entrer dans beaucoup d'autres âmes, que je ne devais en dédaigner aucune. *(Corr,* 23:38)

[There are two schools of thought, I'd even say two religions in the arts. The first one disdains mediocrity, the masses, the public. It states, with reason, that few people can understand lofty things and that you have to work for those few subtle minds without concerning yourself with the others. It calls everything that is a concession to the obtuse and dense intelligence of the masses *vulgar*; this is the school of Beethoven.

The other school tells us that you have to make yourself understood by everyone, because, the moment you put yourself in contact with the pack, you have to be in tune with their hearts and consciences. If you want to be understood only by yourself, then go sing all alone in the woods! But if an audience flocks to you, even if it's made up of deer, and you go on singing, you have to resign yourself to speaking to uncultured people in such a way as to elevate them above themselves by use of transparent or at least accessible parables.

I hesitated a long time between these two schools. I took my place in the ranks of Mozart's, telling myself that if I had in my soul a good or a beautiful sentiment, I needed to find an expression that would unmask it to many other souls, and that I should not disdain a single one of them.]

This sentiment, which Sand expresses privately as advice from an experienced to a fledgling writer in 1872, recalls the counsel Consuelo gave Anzoleto thirty years earlier. Her appreciation of the public and of the artist's responsibility toward the public remains constant. The importance of communication overshadows that of artistic integrity; even though the artist cannot entirely forsake aesthetic ideals. She concludes, "L'art pour l'art est un vain mot. L'art pour le vrai, l'art pour le beau et le bon, voilà la religion que je cherche. . . . C'est mon plaidoyer" [Art for art's sake is a vain term. Art for truth, art for beauty and good, that's the religion I seek. . . . That's my plea] *(Corr,* 23:39).[13]

Many of Sand's musicians are outsiders. This is an especially paradoxical position since the dialectic of self and other plays both ways. On the one hand, the public is Other, the non-initiated desperate to be guided by the artist, who in turn must keep them from falling into the abyss of entertainment. On the other hand, it is the artist who is the Other, representing at once someone who is different and therefore dangerous, but also someone who is exotic and therefore attractive. While this aspect of the artist does not differ so much from the romantic ethos of the outlaw, it seems to diverge from Sand's insistence on the musician's role in social progress. If the musician contributes to a new social order made possible through the unifying language of music, how can she or he remain outside society?

Those Sandian musicians who best fit the profile of the outsider represent an exotic appeal not unlike Vigny's poet in "Le Mont des Oliviers," or Hugo's in "Tristesse d'Olympio," or even in Baudelaire's "Albatros." Joset certainly qualifies as an outsider, but so do Abel and Consuelo, and even Adriani to a certain degree. These outsider musicians create a space where music at once comforts and disturbs, an essential quality of art. They lure music lovers and others into a place where the ills of the material world can be momentarily forgotten and from where they reemerge fortified against individual and social doubt. But different from the standard outsider of the romantic tradition, Sand's musicians are not on a higher plane than other humans. Even Consuelo, Sand's ideal musician, remains entirely human throughout the novel, especially in her incarnation as "la bonne déesse de la pauvreté." Again Sand innovates from a known quantity to the delight of her reading public, creating a world of attainable goals and thus a real promise for social progress.

SAINT-SIMONISM, THE "NEW RELIGION," AND THE ARTIST'S ROLE IN SOCIETY

Rambeau observes that after *Mauprat* (1834), having met Liszt, Lamennais, Leroux, and finally Chopin, and having been introduced to Ballanche's works and Saint-Simonism, Sand finds a new direction in her writing. This burgeoning theme, the problem of art and of the role of the artist in society, establishes an important coherence in Sand's writings on art and artists. I agree with Cœuroy, Marix-Spire, and Rambeau about the importance of Saint-Simonism in the formulation of Sand's aesthetics, finding more influence

from the doctrines of Saint-Simonian disciples than has been inti-
mated by recent scholars.[14]

George Sand's involvement with Saint-Simonians in the early
1830s was brief and limited. The now-famous quotation from the
1852 preface to *Valentine*, wherein Sand refers to her critics' accusation of her having been involved in Saint-Simonism, evinces her
ironic acknowledgment of such influence without at the same time
adhering to it wholesale, "Il paraît que, croyant faire de la prose,
j'avais fait du saint-simonisme sans le savoir" [It seems that, thinking I was writing prose, I had unwittingly been practicing Saint-
Simonism] (*V*, 29). While she wrote in her novels of the slavery of
women in marriage, she did not believe in the abolition of the institution of marriage, as some had thought as early as the publication
of *Indiana* in 1832. Ten years later she defends her purpose, "Je
n'avais point à faire un traité de jurisprudence, mais à guerroyer
contre l'opinion; car c'est elle qui retarde ou prépare les améliora-
tions sociales." [It was not my intention to write a treatise in jurisprudence, but to wage war against public opinion, because that's
what slows down or prepares social improvement].[15] Her criticism
of public opinion will occupy an important place in *Histoire de ma
vie*.[16] When rumor gave Sand's name as a possible wife to the Saint-
Simonian Pope, Prosper Enfantin, she scoffed and politely refused
the invitation to become the "Mère" of the movement. While she
was reputed to have shunned its progressive ideas, or even its reputation for sexual unfettering, perhaps she had already seen some of
the problems of Enfantin's designs.[17]

Michèle Hecquet artfully explains the degree to which Sand di-
vorces herself from Saint-Simonian doctrine. Especially in matters
of art, Sand does not see herself, or any true "poet," as a leader of
the people; neither does she endorse the role of entertainer. She
does adhere to the notion of the artist as a medium through whom
the voice of the suffering people can be heard. Yet, Hecquet continues, she maintains the poet's right to change opinion based on
doubt and faith. The poet is a bother, a grain of sand in the well-
oiled mechanism of the State, whose job it is to expose problems in
the system for the consideration of all.[18]

Despite this apparent distancing from the "cult," and in contrast
to Hecquet's and Perrot's assertion that the only aspect of Saint-
Simonism Sand retains is the criticism of property and Saint-Simon's sense of syncretism,[19] several other precepts of Saint-Simonian doctrine do surface in Sand's works. In particular, and
especially important for my purposes, Sand recognized the domi-
nant role of music in later Saint-Simonian doctrine as detailed by

one of the main Saint-Simonian disciples, Émile Barrault. Following the comments of Bazard that the fate of society was not so much in the hands of the rational as in those of the feeling and loving, and those who have the power to cause others to feel and love,[20] Barrault continued to study the role of the fine arts in the history and the future of humanity. He posited that music is "la seule langue commune entre les hommes" [the only common language among men].[21]

For Sand the importance of the musician as the symbol of the artist and of the positioning of the artist in society, especially after *La Dernière Aldini* (1837), cannot be dismissed. Having already shown her devotion to the importance of music, she assigned an almost priestly role to the musician. Such a position of importance can certainly be seen in Albert and Consuelo, but also in Père Bastien of *Les Maîtres Sonneurs*. The terms "artiste" and "prêtre" were often synonymous in late Saint-Simonian vocabulary; and many instances of the poet-*vates* can be found in the poetry and fiction of the time. But Sand's adaptation of this model responds not only to a Saint-Simonian ideal and a romantic ethos but also to her own idealism. Other elements of Saint-Simonism emerge in Sand's writings in relationship to music. I offer here a brief discussion of the notions of industrialism, the progress of society, the new religion of the Saint-Simonians, and the function of social art as portrayed in Sand's musical texts.

In the 1820s and 1830s, as Saint-Simon and later his disciples assimilated the ideals of the Revolution and distanced themselves from the romantic tendencies for solitude, they attached more and more importance to the role of industry in the progress of society. The impending Industrial Revolution, already in full swing in England, caused Saint-Simonians to privilege the place of industrial engineers and concerns in the new social order they contemplated. Industrialists (*industriels*) and scientists (*savants*) were to become the leaders of the new society, accompanied by artists on a secondary level. Barrault, opposing Enfantin's and Saint-Simon's original thinking, considered the arts on an equal plane with the other two components. Along with Lamartine, Vigny, and Hugo, Sand recognized and encouraged the importance of art for society. She espoused Barrault's beliefs and incorporated them into her writings.

Her first published text on the philosophical aspects of music, *Les Sept Cordes de la lyre* (1839), demonstrates considerable concern about the Saint-Simonian privileging of the industrial state. The title suggests to what degree she places industrial progress as the basis of a new society, since the seven strings of the lyre are made

of gold (two), silver (two), steel (two), and bronze (one). The metallic symbolism of the novel in dialogue form recalls the ages of humanity (the Iron Age, the Bronze Age), with the notable addition
of precious metals (gold and silver) and the more modern, industrial
metal, steel.[22] In the fourth act, entitled "The Steel Strings," Sand
depicts the ills of urban life amid the disarray of modern technology. Clearly, industrial progress alone cannot save society. Only
music and the arts can redeem the human race from the dangers of
such an existence.[23]

In the fourth act, Hélène climbs to the top of a cathedral spire,
symbolizing her desire to remove herself as much as possible from
the world and to approach God. From her vantage point, she observes what the Spirit of the Lyre calls "l'empire des hommes"
("the empire of men"):

> Je ne vois rien qu'une mer de poussière embrasée que percent çà et là
> des masses de toits couleur de plomb et des dômes de cuivre rouge où
> le soleil darde ses rayons brûlants! Je n'entends rien qu'une clameur
> confuse, comme le bourdonnement d'une ruche immense entrecoupé
> par instants de cris aigus et de plaintes lugubres! (*SC*, 156)

> [I see nothing but a sea of burning dust pierced here and there by the
> mass of leaden roofs and copper domes where the sun hurls its blazing
> rays. I hear nothing but a cluttered commotion like the buzzing of a
> huge beehive momentarily interrupted by the sharp wailing of mournful
> laments!]

The use of metals in this description of the city echoes the materials of the eponymous strings with the additional painterly effect of
chiaroscuro. Sand portrays the city in the evocative oxymoron of a
sea of burning dust. What emerges is a confused visual and auditory mass that represents the maelstrom of humanity. The use of
"ruche" is interesting; it not only implies a swarming, noisy mass
of industriousness, it is also a common metaphor for the disorder of
society. At the same time, it is a metaphor used by contemporary
socialist thinkers to designate groups of workers living in commu-
nities according to various socialist models. (Fourier designated
similar living and working groups as "phalanstères.") But the Spirit
of the Lyre urges Hélène to examine more closely "la puissance de
l'homme . . . les merveilles de son infatigable industrie! . . . la voix
de l'industrie, le bruit des machines" [the power of man . . . the
marvels of his tireless industry! . . . the voice of industry, the noise
of machines"] (*SC*, 156–57). This long speech is sung by the Spirit
of the Lyre. Wilhelm hears and understands it: "Jamais la lyre n'a

été plus sonore, jamais le chant n'a été plus mâle, et l'harmonie plus large ou plus savante" [Never had the lyre been more sonorous, never had the song been more masculine and the harmony more abundant or more enlightened]. Even Albertus begins to hear and understand the music: "Oui, maintenant enfin, je comprends le langage de la lyre" [Yes, now I finally understand the lyre's language].

But Hélène sees and hears something different: "Je ne vois au-dessous de moi que les abîmes incommensurables du désespoir, je n'entends que les hurlements d'une douleur sans ressource et sans fin!" [Below me I see only the immeasurable chasm of despair, I hear only the wailing of suffering without resource or end] (SC, 158). The money she hears rolling on the tables of rich men is the tears of the poor, the sweat of the worker, the blood of the soldier. Disgusted by what the Spirit of the Lyre has shown her, despite his efforts to reveal the good hidden by evil and to convince her of the need to endure suffering in order to find justice, Hélène throws the lyre from the spire and comes back down from her pinnacle of elitist observation to go into exile. Similarly, Ballanche, whose Orphée Sand was reading at the time, explores in book 8 the inexplicable human suffering that seems to be the price to be paid for progress. Throughout this passage Sand has been careful to supply equal doses of visual and auditory images and references. Music always accompanies and often dictates the transmission of communication. When Hélène throws down the lyre, the crowd gathered below remarks, "La musique a cessé!" [The music has ended!] (SC, 162).

The steel strings symbolize modern, industrial society, and by destroying them Albertus removes the harshness of the industrial revolution from his world. Albertus's act was not inspired by an altruistic and socialist impetus, rather by an egotistical one. Nonetheless, Sand creates a situation where Albertus and Hélène together, though not in complicity, work toward social progress. The expiation of the ills of industrial society through music allows for social and humanitarian progress alongside industrial progress. Industrialization is not destroyed or halted; it is put into a more balanced perspective, equal to the fine arts. The Spirit of the Lyre, who is deified in this text, reveals the good that is to be seen beneath apparent evil. Far from advocating a destruction of a future industrial France, Sand is promulgating the careful balance of technical and humanitarian progress.

The final string symbolizes love. Once again Ballanche's link between the love of a sanctioned union of two people and social progress serves to influence Sand's denouement. In book 3 of Orphée the title character says, "Je vais chercher sur ma lyre les accords qui peignent l'amour, car ils y sont aussi bien que ceux de l'inspiration sociale: et la société conjugale n'est-elle pas la première de toutes les sociétés humaines?" [On my lyre I shall seek chords that paint love, for they must exist as much as the chords of social inspiration; and is not conjugal society the first of all human societies?].[24] Thus a marriage of equals forms the foundation of modern society, an ideal with which Sand agrees wholeheartedly.

By the time Sand became interested in Saint-Simonism, the master himself had died and his work was being preached and developed by his disciples, who did not always agree among themselves. The place of the arts in Saint-Simonism became more defined by the next generation and in most cases took on a more important role. Fromental Halévy also wrote passionately about the social role of music. In a singing primer as well as in the preface of an article on music for the *Encyclopédie nouvelle*, which he was unable to complete, he espouses a sociological influence of society on the arts. He focuses on music's effect on those who make it rather than on the use of music for the needs and goals of society, as the encyclopedia's editors would have preferred.[25] Liszt and Nourrit championed the movement to bring music to the people, thus making them happier and perhaps encouraging them to be more productive human beings. The overlap of the Saint-Simonian goal of productivity and the egalitarian socialist goal of making music accessible to more than just the elite is evident in these musicians' acts. George Sand, encouraged largely by the examples of Liszt and Nourrit, lent her pen to the efforts for egalitarianism in music as in all aspects of society.

The evolution of Saint-Simonian theories of the place of art in the social structure can best be see in a didactic text written by Léon Halévy and Saint-Simon. Léon Halévy, brother of the well-known composer Fromental Halévy, was secretary to Saint-Simon and penned large portions of the pamphlet *Opinions littéraires, philosophiques et industrielles*, specifically a section entitled "The Artist, the Scientist, and the Industrialist: A Dialogue." In this article Halévy writes that art fulfills a human need quite apart from its effect on behavior and attitudes. While Saint-Simon had already written that art civilizes people, Halévy takes the concept to the next stage by positing that "man is still eager for the delights that the fine arts procure."[26] The "Dialogue" (1825) bears witness to a complex network of notions that emerged from the Saint-Simonian experience, not least of which is marketing. Having seen that the general public was no longer interested in industrial politics, Halévy convinced Saint-Simon to endorse art as an instrument of publicity. The extrinsic utility of art was the object of his attentions, placing art in a high position in the socialist hierarchy but solely because of its utilitarian possibilities. The problem of the term *art social* comes to the fore. Is social art just a means to an end? How did artists react to this notion?

Witness Halévy's words as he extols the role of the artist in society:

> Let us combine our forces, and mediocrity. . . . Let us unite. . . . We—the artists—will be your vanguard. The power of the arts is in effect the most immediate and most rapid of all powers. We have all kinds of weapons. . . . We address ourselves to man's imagination and sentiments; consequently we are always bound to have the sharpest and most decisive effect. . . . This is the task, the mission of the artists. . . . Artists, who are men essentially *passionate* by nature, can usefully take their place among the rulers, who are essentially *rational* by nature. We know that in their language *reason* means *power*, and they have such a dread of *passion* that they even fear passion for the public good. But if the capacity for ruling, which no longer directly fulfils one of society's needs, or, to be more exact, which fulfils only secondary needs, were to become subordinate, as it is in reality, and were to relinquish the direction of national interests to the great positive capacities on which the social edifice rests, then not only would the participation of artists, men of imagination, in the direction of public affairs no longer be anomalous, it would be *useful* and *necessary*.[27]

This passage begs some commentary on the mixture of the eighteenth-century dichotomy of reason and nature and the mid-nineteenth-century application of positivism to social progress. Halévy is clearly pulling out all the stops in an effort to convince the (liberal) public of the necessity of art in the overall socialist scheme. The phrase "*useful* and *necessary*" suggests the lengths to which he felt he needed to go in order to win over liberal thinkers—artists and industrialists alike—to the cause of socialism. The opposition of a military vocabulary to imagination suggests the enlistment of that "queen of all faculties" in the service of social reform. We cannot ignore that the very existence of a "ruling" structure is during the Restoration under scrutiny now that the former limits placed on the participation of the arts in political and social organization is to be reversed. This would then allow an important place for the arts in government, if indeed government be needed. The idealistic, utopian thoughts behind these comments do little to convince the modern reader of the importance of the fine arts, and in fact few artists of the period were seduced by the rhetoric. However, Liszt, Nourrit, Béranger, and Sand were not deaf to some of these ideals.[28]

Just before meeting Sand, Liszt had become quite interested in Saint-Simonian ideals as well as in the writings of abbé Lamennais. He learned a great deal from Barrault's teachings and accordingly began to think of the artist as priest, who would play an important role as guide and leader toward social goals in the critical phases of history and as animator of action in the direction of these goals in the organic phases. From Lamennais, Liszt developed a sense of the solidarity of artists, and in this solidarity he saw a common cause in the goals of social reform. His enchantment with the abbé's ideas in *Paroles d'un croyant* (1834), so in tune with Saint-Simonian doctrine and his own unarticulated frustration at the plight of artists, led him to Taitbout to hear the predications of Saint-Simonian speakers. He vowed to realize the popularization of Saint-Simonism and thereby to raise the status of the artist in society. Rather than the provider of entertainment for an elite, Liszt saw the artist as an equal member of society, one who could and should serve as a messenger to tell the public "where we come from, where we're headed, what our mission is."[29] He took as his model Paganini, whom he revered as an artist able to unite beauty with utility. Ballanche, too, inspired Liszt to develop his thoughts about the important role of the arts, especially music, in the development of the public's instruction.[30]

Liszt did not, however, feel capable of this task on his own and enlisted the aid of his newfound friend, George Sand, whom he already admired as an artist. He thought she could convince people to acknowledge and correct the current dismal position of the artist in society. Coincidentally, Sand was at this time, in the autumn of 1834, floundering with her own inarticulate ideals of art and its place in society. Disappointed in Musset as the embodiment of the poet and disillusioned by the ideas of Michel de Bourges on art and artists, Sand found in Liszt the incarnation of her ideal, the artist-musician who would bring the message of art to the people.[31] Despite the jealousies of Musset and Marie d'Agoult, Sand continued to correspond with Liszt and to meet with him to discuss their ideas on art. Liszt persuaded her to meet Lamennais in May 1835. Together they dreamed of a better condition for artists.

Sand refutes the ideas of Michel de Bourges in the sixth letter of *Lettres d'un voyageur*, stating that the effective usefulness of the artist is to give emotions and mystical enthusiasm to those who work by the sweat of their brow. Usefulness, she continues, does not have to be described in terms of social action, but it should involve a conscientious effort to raise humanity to a higher level of reflection and to allow for dreams of a better future.

> Le citoyen austère [Michel] veut supprimer les artistes, comme des su-perfétations sociales qui concentrent trop de sève; mais monsieur aime la musique vocale et il fera grâce aux chanteurs. . . . Mais dis-moi pour-quoi vous en voulez tant aux artistes. L'autre jour, tu leur imputais tout le mal social, tu les appelais *dissolvants*, . . . Est-ce à l'*art* lui-même que tu veux faire le procès? Il se moque bien de toi, et de vous tous, et de tous les systèmes possibles! . . . Si ce n'est pas l'art que tu veux tuer, ce ne sont pas non plus les artistes. Tant qu'on croira à Jésus sur la terre, il y aura des prêtres, . . . tant qu'il y aura des mains ferventes, on entendra résonner la lyre divine de l'art. (*LV,* 2:807–8)

> [The sober citizen wants to remove artists as social superfluities that distill too much sap; but the gentleman likes vocal music and he'll par-don singers. . . . But tell me, what do all of you hold against artists. The other day you attributed to them all social evil; you called them *insurgents*. . . . Is it *art* itself you want to take to court? It doesn't care a whit about you, nor about any of you nor all your reasonable systems! . . . If it's not art you want to kill, then it's not artists either. So long as we believe in Jesus on earth, there will be priests, . . . so long as there are impassioned hands, we'll hear the divine lyre of art resounding.]

Sand's apologia of art, even though an emotional reaction to Mi-chel's vitriolic attack, is a constant element of her ideology. No clearer is the burgeoning concept of social art for Sand than in these statements where she demonstrates her refusal to accept wholesale the utilitarian goal of Michel's socialism. The musical metaphor at the end of the passage, although certainly not original with Sand, mirrors the most common application of her aesthetic principle, which she put at the center of many novels from this time to the end of her career.

This introduces the argument of art for art's sake, which has par-adoxically enjoyed both the reputed support and rejection of Saint-Simonians. Rather than try to resolve this thorny problem of Saint-Simonian ideology, I wish rather to point out that Sand clearly moves away from a utilitarian function of art to a profound appreci-ation of its aesthetic beauty along with a moral and thereby social function. As Barrault states in his *Prédication sur l'art,* "Only the artist, in a word, by the power of that sympathy that causes him to embrace God and society is worthy to guide humanity!"[32] As for the separation of the beauty and usefulness of art that Gautier, among others, so acutely espoused, Sand disagreed and saw an es-sential mixture of both.

It may be suggested that, just as Saint-Simonian doctrine posits the use of art principally for production goals, the socialist view of art is primarily utilitarian. However, if one follows the arguments of Barrault, Halévy, and others, art may be seen as useful and necessary on its own. Pushing the pragmatic interpretation to the extreme, one can arrive at an authoritarian, even a fascist use of art, a criticism that has been levied as the ultimate result of a Saint-Simonian approach to the fine arts. Adopting the aesthetic interpretation, one can conceivably come to a self-serving purpose for art. In fact, one can see both interpretations functioning at the same time in a slightly altered, compromised fashion, insofar as the later Saint-Simonians, and Sand with them, recognized the ability of art to influence and engage the public. This would mean it answered some ineffable need for art. In such a powerful and dangerous capacity, art could either develop in the direction of utilitarianism or instead toward that of abstracted aesthetics. Sand maintains throughout her life that the human need for art commands the artist to produce for the good of the public. It is the artist's responsibility to please the public but also to instruct, to challenge, and to elevate. Hélène, Consuelo, Albert, Cécilia, and several others advance the conscientious obligation of the artist to respond to the public while bringing to it another realm of thought, of feeling, of existence.

Saint-Simonians urged workers to join with industrial leaders for the sake of the "association" and to avoid strikes and political organization. We can see a reflection of this attitude in Sand's treatment of corruption in the guild system of bagpipers in *Les Maîtres Sonneurs*. The *confrérie* of pipers as she presents it in this novel claims to regulate quality and quantity. However, the majority of its members are more preoccupied with nepotism and wages. Sand depicts Carnat and his ilk in a greedy light. Huriel and his father counterbalance the picture, but the difference between them and the former is important: first, they are Bourbonnais while the others are Berrichons; second, while they are master pipers they are not professional musicians, having decided to work instead as woodsmen, whereas the Berrichon pipers are professionals. Even though Sand may not be actively promulgating Saint-Simonian ideals by denigrating this pipers' anachronistic trade union, there is evidence of a lingering influence.

Pierre Leroux, another source of socialist ideology for Sand, had long since left the fold of the Saint-Simonians and had established his own utopian notions based on a mixture of nineteenth-century idealism and eighteenth-century rationalism. The mission of the artist, he maintains, is to reflect the times. He sees among romantic artists two camps: having lost faith in contemporary structure, some express that loss of confidence openly and others return to the past to seek inspiration. Unfortunately, he says, Sand's *Lélia* puts emphasis on despair and discouragement, even though she has something new to say about doubt and pain. *Indiana* showed a more hopeful solution, he says, which was ignored in Léon Halévy's stage rendition, which ends with Raymon's death. Fortoul, a disciple of Leroux, criticizes Halévy's interpretation, which disregards the forward-looking aspect of the novel.[33]

The concatenation of ideas from Saint-Simon and his disciples, from Lamennais, and even from Liszt, causes Sand to reflect on the notion of a new religion and music's place therein. Influenced by the Saint-Simonian use of "priest," largely thanks to Liszt's impressions, she examines this aspect of the artist. Pierre Leroux argues that industry attempts to transform the external nature of humanity, while art represents the internal expression. It is the exteriorization of this expression that must be fostered. Here the role of the artist-priest becomes important. Sand adheres to the notion of the artist's struggle to express, which lies in part in the need to externalize and share. Thus Albert encourages Consuelo to share her talent with others, be it on the stage or in the temple. Thus, too, Adriani returns to the stage as does Célio. Only Joset remains unwilling to share.

Eugène Rodrigues explains the nuance between the terms "artist" and "priest" in the Saint-Simonian *Doctrine*:

> [I]t has even happened that we used the word ARTIST and the word PRIEST interchangeably. . . . But there is nonetheless an important distinction between them. . . . The PRIEST CONCEIVES the future and produces the RULE which LINKS humanity's *past* destinies to its *future* ones. In other words, the PRIEST GOVERNS. The artist grasps the thought of the priest, translates it into his [own] language, and makes it perceptible to everyone. . . . The *artist*, to put it simply, is the *word* [*verbe*] of the PRIEST.[34]

Sand is less concerned with the problem of balanced status than with the transmission of a message. Her artists do not seek power, rather they wish to communicate a vision to the public. Thus Consuelo's move from opera singer to Albert's interpreter can be seen less as a change in power position than as an assertion of efficacy.

The term "priest" underscores the prickly issue in the splintering of the Saint-Simonians. While the adherents of the Taitbout gatherings were troubled by the resurgence of Catholicism under the July

Monarchy, they did not always agree on the nature of a "new religion." The role of Sand's artist in this search is to aid humanity in communion through art, most often music. All the references to "spirit" in *Les Sept Cordes de la lyre* as well as the final scenes where Hélène's apotheosis reveals a heavenly intervention encourage us to view Sand's message as one of sacred importance, one that is not easily heard or understood. Likewise, in *Spiridion* (1838), written just before *Les Sept Cordes*, Sand traces the trajectory of a religious character in search of the truth.

Spiridion, like *Lélia*, especially the 1839 *Lélia*, details a search for the true religion. The vision of a "new religion," clearly inspired by Saint-Simonian precepts, leads the narrators to discuss various forms of religion. Spiridion's studies take him from Judaism to Protestantism and finally to Catholicism. Somewhat like Sand herself, he becomes disillusioned with the lack of piety in the Catholic Church. But failing to find a solution, he continues outwardly to practice Catholicism. He commits his thoughts to paper, passes them on to his disciple, Fulgence, who buries the writings with Spiridion but tells a young monk, Alexis, about them. Alexis, together with his disciple, Angel, unearths the manuscript, entitled *Hic est veritas!*

In *Spiridion*, religious origins and mystical overtones enjoy a brief but significant musical expression. Alexis, the narrator and central figure, represents the novel's religious fervour and intellectual curiosity. In one scene, two-thirds of the way through the book, the hero is contemplating the natural surroundings of the monastery. He is rapturously disturbed by music in the midst of this calm:

[J]'entends un pêcheur qui chantait aux étoiles. . . . Mes oreilles avaient toujours été fermées à la musique, comme mon cerveau à la poésie. Je n'avais vu dans les chants du peuple que l'expression des passions grossières, et j'en avais détourné mon attention avec mépris. Ce soir-là, comme les autres soirs, je fus d'abord blessé d'entendre cette voix qui couvrait celle des flots, et qui troublait mon audition. Mais, au bout de quelques instants, je remarquai que le chant du pêcheur suivait instinctivement le rhythme de la mer, et je pensai que c'était là peut-être un de ces grands et vrais artistes que la nature elle-même prend soin d'instruire, et qui, pour la plupart, meurent ignorés comme ils ont vécu. Cette pensée répondant aux habitudes de suppositions dans lesquelles je me complaisais désormais, j'écoutai sans impatience le chant à demi sauvage de cet homme à demi sauvage aussi, qui célébrait d'une voix lente et mélancolique les mystères de la nuit et la douceur de la brise. Ses vers avaient peu de rime et peu de mesure; ses paroles, encore moins de sens et de poésie; mais le charme de sa voix, l'habileté naïve de son rhythme, et l'étonnante beauté de sa mélodie, triste, large et monotone comme celles des vagues, me frappèrent si vivement, que tout à coup la musique me fut révélée. La musique me sembla devoir être la véritable langue poétique de l'homme, indépendante de toute parole et de toute poésie écrite, soumise à une logique particulière, et pouvant exprimer des idées de l'ordre le plus élevé, des idées trop vastes même pour être bien rendues dans toute autre langue. Je résolus d'étudier la musique . . .[35]

[I hear a fisherman singing to the stars. . . . My ears had always resisted music just as my brain had done for poetry. I had perceived in peasant songs only the expression of vulgar emotions, and I had turned away with disdain. That evening, like the others, I was at first offended to hear this voice covering up the voice of the waves and perturbing my hearing. But after a few moments I noticed that the fisherman's song instinctively followed the rhythm of the sea, and I thought that he was perhaps one of those great and true artists that nature herself takes care to instruct, and who mostly die as unknown as they lived. This thought responded to my habit of making assumptions that until then I was content to carry on, and I listened without intolerance to the half-wild song of this equally half-wild man who, with a slow and melancholy voice, praised the mysteries of the night and the gentleness of the breeze. His verses had little rhyme and little rhythm; his words even less meaning and poetry; but the charm of his voice, the unsophisticated skill of his rhythm, and the surprising beauty of his melody, sad, unlimited, and monotonous like that of the waves, struck me so vigorously that all of a sudden music was revealed to me. Music seemed necessarily to be the true poetic language of man, independent of all language and of all written poetry, governed by a specific logic; nonetheless, it expressed ideas of a loftier order, ideas too vast even to be conveyed in another language. I resolved to study music.]

The passage continues in a monologue that proposes a hierarchy of the arts: first music, then poetry, and finally lyrical prose. While music enjoys only a small place in the novel, in this brief passage Sand expresses a number of her standard theories: the peasant endowed with innocent wisdom and superior musical talents; the glory of the unknown artist; the purity of music as a self-sufficient language superior to verbal communication; the parallel of music and nature; and the religious origins and function of music. The universality of music in Alexis's discovery carries the full weight of the importance Sand gives to that art. Alexis's "revelation" of the powers of music is augmented since as a novice he has already passed through several crises of skepticism. Music brings him to the realization that a higher order of existence is communicated to man in mysterious and often arcane ways. This brief analysis of music corresponds entirely to the principal theme of the novel, which centers on an exhaustive study of the Scriptures, especially of the New Testament and the endless effort to comprehend God's word. Significantly, Alexis insists that it is not the words, which are of little interest, but the music that seems to communicate to him, identical to Albert's thought he shares with Consuelo in the grotto. Herein lies the message of God, the real purpose of music.

While *Spiridion* refers to the ethereal moods the sounds of music evoke, *Consuelo* presents the clearest association of music and religion. Consuelo's characterization prepares the reader for such an interpretation, but Albert's direct comparisons take the analogy to a level of equation. From the discussion of Consuelo's musical gift (chapter 51) proceeds his speech on Protestantism versus Catholicism, Bohemian culture versus high culture, and Bohemia versus Austria. Consuelo's music, along with Zdenko's, communicates religious and political ideas, along with social ideals, in the wider sense of these terms. And the religious connotations of Albert's words seamlessly evolving into violin music underscores the mystical symbolism of music. Religion stands out as one of Sand's major concerns in the novel, evidenced by Consuelo's struggle to reconcile sacred and secular music. In the end, a new religion, the socialist goal Sand inherited from Leroux, Lamennais, Liszt, and the disciples of Saint-Simon, is revealed, communicated, and advanced through music.

Consuelo represents yet another aspect of Sand's religious message, the natural spirit of communion with God. Albert's ability to find a direct path to God through musical meditation corresponds to Consuelo's musical devotion. Together they perfect a musical form of communication they can share with others. Their musical dialogue—and this expression signifies only if "logos" can embrace a musical definition—demonstrates the union of religion and the fine arts in a society where artists are valued. The artist's responsibility remains an important issue, as with any figure who is perceived to wield power. The characterization of the artist in *Les Maîtres Sonneurs* presents another side of the situation, with unfortunate consequences for all concerned.

The religious aspects of Saint-Simonism, which Leroux and Fortoul are quick to point out, influence Sand in obvious ways. It will suffice to point out here that the utopian socialism of Leroux, influenced by Lamennais, was taken up by Liszt and Sand in their compositions of this period and transformed into a mystical, religious interpretation (not always appreciated by Leroux and which took them away from the Saint-Simonian fold in practical terms) but where the essential influence is still clear.

Sand wrote of music before 1834 in contexts that showed little political or social advocacy but certainly the germs of egalitarianism. In both *Rose et Blanche* and *Valentine*, for instance, music serves to bring different social classes together through an understanding and appreciation of musical talent regardless of social status. However, after meeting Liszt and articulating her ideas on the social role of art in dialogue with Michel de Bourges, Sand writes of music with more conviction as to its function in society. In *Les Sept Cordes de la lyre* the strong role of social progress and the concern about losing sight of aspects of society other than technology are communicated through music. In *Consuelo* Sand once again takes up the theme of achieving social equality through music, not only in Consuelo and Albert's principles, but also in the exploration of Zdenko's worth especially in contrast to Anzoleto.

In "Carl," the innkeeper's son is saved from his unenlightened and biased father, and therefore from a lifetime of stagnation and frustration, by the awakening of a dormant musical talent. This text not only exploits music's powers of recovery in terms of emotional convalescence and locating memories, but it also investigates the call to productivity through the vehicle of music. As Carl becomes more energetic by singing, he also becomes more focused, more self-aware, and garners a better self-image. The gain here is for both individual and society.

La Filleule presents a reversal of Sand's typical shift in social class since Moréna is tempted to leave her aristocratic adoptive parents and to respond to the musical yearnings of her cultural memory when she discovers her gypsy birth. This movement is echoed in the mournful and melancholy moods of Stéphen, Moréna's adoptive father, who plays country tunes in memory of his own deceased mother. Although fanciful and idealistic, this novel extols the socialist views Sand gleaned from her readings and her acquaintances.[36]

The socialist ideals portrayed in *Les Maîtres Sonneurs* are mixed with Sand's musico-psychological agenda, to depict the talented but imperious (male) musician. The interaction among the characters thus becomes a struggle between individual and society, ending in a typically tragic fashion with the banishment of the hero. Of the main protagonists, only Brulette and Huriel turn out to be upstanding characters at the end of the novel, even though one has spent almost half of the novel being a coquette and the other has committed a murder. So while music has served to distinguish a social function for the principal character, the unwitting representative of a group, the social concerns in *Les Maîtres Sonneurs* are overshadowed by the antithesis of community and individual music.

One thing remains constant for Sand: music functions in society not just as a means to increase productivity, although she does not ignore this aspect, but as a vital, human need. A need for what? This lingers as the eternal, unanswerable question in aesthetics. Sand does not attempt to answer the query. She contents herself with the equally thorny matter of how to express music, the nature of music, the effects of music, the power of music in verbal language. To this question, she also does not find a satisfying solution, but her writing on music demonstrates a tireless wonder and investigation of the issue.

While many disciples of Saint-Simon moved away from Enfantin's notion of a new religion with its elaborate hierarchy and, in their opinion, skewed principles, the need for religious restructuring was keenly felt. They found the reemergence of Catholicism during the Restoration and at the beginning of the July Monarchy disquieting, though they still adhered to a form of Christianity that remained aloof but not separated from the Church. The fear of an overpowering industrialization caused them to reconsider the place of industry in their social and socialist project. Instead of granting primary importance to the place of the industrialist, perhaps the artist could be enlisted as a marketing agent.

Alongside the redefinition of religion in the new society came a redefinition of the artist. The evolution of religious thought and structure paralleled a new conception and consideration of the fine arts, so that both developed simultaneously in new directions. For these Saint-Simonians, art *is* thought, and the form it takes ought to combine both harmony and discord in order best to affect the listener, viewer, and spectator. Buchez states that the artist has a message to share with the public. Different from previous Saint-Simonian notions, where the artist's job resides in sharing and not in discovering the message, this group of Saint-Simonians places the artist on a par with scientists and industrialists. Barrault, and Sand after him, maintain that the role of the artist is to propagate ideas.

THE FEMALE MUSICIAN

Otherness is an essential element of the Sandian artist, as I have already pointed out. Consuelo's move from the realm of the conventional to the domain of an outcast and later a political outcast exemplifies Sand's notion of the artist as other. Whereas Consuelo remains seemingly unaware of her difference until after her formal training is accomplished, Joset is all too aware of his otherness from an early age. The difference between these two musicians establishes a focal point for the definition of Sand's artist, where difference, training, and devotion form the admixture of aesthetic and narrative. The Sandian musician represents the common people and, with the exception of Joset, provides a positive model for the masses and for society as a whole. The underlying message is that we can all learn from the discipline and devotion of the musician. Consuelo is a model musician and a model person. Joset portrays less than desirable traits, requiring further examination of the gender-based commentary that underlies this distinction.

The female artist holds an especially important position in Sand's universe. Most French romantic authors do not portray female musicians as models or in fact as principal characters. In Balzac there is la duchesse de Langeais; in Stendhal there is Gina in *La Chartreuse de Parme*; Flaubert has none at all, nor does Hugo. Sand's Consuelo, an exemplary musician, represents the model for women and for society in general, but she is not the only one in Sand's fictional universe. Gina ("La Prima donna"), Portia ("Histoire du rêveur"), Blanche (*Rose et Blanche*), Hélène (*Les Sept Cordes de la lyre*), Bianca Aldini (*La Dernière Aldini*), Cécilia (*Le Château des Désertes*), Laure (*Adriani*), and Moréna (*La Filleule*)—all join to present the ideal of the female musician in Sand's world. While not all of these female singers or instrumentalists (Bianca is a harpist) are professional musicians, and not all are from the lower class (Bianca and Laure are, respectively, bourgeoise and aristocrat), Sand makes a strong case for the female musician in a way no other romantic author does. The generally inferior position of the female artist in the French tradition, clearly and ironically alluded to in *Rose et Blanche*, "La Prima donna," and *Lucrezia Floriani*, gives Sand a socioliterary basis for her rebellious, seditious characterization. And the secondary, inferior status of women in nineteenth-century French society provided obvious grounds for Sand's desire/need to develop strong women artists.

Sand portrays women's search for freedom in many of her novels, musical and non-musical. Criticism levied against a supposed tendency to concentrate on sexual liberties while shunning other feminist concerns constantly returns to the notion of a sublimation of sexual instinct. The subject of sexuality in Sand's fiction is a rich subject that has been the focus of several scholars and deserves still more study.[37] Still, I reject the inference that this is Sand's only "feminist" concern. Further, Thibert remarks on Sand's limiting herself to writing about women like herself, belonging to a privileged class with culture and education, forsaking women of more modest classes. Thibert seems to ignore Sand's devotion to the plight of peasant and working-class women in *Claudie, François le champi,* and *La Ville noire,* all of which portray women of modest means and origins and the problems that arise largely due to their status as women. In addition, Thibert states that Sand's principal method for portraying the liberated woman is to virilize her.[38] This, too, is inaccurate, as we can clearly see from the examples I have cited.

Claire Goldberg Moses posits that the Saint-Simoniennes' insistence on sexual difference emerges logically from the romantic desire to separate from the world of the ancien régime, from a universe of sameness. Difference was prized by the romantics, giving rise to individualism and solitude. If the Saint-Simonian feminist movement gave so much importance to sexual difference, the feminists of revolutionary days focused more on the notion of natural rights, as demonstrated by Olympe de Gouges's *Déclaration des droits de la femme et de la citoyenne,* based in part on Condorcet's 1790 essay on the acceptance of women into the establishment. Somehow the feminists of the Saint-Simonian movement, almost all closely linked to male leaders of the movement, felt the need to disassociate themselves from their male counterparts, leading to a pronouncement of difference that was, and will always be, based on difference from men, and thus a construct originating in men.[39]

Sand's adherence to the notion of otherness is most clearly seen in *Lettres à Marcie.*[40] But her inclination to see artists as different from the rest of society hinges somewhat on the same tendency to move away from the mainstream in an effort to establish a specialized subgroup, different from but neither superior nor inferior to the main group. Leslie Wahl Rabine postulates a reconfiguration of the oedipal triangle. Rather than the eternal opposition between father and mother, male and female, subject and object, mind and body, language and silence, especially in the case of daughters, she sees instead a structure where the mother is both object of desire and object of identification, less a system of opposition than one of unstable difference.[41] Sand's fictional mother-daughter relationships follow neatly along these lines. However, in the realm of the musician, the female musician is almost always seen in opposition to the male musician.

Apart from the obvious social and feminist commentary inherent in making female artists so prominent and strong, a study of the linguistic aspect of these female artists' music provides an interesting perspective in which to view the construction of Sand's universe. Insofar as Sand defines music as a language, we can examine the linguistic and connotative use that Sand's women make of music especially as it compares with that of her male artists. Music as a form of escape finds proponents in Sand's Amédée, Albert, and Joset, to name the most obvious. These examples are all men, but it should be noted that women are the musical vehicle for the men's escape in the first two examples. Yet women, too, use music as an escape: witness especially Gina, Consuelo, and Laure. Let us examine Sand's use of music as a language of escape and empowerment and as an expression for women.

For my discussion of the inherently feminine aspect of musical communication, I rely on an essentially Kristevan interpretation of the semiotic as opposed to the symbolic. As music can be traced to pre-oedipal rhythms embedded in a pre-verbal state, the link with the mother is clear, as is the expression of primary narcissism. Plato's *chora* symbolizes a stage of provisional articulation that precedes representation and figuration. It is a nourishing, maternal receptacle, deprived of unity, identity, or deity. Opposed to the law of the symbolic, music as a manifestation of the semiotic precedes the acquisition of language and organizes pre-verbal semiotic space. In this way, the link between music and the feminine seems certain and obvious. Criticism of Kristeva's analysis has identified an overtly masculine slant to her interpretation, from her emphasis on the phallus to her insistence on citing male artists as examples of the semiotic presented through symbolic language. Gail Schwab takes as her point of departure the now-common observation that Kristeva's semiotic is in fact just another phallic privilege. All the while recognizing Kristeva's groundbreaking analysis, Schwab introduces Irigaray's notion of the imaginary, which proposes a promise of a new social order rather than Kristeva's negative and unproductive struggle.[42] Sand can be seen in this light to have forged an inroad to establishing or suggesting a new social order through an understanding of the need for communication—and here "communication" refers not to the symbolic, verbal exchange of knowledge, but rather the pre-verbal and, in Sandian and romantic terms, mystical revelation of an ineffable meaning, ineffable because pre-verbal.

Kristeva's analysis of the *Stabat Mater* insists on the role of primary narcissism in the construction of the ego. The possibilities of communication having been swept away, one is left with sound, touch, and visual traces, older than language, for the battle against death.[43] Therefore music, in Sand's interpretation, provides this primordial "language" in the mouths of women to offer another avenue for developing a new order. Instead of adopting so-called masculine methods of ordering, Lacan's symbolic order attempting to establish control over the universe, women in Sand's world can look to music for an expression of purpose and calm. This approach is not without a sense of control, as evidenced in the case of Cécilia, who obliges Célio to check and redefine his notions of love and responsibility. And it must be said that the musical phenomena of the symbolic—mathematics and discipline, for example—are manipulated just as well by Sand's female musicians as by her male ones.

Hélène's perception of music as language in *Les Sept Cordes de la lyre* presents an interesting test case. Hélène consistently understands the Spirit of the Lyre when he speaks to her. However, the reader is aware that his "speaking" is in fact music without words, that the lyre is playing, and that Hélène hears and understands thoughts communicated by music. The young Hélène once strummed the harp and fell into an ecstatic fever. Her psychosomatic reaction suggests an inexperienced woman's fear of an unfamiliar and newly found power. And that her father should thereafter forbid that she touch the lyre, and that Albertus should counsel prudence, indicates a man's fear of a woman's acquiring power. It is not surprising that Hélène should react with concern since in her world women do not have access to language. Similarly, when Hanz and later Albertus begin to understand the tones of the lyre and the philosophical/intellectual concepts they communicate, it is always through Hélène or along with Hélène that they hear and understand them. In act 3, Hanz hears and understands the music that Hélène hears. He inquires as to Albertus's understanding, "Ne vous semblait-il pas que cette musique exprimait des idées, des images et des sentiments?" [Did it not seem to you that music expressed ideas, images, and feelings?] (*SC*, 132). Earlier, in act 2, Albertus could not fathom the inaccessibility of music, "D'où vient donc que je ne comprends pas cette langue musicale?" [How is it that I cannot understand this musical language?] (*SC*, 128). Now he hears the music and understands feelings and images, but not ideas. Hélène asks in disappointment, "Ne savez-vous pas un seul mot de la langue de Dieu?" [Do you not know a single word of the language of God?] (*SC*, 134). And Hanz says to Albertus, "Eh bien! Maître, cette musique ne parle-t-elle pas à votre âme?" [So, Master, does this music not speak to your soul?] (*SC*, 135).

The message is clear: musical, mystical language belongs more to woman than to man in this text. Albertus represents the rational side of humanity, the "male" side; he cannot understand the language of the lyre. Hélène represents the emotional, mystical side of humanity, the "female" side. She can understand (the) music and tries to help Albertus. Hanz is situated in a median position, understanding the music somewhat but unable to participate. Thus he represents the hope that men can and will, one day, be able to participate in this sort of communication. At the end of the text, Albertus in dialogue with Hélène and the Spirit of the Lyre understands all too well the spiritual/mystical language of the lyre's music, realizing perhaps too late that his lifelong insistence on rationality has deprived him of love, self-awareness, and social understanding. Struggling between the two opposing, masculine influences in her life, Albertus and the Spirit of the Lyre, Hélène can finally articulate her desire and her destiny:

> "[V]ous me parlez des choses finies, et le sentiment de l'infini me dévore! L'un veut que j'aime pour servir d'exemple et d'enseignement aux habitants de la terre; l'autre veut que j'aime pour satisfaire les désirs de mon cœur et goûter le bonheur sur la terre. O Dieu! ô toi dont la vie n'a ni commencement ni fin, toi dont l'amour n'a pas de bornes, c'est toi seul que je puis aimer! . . ." *La corde d'airain se brise avec un bruit terrible. Hélène tombe morte.* (*SC*, 186–87)

> ["You speak to me of finite things, and the feeling of the infinite devours me! One of you wants me to love so that I may serve as an example to teach the inhabitants of the earth. The other one wants me to love to satisfy the desires of my heart and to taste happiness on earth. O God, you whose life has no beginning or end, you whose love knows no bounds, you alone can I love! . . ." *And the brass string breaks with a horrible noise. Hélène falls dead.*]

Both Albertus and the Spirit of the Lyre try to seduce Hélène for their own purposes, supposedly "for her own good." The surprising association of the Spirit's desires with Albertus's shows Sand's interpretation of music as a vehicle of communication with God and not an end in itself. There is no question that the gifted and strong character in *Les Sept Cordes de la lyre* is Hélène, despite her apparent madness. Hélène, like Consuelo, finds the strength to detach and distinguish herself from the men in her life, and she finds the source and the courage to do so through music.

The mystical and narrative need to destroy the last string, indeed all the strings of the lyre, represents undoing the male definition of order. Breaking the strings is a device of Méphistophélès to annul the order of man on earth. I use the term "man" advisedly, not because I see Méphistophélès as a feminist vehicle, rather because Sand's use of the character fulfills the feminist goal of restructuring society by removing the patriarchal model. In order to gain control over the souls of men, Méphistophélès convinces Albertus that the strings should be broken, thus breaking the "spell" that music has over them. That Albertus should be incapable (or rather uninterested) in breaking the strings of the lyre bears testimony to his unilateral dedication to the rational. Only Hélène, who is forbidden access to the rational, can effectively overcome the domination of reason by breaking the last string and accepting to abandon her earthly existence for a new, divine one. In so doing, Hélène destroys the notion of order, man's notion of order. But instead of a new order of the devil, it is a new order of woman that reigns.

It is noteworthy that the strings seems to break of their own accord. In the preceding quotation, the stage directions state, "la corde d'airain se brise" [the brass string breaks]. While it seems clear that Hélène is the perpetrator, the passive reflexive verb allows for some ambiguity. In other instances, the strings break by themselves in similar fashion or the act simply ends and they are broken at the opening of the subsequent act. Hélène is always present and always tempted to touch or break the lyre, but a doubt remains. Sand is surely playing with her heroine's powers here: while Hélène will become the mediator of (musical) understanding, and in so doing the one who puts into balance the opposition between science and art, at the same time she cannot be perceived as the destructor of order or philosophy. Rather she is responsible for reordering, for urging society to go beyond its present limits, to progress. In this view, since the music continues, breaking the seven strings of the lyre is not so much a destruction as a new conception of the place of aesthetics. Ambiguity in how the strings are broken serves Sand's illusive narrative and feminist goals well by allowing the reader/spectator to appreciate Hélène's desire for and acquisition of control over her own destiny without that control being perceived as destructive.

Interesting, too, is the movement from the rigid linguistic value Sand assigns music in this relatively early work to the more encompassing understanding of music she demonstrates in later works. In *Consuelo* the power of music as language is portrayed as strong and clear. Yet, it communicates more subtly and less intellectually than in *Les Sept Cordes de la lyre*. And while Albert is an equally talented musician, it is to Consuelo that the position of leader falls. It is she who functions as the intermediary, the Saint-Simonian priest-(ess), the communicator. Brulette, although not a producer of music, demonstrates a natural ability to "understand" music, and not just the composer's intent, but the further-reaching levels of meaning that belie Joset's real purpose. Similarly, Laure (*Adriani*) will also understand and communicate in the language of music. In these two examples, communication remains certain, but it is less an exchange than a realization of emotions and spiritual comprehension—ideas of another order.

Cécilia's situation in *Le Château des Désertes* deserves some discussion. She is a major character and an important influence on Célio's musicianship, although her own musical career remains subordinate to her function as a paradigm of moral and professional fibre. Her relation to the musical world assembles a network of people and concerns more extensive than her own profession. She remembers fondly the time spent with Lucrezia Floriani, Célio's mother, and her own father, Boccaferri, a retired director who leads his merry troupe on the stage at the château in Les Désertes. The first evaluation of her as a singer comes from the duchess of ***, who finds her second-rate. But for Adorno she brings the opera to life. Her aria, "Vedrai carino," enchants him and later haunts him when he hears her singing it below his window in Turin. Thanks to this unwitting intervention, he leaves behind the duchess and pursues Cécilia. Béatrice Didier points out that while the famous aria serves as a leitmotif for the character of Cécilia, and thus brings a musical effect to the text, it does not resolve all the problems of the presence of music in a literary text.[44] I agree that Sand's technique of including such a leitmotif relies on the reader's memory of Mozart's music and thus inserts a memory of music into the reading of the text. Moreover, I would posit that Sand establishes a deliberate frustration for the reader, who "hears" the familiar music while reading. The desire to hear the music combined with the memory of having heard it enhances the reading of the literary text and thus establishes an intermediary form of artistic appreciation. There is nothing inherently feminine about this appreciation, but that Sand gave that role to a female character is in itself noteworthy.

In Les Désertes, where Boccaferri brings together a complex admixture of Molière's, Hoffmann's, and Mozart's Don Juans, Cécilia sings Ottavio whereas she sang the role of Zerlina in Vienna. There is nothing surprising in the change of role, since this is a different production, and such changes are common in the theater/ opera world.[45] Further, the fact that Cécilia should sing a man's role is not startling, as so-called trouser roles were common in operatic performances of the time, especially as Ottavio is a tenor, not an unprecedented enterprise for a female singer. What is astonishing, however, is that Zerlina is a soprano, which would mean Cécilia would have to have an enormous range in order to deftly accomplish both roles unless she sings the tenor role an octave higher. The performance she gives impresses her father: "elle traduisit la pensée du maître dans un langage aussi élevé que sa musique" [she translated the master's thought into a language just as lofty as his music] (*CD*, 116). Furthermore, her father's appreciation focuses on musicality and theatricality, since first he zeros in on a single word that Cécilia interprets with wondrous mastery, in his opinion, and second, since the role of Ottavio is one easily eclipsed by those of don Juan, donna Anna and donna Elvira.

What interests me especially is the change of gender in the roles her character sings. What are we to understand from a gifted singer and an even more consequentially influential person who receives more praise singing a man's role than a well-known and challenging female role? Sand makes an important statement about women in the musical profession by shifting emphasis from the role to the singer. Furthermore, she focuses on the multiple abilities of a woman not only capable of singing different roles of both genders, but also of putting aside any thoughts of ambition as well as helping others to perform better and to understand their own limitations, in their moral and professional makeup. Cécilia represents a substantial message on the varied capabilities of women. No man in Sand's universe displays such manifold talents and such largesse.

Cécelia's mature and progressive attitude also offers a positive image of the female artist. Her calm nature, devoid of ambition and jealousy, serves as a model for social progress. Her ability to present her thoughts in music and words helps her guide Célio through his egoism, allowing him to find his way in his profession and his life. Cécilia's breakthrough with Célio represents much less a revolution, either personal or societal, than Consuelo's. She simply waits for the right moment. Significantly, Cécilia is Sand's last musical heroine in a series of strong women musicians. And rather than anarchy, she demonstrates a calm and subtle approach. Her position as a lesser musician than Célio remains, however, different from Consuelo's, who equals Albert's in musicality to the end. Cécilia's apparent musical inferiority manifests another aspect of Sand's appreciation of music, that is, that the most successful exchange relies less on musical talent than on sincerity in music.

Music often serves a woman in Sand's world as a form of escape from a man's world or as a means of communication, whereas using verbal language would entail tackling a man's world. Yet, we must be careful not to define music too easily as woman's *parole* in a domain of man's *langue*, for Sand's conception of the musician in society remains inclusive. Women musicians are in fact presented in Sand's world as privileged figures who experience music in a way men do not, or perhaps cannot. However, this does not imply that women in Sand's universe lack verbal acumen. Many female characters in Sand's œuvre, musicians and others, demonstrate linguistic acuity or depict the struggle for linguistic assertion. From Indiana, who works slowly through her feelings to the point where she can articulate her unhappiness and discover the route of lost dreams, to Mademoiselle de Marquem, whose life experience is demonstrated in part through her ability to talk to fishermen and Armand with confidence and determination, many of Sand's women display the qualities usually denied women in mid-nineteenth-century France, in fiction as well as in historical French society, and to which Sand herself aspired. But the female musician provides an additional instance wherein women can effect a *prise de parole* devoid of the patronizing spin often given to such women in male authors' works. And in this case, where music is both *langue* and *parole*, Sand's female characters are superior to the male ones. Only Albert stands out as a vigorous male communicator in music, and as we have seen, he still needs Consuelo to act as interpreter, for without her, the effectiveness of his musical communication remains mitigated even for the most ardent of followers.

Criticism has been levied that the privileged position of Albert sets him up as the Priest—to adopt Saint-Simonian terminology—relegating Consuelo to the role of Artist, that is, in service to the Priest, the message-giver but not the message-diviner. However, what Sand clearly wants for her artists, male and female, is to be able to communicate the promise of hope to society. While late-twentieth-century feminists might find fault with this tactic, the anachronistic application of postmodern feminist concepts on Sand and her society does not advance the understanding of the social struggles of the mid-nineteenth century. The annunciatory role inherent in the priestess, the sibyl, and the initiatrix enhances the female role in social progress at the same time as it links social progress to religion—a new religion similar to the one proposed by Saint-Simon's disciples, where the artist both predicts and encourages social progress. Sand's statement about the role of women in social progress remains one of understanding, in the sense of comprehension as well as sensitivity, and one of communication—*entendement* in its fullest sense. And we cannot forget that the ballad at the end of *La Comtesse de Rudolstadt* that announces the future of a new society is Consuelo's musical composition. Music, and therefore the musician, remains for Sand a matter of communication.

Consuelo struggles with the direction of her future: success on the stage and thus glory for Porpora, or marriage and thus happiness and consolation for Albert? Always her goal is to make a man happy. Repulsed by the politics of the Viennese musical world, she attempts to write to Albert of her decision to reject the professional world. But she realizes she does not feel for him the same "violent passion" (*C*, 2:180) that music gives her. Not only does this dilemma point to a clear identification of music and emotions, and the intensity of the musical experience and its capacity for stimulating *jouissance*, it also makes a strong comment on the development of Consuelo as a woman with desires. When later she is offered a position at the Italian theater in Vienna, she must choose between devotion to a person or to art:

Ainsi partagée entre deux forces contraires, ma vie s'use, et mon but est toujours manqué. Si je suis née pour pratiquer le dévouement, Dieu veuille donc ôter de ma tête l'amour de l'art, la poésie, et l'instinct de la liberté, qui font de mes dévouements un supplice et une agonie; si je suis née pour l'art et pour la liberté, qu'il ôte donc de mon cœur la pitié, l'amitié, la sollicitude et la crainte de faire souffrir, qui empoisonneront toujours mes triomphes et entraveront ma carrière! (*C*, 2:192–93)

[Thus torn between two contrary forces, my life is deteriorating and my goal has still not been met. If I was born to practice devotion, then may God remove love of art, poetry, and the instinct of freedom from my head; they make torture and anguish of my devotions. If I was born for freedom, then may he remove pity, friendship, concern, and the fear of causing pain from my heart; they will always poison my triumphs and hinder my career!]

In this passage Sand presents the classic feminist predicament: a woman whose own aspirations are restricted by pleasing either husband or father, where she must choose between satisfying her own desires or societal conventions and duty. This remains one of the characteristics of the female Bildungsroman, that "female protagonists must frequently struggle to voice any aspirations whatsoever."[46] Consuelo defines her dilemma in terms of freedom, which she associates with the world of art and not at all with the world of marriage. Her desires are obscured by her sense of duty, which even she is beginning to perceive.[47]

These personal politics are aggravated by the external politics of the theatrical world, which are in turn exacerbated by those of the ruling government. Music lies at the nexus of the political quandary of all these worlds in *Consuelo*. The protagonist must understand her role in this complex web of politics in order to define and fulfill her artistic desires. Mozet refers to Moréna as the anti-Consuelo,[48] which I take to indicate a singer that Sand would not wish to offer as a model of artistic or moral integrity. I might add that while this is true, Moréna does undergo a series of changes throughout the novel, from the adoring adoptive daughter, to the adoptive daughter in love with her adoptive father—wherein we cannot deny the reminiscences of Sand's perception of Solange's relationship with Chopin—to the rebellious daughter who wants and needs to recapture her heritage, and finally to the devoted and grateful daughter of the denouement. Her *Bildung* is not so very different from that of any (female) character, but it is worth noting the role of music in the phase where she discovers and explores her cultural roots.[49]

Other female artists, particularly the painters and drawers in "La Fille d'Albano," *Elle et Lui,* and "Le Château de Pictordu," provide another point of comparison for the representation of artistic expression by women.[50] These females see clearly, especially Diane, the young girl in the last text. This miniature Bildungsroman, perhaps a "Bildungsnovelle," puts Diane, the daughter of a portraitist, on a quest to discover the face of a woman who appears to her as a veiled statue in a dream/vision. Attempting to render the portrait of her "fairy godmother," Diane discovers she cannot remember the face. At the end of the text, Diane is finally able to remember her mother's face, drawing it to perfection, by far surpassing her father's gifts in portraiture. Friends of the family and Diane's father stand in amazement at the striking similarity between Diane's drawing and the face of her mother, of whom she has never seen even a picture. Sand's female artists, young and mature, display a gift for seeing and translating essential information into a language others can understand. Sand will also use a dancer in her unfinished novel, *Albine Fiori* (1876), where it seems that the artistry of the heroine attracts the male protagonist and perhaps sparks love.[51]

One last female musician in Sand's universe, the eponymous character in *Ma Sœur Jeanne*, uses music as a substitute for passion. The romantic ethos of passion expressed in a musical metaphor has nothing new for literature, especially in 1874 when the novel was published. However, Jeanne's explicit choice of music over physical passion, since she could not abandon herself to her true passion—her love for her "brother" Laurent, who she suspected, and rightly so, was not her brother at all—represents an innovation in the cognizance of the decision. Music explicitly replaces passion in Jeanne's world until the lies and secrets of her family drama have been revealed and she can fully venture into a passionate relationship with Laurent. The independence of the protagonist can be seen constantly in her attitude toward her "brother," her "mother," herself, and especially in her resolute stalwartness and patience while she waits for the truth to emerge. Music provides Jeanne with not only a replacement, not only with an alternate means of expression, but also with the strength to sustain her desires and the hope they will be realized.

A brief look at Sand's depiction of male musicians and their use of music will round out this commentary on the female musician. Competent male musicians also have their place in Sand's universe. They also have issues with the public they must resolve. Célio, the son of the actress Lucrezia in *Lucrezia Floriani*, becomes the hero and focus of moral and musical development in *Le Château des Désertes*. As we have already seen, his debut in Vienna is similar to Anzoleto's debut in Venice, and Célio shows disdain for the public at the same time as he appeals to its tastes:

> Célio s'achemin[ait] vers une de ces chutes dont on ne se relève guère, ou tout au moins vers un de ces *fiasco* qui laissent après eux des années de découragement et d'impuissance. En effet, ce jeune homme se présenta avec un aplomb qui frisait l'outrecuidance. On eût dit que le nom qu'il portait était écrit par lui sur son front pour être salué et adoré sans examen de son individualité; on eût dit aussi que sa beauté devait faire baisser les yeux, même aux hommes. Il avait cependant du talent et une puissance incontestable: il ne jouait pas mal, et il chantait bien; mais il était insolent dans l'âme, et cela perçait par tous ses pores. (*CD*, 44–45)

> [Célio was heading for one of those declines from which one hardly ever recovers, or else for one of those *fiascos* that are followed by years of dejection and helplessness. In fact, this young man performed with a confidence that bordered on impertinence. One might have said that he had written the surname he bore on his forehead to be acknowledged and adored without any scrutiny of his individuality; one might have also said that his beauty commanded eyes, even men's eyes, to be lowered. However, he had talent and a indisputable power: he didn't act badly, and he sang well; but he was arrogant in his soul, and that seeped out of his every pore.]

Célio's attitude springs from Sand's disdain for the overly confident artist. (She will take up this discussion in greater detail in *Les Maîtres Sonneurs*.) Célio's nature is not so different from Karol's

(*Lucrezia Floriani*) or from Joset's. Yet, some interesting differences do stand out, in particular Célio's ability to learn and mature
on the emotional level and eventually to set aside his selfishness for
the good of a worthy relationship. This psychological progress in
turn provides the opportunity for expansion on the musical and professional level. Rambeau posits that "if man's social situation is ap-
preciably the same as woman's, then the difference occurs at the
level of the quality of intelligence and heart."[52] While her terms
remain vague, she goes on to discuss the male's immature traits in
contrast to the female's maternal ones: "Though adolescents, Joset
and Sylvinet have an attitude of regression that is characteristic of
early childhood."[53] Joset, Albert, Zdenko, Adriani, Favilla, and several others provide us with enough masculine models to contrast
with Sand's female musicians. Adriani and Célio, as we have seen,
are able to portray love convincingly in their singing only after having experienced the emotion themselves. These characters nonetheless must have the experience of the emotion before knowing what
is involved and thus what to convey on the stage. Both learn the
depths and heights of this emotion and thereafter are able to communicate love cogently. Laure and Cécilia, the women with whom
they experience love, are musicians in their own right and communicate to the men a need for sensitivity and expressivity not only in
their relationships but also in music. Neither Célio nor Adriani can
conjur up the emotion they are to communicate through music until
they have experienced the emotion and thus have a memory upon
which to draw.[54]

It is the memory of the emotion that is important at the time of
performance. Diderot wrote in *Le Paradox du comédien* that we
cannot adequately portray an emotion while actually experiencing
it. But the memory of that emotion is nonetheless essential. Similarly, the musical memory of a phrase or of the moment when we
first heard a piece provides the basis for subsequent recollections.
On these occasions, we do not so much relive the emotion as we
recall having experienced the emotion. Sand creates women artists
who understand the value of memory and its application in aesthetic expression. For example, in *Les Maîtres Sonneurs* the importance of memory for the master pipers, all men, is as a technical
prowess to be conquered and displayed. Brulette, and to a lesser
degree Thérence, value the memory for how it speaks to their personal experiences, in this case through music. The role of the memory occupies less an ideal of external show*man*ship than of internal
expansion.

Favilla represents the kind of musician who enjoys music for himself and for the communion it provides him with other musicians. His music is not for the public, and the music he produces does not extend to others uninvolved in music making. When his close friend and fellow musician dies, he is unable to explain the intensity of their musical communication to others. Only when he hears the music of Handel, which he had played with his deceased friend, can he even recall the feelings. But, he is still unable and uninterested in sharing them with those around him.

Albert presents perhaps Sand's most far-reaching male musician. He is capable not only of hearing and understanding spiritual messages from God but also of encouraging Consuelo, and eventually their children, to develop and share their musical skills. Still, he is so involved with the past or with the beyond, that he remains rather ineffective as a communicator of current socialist thought. For this reason, Consuelo surpasses him despite her apparently reduced musical role. Her vision is in fact larger than Albert's, enabling her to encompass more conventional communication as well as musical expression. From travels with her mother throughout Europe to her sentimental disillusionment in Venice, to her opera disappointments in Vienna, Consuelo's experiences in the world have provided her with a more practical and effective basis for developing her communication skills. In the end, she holds the power even though Albert remains the object of awe. While some might see in this paradigm a representation of the conventional roles of the "speaking" male and the "doing" female, Sand assigns a semiotic value to Consuelo's acts and talents wherein she does not attempt to usurp the "masculine" role and does not interfere with the "masculine" presentation. Nevertheless, she is responsible for the personal communication that allows for progress.

Joset, the outsider of Sand's musical universe, is still a gifted musician. In this way he commands the narrator's and Sand's mitigated respect. However, his inability to share with those around him, be they other pipers or friends or his own beloved, reduces his talent to a sterile gift that dies with him. The real goal of music, according to Sand, is to communicate with others, to convey hope and encourage progress. Musical talent alone does not raise one to divine heights in Sand's universe, rather it is the informed use of music for human and divine exchange that qualifies as communication.

Of particular interest is Rambeau's observation that in the decade 1843 to 1853 Sand no longer places musical genius with women but with men: Carl, Stéphen, Adriani, and Joset. Significantly Sand was planning her autobiography about this time, specifically the chapter on Chopin. Should we conclude that she was reconsidering the definition of musical genius in terms of an apotheosis of Chopin? I think rather her reexamination is proof of her satisfaction with her ideal female musician, Consuelo, in contrast with the all-too-real and multifaceted model of the male musician, who resisted a definitive categorization. Rambeau points out multiple ways in which Chopin is reflected in the characters of Adriani, Joset, Albert, and Carl. Traits of nobility tinged with frailty do, in fact, character-ize all but the first of these, who although noble of birth and stature is not sickly. Rambeau goes on to say that Joset is at once the most and the least like Chopin and as such is the epitome of a novelistic character. Joset also brings to the surface the flaw of jealousy, not unlike Sand's view of Chopin as well as a trait to be found in nu-merous Sandian male characters. Karol presents perhaps a stronger example of the jealous male, what Rambeau calls the evidence of a "masculine mentality." Sand always maintained that *Lucrezia Floriani* was not a translation into fiction of her relationship with Chopin. The eminent Sand scholar Georges Lubin defends her stance. I can only disagree, citing along with Rambeau the multi-tude of similarities in Chopin's and Karol's characters as well as the fact that *Lucrezia Floriani* is the only Sand novel for which Chopin expressed any reservation.[55]

One wonders about the objectivity of Sand's portrayal of male and female musicians. Consuelo presents a positive image, albeit idealistic. Joset, on the other hand, displays a more troubled and unsuccessful portrait. They are the extremes of what Sand submits as a definition of the musician. The indisputable truth of the impos-sibility of describing music also inhibits Sand's attempts to de-scribe the musician. The nature of the artist, especially the musician, cannot be summed up in one character. In the early 1840s Sand believed Consuelo to be that definition, but she soon discov-ered other facets equally "true," equally important, which war-ranted exploration. Finally Sand's musician represents a conglomeration of traits that proffers a more realistic—even though Sand would resist the term—definition of the social and aesthetic construct we know as the fictional musician.

Not unlike Sand's controversial brand of feminism,[56] her position concerning the female musician presents a stance that clearly af-firms the individuality of women demonstrated largely through ar-tistic expression. What is important for these female artists is not that they occupy positions equal to men, but that they exhibit their own abilities and develop their own talents. Just as Sand did not accept the candidacy for a seat in the Académie or for a position as

Minister, her female musicians will not seek to surpass or even to compete with men. Far more important is that they should first become comfortable with their own strengths so that when the day comes that they can claim the same education as men, they will be psychologically ready to assume positions of power.

♫ ♫ ♫

As we have seen, George Sand incorporates music in her statements on social(ist) progress, rendering much of her socialist commentary in musical terms. Hers is a vision that engulfs society, industry, and the fine arts in an effort to communicate to her readers the necessity of working together for the good of France. And as "France" remains always a collective social construct for Sand, as for all social democrats of the mid-nineteenth century, this conception, which incorporates the arts into all other realms of social progress, bespeaks her belief that music holds not only a utilitarian role but a sociological one, in the sense that it encompasses all aspects of life.

In a more encompassing way than Félicien David or Jules Vinçard, Sand retains the aesthetic as well as the utilitarian appreciation of music. Music for Sand continues to play the role it always has throughout history. Her many uses of eighteenth-century musical contexts demonstrates a continuity of tradition rather than a revolution. Nonetheless, transposing the use of music from entertainment for an elite to an art form for all people, or in socialist terms the shift from a society geared toward the amusement of the aristocracy to one that encompasses all people, remains the mainstay of Sand's socialist musical message. Music of the people, by the people, and for the people remains an important aspect of Sand's objective.

So why do we find so few references to music in the so-called socialist novels? This remains a baffling issue. The "socialist" novels shy away from an aesthetic commentary (with the exception of *Le Compagnon du tour de France*), perhaps because they are imbued with a "modern" vocabulary and a "modern" conceptualization of society, in which Sand made little room for music. This seems strange, since she did not hesitate to incorporate music and art in other novels with nonaesthetic themes, for example, *Spiridion, Lélia,* and *Le Meunier d'Angibault.* Still, *Simon* (1836), *Horace* (1841), *Le Compagnon du tour de France* (1840), and *Le Péché de Monsieur Antoine* (1845) do not lend space to musical expression. A practical reason for this phenomenon is that Sand was pooling all her musical efforts about this time into *Consuelo* and *La Comtesse de Rudolstadt.* The amount of musical—as well as historical, religious, and topographical—research that went into this series could have deterred Sand from risking repeating statements she felt she had already made. In a similar vein, her rustic-novel series had also exploited the area of folk music. Michelle Perrot's perspicacious collection of Sand's political writings suggests that the period of the late 1840s represents a more devoted reflection of politics, which would also explain less attention to art and music. That she was moving away from Leroux at the same time, and thus from any attachment she might have had to Saint-Simonian ideals, reinforces the notion of a temporary movement away from music.[57]

Perhaps the most obvious reason for Sand's not including music in the socialist novels is to be found in the perceived need to concentrate on the complicated (and often convoluted) utopian and socialist theories of the day. From Rousseau to Lamennais, from Leroux to Fourier, Sand found multiple references to utopian socialism that preceded her own that she could not and did not wish to ignore. Already her religious allusions had gathered a force that could not be separated from her socialist commentary,[58] and since such a conflation of ideals is far from original in this generation of romantics, Sand had her work cut out for her to develop ideas in this area. Indeed, most of her socialist thought is a reworking of Leroux and Lamennais with the prevalent underpinnings of Saint-Simon, which prevailed in most socialist writings of the time. In her essay "Lamartine utopiste," a commentary on Lamartine's *Recueillements poétiques* (1839; Sand's essay is from 1841), Sand states:

> Quel admirable instrument que M. de Lamartine! Comme il répond, comme il chante, quand la main divine presse son clavier facile, et que le souffle de l'inspiration remplit ses tubes sonores! Ce n'est point à la lyre antique que je voudrais le comparer. Il a moins de simplicité et plus d'étendue. C'est l'orgue chrétien, avec toutes ses ressources, sa puissance infinie, ses jeux divers, ses voix célestes, ses grands déchirements, toutes les fictions que ses vastes flancs recèlent. Mais cette grande musique, que nous écoutons dans l'extase, n'est-ce que la voix d'un instrument et, pour nous débarrasser de la métaphore, cette superbe déclamation prophétique n'est-elle que le trop-plein d'une intelligence de poète?[59]

> [What a commendable instrument is M. de Lamartine! How he responds, how he sings when the divine hand strikes his effortless keyboard and when the breath of inspiration fills his resonant pipes! This is no ancient lyre that I compare him to. He has less simplicity and more breadth. It is the Christian organ, with all its possibilities, its infinite power, its various stops, its celestial voices, its magnificent havoc, all

the fables that its substantial flanks contain. But this great music that we listen to in ecstasy, is it not the voice of an instrument; and to rid ourselves of the metaphor, this exquisite prophetic declamation, is it anything other than the excess of a poet's intelligence?]

Most flagrant in this passage is, of course, the extended musical conceit that permeates it, all the more remarkable given the relative lack of musical references in Sand's own "socialist" writings. Preparing the metaphor of the organ, the instrument that encompasses all instruments, and the romantic instrument par excellence, she introduces "clavier," "souffle," and "tubes sonores." But more interesting still is the rejection of the metaphor at the end, signaling a detachment from aesthetics as an excess too rash for such a serious topic. Her statement that Lamartine has less simplicity as an organ than the ancient lyre must be taken as less than laudatory, given all we have seen about her praise of simplicity. She continues in the essay to say that while such noble thoughts occupy his mind, and that of others of the time, Lamartine's ego occupies too important a place in the work. Citing the piece "Utopie," Sand points out that, in her opinion, Lamartine focuses too much on poetics and not enough on socialist philosophy. Perhaps this is the inverse of her own fear in her socialist writings of the period, written mostly after this essay. She is keenly aware of the tendency to become caught up in extended metaphors and to devote more attention to form than to content. Her prose often demonstrates a lyrical penchant of which she is not unaware. Such is the pitfall she wishes to avoid. Thus, music remains an undeveloped element of the socialist commentary of these novels.

Having said this, I remain convinced that Sand could not relegate music to the margins of her universe, not even in socialist contexts. While the dearth of musical elements in the socialist novels might suggest a movement away from aesthetic reflection, numerous other musical references inhabit socialist contexts in other texts, as has been noted. The vision of social progress as seen and understood through musical communication characterizes Sand's works before and after her so-called socialist phase. This trait exhibits the importance of music to her worldview, to her mode of expression, and to her hopes for the France of the future. Sand's musician must therefore represent a central member of society who is responsible for both seeing and understanding that which the average population glosses over too easily, and for communicating these observations to society. More important, she or he must teach the people to communicate, that is to say, to exchange ideas and feelings in order to move toward a better society. And this can be accomplished in part through music.

Conclusion
♫♫ The Indescribable Mysteries of Music ♫♫

[le] pays [de] la musique. Ce doit être
le paradis des hommes.

[The musical realm must be a human paradise.]
—Letter to Liszt, 21 April 1835

IF THERE BE A REALM OF MUSIC, ITS LANGUAGE, ACCORDING TO SAND, would be divine and universal. The social-sociological-socialist goal Sand sets for humanity envisions better relations through better communication, for which music is the ideal medium. From her earliest writings, she expresses her need to investigate her thoughts about music. As she writes to Casimir Dudevant in February 1831, "j'écris sur la musique" [I'm writing about music].

For Sand, music is the central vehicle of communication among humans. She examines the various ways music can be considered a language, but the underlying essence of this language remains unfathomable. Sand sees the universality of music as something much more fundamental than an Esperanto-like mode designed to avoid the pitfalls of conflicting verbal languages. She is not interested in establishing schools of musical interpretation and translation. Her goal, her dream goes much deeper, for it focuses on the very rudiments of understanding. To learn music for Sand is to learn to hear, to listen, and to understand perhaps not a philosophical or metaphysical message, but the most basic exchange between two individuals. Such listening, such communication is an essential element in Sand's formula for political harmony. This standard political discourse, a musical metaphor made political, is exemplary of Sand's attention to music and social progress and their inextricable association.

Sand has considerable respect for the socialized community of musicians, all the while recognizing they remain separate and different from the rest of society and even from other artists. In the seventh of the *Lettres d'un voyageur*, writing to Liszt who is leaving for Geneva, she states:

326

Je présume que vous allez fonder, dans la belle Helvétie ou dans la verte Bohème, une colonie d'artistes. Heureux amis! que l'art auquel vous vous êtes adonnés est une noble et douce vocation, et que le mien est aride et fâcheux auprès du vôtre! Il me faut travailler dans le silence et la solitude, tandis que le musicien vit d'accord, de sympathie et d'union avec ses élèves et ses exécutants. La musique s'enseigne, se révèle, se répand, se communique. L'harmonie des sons n'exige-t-elle pas des volontés et des sentiments? Quelle superbe république réalisent cent instrumentistes réunis par un même esprit d'ordre et d'amour pour exécuter la symphonie d'un grand maître! (*LV,* 2:818)

[I presume that you're going to establish an artists' colony in beautiful Switzerland or green Bohemia. Fortunate friends! What a noble and gratifying vocation is the art to which you have devoted yourselves, and how arid and inauspicious is mine compared to yours. I have to work in silence and solitude, whereas musicians live in accord, in sympathy, and in union with their pupils and their performers. Music is taught, revealed, disseminated, and communicated. Does the harmony of sounds not demand the determination of feelings? What a splendid republic is realized by a hundred instrumentalists brought together by a single spirit of order and love to perform a great master's symphony!]

Sand's admiration for and envy of the community of musicians and their association discloses her desires to make music. But is Sand unreasonably harsh on the community of *littérateurs*? Are they not also somewhat prone to communing? And is the musical community as socially motivated as Sand believes? The collective nature of music emphasizes the union of a group of musicians who play a common score together; the transitory, ephemeral and evanescent nature of music suggests a solitary reaction in the midst of common production. But what of the soloist, a pianist for instance, playing alone for her/himself without any public of any kind? Isolation in music can also be a refuge. Thus, the nature of the musical experience is sometimes sequestering rather than uniformly social, as Sand would have us believe.

As a writer of literature, Sand feels isolated, alone with her head in the cupboard-desk of Nohant. Nicole Mozet observes in the discourse of this letter as well as in *Histoire de ma vie* and "Mouny-Robin" the need for isolation. The motif of "la maison déserte" in letter 7 of *Les Lettres d'un voyageur* serves as a metaphor for this recurring theme, often replaced by the topos of the traveler. It is an isolation that Sand both requires and regrets.[1] Music, at least expressing feelings about music, provides Sand with an externalization of thoughts, sentiments, and sympathies that would otherwise remain stifled. Music represents freedom for Sand, freedom to think and to express in association with others.

This does not necessarily imply a society made up solely of musicians. Brulette learned to listen. So did Gottlieb (*Consuelo*) and Adorno (*Le Château des Désertes*) and others in Sand's universe. These non-musician enthusiasts are in some ways just as important as the musicians for our understanding of Sand's conception of music, for without the contrast the reader might assume only accomplished musicians are admitted to Sand's circle of divine communicators. Other mediating characters, such as Bianca Aldini and even Cécilia Boccaferri, represent an intermediary position, that of the musician, amateur or semi-professional, who does not embrace the professional musical world. Sand provides a spectrum of musicians and nonmusicians into which readers, musician or not, musically talented or not, Parisian or provincial, French or other, can comfortably inscribe themselves. The message of the universality of music continues to shine through the polyphony of communication possibilities for a panoply of participants.

Nonetheless the musician does occupy a privileged position in Sand's world. Those who respect their innate talent enough to suffer the long and disciplined training required reap the author's most profound respect. She grants them the status of guides who demonstrate the potential beauty and purity of divine and human communication. Our task as lay listeners is to apprehend and appreciate the art of the musician, and in so doing to comprehend and assimilate the beauty of music and its message. In this way we learn what to expect in terms of art, beauty, and human relationships. We learn how to view society and how to seek better communication by giving sincere and concentrated attention to music. Musicians for Sand, both performers and composers, offer not just a model of artistic performance, but a model for the rest of humanity, a model of meaningful exchange and progress. The musician or interpreter—in the musical sense of performer, but also in the sense of a linguistic intermediary—furnishes a direction for everyday transactions. The composer or inventor, according to Sand and contrary to the earlier generation of Saint-Simonians, supplies original messages and honest, direct paths to God. The Sandian concept of inventor, which includes peasant as well as academic musician, encompasses the notion of inspiration and hard work. Her romanticism does not totally eclipse her practicality. But she warns us against the musician who loses touch with society, as in Joset's case. This is not so different from her thoughts of Chopin, about whom she writes, "Il est musicien, rien que musicien. Sa pensée ne peut se traduire qu'en

musique" [He's a musician, nothing but a musician. He can translate his thoughts only into music].[2] On the other hand, musicians
like Célio and Lélio (*La Dernière Aldini*) remind us that the potential for (musical) exchange abides in us all.

Baudelaire offers an articulate expression of the exchange between the material and the ethereal worlds in the synesthesia theme
of "Correspondances" and again in the *Salon de 1846*. Here he
comments at length on the qualities of the colorist and on the nature
of color, finding abundant analogies with music, "On trouve dans
la couleur l'harmonie, la mélodie et le contrepoint" [In color one
finds harmony, melody, and counterpoint], and further, "La couleur
est donc l'accord de deux tons" [Color is therefore a chord
with—or a pact between—two tones or hues], and again "L'harmonie est la base de la théorie de la couleur. La mélodie est l'unité
dans la couleur, ou la couleur générale" [Harmony is the basis of
color theory. Melody is the unity within color, or color generally].
The best-known passage is this articulate paragraph after Hoffmann's *Kreisleriana*:

> Ce n'est pas seulement en rêve, et dans le léger délire qui précède le
> sommeil, c'est encore éveillé, lorsque j'entends de la musique, que je
> trouve une analogie et une réunion intime entre les couleurs, les sons et
> les parfums. Il me semble que toutes ces choses ont été engendrées par
> un même rayon de lumière, et qu'elles doivent se réunir dans un mer-
> veilleux concert. L'odeur des soucis bruns et rouges produit surtout un
> effet magique sur ma personne. Elle me fait tomber dans une profonde
> rêverie, et j'entends alors comme dans le lointain les sons graves et pro-
> fonds du hautbois.[3]

> [It's not just while dreaming and in the light delirium that precedes
> sleep, it's while still awake, when I hear music, that I find an analogy
> and an intimate reunion between colors, sounds, and scents. It seems
> that all these things were generated by a single ray of light, and that they
> must come together in a spectacular concert. The odor of brown and red
> marigolds produces an especially magical effect on my person. It puts
> me into a deep reverie, and then far off I hear the deep and profound
> sounds of the oboe.]

All the elements of Sand's universe are here: nature and art; synesthetic mixture of the senses; half-dream; and of course music
everywhere. As strange as it might seem to the informed reader to
compare Sand and Baudelaire, many of the same themes inhabit
both universes.[4] In an extraordinary and little-known tale, "Ce que
disent les fleurs" [What the Flowers Say] (1875) published in
Contes d'une grand'mère, Sand provides an analogy between scent

and language, a divine language similar to what she calls music in other texts. The flowers speak to the grandmother-narrator, who states, "il me sembla même que je comprenais mieux ce langage que tout ce que j'avais entendu jusqu'alors" [it even seemed to me that I understood this language better than anything else I'd heard up till then].[5] While music is never mentioned in the story, the juxtaposition of this text just after "L'Orgue du titan" recalls the multitude of musico-linguistic references in Sand's œuvre.

But it is in *Consuelo,* three years before Baudelaire's *Salon,* that we find a better example of these same correspondences. Consuelo is examining the garden at the Bohemian home of the old canon, a horticulturist and music-lover who has offered rest and sustenance to her and Haydn in exchange for music and conversation about music. She is nonplussed at the beauty of nature in the light of dawn and in particular of the multitude and variety of flowers:

> En examinant leurs diverses attitudes et l'expression du sentiment que chacune de leurs physionomies semblait traduire, elle cherchait dans son esprit le rapport de la musique avec les fleurs, et voulait se rendre compte de l'association de ces deux instincts dans l'organisation de son hôte. Il y avait longtemps que l'harmonie des sons lui avait semblé répondre d'une certain manière à l'harmonie des couleurs; mais l'harmonie de ces harmonies, il lui sembla que c'était le parfum. Et cet instant, plongée dans une vague et douce rêverie, elle s'imaginait entendre une voix sortir de chacune de ces corolles charmantes, et lui raconter les mystères de la poésie dans une langue jusqu'alors inconnue pour elle. (*C,* 2:132)

> [By examining their various attitudes and the expression of feelings that each of their faces seemed to translate, she sought in her mind the relationship between music and flowers and wanted to become aware of the association between these two instincts in her host's design. For a long time the harmony of sounds had seemed to answer the harmony of colors in a particular way; but the harmony of these harmonies, it seemed to her, was fragrance. And at that moment, plunged into a obscure and gentle reverie, she imagined she heard a voice from each of the enchanting blossoms telling her the mysteries of poetry in a language that until then she did not know.]

Not only are all the elements of correspondences present in this passage, so are instances of personification, linguistic attributes of music and scent, the symbiotic relationship between dream and the senses, and even mysticism and fantasy. The double layer of harmonies, a sort of hierarchy that places music and color on the same plane and then puts that coupling on a higher plane with scent, completes the analogy. The result is more ordered than Baudelaire's evocations, more systematic and richer in its admixture of human and natural elements. Sand's (re)presentation of music, or more precisely its "sounds," as perceived or sensed through flowers and the identifying attribute of flowers, "scent," coincides with Baudelaire's correspondences while privileging music. The so-called tricks music plays on us constitute for Sand a network of ill-defined and ineffable advantages that music holds over other expressions and languages. That Consuelo "hears" a language from the flowers—and there is no doubt that the language is expressed in scents—that communicates to her better than any other she knows underscores the now-familiar Sandian theme of nonverbal language, which here music shares with perfume.[6]

Once again Consuelo, Sand's model female musician, an exemplar not only of the artist but also of the communicator, portrays the pinnacle of idealism. The female musician in Sand holds a privileged position, one to which other musicians aspire but do not attain. Hélène displays an early stage of the model, and Cécilia and Laure exhibit other qualities of the aptitude. But Consuelo remains the fictive incarnation. It is significant, however, that Sand creates Consuelo in the middle of her career, and once she moves past her forties, she looks beyond this ideal to the multi-faceted nature of the musician-artist. She now creates the musician that is Joset, but also Adriani and Abel. While the insistence on the *vates* nature of her musical model ebbs, her conviction that the musician stands as the artist *par excellence* does not. The musician remains the paragon of communication and the embodiment of hope for all humanity, or at least for nineteenth-century French society. If the number of musicians whose musicianship is the focus of the narrative diminishes in the last two decades of Sand's career, music remains the best vehicle for communication in her universe right up to *Ma Sœur Jeanne* (1874). Music stands pure and sincere, a language we can all learn, as performers and/or as listeners, giving us the hope to apprehend a deeper understanding of God, of ourselves, of others, and of our place in society. "La beauté du langage musical consiste à s'emparer du cœur ou de l'imagination, sans être condamné au terre à terre du raisonnement" [The beauty of musical language consists in taking hold of the heart or the imagination without being condemned to the banality of reasoning].[7]

Still, Sand stumbles against the ever-present problem of representing music and musical communication. While not impossible, it would require a training and a practice quite different from her career in literature. As she wrote in 1837:

Toutes [les compositions musicales des grands maîtres] ont un sens tra-
duisible à la pensée, car toutes ont été inspirées par des sentiments. . . .
Il y en a de si réels, de si palpables, pour ainsi dire, qu'il n'est pas impossible de les saisir, de les noter pour l'oreille de l'artiste et même de
les expliquer, de les traduire en langue vulgaire, de les faire comprendre
au public. Mais ceci demanderait toute une vie de musicien et de poète.[8]

[All the musical compositions of the great masters have a meaning that
can be translated into thought, because all of them were inspired by feeling. . . . There are those that are, so to speak, so real, so palpable, that
it's impossible to grasp them, to note them for the artist's ear, or even
to explain them, to translate them into a common language, to help the
public understand them. But this would require the whole lifetime of
both a musician and a poet.]

A pertinent example of the incapacity of language to transmit the
depth of musical communication comes in *Adriani* (1854). Adriani
often writes his own poetry for his music, and he maintains that a
simple thought reserves the greatest degree of freedom for the
music and allows for greater appreciation and imagination on the
part of the listener. The combination of words and music, a problem
that haunted Wagner and became an important question in the second half of the century, remains a matter for careful contemplation.
"Pour moi, les idées *latentes*, si je puis parler ainsi, ont un charme
que la réalisation détruit" [For me, latent ideas, if I may, have a
charm that their realization destroys] (*A,* 63). And later, "[Q]uand ,
par le sens éminemment contemplatif qui est en elle, la musique
s'élève à des aspirations qui sont véritablement des idées, il faut
que l'expression littéraire soit d'autant plus simple, et procède,
pour ainsi dire, par la lettre naïve des paraboles. Autrement, les
mots écrasent l'esprit de la mélodie, et la forme emporte le fond"
[When, by the eminently meditative meaning that it holds, music
rises to aspirations that are truly ideas, it is necessary for literary
expression to be even more simple and to proceed, so to speak, by
the naive message of parables. Otherwise, the words crush the spirit
of the melody, and the form overtakes the content] (*A,* 114). From
this commentary two important notions emerge: first, the hierarchy
of music over poetry, and second, the concept of artistic essence.
Defining parable as the preferable form of language to be set to
music, she identifies her requirement of simplicity and morality as
the essence of art. At the same time, she privileges metaphoric expression over direct communication by referring to a parabolic trajectory from the source to the goal of the communication,
suggesting that the path of expression is as important as the expres-

sion itself, the admixture of which she calls "l'esprit de la mélodie" [the spirit of melody]. Thus the essence of art resides in the balanced marriage of both form and content, neither one dominating and both constantly cooperating.[9] She is not interested in portraying society as it is but as it should be.[10]

Sand's works, too, resisted attempts by others to set them to music. Apart from the musical setting of *La Petite Fadette*, plans by Berlioz, Liszt, Rossini, Meyerbeer, Auber, Viardot, and Gounod all failed to find realization. Are we to consider this a failure of the musical qualities of Sand's texts? Or on the contrary should we esteem the literary value of her writing as too developed to permit the infiltration of another art form? Would Sand have been happy to see another of her works set to music? She certainly reveled in the setting of *La Petite Fadette* and continually encouraged Pauline Viardot to produce a musical setting of *La Mare au diable*. Still, the plans to set *Consuelo* and other texts to music never saw the footlights. Further study into this question would certainly prove interesting.

Sand returns ceaselessly and assiduously to the notion that musical expression and musical experience remain outside the realm of verbal language, and she is incapable of representing it faithfully. For this she is not sorry. On the contrary, she revels in the polyvalence of the quandary and enjoys maneuvering through it, only to arrive back at the point of departure—all the more satisfied at not having discovered an adequate expression. For the indescribable effects of music, of listening to music, of making music, can be perceived and grasped only while the music lasts—after it fades there is only the memory of music and the hope of experiencing it again. It is the lesson of listening to music that renders musical memories valuable and useful for human(itarian) and social(istic) purposes. "[L]a musique, c'est l'imagination même" (*A*, 115). Music *is* the path of progress for Sand, a path that requires hard work and talent but that also promises unlimited reward. And from these experiences Eliot tells us we can hope only for understanding and a glimpse of the future.

> But you are the music
> While the music lasts. These are only hints and guesses,
> Hints followed by guesses; and the rest
> Is prayer, observance, discipline, thought and action.
> The hint half guessed, the gift half understood, is
> Incarnation.
>
> —T. S. Eliot

♫♫ Notes ♫♫

INTRODUCTION

1. I cannot neglect to mention here the famous line from *Histoire de ma vie* where Sand describes her birth, her mother in a pink dress and her father playing the violin in the next room. Her Aunt Lucie, Sand recounts, is reported to have said, "*Elle est née en musique et dans le rose*; elle aura du bonheur" [*She was born in music and in pink*; she'll be happy] (*OA*, 1:464).

2. Cassou, "George Sand et le secret du XIXe siècle," 603.

3. Bailbé, *Le Roman et la musique*.

4. For the music commentaries of Herder, Kant, Schopenhauer, Wagner, and Kierkegaard, as well as Nietzsche, Hanslick, Hoffmann, Hegel, and others, see Hermand and Gilbert, eds., *German Essays on Music*.

5. Treitler, "Musical Analysis in a Historical Context," in *Music and the Historical Imagination*, 67–78.

6. Critics who study the works of George Sand hesitate between the French terms *sandiste* and *sandien*. I use the term "Sandist" when I refer to critics and criticism, "Sandian" when I speak of Sand and her works.

7. Marix-Spire, *Les Romantiques*.

8. Rambeau, *Chopin*.

9. A special issue of *Présence de George Sand*, no. 12 (1981), devoted to "George Sand et la musique," presents a collection of studies on the subject. In addition, articles with diverse approaches specifically devoted to Sand and music have been published in recent years by James Dauphiné, Béatrice Didier, François Laforge, Francine Mallet, Arlette Michel, Albert Sonnenfeld, and others.

1. BALLAD AND *BILDUNG*—MUSIC AND NARRATIVE

1. Abbate, *Unsung Voices*, x.

2. Dällenbach, *Mirror in the Text*, 43–44.

3. Abbate, *Unsung Voices*, 62.

4. Bal, *Narratology*, 142–61.

5. Prince, *Narratology*, 146.

6. Frappier-Mazur insists on the difference between the Bildungsroman and the novel of initiation ("Desire, Writing, and Identity," 333 ff.). This is a valid distinction, but I find in *Consuelo* a confluence of the two. There is certainly a mystical sense to the novel, a descent into hell, and a spiritual rebirth; but there is also an adjustment to social identity and a sense of compromise, leading to a true religious reform. It is music, in fact, that allows for the nexus of these two genres.

Frappier-Mazur alludes to as much, and in what follows I shall demonstrate how Sand accomplishes this conflation.

7. Baldauf-Berdes discusses the various populations the *figlie del coro* were drawn from throughout the centuries in the Venetian *ospedali*, chapter 8 in *Women Musicians of Venice*. See also Didier, *George Sand écrivain*, 254–55.

8. Baldauf-Berdes reviews the documents required for admittance to an *ospedale*, including legitimation of birth and citizen status in the Republic of Venice, *Women Musicians of Venice*, 121.

9. The poetic licence of historical fiction allowed Sand to take some liberties with the historical Porpora. See Didier, *George Sand écrivain*, 251–52.

10. Sand, *Consuelo* and *La Comtesse de Rudolstadt*, 1:48. Subsequent quotations will be noted parenthetically in the text with the abbreviation *C* and *CR*.

11. Nerval's "proverbe" of 1839, entitled *Corilla*, might have provided Sand with some inspiration for the character in *Consuelo*. Even though the moral makeup of the two Corillas is quite different, some interesting details do link the characters and thus the texts: both Corillas are *prime donne* who charm the public with their beauty as well as their voice; both are strong women who look out for themselves; both sing in first-rate Italian musical centers, Naples and Venice respectively; both texts portray the adoration of a man for an opera singer. Given the date of publication in *La Presse* of *Corilla* (under the original title of *Les Deux Rendez-vous*), it is probable that Sand had read Nerval's text before writing *Consuelo*. Incidentally, Corilla was the stage name of Maria-Maddalena Morelli-Fernandez (1738–1800), a well-known Parisian actress. Her name most likely provided both authors with the name of their characters.

12. See also: "les qualités qu'il exigeait dans un élève: d'abord une nature d'intelligence sérieuse et patiente, ensuite une modestie poussée jusqu'à l'annihilation de l'élève devant les maîtres, enfin une absence complète d'études musicales antérieures à celles qu'il voulait donner lui-même," [the qualities he demanded of a student: first of all a naturally serious and patient intelligence; next, modesty exaggerated to the point of annihilating the student before her masters; and finally total absence of previous musical studies before coming to him] (*C*, 1:55).

13. I would like to point out in passing the double level of derision in these comparisons, where Sand benefits from the conventional mockery of boys by comparing them to girls as well as the more subtle disdain for the aristocracy. This dual irony, sometimes working in tandem and sometimes in conflict, is typical of Sand's style in *Consuelo*.

14. Sand, *Le Château des Désertes*, 44–45. Subsequent quotations will be noted parenthetically in the text with the abbreviation *CD*.

15. For more on the symbolism of improvisation and freedom, see my "Improvisation(s) dans *Consuelo*," 131–34.

16. Sand's interest in the history of Bohemia continues in two other texts, *Jean Ziska* (1843) and *Procope le Grand* (1844). As neither of these texts deals with music, I do not treat them here, though they are worthy of further investigation.

17. This is not the place to enter into a discussion of Sand's use of the same first name for Albert's cousin and Frederick's sister, though the inquiry might prove interesting.

18. While sticking fairly close to the biography of Haydn, Sand does rearrange events to fit her narrative. Bailbé points out that she used Fétis's rather embellished biography as her reference, *Le Roman et la musique,* 300.

19. For more details on this parody, see my "Une fausse note."

20. Porpora's treatises on vocal education are well known and respected, see Baldauf-Berdes, *Women Musicians of Venice*, 128.

21. For more information on the *Querelle des Bouffons*, see the discussion of Rousseau's *Essai sur l'origine des langues* by Scott, "Rousseau's Musical Theory and his Philosophy"; DeJean, *Ancients against Moderns*; and for an interesting discussion of the position of Parisian salon women on the "querelle," see Pekacz's "Salonnières and the Philosophes."

22. See Balayé's excellent treatment of the role of poverty in *Consuelo* in "Consuelo."

23. *Les Maîtres Sonneurs*, 491. Subsequent quotations will be noted parenthetically in the text with the abbreviation *MS*.

24. The bagpipes themselves are different in the two provinces, which is initially the source of a physical and technical problem for Joseph until he readjusts, as Bastien's son, Huriel, explains to Brulette, "et malgré que mon père, conseillé par son expérience, le voulait retenir, Joseph, pressé de réussir, a un peu usé de son souffle dans nos instruments, qui sont, comme vous avez pu voir, d'autre taille que les vôtres, et qui fatiguent l'estomac, tant qu'on n'a pas trouvé la vraie manière de les enfler: si bien que les fièvres l'ont pris et qu'il a commencé de cracher du sang," [and even though my father tried to hold him back, Joseph was in such a hurry to succeed, he wore his lungs out a bit on our instruments, which are, as you've seen, bigger than yours, and tax the gut if you don't learn the right way to fill them. And so he got feverish and started spitting up blood] (*MS*, 178).

25. For details on musical training at the Venice schools such as the Mendicanti, see Baldauf-Berdes, *Women Musicians of Venice*. Balzac's use of untrained but excellent musicians, usually women, falls more into the cliché of the romantic penchant for music, not devoid of his signature irony. See especially *Modeste Mignon*, 1:388; *Ursule Mirouët*, 3:384.

26. Rambeau, *Chopin*, 260–62.

27. Sand, *Adriani*, 191–92. Subsequent quotations will be noted parenthetically in the text with the abbreviation *A*.

28. Sand, *Lettres d'un voyageur*, *OA*, 2:900. Subsequent quotations will be noted parenthetically in the text with the abbreviation *LV*. See also Mozet, *George Sand*, 43, 62.

29. The well-documented trips to Venice (1834) and to Majorca (1838–39) constitute Sand's most distant wanderings. While these trips, as well as sojourns to Spain as a child (1808) and to the Pyrénées (1825) and Auvergne early in her marriage (1829), provided material for texts such as *Voyage en Espagne*, *Voyage en Auvergne*, *Un Hiver à Majorque*, *Lettres d'un voyageur*, and *Histoire de ma vie*, travel in *Les Contes d'une grand-mère* is purely imaginary and often fantastic. For more on travel in Sand's works, see *George Sand Traveller*, ed. Tamara Alvarez and Michael Paulson (Troy, NY: Whitston, 1994).

30. Mozet points out the importance of the travel theme in Sand's works, *George Sand*, 64. See also Mozet's excellent articles on this topic, "Signé le voyageur" and "Le voyageur sandien." See also Naginski, *Writing for Her Life*, 41.

31. See Cocker, "*Corinne* and *Consuelo*."

32. Bailbé points to the episode where Consuelo and Haydn discuss music (beginning of volume 2) as a simple adventure full of charm and rich in reflections; he terms this passage "Artistes vagabonds:" *Le Roman et la musique*, 299–303.

33. The narrative present of *Les Maîtres Sonneurs* is situated in approximately 1770.

34. Célio returns to Vienna after the close of the novel. The narrator is surprised that Célio's fiancée and future parents-in-law "songeassent sérieusement à lui faire reprendre ses débuts: mais je le compris, comme eux, en étudiant son caractère, en

reconnaissant sa vocation et la supériorité de talent que chaque jour faisait éclore en lui," [were seriously thinking of having him make his debut again. But I understood him, as did they, by studying his character, by recognizing his vocation and the superiority of talent that blossomed each day in him] (*CD*, 150).

35. Both Morgenstern's and Dilthey's definitions are quoted by Swales in *German Bildungsroman*, 12 and 3 respectively.

36. See the commentary by Charles-Dominique, "Dans les caves de Saint-Chartier."

37. Schor, *Idealism*, 32.

38. Schor, *Idealism*, 138.

39. Translations of "Bildungsroman" in French have resulted in various terms depending on the direction of the interpretation. "Roman d'éducation," "roman de formation," or "roman initiatique" can thus all be found, sometimes within the same argument. The "roman initiatique" offers perhaps a more restricted subset of the Bildungsroman insofar as it applies strictly to the role of initiation in the protagonist's development. For further discussion of the "roman initiatique" and transcendence, see Cellier, *Parcours initiatiques*; Vierne, *Rite, roman, initiation*; and Frappier-Mazur, "Desire, Writing, and Identity."

40. Swales, *German Bildungsroman*, 4.

41. Even though Joset dies young, there is no doubt that he has progressed considerably from the beginning of the novel. Still, the degree of maturity in his case remains problematic.

42. Rather than the typical trials of the male *Bildung*—travel, amorous conquests, and tests of courage—Marrone finds women's texts tend to deal more with interpersonal relationships rather than reactions to society. See her insightful article, "Male and Female *Bildung*." Marrone further posits that "women's journeys are often accompanied by introspection and self-discovery," 336. I find such use of travel an essential aspect of the Bildungsroman, both male and female.

43. Marrone, "Male and Female *Bildung*," 336.

44. Further discussion of female *Bildung* can be found in Huf, *Portrait of the Artist as a Young Woman*; Joeres and Maynes, *German Women*; and Pearson and Pope, *Female Hero*.

45. Naginski, "La Comédie féminine."

46. See my treatment of the foreshadowing of Consuelo's loss of voice in "Improvisation(s) dans *Consuelo*." For a contrasting interpretation, see Sourian's "Opinions religieuses."

47. Mozet, *George Sand*, 42. Mozet also suggests that the loss of Consuelo's voice characterizes a fulfillment of the central themes of the novel, "this devotion is the opposite of a renunciation. It constitutes the culmination of a double apprenticeship: that of art and love," 188.

48. One can see a decided diversion from this hypothesis in *Les Sept Cordes de la lyre*.

49. Mozet, *George Sand*, 190.

50. Sand intended this element to be the focus of her original story, entitled "La mère et l'enfant." As the story become a novel with other themes, the topic of rumor about a child's purported mother, an unmarried young woman, is eclipsed by the musical and psychological themes. This aspect of *Les Maîtres Sonneurs* merits further investigation.

51. See my "Discord, Dissension, and Dissonance."

52. Naginski minimizes the autobiographical import of suicide in *LV* and labels it a literary exercise: *Writing for Her Life*, 43–45.

53. Cellier, "Le Roman initiatique en France du temps du Romantisme," in *Parcours romantiques*, 118–37; see also his "L'occultisme."

54. See Higonnet, "Speaking Silences."

55. For more on the guild system and its rites, see H. Boyer, "Histoire des corporations et confréries"; Dindinaud, "Les Sociétés secrètes"; Lesure, "Communauté des 'joueurs d'instruments'."

56. The moral question is present in "La Fille d'Albano," *Les Maîtres mosaïstes, Le Piccinino, Elle et Lui,* "Le Château de Pictordu," and other texts. While music is the highest artistic expression in Sand's universe, the matter of a painter's moral obligation is important and requires further study.

57. Balzac, *Œuvres complètes*, 5:129.

58. See Bailbé, *Le Roman et la musique*, 255. Also see his comments on *Gambara*, 76–78 and passim.

59. See in particular Nattiez, *Proust as Musician*.

2. Musical Language

1. I do not wish to ignore the texts that treat the problem of music and language before or after the Enlightenment, notably Aristotle, Boethius, Baïf, Joukovsky, Molinet, Palisca, Ruwet, Tyard, and others. For a treatment of the question of music and Renaissance poetics, see Helgeson, *Ensemble discors*.

2. "Le Théâtre italien de Paris," 361–63.

3. Musset, "Concert de Mlle Garcia" (Jan. 1839; rpt. in Musset, *Œuvres complètes* [Paris: Seuil, 1963], 909); "Débuts de Mlle Pauline Garcia au Théâtre-Italien" (Nov. 1839; rpt. in Musset, *Œuvres complètes*, 915).

4. It is clear that Balzac refers here to a metaphysically perfect synchronization of souls and not a perfect chord, such as an octave or a perfect fifth. *Œuvres complètes*, 9:350.

5. For further discussion of bel canto, see Celletti, *History of Bel Canto*, and Osburne, *Bel Canto Operas*.

6. This is not to say that the *Querelle* does not have a certain influence on some of Sand's characters and many of the musical discussions in her work, especially in *Consuelo*, which takes place in the mid-eighteenth century. For instance, Sand's Porpora fears that Hasse is usurping his place in popular opera, thus playing on a personal anxiety exacerbated by a perceived preference of German over Italian music. Johann Hasse was Porpora's student and went on to great fame as the principal composer of Metastasio's libretti. Despite his cultural origins, his style and humor are quite Italian, which weakens Sand's example. And in a sociopolitical context, when Consuelo first meets Frederick the Great, he engages her in a conversation on the merits of German and Italian music (*CR*, 3:50). The purpose of the discussion has nothing to do with music, as the king cares little about the singer's aesthetic opinions. It is a diversion to put her at ease while he sees whether he can catch her in some political plot.

7. I have written on Sand's borrowing of Balzac's character and the comparative musicality of the two characters, "Schmucke and Schwartz: Cultural Commentary in a Musical Mode" (paper presented at the 14th International George Sand Conference, Brandeis, April 1999).

8. For more on Gluck's determination to introduce an element of emotion, perceived in 1767 as non-German, into an "opera seria," see Howard's "*Alecste*," in *Gluck*, 78–86.

9. *Verismo* would not become popular at the Opéra until later in the century, but the current of realism can already be sensed in the musical journalism of the July Monarchy.

10. See Bailbé, "Les Virtuoses," in *Le Roman et la Musique*, 79–89.

11. The context of this discourse of simplicity should be remembered. The relative simplicity of, say Chopin in comparison with Handel, for example, is the basis for this judgment. Twentieth-century notions of simplicity or minimalism clearly do not apply here.

12. See Didier, *George Sand écrivain*, 258–68.

13. Sand also posits the natural component of simplicity of folk music in *La Mare au diable*, stating it reflects the natural simplicity of the Berrichon character. Rambeau focuses on the importance of simplicity in *La Mare au diable* and cites Delacroix's estimation that it was fitting for Sand to have dedicated this novel to Chopin since his compositions embody the search for simplicity: *Chopin*, 188.

14. It will be remembered that Consuelo's first solo performance in the novel was Palestrina's *Salve Regina*.

15. This historical castrato and a secondary character in *Consuelo* was made popular in *Farinelli, il castrato*, a film by Gérard Corbiau, musical direction by Christophe Rousset (1993).

16. *Lettres d'un voyageur*, 2:928. For a contextualization of the function of music in the *Lettres d'un voyageur*, especially in the matter of the traveler and the question of writing, see Bozon-Scalzitti's perspicacious "La Pierre, l'eau, le sable," 351.

17. Sand may stipulate, "N'imaginez donc pas, je vous en supplie, que je songe à vous donner un conseil" [Don't think, I beg of you, that I'm thinking of giving you advice] (928), but her use of preterition is not lost on the reader.

18. Sand cites Liszt's comparison of the convention of the coda to the French practice of ending formal letters with "J'ai l'honneur d'être votre très humble et très obéissant servitor" ["I have the honor of being your most humble and most obediant servant." The convention relates to the English use of "Sincerely yours"]; *Lettres d'un voyageur* (929). Bailbé suggests that Sand's call for greater sobriety may have given Meyerbeer pause, since he seems to have effected a greater paring down of ornamentation in *Le Prophète* eleven years later: *Le Roman et la musique*, 31.

19. On this subject, one should consult Chevereau's thorough study, *George Sand*.

20. Springer, "Language and Music," 507.

21. Sand, *La Filleule*, 84. Subsequent quotations will be noted parenthetically in the text with the abbreviation *F.*

22. See *Histoire de ma vie*, 1:812–13, 839, 853. Subsequent quotations will be noted parenthetically in the text with the abbreviation *HV.*

23. Frappier-Mazur evokes this passage of *Histoire de ma vie* as a sign of the links between narrating, writing, and music and the desire to represent an absence that is fiction in the making, "Desire, Writing, and Identity," 330.

24. Sand, *Entretiens journaliers*, 2:981.

25. Rambeau, *Chopin*, 156–62. Rambeau's argument here and elsewhere is limited by her having constrained her study to the nine years of the Chopin-Sand relationship.

26. *Rondeau fantastique sur un thème espagnol.* Originally for piano and orchestra, the piano score can be found at the Département de Musique in the Bibliothèque Nationale, B.L. 1031.

27. Variations are often improvisations. The form of theme and variations presents an intriguing aside here. Playing or creating variations on a theme, an enterprise with which a nineteenth-century soloist often delighted a concert or recital public, consists of improvisation; but the formulaic manner of improvisations that usually characterize this form interests me less than the ornamentation that embellishes a melody. Incorporating decoration in a melody rather than taking the whole melody as the basis of adornment is closer to Sand's thoughts on improvisation.

28. Sand, "Le Contrebandier," in *La Coupe*, 262. Subsequent quotations will be noted parenthetically in the text. Langer will make similar conjectures in her *Feeling and Form*, 153–54.

29. Another instance of piano improvisation turning to storytelling occurs in Sand's *Jacques*, where Sylvia's "improvisations étranges" [strange improvisations] give rise to Jacques's and Octave's account of "les divers rêves poétiques qu'ils ont fait [sic] pendant le chant et les modulations du piano" [the various poetic dreams they had during the singing and the piano modifications] *Jacques*, 944.

30. For a detailed analysis of the musical nature of Sand's story, see my "Musical-Literary Intertextuality."

31. Bailbé, *Le Roman et la musique*, 281–340.

32. *Teverino*, 69–70.

33. The language Consuelo and Zdenko speak here is politically and aesthetically important for the novel: a mark of marginality, since German is not only a symbol of the Austro-Hungarian domination of Bohemia but also a symbol of the problems of verbal communication that are circumvented by musical communication. That they speak first in German and later in Bohemian, which he teaches her, then in folk tunes, bears witness to the importance of language—and here music as language is clearly the thesis.

34. For a commentary on classical musical training as the worst thing for learning improvisation, see Bailey, *Musical Improvisation*, 84.

35. It is interesting to note that *Les Maîtres Sonneurs*, as it appeared in *Le Constitutionnel* as well as in volume, comprises thirty-two chapters (called *veillées* in accordance with the tradition of telling stories throughout the long winter evenings otherwise spent in work), a noticeably musical number. The most explicit discourse on music occurs at the midpoint, in chapters 17 and 18. And for further commentary of the major-minor alternance, see Ramaut-Chevassus, "Le Postminimalisme."

36. Guichard, *La Musique et les lettres*, 379 n. 119.

37. See preface to *François le champi*.

38. Rambeau, *Chopin*, 264.

39. Sand, "L'Orgue du titan," 107. All subsequent references will be indicated parenthetically in the text with the abbreviation "Orgue."

40. Sand, "Histoire du rêveur," here 13. I respect the spelling and punctuation of the edition listed in the bibliography. Subsequent quotations will be noted parenthetically in the text with the abbreviation "Rêveur."

41. Sand, *Les Sept Cordes de la lyre*, 129. Subsequent quotations will be noted parenthetically in the text with the abbreviation *SC*.

42. Juden, *Traditions orphiques*, 508.

43. I refer, of course, to the response of the general public and not to that of an informed and analytical listener who may remember and analyze during the listening experience.

44. See my "Improvisation(s) dans *Consuelo*," 130, and Brombert, *Romantic Prison*.

45. One recalls the unsuccessful efforts of Chopin to commit to paper some of Sand's favorite Berrichon melodies. Viardot, too, was frustrated by the difficulty of notating the folk tunes, although she did manage to write down some of them. See Tiersot, *Chanson populaire*.

46. Folk music reminds Albert of his earlier meeting with Consuelo and her mother, punctuated by the memory of their broken guitar, which he replaced with his own. Consuelo remembers then the beautiful guitar, marked with the initials "A. R.," that her mother always had with her and that remained in Venice when she left.

47. The Rudolstadt family, formerly Bohemian of the name Podiebrad, stand as living proof of the hypocrisy and frustration of the unsatisfying fight. George de Podiebrad was an ancestor of George Sand, as Lubin has proven in *Présence de George Sand*. See also Bourgeois' and Vierne's note on the fictionality of this character (*C*, 1:486).

48. The hint of incest proves false when Algénib reveals that he is not Moréna's brother. This is similar to the situation Sand will describe in *Ma Sœur Jeanne* (1874).

49. Molière's, Mozart's, and Hoffmann's.

50. Didier states that rehearsals, like improvisation, are more important than the performance since they better display the creative momentum, "George Sand et *Don Giovanni*," 50.

51. Normally it is the ankles that swell from pride according to the French idiom, but the fingers provide a more appropriate metonymy here. The phallic symbolism is evident.

52. *Le Dernier Amour*, 293–94. Subsequent quotations will be noted parenthetically in the text with the abbreviation *DA*. In *Adriani* (1854), Sand had already referred to the passage from Dante's *Inferno* (via Rossini's *Otello*), that no suffering can be worse than the memory of past happiness: "Nessun maggior dolor." See infra, 159.

53. Dauriac, *Essai sur l'esprit musical*, 183.

54. G. Guillaume, "*Les Maîtres Sonneurs*," and L. Charles-Dominique, "Dans les caves de Saint-Chartier."

55. For an excellent discussion of the sensual evocations of music in Proust, see Nattiez, *Proust as Musician*.

56. The bibliography for the question of music and mimesis, like that for music and language, is endless. Following is an abbreviated but by no means exhaustive list of pertinent titles: Adorno, *Aesthetic Theory*; Baldensperger, *Sensibilité musicale*; Barricelli, *Melopoiesis*; Barry, *Language, Music and the Sign*; Bloch, *Philosophy of Music*; Brown, *Music and Literature*; Burrows, *Sound, Speech, and Music*; Cook, *Music, Imagination, and Culture*; Cooke, *Language of Music*; Dahlhaus, *Nineteenth-Century Music*; DeBellis, "Representational Content of Musical Experience"; Despringre, "Démarche, concepts et méthodes"; Hanslick, *On the Musically Beautiful*; Hegel, *Aesthetics*; Hertz, *Tuning of the Word*; Jordan, "Augustine on Music"; Kivy, *Sound and Semblance*; Kramer, *Music and Poetry*; Le Huray and Day, eds. *Music and Aesthetics*; Lippman, *History of Western Musical Aesthetics*; Minehan, *Word Like a Bell*; Nattiez, *Fondements d'une sémiologie de la musique*; Neubauer, *Emancipation of Music*; Pagnini, *Lingua e musica*; Pousseur, *Musique, sémantique, société*; Said, *Musical Elaborations*; Saloman, "Chabanon and Chastellux"; Schelling, *Philosophy of Art*; Scher, ed. *Music and Text*; Springer, "Language and Music"; Steiner, ed., *The Sign in Music and Literature*; Storr, *Music and the Mind*; Zuckerkandl, *Sound and Symbol*, vols. 1 and 2.

57. Sand, *La Mare au diable, Francois le champi*, "Avant-Propos," 205. Subsequent quotations will be noted parenthetically in the text with the abbreviations *MD* and *FC*.

58. No reference to Musset's poem of 1837 (ten years earlier), which tells the story of the poet's bitterness at unrequited love. The tone of Sand's text represents quite the opposite feeling, a joyful celebration of beauty.

59. *Dialogue familier sur la poésie des prolétaires* and *Second dialogue familier sur la poésie des prolétaires*, published in the *Revue indépendante* in January and September 1842.

60. Sand will again refer to escape into the pastoral—in a Rousseauian sense this time and not à la Marie-Antoinette—in the preface to *La Petite Fadette*, 10. Here she makes an effort to rejoice in the amusement of the countryside, in "la musique de la nature," far from the political turmoil of Paris in the post-1848 disappointment.

61. See Sand's recounting of a conversation among Chopin, Delacroix, and Maurice about imitation in art, reported in *Impressions et Souvenirs*, 83–89. "[Chopin] ne connaît pas cette puérilité [l'harmonie imitative]. Il sait que la musique est une impression humaine et une manifestation humaine. C'est une âme humaine qui pense, c'est une voix humaine qui s'exprime. C'est l'homme en présence des émotions qu'il éprouve, les traduisant par le sentiment qu'il en a, sans chercher à en reproduire les causes par la sonorité. Ces causes, la musique ne saurait les préciser; elle ne doit pas y prétendre. Là est sa grandeur, elle ne saurait parler en prose" [Chopin does not fool with this childishness. He knows that music is a human impression and a human manifestation. It is a human soul that thinks, a human voice that expresses itself. It is man in the presence of the emotions he feels, translating them by the feelings he has without seeking to reproduce the cause through sound. Music would not be able to specify the cause, it does not claim to. Therein lies its greatness; it could never speak in prose] (86–87).

62. Rousseau, *Œuvres complètes*, vol. 5, *Écrits sur la musique, la langue et le théâtre*, 383. I respect the spelling and punctuation of the edition listed in the bibliography; subsequent quotations will be noted parenthetically in the text with the abbreviation *Discours*. For his definition of "accent," see the entries "Accent" and "Mélodie" in *Dictionnaire de musique*, 613–17, 885.

63. Rousseau belonged to the melody camp, which is but one component of current arguments that separated him from Rameau, who propounded on behalf of harmony as the most important element of music.

64. *Lettre sur la musique françoise* in *Œuvres complètes*, 5:316. Subsequent quotations will be noted parenthetically in the text with the abbreviation *Musique*.

65. For pertinent readings of Rousseau's painting metaphor, see de Man, "The Rhetoric of Blindness: Jacques Derrida's Reading of Rousseau," in *Blindness and Insight*, 102–41.

66. Balzac must have been thinking of Rousseau's dismissal of French when writing a passage of *Les Deux Poètes*, where a brief discussion revolves around the perfect suitability of French for music: "La vraie poësie française est la poësie légère, la chanson . . . —La chanson prouve que notre langue est très musicale" [True French poetry is light poetry, song. . . . Song proves that our language is musical.] (4: 541).

67. It is interesting to note that George Sand's paternal grandfather, Louis-Claude Dupin de Francueil, may have contributed to some of the composition of *Le Devin du village*. Several critics, Marix-Spire and Karénine, among others, have commented, without any conclusion, on the association between Rousseau and Francueil. See also passages of Rousseau's *Les Confessions*, book eight.

68. Langer, *Feeling and Form*, 153–54.

69. Baudelaire, *Les Fleurs du mal* (Paris: Seuil, 1968), 82.

70. Sand, *Rose et Blanche*, 1:51; my emphasis. I respect the spelling and punctuation of the 1831 edition. Subsequent quotations will be noted parenthetically in the text with the abbreviation *RB*.

71. In *Histoire de ma vie*, Sand has the following to say about working with Sandeau: "La collaboration est tout un art qui ne demande pas seulement, comme on le croit, une confiance mutuelle et de bonnes relations, mais une habileté particulière et une habitude de procédés *ad hoc*. Or, nous étions trop inexpérimentés l'un et l'autre pour nous partager le travail. Quand nous avions essayé, il était arrivé que chacun de nous refaisait en entier le travail de l'autre, et que ce remaniement successif faisait de notre ouvrage la broderie de Pénélope" [Collaboration is a whole art that does not require only, as is thought, for mutual confidence and good relations, but for a particular skill and a habit of ad hoc proceedings. However, we were both too inexperienced to share the work. When we had tried, we ended up completely rejecting the other's work and the subsequent redrafting made our work into Penelope's embroidery] (*OA*, 2:174).

72. Sand's insecurity about her own musical abilities surfaces here. She writes in *Lettres d'un voyageur*, "je comprends cette langue divine et ne puis la parler" [I understand this divine language and cannot speak it.] (*OA*, 2:845). Mozet relates this fear to her interpretation of "Mouny-Robin," *George Sand*, 35.

73. Sand speaks out here and elsewhere against journalistic criticism by advising her readers to listen to music instead of reading what music critics have to say. In the first act, when the critic explains that the arts are dead and that only criticism survives, the painter replies, "C'est-à-dire que vous faites un métier de croquemort" [That is to say that you are exercising a undertaker's trade] (*SC*, 86). Sand's opinion of critics does not change considerably throughout her career. Despite her invective against literary critics, I shall nonetheless persevere.

74. See chapter 4 for a more detailed analysis of the fantastic elements of this tale.

75. Balzac makes similar use of music in what is perhaps the most lyrical passage he ever wrote on music. In *Le Cousin Pons*, when Pons is on his deathbed he asks Schmucke to play for him: "Il trouva des thèmes sublimes sur lesquels il broda des caprices exécuté tantôt avec la douleur et la perfection raphaëlesques de Chopin, tantôt avec la fougue et le grandiose dantesque de Liszt, les deux organisations musicales qui se rapprochent le plus de celle de Paganini" [He discovered sublime themes on which he embellished fantasies, sometimes played with the Raphaël-like pain and perfection of a Chopin, sometimes with the wildness and the Dante-like majesty of a Liszt, the two musical organisms that come closest to Paganini] (2:743).

76. Stendhal, *Romans. La Chartreuse de Parme* (Paris: Gallimard, 1952), 2:329. The serenade style of communication is used again later in the novel.

77. A similar situation can be found in *La Daniella*. While hiding from the pontifical police, Jean Valreg thinks he hears a Bertini piano study being played badly. The strangeness of such music and such an instrument in the area causes him to doubt his ears; perhaps it was a gypsy's *cembalo*. But he is obliged to admit that it was the "son du piano fantastique, dans cette masure, que l'on pourrait appeler le château du diable" [sound of the fantastic piano in this hovel that could be called the devil's castle.] 1:301–2. Subsequent quotations will be noted parenthetically in the text with the abbreviation *LD*. Both volumes are published together in the edition I use, but the original pagination is retained.

78. See Balayé's excellent article, "Consuelo."

79. Daly, *Heroic Tropes*, 116–125.

80. Dauriac, *Essai sur l'esprit musical*, 183.

81. It would be revealing to take a census of the number of times such verbs appear in a metaphoric usage. Since my methodology is not quantitative, I leave that task to others.

82. For further discussion on music as language in *Les Maîtres Sonneurs*, see my " '*La langue de l'infini*'."

83. Sand, *Malgrétout*, 13. Subsequent quotations will be noted parenthetically in the text with the abbreviation *M*.

84. One also notes the phonetic resemblance between Albert and Abel.

85. In another case, Didier makes an interesting remark about Sand's unconventional quoting from *Don Giovanni* in *Le Château des Désertes* in Italian, unusual for the time, with a use of italics comparable to that used to indicate a foreign language; therefore foreign language would be analogous to music, or a language other than a verbal language; "George Sand et *Don Giovanni*," 52.

86. Sand, *Ma Sœur Jeanne*, 55. Subsequent quotations will be noted parenthetically in the text with the abbreviation *SJ*.

87. See Didier, *George Sand écrivain*, 261–74 and 268–70.

88. See Berlioz's comments on Balzac's *Gambara* in *Les Grotesques de la musique*, 19.

89. See quotation from the eleventh of the *Lettres d'un voyageur*, "Comment croirais-je que la musique est un art de pur agrément et de simple spéculation, quand je me souviens d'avoir été plus touché de ses effets et plus convaincu par son éloquence que par tous mes livres de philosophie?" [How could I believe that music is only an art of entertainment and of simple speculation when I remember being more touched by its effects and more convinced by its eloquence than by all my philosophy books?] (*LV*, 2:925–26).

90. Mozet, *George Sand*, 36–37. See also *Consuelo* (2:42).

91. Curtius, *European Literature*, 159–62.

3. Love, Madness, and Music

1. Balzac, *Modeste Mignon*, 1:448.

2. It must not be forgotten that this novel was a collaborative work, written with Jules Sandeau. Had Sand been writing alone, the outcome of the love plots and how the women were punished or rewarded for their love might have been different.

3. Sand, *Valentine*, 54. Subsequent quotations will be noted parenthetically in the text with the abbreviation *V*.

4. Jeanne, in *Ma Sœur Jeanne*, expresses a similar opinion (*SJ*, 268–69). A comparable remark comes from the mouth of a man, Jean Valreg in *La Daniella*, "La musique met trop l'individu en vue du public . . . le jour où je serais un virtuose distingué, il faudrait me produire et me montrer; cela me gênerait. Il me faut un état qui me laisse libre de ma personne. Si je fais de la mauvaise peinture, on ne me sifflera pas pour cela. Si j'en fais d'excellente on ne m'applaudira pas quand je passerai dans la rue," [Music puts an individual too much in the public eye . . . the day I become a distinguished virtuoso, I'd have to play in public and show myself, which would distress me. I need an profession where I can be free. If I paint badly, I won't be hissed at for it. If I paint well, I won't be applauded when

I pass by in the street] (1:17). Valentine's fear—a fall in social standing, thus a fear imposed from without—differs from Valreg's—a loss of privacy, Thus a fear felt from within—insofar as it reflects the social structure of mid-nineteenth-century France.

5. Marix-Spire points to a similar piano-tuning scene in Hoffmann's "Le Majorat": *Les Romantiques et musique*, 257. In actual fact, this scene (part 7 of the Loève-Veimars translation) represents a fix-up between two young musicians by a third party. This configuration radically differs from Sand's use of the piano-tuning ploy, where it always benefits two (would-be) lovers. Sand will use the device again in *La Dernière Aldini*.

6. In *La Coupe*, 222.

7. Another Sandian heroine is said to sing beautifully and only in service to the Church, the protagonist of *Mademoiselle La Quintinie* (Paris: Michel Lévy Frères, 1863), 58–63.

8. The reader notices the phonetic proximity between the name of the unknown savior and *libertà*, which recurs regularly in the Italian arias Consuelo sings.

9. Frappier-Mazur, "Desire, Writing, and Identity," 345–51.

10. Franz Benda (1709–1786) was a Bohemian violinist who became *Konzertmeister* to Frederick the Great. Sand's use of his name in the context of the *Invisibles* initiation supports Consuelo's evocation of the king's fears of being surrounded by plots of political overthrow.

11. See Leonardi and Pope, *The Diva's Mouth*, 81–82.

12. Music also serves a complex function in the love plot of *La Daniella*, in which the protagonist, Valreg, is pleased to teach Daniella to develop her innate vocal talents. While the musical link enforces the love relationship, it is also, in Daniella's eyes, a means to raise her to a socially acceptable rank, equal to Valreg's. At the same time, Valreg retains the superior role as he who knows (official) music. See *LD*, 2:205–8.

13. Sand, *Teverino*, 125.

14. *Teverino*, 160–61.

15. It is curious that Célio's role in the Vienna production, where he performed "dans un rôle bien fort" [in a strong role] (*CD*, 41), is never named. He is call a *primo basso cantante* (*CD*, 41), which would limit him to the roles of the Commandatore, for which he is much too young, or Leporello, much more appropriate for his age and demeanor.

16. While *Le Château des Désertes* was written in 1847, six years earlier than *Les Maîtres Sonneurs* (1853), it was published only in 1851, two years earlier than the bagpiping novel.

17. Bailbé speaks of the intimacy that turns to lyricism between Joset and Brulette, reminiscent of that between Consuelo and Haydn, Bailbé, "Écriture intime."

18. See the two versions found by Allier and Vincent, which Salomon and Mallion give in a note in their edition (Paris: Garnier, 1958), 264–65. Sand's version is quite different and much more poetical, though clearly rearranged to suit her narrative.

19. I discuss the ethnomusicological aspects of this song in chapter 5.

20. The line is inspired by Dante's *Inferno*, canto V, l. 121, which originates in Boethius's "in omni adversitate fortunæ infelicissimum . . . ," *Consolatio philosophæ*, II, iv, 4.

21. For contrast, see how music sparks jealousy and memories of former love at the moment of burgeoning love in *Jacques*, 880–82.

22. Balzac, *La Duchesse de Langeais*, 5:133–34.

23. See Berlioz's discussion of *Gambara* in *Les Grotesques de la musique*, 19.

24. One of course thinks of Hélène having inherited her grandfather's lyre.

25. Produced in Paris in 1827.

26. Balzac, *Œuvres complètes*, 9:334. Subsequent quotations will be noted parenthetically with the abbreviation *Doni*.

27. For further discussion on the function and correspondence of painting and musical metaphors, see the recent article by Saint-Gérand, "Métaphores correspondancielles." Also not to be neglected is the "clavecin oculaire" [ocular harpsichord] of Père Castel (1688–1757), which produced a different color for each step of the chromatic scale.

28. Didier points out that Sand avoided the trap of "l'analyse musicale . . . qui risque toujours de passer à côté de l'indicible" [musical analysis . . . which always runs the risk of sidestepping the ineffable]: "George Sand et *Don Giovanni*," 52–53.

29. Rambeau, *Chopin*, 298.

30. See Feder, *Madness in Literature*, 204, 208. See also pertinent remarks about Nerval's *Aurélia*, 252.

31. Felman, *La "Folie,"* 69.

32. Foucault, *Madness and Civilization*, 33.

33. Sand, "La Prima donna," signed "Jules Sand," 42. Subsequent quotations will be noted parenthetically in the text with the abbreviation "Prima." I respect the spelling and punctuation of the original text (*Revue de Paris*, April 1831), which the edition cited in the bibliography reproduces.

34. For an insightful discussion of women's silence and a female singer's voice, see Leonardi and Pope, *The Diva's Mouth*, especially chapter 3.

35. See my "Le Fantastique musical chez George Sand"; chapter 4 of the present volume gives a full discussion of the fantastic elements of this tale.

4. The Musical Fantastic

Portions of this chapter originally appeared as " 'Music Conducive to Dream': Sand and the Musical Fantastic," in *Le Siècle de George Sand*, ed. David A. Powell (Amsterdam: Rodopi, 1998), 321–33.

1. Hoffmann's astounding success in France has been widely documented. Michel,"Musique et poésie," demonstrates the affinities between Hoffmann and Balzac and Sand, where she identifies the importance of the musician, language, and expression. Castex, in his landmark study *Le Conte fantastique en France de Nodier à Maupassant*, recalls the importance of Hoffmann but also that of Swedenborg, Mesmer, Lavater, Comte, Lévi, and Poe on the French authors of the period. Milner points out in his significant work, *Le Diable dans la littérature française, de Cazotte à Baudelaire*, that French romantic authors tended to make the devil a figure of the fantastic more than Hoffmann. He then devotes several pages of study to Sand's use of the devil: 1:556–79; 2:164–72; 236. See also his *La Fantasmagorie*. Lloyd, *Baudelaire et Hoffmann*.

2. We should remember that "unheimlich" (uncanny) comes from "un-" (not) and "-heim, die Heimat" (home).

3. Avni, "Fantastic Tales"; Bellemin-Noël, "Notes sur le fantastique"; "Des formes fantastiques"; Castex, *Anthologie*; Cixous, "La Fiction et ses fantômes"; Freud, "The Uncanny"; Nodier, "Du fantastique en littérature"; Schneider, *La Lit-*

térature fantastique; Schuerewegen, "Histoire de pieds"; Siebers, *Romantic Fantastic*; Todorov, *Littérature fantastique*.

4. "Les Visions de la nuit dans les compagnes." The work on Breton folklore she refers to is M. de la Villemarqué's *Barza-Breiz* (1839), which most studies on French folklore acknowledge as a pivotal work in ethnomusicology.

5. Much of musico-literary criticism from the 1950s and 1960s attempted just this sort of correspondence.

6. Bellemin-Noël, "Des formes fantastiques," 105.

7. Todorov specifies that the fantastic is not a separate genre since what characterizes it is its hesitation between two genres, the uncanny and the marvelous. While I appreciate the tenuous nature of the fantastic, that in itself does not detract, I feel, from its status as a unique form. I therefore consider the fantastic a separate genre and classify the musical fantastic as a subgenre of the fantastic.

8. Hanslick, *On the Musically Beautiful*; also Dahlhaus, *Nineteenth-Century Music*, 92.

9. While theoretical writings on a nonconceptual understanding of music would not appear for another 150 years (e.g., Ruwet, Scruton, Eggebrecht), formalist theories were already beginning to crystalize in the late nineteenth century; and Lippman recently posited that the romantic tendency to combine opposites in a syncretic, eclectic system encourages viewing music at once as formal and ideational; Lippman, *History of Western Musical Aesthetics*.

10. Mozet, *George Sand*, 21.

11. See Baudelaire's "De l'essence du rire."

12. See Kennedy's perspicacious introduction to his translation of Sand's *Sept Cordes de la lyre*.

13. *OA*, 2:983–85.

14. For a more general discussion of Hoffmann's influence on Sand, see Kreitman's doctoral dissertation, "George Sand's Symbolic Vision."

15. For further commentary on Sand's use of a French narrator as a foreigner, see my article, "Eux et nous."

16. While the gender of the singer remains explicitly unclear, the masculine form is used throughout. Such use of the masculine is not uncommon in Sand's writing; witness *Les Lettres d'un voyageur* and some of her correspondence.

17. This trait also appears in "L'Orgue du titan." Célio, in *Le Château des Désertes*, learns to go beyond his technical bravura to a level of musical understanding and communication that will make of him a *real* musician. Joset, in *Les Maîtres Sonneurs*, will not lose his arrogance and therefore fails to develop as a *true* musician in Sand's eyes.

18. As I have suggested elsewhere, perhaps the only reason Sand did not also use the symbol for flat, "♭" is that it resembles the letter "b" too much. See my "Le Fantastique musical chez George Sand," 518; also, for a preliminary reevaluation of the musical fantastic, see my " 'Music Conducive to Dream'."

19. The title of chapter 2 is "Le Chanteur," although Bodin notes that it might actually read "Le Chévrier" ["goatherd"]. Later, another manuscript adds "l'inconnu, qui n'était autre que le Chanteur" (15,n80). The manuscript in the Bibliothèque Nationale (N. a. fr. 13642, fol. 13²) clearly reads "Le Chanteur."

20. Bellemin-Noël, "Des formes fantastiques," 112.

21. *La Comédie humaine*, 6: 90.

22. In like fashion, Mallarmé's faun will awaken from a dream and wonder to what degree his sexual desires have actually been aroused, "Aimai-je un rêve?" *L'Après-midi d'un faune*, (line 3) [Did I love a dream?]. Nerval's narrator in *Auré-*

lia never really seeks to awaken from his dreams; here the "épanchement du songe dans la vie réelle" [effusion of the dream into real life] all too clearly reinforces the search for an ambiguous state.

23. The reference to Sand's cricket, in the well-known passage from *Histoire de ma vie* (2:100–1), is obviously the first-level referent for the second narrator, Tricket. However, in my oneiric analysis, the reference to Corambé is more evident.

24. I spoke on the topic of illusion and performance in "On and Off Stage: Performances of La Portia in 'Histoire du rêveur' " (paper presented at the annual MLA, Washington, D.C., December 1996).

25. From evidence in a letter from Sand to Pauline Viardot, Glasgow suggests that the inspiration for the death of a friend comes from Chopin's loss of a friend, Matasynski. She also suggests that the name Carl recalls Karol from *Lucrezia Floriani*, a character largely considered to be inspired by Chopin, "Sand's Imaginary Travels in 'Carl'," 99.

26. There is one instance of actual musical notation in a text by Balzac, in *Modeste Mignon*, where Modeste's song, "Chant d'une jeune fille," appears with lyrics and piano score, over more than five pages in the Pléiade edition (1:448–54). On the CD-ROM *Explorer "La Comédie humaine"* (Paris: Acamedia, 1999) there is a piano and vocal recording of the music. Contrary to Sand's use in "Carl," however, no narrative imperative requires that the music be in Balzac's text.

27. Sand's dislike of Halévy's music has been noted by Marix-Spire, *Les Romantiques*, 537. See also Sand's letter to Delacroix, *Corr*, 5: 529–30.

28. Sand, "Carl," 242. Subsequent quotations will be noted parenthetically in the text.

29. An obligatory comment on the allusion to the nativity scene is in order, where the holy family is portrayed by the narrator, Carl-the-boy, and the spirit of Carl-the-friend. This is actually closer to the Trinity, because of the spirit, and therefore an allusion to Easter, where death and rebirth are the major themes.

30. Glasgow reviews Sand's correspondence at the time of the publication of "Carl." Schlésinger failed to return the manuscript with the proofs. Consequently she could not remember exactly where the musical phrases went. She suggests to the editor that he either give the proofs to Halévy to insert the music, or else return to her the original manuscript: "Sand's Imaginary Travels in "Carl," 98–99. The position of the musical quotations is thus important to their semiotic contribution to the story. A recent collection of *Nouvelles musicales*, collected by Martine Kaufmann (Paris: Liana Levi, 1992), 37–52, claims to reproduce the 1843 edition of "Carl," but the musical notations have been excised. The result is an eviscerated text, where a whole level of significance is missing.

31. See Rambeau, *Chopin*, 266.

32. Glasgow, Sand's Imaginary Travels in "Carl," 100.

33. Another auditory memory Sand mentions in her autobiography is the sound of the flageolet she heard from the window of an apartment outside Paris. As she could not see anything but the rooftops and the sky, she remained clueless as to the origin of the music, yet the sounds mesmerized her: "Quoi qu'il en soit, j'éprouvais d'indicibles jouissances musicales, et j'étais véritablement en extase devant cette fenêtre, où, pour la première fois, je comprenais vaguement l'harmonie des choses extérieures, mon âme étant également ravie par la musique et par la beauté du ciel" [Whatever it was, I experienced an ineffable musical pleasure, and I was truly in ecstasy in front of this window where, for the first time, I vaguely understood the harmony of external things, my soul being equally thrilled by the music and the beauty of heaven] (*HV,* 1:547).

34. Sand and Lévy had discussed calling these tales *contes fantastiques*, a term Sand ended up rejecting since "le fantastique est [dans mes contes] sous une forme d'allégorie si transparente que j'aurais voulu un adjectif plus modeste et mieux approprié, mais je ne le trouve pas" [in my stories the fantastic is in such a transparent form of allegory that I would prefer a more modest and more appropriate adjective, but I can't find one], letter to Lévy, June 1873, *Corr*, 23: 544. Despite her objection to the term, I include the discussion of this tale with those I designate as fantastic.

35. Here the term "master" is ironic, as opposed to its use in *Les Maîtres Sonneurs*.

36. Kreitman rightly points out that Sand also uses the symbol of a stone imbued with supernatural powers in *Consuelo* and *Jeanne*, "George Sand's Symbolic Vision," 63.

37. Sand, L'Orgue du titan," 120. Subsequent quotations will be noted parenthetically in the text with the abbreviation "Orgue."

38. Sand has used the phenomenon of music emanating from rocks before, in *Jeanne* (1844). See my discussion in chapter 5.

39. A quick search of atlases uncovers no such town. Given the phonetic nature of Sand's use of the name, it is likely that she invented it.

40. Perrot, *George Sand*, 17.

41. I disagree with Rambeau, who claims that these musicians from modest backgrounds forego a musical training and enter into the professional life as autodidacts, On the contrary, in all instances Sand's musicians rely heavily on proper musical training, which, coupled with natural talent, is a mainstay of Sand's image of the musician. *Chopin*, 260–61.

42. For further reading on this play as well as for its critic, see Bessière, *Récit fantastique*, 14, and Manifold, *Sand's Theatre Career*, 90–92.

43. Gounod wrote the music for the original version of this play in 1851.

44. Sand, "Maître Favilla," 191. Subsequent quotations, respecting the spelling and punctuation of the edition cited in the bibliography, will be noted parenthetically in the text with the abbreviation *MF*.

45. The character of Favilla is based on Joseph Dessauer, a German musician in Paris in the 1840s reputed to be idealistic and slightly mad. He was a personal friend of Sand: Cœuroy, "L'Inspiration musicale de George Sand," 49.

46. In the original version, where Favilla is called Nello, the sheet music was hidden in Nello's violin: Aroldi, "De *La Baronnie de Muhldorf* à *Maître Favilla*, 2:860.

47. The parallel with *Le Péché de Monsieur Antoine* and *Monsieur Sylvestre* is subtle but clear.

48. Bessière, *Récit fantastique*, 14.

49. Sand, *Théâtre de Nohant*, 211. Subsequent quotations will be noted parenthetically in the text with the abbreviation *NN*.

50. Sand states in "Les Visions de la nuit dans les campagnes," 89, that Christmas Eve is the time of "la plus solennelle crise du monde fantastique" [the most solemn climax of the fantastic world]. During the hour between midnight and one, evil spirits are at the mercy of those who know where to find them, and the devil offers gifts to humans. However, the devil is no dupe to human trickery, and the fantastic animals who might unwittingly lead humans to their hidden treasures will kill the human who is not gone from their territory at the stroke of one o'clock. The time element is essential to the cultural background of the play.

51. There is some confusion about the *bûche*. Manifold (*Sand's Theatre Career*,

142) refers to the regional ritual of placing a blessed yule log in the fire, which would account for the noise it makes. That the *bûche* is in the oven supports the interpretation of the more modern, seasonal pastry, fashioned to look like a yule log.

52. Milner, *Diable*, 1:167, 203.

53. Milner, *Diable*, 1:485.

54. The devil is indeed a character in Sand's novel in dialogue form, *Le Diable aux champs* (1851). Since this is not a musical text, I forego discussion of this instance of the devil.

55. Rambeau, *Chopin*, 241–67.

56. Berlioz's arrangement of *Der Freyschütz* (*Robin des bois*) was performed at the Opéra de Paris in 1841.

57. Mozet, *George Sand*, 65.

58. Sand, "Mouny-Robin," 276–77. I respect the spelling and punctuation of the edition cited in the bibliography.

59. Sand, *Légendes rustiques*, 185–91.

60. See Cellier's introductory essay to his edition of the novels, "L'Occultisme," 1:xlvii–lxxviii.

61. Juden, *Traditions orphiques*, 719. Juden's magisterial study provides many other perspectives under which to examine Sand's use of the Orpheus myth.

5. Folk Music

1. Recent scholarship has begun to unearth information about the "*trobairitz,*" or women troubadours. See Anne Callahan, "The Trobairitz." While Sand was probably unaware of this fact, the troubadour aspect of her writing, and of her life, takes on new meaning. See Reid's article, "Troubadoureries," based on the correspondence between Sand and Flaubert, for another pertinent usage of the term.

2. Johann Herder's concept of "national spirit" did much to launch a notion of history, culture, and nationhood; see Dahlhaus, *Nineteenth-Century Music*, 40, 81.

3. Guillaume, "*Les Maîtres Sonneurs.*"

4. In this chapter, as elsewhere, I struggle with an English equivalent for "paysan." Here I freely use "peasant" as a substantive, I alternate between "peasant" and "country" for the adjectival form.

5. Bancquart, "Préface," 5.

6. See, among others, Charron, "George Sand and the Revolution of 1848"; "De Fadette à Nanon"; "Rivières et fontaines"; Van Slyke, "History in Her Story."

7. The principal works on this question are Vincent, *La Langue et le style rustiques de George Sand* and Parent, "George Sand et le patois berrichon."

8. Memnon is an Ethiopian prince, ally of the Trojans. The statue of Amenhotep III at Thebes was associated with him and is known as vocal Memnon. Ancient writers record that when the first rays of the rising sun fall upon this statue, a sound is heard to issue from it, which they compare to the snapping of a harp string. It has been suggested that sounds produced by confined air making its escape from crevices or caverns in the rocks may have given some ground for the story. The statue is in fact hollow, and when struck, the stone emits a metallic sound, "that might still be made use of to deceive a visitor who was predisposed to believe its powers": *Bullfinch's Mythology* (New York: Avenel Books, 1979), 209. See Horace's commentary of Amphion, *Ars poetica*: "dictus et Amphion, Thebanae condi-

tor urbis, / saxa movere sono testudinis et prece blanda / ducere quo vellet," lines 394–96.

9. See Naginski for a discussion of mythological reworkings, especially of the Orpheus myth, *Writing for Her Life*, 205–15. For Amphion's powers to move stones with his lyre, again see Horace, *Ars poetica*.

10. A precept of Saint-Simonian doctrine that Sand co-opts is the use of music to inspire the masses to be good workers and thus to enhance social progress. Rouget de Lisle suggested to Saint-Simon as early as 1820 that music could be employed in the rehabilitation of society, and to that end he composed the "Chant des industriels," to be sung by a three-part men's chorus (workers), designed to develop subliminally their feelings of cooperation. Sand, subtler than Rouget de Lisle, includes farmers' songs in *La Mare au diable,* taking existing *chants de métiers* and molding them to express the socialist purpose of her novel: to exhort the farmer (i.e., all individuals) to contribute to society as a whole. Conceived to increase production as well as to lighten the animals' and the workers' burden, these songs enlist the cultural heritage of the masses in the exploitation of the doctrine of social reformers. Typical for the mid-nineteenth century, when much attention was paid to folklore and the culture of the provinces, such images contributed considerably to the understanding of social progress insofar as it ostensibly found its origins with the people.

11. *Le Courrier de Paris*, 2 September 1857. See text of "Le Réalisme" in *Questions d'art et de littérature*, 211–22. Also see the correspondence of Sand and Flaubert, passim.

12. Tiersot, *Chanson populaire*, 218.

13. Sand, *La Petite Fadette*, 9. Subsequent quotations will be noted parenthetically in the text with the abbreviation *PF*.

14. *Questions d'art et de littérature*, 206.

15. Commenting on *Le Compagnon du tour de France*, Hecquet points out the relation between the worker's art and its relation to national history, a phenomenon that has become legend: *Poétique du la parabole*, 115–17. In similar fashion, peasant music occupies an important place in Sand's presentation of art and social progress.

16. Sand wrote in a preliminary draft of the text: "sur un rythme à 6 ou 8 temps facile à observer" [on a 6– or 8–beat rhythm that's easy to keep to], which provides more musical detail but remains less descriptive of the topographical application of music.

17. Sand, *Jeanne*, 36. Subsequent quotations will be noted parenthetically in the text with the abbreviation *J*.

18. Chapter 27; there is an interesting study to be done on the function of eavesdropping in this novel.

19. A similar scene in *Valentine*, which I have already discussed, reveals the sociological ramifications of the ritual kiss at the opening of the bourrée. The bourrée in process, the obligatory kiss has already taken place, but the mischievous vielle player stops in mid-phrase and takes up the initial trill again, which demands the kiss again. Bénédict and Valentine are both embarrassed at the musician's injunction, but he remains constant to his prankish command and will not continue the dance music until the kiss has been delivered. As the count consents and indeed encourages Bénédict to perform his duty, Bénédict kisses Valentine, who blushes and laughs. The reactions to this kiss set off a series of attitudes that will affect the plot development. Bénédict notices that, while Valentine blushed at the count's "baisemain" [hand-kissing], she did not laugh, from which he concludes that she

truly loves the count. Based on this illogical deduction, Bénédict decides that he is less interested in dancing with Valentine than he was initially, and he encumbers the relationship between the two with unnecessary pride. In a different way, la comtesse de Raimbault, Valentine's mother, is mortified at Bénédict's brashness, at Count de Lansac's lack of judgment, and at Valentine's imprudence in allowing the kiss. Her haughty disposition in matters of class structure and mores prohibits any discussion of the practicality of the situation, and she remains poorly inclined toward Bénédict. So it is from music to dance, from dance to social customs, and from social customs to social prejudices, that we arrive at the sociological perspective that shapes the narrative. The prominent role of music prepares the socio-moral network of the novel.

20. In "Les Visions de la nuit dans les campagnes," Sand notes that "Le follet, fadet ou farfadet n'est point un animal . . . mais il a le corps d'un petit homme, et, en somme, il n'est ni vilain ni méchant, moyennant qu'on ne le contrariera pas" ["The sprite, pixie, or elf is not an animal . . . but it has the body of a small man and all in all is neither ugly nor mean, so long as he is not annoyed"] (82). Jaubert gives only "fade, fadette—fée, sorcière . . . le même au féminin que *fadet*, s. m. sylphe, génie rustique, esprit follet. (En français *farfadet*)," [fairy, witch . . . the same in the feminine as *fadet*, n.m. sylph, pixie, flighty creature. (In French *elf*)] (*Glossaire*, 1:419). He does give the term "folleté" (1:445), "étourderie, caprice" [careless mistake, whim] for which he cites from *François le champi*. None of these terms appears in his 1842 *Vocabulaire du Berry*.

21. Tiersot, *Chanson populaire*, 241.

22. See the discussions of Tiersot, *Histoire de la chanson populaire*, 241–43; Vincent, *Le Berry dans l'œuvre de George Sand*, vol. 1 of *George Sand et le Berry*, 279–80; and Bénichou, *Nerval et la chanson folklorique*, 158–60.

23. See Charles-Dominique, "Dans les caves de Saint-Chartier," 100–21. He goes on to say that Sand was certainly influenced by Cazotte's *Le Diable boîteux* in terms of the role of the devil in her novel. See also Heintzen, "La Musique pousse dans les bois," 136–47.

24. See my "Musique et musiquette."

25. A similar appreciation of Venetian folk music can be found in "Mattea," where we read, "La guitare est un instrument qui n'a son existence véritable qu'à Venise, la ville silencieuse et sonore" [The guitar is an instrument whose true existence can be known only in Venice, that silent and sonorous city] in *George Sand: Nouvelles*, ed. Eve Sourian, 298 (Paris: des femmes, 1986).

26. Sand, *Un Hiver à Majorque*, in *OA*, 2:1043.

27. Le Vot discusses the discrepancy between Sand's treatment of folk music in Venice and in Mallorca. "Berlioz écrivain et les musiques 'autres'."

28. See Marix-Spire's article "La musique naturelle." Another interesting discussion on *musique naturelle* occurs in *La Daniella*, 1:313–16.

29. According to the *Robert* dictionary, "bourrée" came into the French language in the fourteenth century and can be found in *Les Châtiments* by Hugo; there is no mention of regionalism. Littré gives examples from Mme de Sévigné and Chateaubriand. Neither "accent" or "bourrée" appears in Jaubert's *Glossaire* nor in his *Vocabulaire*, so we must assume the standard French definitions and etymologies apply. See Rousseau's *Dictionnaire de la musique* for a discussion of "accent."

30. Perrot, *George Sand*, 20.

31. Sand, *Le Meunier d'Angibault*, 39. Subsequent quotations will be noted parenthetically in the text with the abbreviation *MA*.

32. Hecquet, *Poétique de la parabole*, 16.

33. In actual fact, "fautes d'orthographe" refer to more than what in English we call "spelling mistakes." The French include under this rubric mistakes of agreement and tense that show up in spelling. Therefore it is as much grammar as spelling that is in question. "Grammar" being the essence of a language's ability to communicate, the allusion here is more destabilizing than the translation "spelling errors" connotes.

34. For a closer study of Schwartz's role in Stéphen's musical development as well as in communicating a cultural sense of the place of music in French society of the July Monarchy, especially in comparison with Balzac, whose character Schmucke (*Le Cousin Pons*) Sand borrowed, see "Schmucke and Schwartz: Cultural Commentary in a Musical Mode" (paper I presented at the Fourteenth International George Sand Conference, Brandeis University, April 1999).

35. For more on Sand's use of gypsy stereotypes and especially in comparison with Mérimée's, see Rea, "An Apolitical Sand?"

36. *Théâtre complet de George Sand*, 1: 20.

37. This song appears in toto in *Les Maîtres Sonneurs*. Tiersot comments on Sand's transformation of the original, *Chanson populaire*.

38. *Théâtre complet*, vol. 2, act 1, viii.

39. Sand seems to have been pleased with the production. In a letter to Maurice and Lina, she writes that she had been to a rehearsal; "C'est très joli, musique, décor, costumes, et le poème est gracieux et attendrissant" [It's very pretty, music, sets, costumes, and the book is gracious and compassionate]. On the evening of the premiere, she writes to Lina, "Immense succès, de poème, de musique, d'artistes, sans défaillance d'un instant, sans contestation d'une minute, une bienveillance et un enchantement continus. La partition a été vendue entre le 1er et le 2d acte et très bien vendue. J'ai déjà touché une somme et on dit que la pièce fera beaucoup d'argent. . . . On a bissé tous les morceaux d'une dimension possible. . . . La salle était comble et a fait bonne recette malgré les billets donnés" [An immense success, book, music, actors, without a moment's faltering nor a minute's protest; continual benevolence and enchantment. The score was sold between acts 1 and 2, and it sold very well. I've already made a certain amount and they say the play will make a lot of money. . . . They encored all the pieces they possibly could. . . . The house was full and made good money despite the comp tickets"] (*Corr,* 21:606, 617). The opera continued to be a financial success.

40. I refer throughout this section to the piano score of *La Petite Fadette* (Paris: Brandus and Dufour, 1869), B.N. manuscript number M1503/S373P4/1869.

41. See in particular the insightful article by Schor, "Reading Double."

42. In a letter to Adolphe de Leuven, the manager of the Opéra-Comique, Sand sends her approval of the manuscript of the opera, with some important suggestions, e.g., making it clearer how much Sylvinet wants to separate Landry from Fadette, thus better explaining Landry's madness and Sylvinet's lie. She also suggests an additional aria for Sylvinet in the second act to explicitly disclose his jealousy (*Corr,* 21:526–27). These suggestions clearly went unheeded.

43. See Marix-Spire, "Vicissitudes d'un opéra-comique."

44. Sand, *Promenades autour d'un village, suivies du Journal de Gargilesse,* 87.

45. "Le meneu' de loups," in *Légendes rustiques,* 185–91. Subsequent quotations from the text will be noted parenthetically with the abbreviation "Meneu'. Sand's "Mouny-Robin" also exploits the legend of the *meneux de loups*. Instead of folk music, however, it is Weber's *Freyschütz* that Sand uses as the musical backdrop.

6. Musician, Public, and Society

1. Hecquet, *Poétique de parabole*, 11.
2. See Didier, *George Sand écrivain*, 373.
3. For more on the narratological function of the narrators, see my "Nous et Eux."
4. See Sand's discussion of the public's response to Viardot's singing and acting in "Le Théâtre italien de Paris et Mlle Pauline Garcia," 364. Also see Didier, *George Sand écrivain*, 265–66.
5. FitzLyon, *Maria Malibran*, 65.
6. Didier, "George Sand et *Don Giovanni*," 51.
7. See Capasso, "Empress Eugénie."
8. The terms *mélomane* (music-lover) and *mélomanie* (music mania) are always used in a pejorative sense in this novel. Only the characters who disdain the condition of the artist employ the terms, which presents an interesting note on Sand's effort to characterize the controlled enthusiasm of her music lovers. Sand never talks about *mélomanes* in any other text.
9. A quick comparative study between this analogy and Sand's account of her discussion with Michel about art in the sixth of the *Lettres d'un voyageur* (*LV,* 2:807–13) would doubtless uncover interesting similarities and contrasts.
10. Guillaume points out that by the mid-nineteenth century, most peasant musicians actually exercise a craft full-time and play gigs on the side.
11. See Diaz's excellent and thorough treatment of Sand's relationship with Poncy through their correspondence in "Portrait de l'artiste en maçon."
12. Lubin notes the manuscript is unclear, and that this is perhaps "gens."
13. Hecquet affirms that Sand's argument in many of her novels treats the issue of how best to portray her message, especially when carried by peasant characters: *Poétique de la parabole*, 325–26.
14. Rambeau, *Chopin*, 204; André Cœuroy points to the importance of the Saint-Simonian doctrine of "progress through art" to be found in abundance in Sand's work: "L'Inspiration musicale de George Sand"; Marix-Spire, *Les Romantiques*, and Rambeau, *Chopin*, affirm and develop this conclusion. Perrot, *George Sand*, and Hecquet, *Poétique de la parabole*, attest the role of Saint-Simonism in Sand's concept of social progress, but gloss over with little or no commentary its influence on her aesthetics.
15. *Indiana*, 1842 preface, xv–xvi. For these and other prefatory texts, see Szabó's recent publication, *Les Préfaces de George Sand*.
16. See *HV,* 1: 1084–89.
17. Moses, " 'Difference' in Historical Perspective: Saint-Simonian Feminism," in Moses and Rabine, *Feminism, Socialism, and French Romanticism*, 17–84.
18. Hecquet, *Poétique de la parabole*, 320–23. For more about Sand's views on Saint-Simonism, see her *Lettres à Marcie*, in particular letter 3. See also Goldin's exhaustive article, "Le Saint-Simonisme."
19. Hecquet, *Poétique de la parabole*, ch 1; Perrot, *George Sand*, 17–19, passim.
20. Bazard, in Thibert, *Le Rôle social de l'art*, 27–28.
21. Cited by Marix-Spire, *Les Romantiques*, 430.
22. An allusion to a "Golden Age" could perhaps be posited, though I prefer to think Sand refers to the ills of gold and silver as well as those of steel, as embodied in the impending Industrial Age. The symbolism of the text also recalls Hesiod's theory of the four ages of humanity.

23. I cannot resist a comment, as I type on a laptop and print out on a laser printer, to urge policy makers at the time of this writing to contemplate similarly the dangers of investing in technology at the cost of the arts.

24. Ballanche, *Œuvres complètes*, 454.

25. Locke, *Music, Musicians and the Saint-Simonians*, 96–97.

26. See Locke's discussion in *Music, Musicians and the Saint-Simonians*, 37–42.

27. " 'The Artist, the Scientist, and the Industrialist: A Dialogue', by Saint-Simon and Léon Halévy (*Opinions littéraires, philosophiques et industrielles*)," in Saint-Simon, *Selected Writings*, 279–88.

28. See Locke, "Liszt's Saint-Simonian Adventure."

29. Liszt, "De la situation des artistes," cited in Marix-Spire, "Du Piano à l'action sociale," 205.

30. See Liszt's *Lettres d'un bachelier ès musique* (1835–41), trans. Charles Suttoni as *An Artist's Journey*. Although much of this text is said to have actually been penned by Marie d'Agoult, it details Liszt's socialist and aesthetic thought during his time in Paris.

31. Marix-Spire, *Les Romantiques*, 207.

32. Cited in Thibert, *Le Rôle social de l'art*, 33.

33. See Hunt, *Politics, Culture, and Class*, 95–104 and 271–78. See also Naginski's discussion of Fortoul in *George Sand*, 109–11.

34. Locke, *Music, Musicians and the Saint-Simonians*, ch. 6, esp. 45–52.

35. *Spiridion*, 229–30. I respect the spelling of the edition in the bibliography. Subsequent quotations will be noted parenthetically in the text with the abbreviation *S*.

36. See Rea's treatment of the political aspect of this novel: "An Apolitical Sand?"

37. See Mozet's treatment of this subject throughout her *George Sand*, and Frappier-Mazur's articles.

38. Thibert, *Le Rôle soial de l'art*, 274–75, 277.

39. See Moses, *French Feminism in the Nineteenth Century*; also Moses and Rabine, *Feminism, Socialism, and French Romanticism* (Bloomington, IN: Indiana University Press, 1993).

40. See Schor, *George Sand and Idealism*, 76–80, and "Le Féminisme et George Sand"; also Nigel Harkness, "Sand, Lamennais et le féminisme: Le Cas des *Lettres à Marcie*," in Powell, ed., *Le Siècle de George Sand*, 185–92.

41. See Moses, *French Feminism in the Nineteenth Century*, intro.

42. Schwab, "Mother's Body, Father's Tongue."

43. Kristeva, "Stabat Mater," in *The Kristeva Reader*.

44. Didier, "George Sand et *Don Giovanni*," 52.

45. Taviani and Schino tell that contrary to the accepted belief, commedia dell'arte actors frequently changed roles—in fact, the public applauded that very gift of being able to change masks: *Le Secret de la commedia dell'arte*, 315–23.

46. Abel, Hirsch, and Langland, eds., *The Voyage In*, 7. Marrone writes of the stifling nature of society in the female Bildungsroman, "Male and Female *Bildung*," 339. For Consuelo the microcosm of the Viennese opera world represents this repression.

47. For a discussion of how music symbolizes a search for freedom in this text, see my "Improvisation(s) dans *Consuelo*." See also Didier, *George Sand écrivain*, 278–90.

48. Mozet, *George Sand écrivain*, 158.

49. See the section on Bildungsroman in chapter 1, where I discuss at length differences between male and female *Bildungen.* Mozet points out Solange Sand-Clésinger's revealing choice of an opera singer for the heroine of her novel *Jacques Bruneau* (1870). The nature of this heroine differs considerably from any of Sand's singers; still, it is interesting that Solange should exploit a musical career she knew little about, certainly less than her mother. While Sand's critiques of her daughter's novel as well as her reformulation of some of the material found therein add little to my discussion about music, Mozet's examination of the literary aspect of Sand and Solange's relationship provides a provocative analysis: *George Sand*, ch. 5: "Solange ou la déchirure"; for the singer reference, see 121–22.

50. These texts cover the chronological scope of Sand's work: "La Fille d'Albano" in 1831, *Elle et Lui* in 1859, and "Le Château de Pictordu," in *Contes d'une grand'mère*, 1873.

51. See the interesting remarks on Sand's sole dancer in Aline Alquier's notes to her edition of *Albine Fiori*, 119–37.

52. Rambeau, *Chopin,* 252.

53. Rambeau, *Chopin*, 253.

54. See Didier, *George Sand écrivain*, 364–69.

55. Rambeau, *Chopin*, 176, 259, 314, 321, 327. See also Sand's letter to Hortense Allart (22 June 1847) on this issue: *Corr*, 7: 757–58).

56. An excellent treatment of this volatile issue can be found in Perrot's *George Sand*, 39–48 and passim.

57. Perrot, *George Sand*, "Présentation," 7–57. Also Hecquet, *Poétique de la parabole,* especially chs. 1 and 8.

58. See Bowman, *Le Christ des barricades*, esp. 264–69; also Naginski, *Writing for Her Life*, 142–44.

59. "Lamartine utopiste," in Sand, *Questions d'art et de littérature*,124.

CONCLUSION: THE INDESCRIBABLE MYSTERIES OF MUSIC

1. Mozet, *George Sand*, 33–53.

2. *Impressions et Souvenirs,* cited in Rambeau, *Chopin*, 80.

3. Baudelaire, *Œuvres complètes*, 231–32.

4. Gérard Gasarian, in his paper, "Baudelaire et ses sœurs" (paper presented at the annual MLA, Washington, D.C., 1996), discusses the similarities between these otherwise antipodal authors, particularly Sand's influence on Baudelaire.

5. Sand, *Contes d'une grand'mère*, 2:130.

6. See *Impressions et Souvenirs*, in which Sand recounts Delacroix's conversation with Chopin and Maurice Sand about the analogies between color, moonlight, and music, 85–86.

7. *Impressions et Souvenirs*, 88.

8. Sand, *Entretiens journaliers*, *OA*, 2:985.

9. Hecquet discusses the role of art and artists in the literary tradition as equally central to the problems of social structure and social exchange as to matters of aesthetic expression, *Poétique de la parabole*, 326. To this argument I would of course add music and musicians.

10. See Sand's essay "Réalisme," in *Questions d'art et de littérature*, 211–22; also Perrot, *George Sand*: "il n'est pas question pour elle de 'réalisme', fût-il social; mais d'une modification de l'art en profondeur, dans ses structures mêmes, qui le rende plus 'vrai,' " (19) and further on, "Le rôle des écrivains et des artistes

est d'y participer [à la diffusion des lumières] par les mots et les images [and here I would add 'music']. Sand puise là sa certitude de l'utilité de l'art et sa conception d'un roman 'idéaliste', dans la mesure où il cherche à susciter chez le lecteur des émotions génératrices de sentiments altruistes . . . Elle entend se mettre 'au service' d'une 'cause' : celle du peuple, selon le titre de son journal" [for her, it's not a matter of realism, even if social, rather of a profound modification of art, in its very structures, which makes it more 'true.' . . . The role of writers and artists is to participate in the dissemination of enrichment by words and images. This is where Sand derives her confidence in the utility of art and her conception of an 'idealist' novel in so much as it seeks to elicit the reader's propagative emotions of altruistic feelings. . . . She intends to put herself 'into service' of a 'cause': that of the people, according to the title of her newspaper] (37–38).

♫♫ Bibliography ♫♫

PRIMARY SOURCES: WORKS BY GEORGE SAND

Adriani. Edited by Maurice Toesca. Paris: Editions France-Empire, 1980.

Albine Fiori. Edited by Aline Alquier. Tusson: Du Lérot, 1997.

"Carl." In *Œuvres de George Sand*, 31:235–60. Paris: Hetzel-Lecou, 1852–55.

Le Château des Désertes. Edited by J.-M. Bailbé. Meylan: Editions de l'Aurore, 1985.

Consuelo and *La Comtesse de Rudolstadt*. 3 vols. Edited by Simone Vierne and René Bourgeois. Meylan: Editions de l'Aurore, 1983.

Contes d'une grand-mère. 2 vols. Edited by Philippe Berthier. Meylan: Editions de l'Aurore, 1982, 1983.

"Le Contrebandier." In *La Coupe*. Paris: Calmann Lévy, 1876, 261–98.

Correspondance de George Sand. 25 vols. Edited by Georges Lubin. Paris: Garnier, 1964–95. Also vol. 26, *Supplément*. Edited by Georges Lubin. Paris: Bordas, 1991.

La Coupe. Paris: Calmann Lévy, 1876.

La Daniella. Geneva: Slatkine, 1979.

Le Dernier Amour. Paris: Calmann Lévy, 1876.

La Dernière Aldini. Paris: Michel Lévy, Frs., 1857.

"Dialogue familier sur la poésie des prolétaires." *Revue indépendante* (January 1842); also "Second dialogue familier sur la poésie des prolétaires." *Revue indépendante* (September 1842).

Elle et Lui. Edited by Thierry Bodin. Meylan: Editions de l'Aurore, 1986.

Entretiens journaliers avec le très docte et très habile docteur Piffoël, professeur de botanique et de philosophie. In *Œuvres autobiographiques*, 2: 973–1025.

"La Fille d'Albano." In *Œuvres de George Sand*, 31: 154–71. Paris: Lévy, 1856–57.

La Filleule. Edited by Marie-Paule Rambeau. Meylan: Editions de l'Aurore, 1989.

François le champi. Paris: Garnier, 1981.

Histoire de ma vie. In *Œuvres autobiographiques*. Edited by Georges Lubin. 2 vols. vol. 1, 2:1–465. Paris: Gallimard, 1970–71.

"Histoire du rêveur." Edited by Thierry Bodin. *Présence de George Sand* 17 (June 1983): 9–39.

Un Hiver à Majorque. In *Œuvres autobiographiques*, 2: 1027–77.

L'Homme de neige. 2 vols. Edited by J.-M. Bailbé. Meylan: Editions de l'Aurore, 1990.

Impressions et Souvenirs. Paris: Lévy, 1873.

Indiana. Plan de la Tour: Editions d'aujourd'hui, 1976.

Jacques. In *George Sand: Romans 1830.* Paris: Omnibus/Presses de la Cité, 1991.

Jeanne. Edited by Simone Vierne. Meylan: Editions de l'Aurore, 1986.

Légendes rustiques. In *Promenade dans le Berry: Mœurs, coutumes, légendes,* 119–223. Brussels: Editions Complexe, 1992.

Lettres d'un voyageur. In *Œuvres autobiographiques,* 2: 633–943.

Lucrezia Floriani. Paris: Editions de la Sphère, 1981.

Maître Favilla. In *Théâtre de George Sand,* 1: 167–255. Paris: Lévy, 1860.

Les Maîtres Sonneurs. Edited by Marie-Claire Bancquart. Paris: Folio/Gallimard, 1979.

Malgrétout. Edited by Jean Chalon. Meylan: Editions de l'Aurore, 1992.

La Mare au diable. Paris: Garnier, 1981.

"Mattea." In *George Sand: Nouvelles.* Paris: des femmes, 1986.

Le Meunier d'Angibault. Verviers: Marabout, 1977.

"Mouny-Robin." *Revue des deux mondes* (15 June 1841): 251–77.

Œuvres autobiographiques. 2 vols. Edited by Georges Lubin. Paris: Gallimard, 1970–71.

"L'Orgue du titan." In *Contes d'une grand-mère,* 2: 105–25. Meylan: Editions de l'Aurore, 1983.

La Petite Fadette. Edited by Pierre Salomon and Jean Mallion. Paris: Garnier, 1958.

La Petite Fadette. Lyrics by Michel Carré. Music by Théophile Semet: Arranged by Bazille. Paris: Brandus and Dufour, 1869. Département de Musique, Bibliothèque Nationale, M1503 / S373 P4 / 1869.

"La Prima donna." *Présence de George Sand* 17 (June 1983): 40–45.

Promenade dans le Berry: Mœurs, coutumes, légendes. Prefare by Georges Lubin. Brussels: Editions Complexe, 1992.

Promenades autour d'un village, suivies du Journal de Gargilesse. St-Cyr-sur-Loire: Christian Pirot, 1984.

Questions d'art et de littérature. Edited by Henriette Bessis and Janis Glasgow. Paris: des femmes, 1991.

Rose et Blanche. 2 vols. Brussels: Méline, 1833.

Les Sept Cordes de la lyre. Edited by René Bourgeois. Paris: Flammarion, 1973.

Ma Sœur Jeanne. Paris: Lévy Frères, 1874.

Spiridion. Presented by Oscar A. Haac and Michèle Hecquet. Geneva: Slatkine Reprints, 2000.

Teverino. Plan de la Tour-Var: Editions d'aujourd'hui, 1977.

Théâtre complet de George Sard. 4 vols. Paris: Lévy, 1860.

Théâtre de Nohant. Paris: Lévy, 1864.

"Le Théâtre italien de Paris et Mlle Pauline Garcia." In *Autour de la table,* 351–67. Paris: Michel Lévy Frères, 1876.

Valentine. Edited by Aline Alquier. Meylan: Editions de l'Aurore, 1995.

"Les Visions de la nuit dans les compagnes." In *Promenade dans le Berry: Mœurs, coutumes, légendes,* 54–93. Brussels: Editions Complexe, 1992.

SECONDARY SOURCES

Abbadie, Christian. "Le Thème du *Contrebandier.*" *Présence de George Sand* 12 (October 1981): 34–45.

Abbate, Carolyn. *Unsung Voices: Opera and Musical Narrative in the Nineteenth Century.* Princeton: Princeton University Press, 1991.

Abdelaziz, Nathalie. *Le Personnage de l'artiste dans l'œuvre de Geroge Sand avant 1848.* Villeneuve d'Ascq: Presses Universitaires du Septentrion, 1997.

———. "Quelle fin pour l'artiste: Spécificités d'écriture de la clôture des romans sur l'artiste." In *George Sand et l'écriture du roman,* edited by Jeanne Goldin, 325–35. Montréal: Paragraphes, 1996.

Abel, Elizabeth, Marianne Hirsch, and Elizabeth Langland, eds. *The Voyage In: Fictions of Female Development.* Hanover, N.H.: University Press of New England, 1983.

Adam, B., and J.-M. Adam. "Pour une analyse structurale du texte romanesque: Lecture des *Maîtres Sonneurs* de George Sand." *Le Français aujourd'hui* (January 1972): 36–41.

Adorno, Theodor W. *Aesthetic Theory.* Edited by Gretel Adorno and Rolf Tiedemann. Translated by C. Lenhardt. 1970. Reprint, London: Routledge & Kegan Paul, 1984.

Agoult, Marie d'. *Mémoires.* Edited by Daniel Ollivier. Paris: Calmann-Lévy, 1927.

Alvarez-Detrell, Tamara, and Michael Paulson, ed. *The Traveler in the Life and Works of George Sand.* Troy, N.Y.: Whitston, 1994.

Aroldi, Maria Pia. "De *La Baronnie de Muhldorf* à *Maître Favilla* de George Sand: Un Ours qui change de peau." In *George Sand et son temps: Hommage à Annarosa Poli,* edited by Elio Mosele, 2: 857–85. Geneva: Slatkine, 1992.

Avni, Ora. "Fantastic Tales." In *A New History of French Literature,* ed. Denis Hellier, 675–81. Cambridge: Harvard University Press, 1989.

Bailbé, Joseph-Marc. "Le Bourgeois et la musique au XIXe siècle." *Romantisme* 17–18 (1979): 123–36.

———. "Écriture intime et mouvements lyriques dans *Les Maîtres-Sonneurs.*" In *George Sand et l'écriture du roman,* edited by Jeanne Goldin, 279–85. Montréal: Paragraphes, 1996.

———. "Musique et personnalité dans *Consuelo.*" In *La Porporina,* edited by Léon Cellier, 119–28. Grenoble: Presses Universitaires de Grenoble, 1976.

———. *Le Roman et la musique en France sous la Monarchie de Juillet.* Paris: Lettres Modernes, Minard, 1969.

———. "Le Théâtre et la vie dans *Le Château des Désertes.*" *Revue d'histoire littéraire de la France* 79 (1979): 600–12.

Bailey, Derek. *Musical Improvisation: Its Nature and Practice in Music.* Englewood Cliffs, N.J.: Prentice-Hall, 1980.

Bal, Mieke. *Narratology: Introduction to the Theory of Narrative.* 2d ed. Toronto: University of Toronto Press, 1997.

Balayé, Simone. "Consuelo: De la mendiante à la déesse de la Pauvreté." *Revue d'histoire littéraire de la France* 74 (1974): 614–25.

Baldauf-Berdes, Jane L. *Women Musicians of Venice: Musical Foundations, 1525–1855.* Oxford: Clarendon Press, 1993.

Baldensperger, Fernand. *Sensibilité musicale et romantisme.* Paris: Presses Françaises, 1925.

Ballanche Pierre-Simon, *Œuvres complètes.* Geneva: Slatkine, 1967.

Balzac, Honoré de. *Œuvres complètes.* Edited by Marcel Boutereau. Paris: Gallimard, 1952.

———. *Le Cousin Pons. La Comédie humaine.* Vol. 2. Edited by Marcel Boutereau. Paris: Gallimard/Pléiade, 1952.

———. *Les Deux Poètes.* Part 1 of *Illusions perdues. La Comédie humaine.* Vol. 4. Edited by Marcel Boutereau. Paris: Gallimard/Pléiade, 1952.

———. *La Duchesse de Langeais. La Comédie humaine.* Vol. 5. Edited by Marcel Boutereau. Paris: Gallimard/Pléiade, 1952.

———. *Gambara. La Comédie humaine.* Vol. 9. Edited by Marcel Boutereau. Paris: Gallimard/Pléiade, 1952.

———. *Massimilla Doni. La Comédie humaine.* Vol. 9. Edited by Marcel Boutereau. Paris: Gallimard/Pléiade, 1952.

———. *Modeste Mignon. La Comédie humaine.* Vol. 1. Edited by Marcel Boutereau. Paris: Gallimard/Pléiade, 1952.

———. *Sarrasine. La Comédie humaine.* Vol. 4. Edited by Marcel Boutereau. Paris: Gallimard/Pléiade, 1952.

———. *Ursule Mirouët. La Comédie humaine.* Vol. 3. Edited by Marcel Boutereau. Paris: Gallimard/Pléiade, 1952.

Bancquart, Marie-Claire. "Introduction." In *Les Maîtres Sonneurs.* Paris: Folio/Gallimard, 1979.

Barricelli, Jean-Pierre. *Melopoiesis: Approaches to the Study of Literature and Music.* New York: New York University Press, 1988.

Barry, Joseph. *Infamous Woman: The Life of George Sand.* New York: Doubleday, 1971.

Barry, Kevin. *Language, Music and the Sign: A Study in Aesthetics, Poetics and Poetic Practice from Collins to Coleridge.* Cambridge: Cambridge University Press, 1987.

Baudelaire, Charles. "De l'essence du rire." In *Œuvres complètes,* 370–78. Paris: Seuil, 1968.

Bellemin-Noël, Jean. "Des formes fantastiques aux thèmes fantasmatiques." *Littérature* 2 (May 1971): 103–18.

———. "Notes sur le fantastique." *Littérature* 8 (December 1972): 3–23.

Belmont, Nicole. "L'Académie celtique et George Sand: Les Débuts des recherches folkloriques en France." *Romantisme* 9 (1975): 29–38.

Bénichou, Paul. *Nerval et la chanson folklorique.* Paris: José Corti, 1970.

Berlioz, Hector. *Les Grotesques de la musique.* Paris: Calmann-Lévy, 1927.

Bessière, Irène. *Le Récit fantastique: La Poétique de l'incertain.* Paris: Larousse, 1973.

Blaze, François-Joseph (dit Castil-Blaze). *De l'opéra en France.* Paris: Chez l'Auteur, 1826.

Bloch, Ernst. *Essays on the Philosophy of Music.* Translated by Peter Palmer. Cambridge: Cambridge University Press, 1985.

Bohlman, Philip J. *The Study of Folk Music in the Modern World.* Bloomington: Indiana University Press, 1988.

Boulez, Pierre. *Orientations: Collected Writings.* Edited by J.-J. Nattiez. Translated by Martin Cooper. Cambridge: Harvard University Press, 1986.

Bourgeois, René. "Les Deux Cordes de la lyre: Ou Goethe jugé par George Sand." In *Hommage à George Sand,* edited by Léon Cellier. Grenoble: Presses Universitaires de Grenoble, 1969.

———. "Le Voyage heureux: Feinte et naturel." In *La Porporina,* edited by Léon Cellier, 69–75. Grenoble: Presses Universitaires de Grenoble, 1976.

Bowman, Frank Paul. *Le Christ des barricades, 1789–1848.* Paris: Editions du Cerf, 1987.

———. *Le Christ romantique.* Gevena: Droz, 1973.

———. "George Sand, le Christ et le Royaume." *Cahiers de l'Association Internationale des Études Françaises* 28 (May 1976): 246–62.

———. "Notes towards the Definition of the Romantic Theater." *L'Esprit créateur* 5 (1965): 9–13.

Boyer, H. "Histoire des corporations et confréries d'art et métier de Bourges." *Mémoires de la société historique, littéraire et scientifique du Cher* (1909): 47–51.

Bozon-Scalzitti, Yvette. "George Sand: Le Bruit et la musique." *Orbis Litterarum* 41 (1986): 139–56.

———. "La Pierre, l'eau, le sable: L'Écriture sandienne dans les *Lettres d'un voyageur.*" *Nineteenth-Century French Studies* 21, nos. 3–4 (spring–summer 1993): 339–56.

Brombert, Victor. *The Romantic Prison.* Princeton: Princeton University Press, 1987.

Brooks, Peter. *Reading for the Plot: Design and Intention in Narrative.* New York: Knopf, 1984.

Brown, Calvin. *Music and Literature: A Comparison of the Arts.* Rev. ed. Hanover, N.H.: University Press of New England, 1987.

Brown, Marshall. "Origins of Modernism: Musical Structures and Narrative Forms." In *Music and Text: Critical Inquiries,* edited by Steven Paul Scher, 75–92. Cambridge: Cambridge University Press, 1992.

Brzoska, Matthias. "Musikalische Form und sprachliche Struktur in George Sands Novelle 'Le Contrebandier.' " In *Musik und Literatur,* edited by Albert Bier and Gerold W. Gruber, 169–84. Europäische Hochschulschriften, vol. 127. Frankfurt: Peter Lang, 1995.

Burrows, David. *Sound, Speech, and Music.* Amherst: University of Massachusetts Press, 1990.

Callahan, Anne. "The Trobairitz." In *French Women Writers: A Bio-Bibliographical Source Book,* edited by Eva Martin Sartori and Dorothy Wynne Zimmermann, 495–502. New York: Greenwood Press, 1991.

Canteloube, Joseph. *Anthologie des chants populaires français groupés et présentés par pays ou provinces.* Paris: Durand, 1951.

———. *Chants d'Auvergne.* 5 vols. Paris: Heugel, 1925–55.

———. *Les Chants de provinces françaises.* Paris: Didier, 1947.

———. *Le Tour du monde: Des petits chanteurs à la croix de bois.* N.p.: Mame, 1955.

Capasso, Ruth Carver. "The Empress Eugénie in Sand's *Malgrétout.*" In *Le Siècle de George Sand,* edited by David A. Powell, 253–60. Amsterdam: Rodopi, 1998.

Cassou, Jean. "George Sand et le secret du XIXe siècle." *Mercure de France* 343 (December 1961): 601–18.

Castex, Pierre-George. *Anthologie du conte fantastique français.* Paris: José Corti, 1947.

———. *Le Conte fantastique en France de Nodier à Maupassant.* Paris: José Corti, 1951.

Cate, Curtis. *George Sand: A Biography.* Boston: Houghton-Mifflin, 1975.

Celletti, Rudolfo. *A History of Bel Canto.* Translated by Frederick Fuller. Oxford: Clarendon Press, 1991.

Cellier, Léon. "L'Occultisme dans *Consuelo* et *La Comtesse de Rudolstadt.*" In *Consuelo,* by George Sand. Paris: Garnier, 1959.

———. *Parcours romantiques.* Edited by Ross Chambers. Grenoble: Presses Universitaires de Grenoble, 1977.

———, ed. *La Porporina: Entretiens sur "Consuelo."* Grenoble: Presses Universitaires de Grenoble, 1976.

———. "Le Romantisme et la mythe d'Orphée." *Cahiers de l'Association Internationale des Études Françaises* 10 (1958): 138–57.

Cellier, Léon, and Léon Guichard, eds. "Introduction." In *Consuelo,* by George Sand. Paris: Garnier, 1959.

Champagne, Roland A. "The Enchantment of Orpheus: Music and Words in Contemporary French Fiction." In *French Literature and the Arts,* edited by Phillip Crant. Columbia: University of South Carolina Press, 1978.

Charles-Dominique, Luc. "La Cornemuse dans l'espace ménétrier français de l'Ancien Réglme." In *Les Cornemuses de George Sand,* edited by Sylvie Douce de la Salle, 19–21. Montluçon: Mame, 1996.

———. "Dans les caves de Saint-Chartier, ou la mythification scénarisée de l'altérité sociale et culturelle." In *À la croisée des chemins: Musiques savantes—musiques populaires, Hommage à George Sand,* edited by Joseph LeFloc'h, 100–21. Saint-Jouin-de-Milly: FAMDT, 1999.

———. *Les Ménétriers français sous l'Ancien Régime.* Paris: Klincksieck, 1994.

Charlton, David, ed. *E. T. A. Hoffmann's Musical Writings: 'Kreisleriana,' 'The Poet and the Composer,' Music Criticism.* Translated by Martyn Clarke. Cambridge: Cambridge University Press, 1989.

Charron, Sylvie. "De Fadette à Nanon: Révolutions et écritures." *Geroge Sand Studies* 13, nos. 1–2 (1994): 37–44.

———. "George Sand and the Revolution of 1848: Rereading *La Petite Fadette.*" *George Sand Studies* 10, nos. 1–2 (1990–91): 60–66.

———. "Rivières et fontaines dans les romans champêtres." In *George Sand Today,* edited by David A. Powell, 145–52. New York: University Press of America, 1992.

Chevereau, Anne. *George Sand: Du Catholisicisme au paraprotestantisme.* Typescript copy. Paris: Amor, 1988.

Christensen, Peter G. "*Consuelo, Wilhelm Meister,* and the Historical Novel." *George Sand Newsletter* 5, no 2 (fall-winter 1982): 69–75.

Cixous, Hélène. "La Fiction et ses fantômes: Une Lecture de l'*Unheimliche* de Freud." *Poétique* 10 (1972): 199–216.

Claudon, Francis. *La Musique des romantiques.* Paris: Presses Universitaires de France, 1992.

Cocker, Erica. "*Corinne* and *Consuelo*: Women Artists in Dialogue with the World." In *Le Siècle de George Sand,* edited by David A. Powell, 247–53. Amsterdam: Rodopi, 1998.

Cœuroy, André. *La Musique et le peuple en France.* Paris: Editions Stock, 1941.

———. *Musique et littérature.* Paris: Blond et Gay, 1923.

———. "Notes brèves sur l'inspiration musicale de George Sand." *La Revue musicale* 9 (July 1926): 46–53.

Constable, M. V. "The 'Figlie del coro': Fiction and Fact." *Journal of Euorpean Studies* 11 (1981): 111–39.

Cook, Nicholas. *Music, Imagination, and Culture.* Oxford: Clarendon Press, 1990.

Cooke, Deryck. *The Language of Music.* Oxford: Oxford University Press, 1959.

Crant, Phillip, ed. *French Literature and the Arts.* Columbia: University of South Carolina Press, 1978.

Crecelius, Katheryn J. *Family Romances: George Sand's Early Novels.* Bloomington: Indiana University Press, 1987.

Curtius, Ernst R. *European Literature and the Latin Middle Ages.* Translated by Willard R. Trask. New York: Pantheon Books, 1953.

Dahlhaus, Carl. *Nineteenth-Century Music.* Translated by J. Bradford Robinson. Berkeley: University of California Press, 1989.

Dällenbach, Lucien. *The Mirror in the Text.* Translated by Jeremy Whiteley. Chicago: Chicago University Press, 1989.

Daly, Pierrette. *Heroic Tropes: Gender and Intertext.* Detroit: Wayne State University Press, 1993.

Dauphine, James. "La Mythe d'Orphée et l'écriture musicale dans *Les Maîtres Sonneurs* de George Sand." In *Hommage à Jean Onimus,* edited by J.-B. Guiran, 113–17. Nice: Belles-lettres, 1979.

Dauriac, Lionel. *Essai sur l'esprit musical.* Paris: Alcan, 1904.

DeBellis, Mark. "The Representational Content of Musical Experience." *Philosophy and Phenomenological Research* 51, no. 2 (June 1991): 303–24.

DeJean, Joan. *Ancients against Moderns: Culture Wars and the Making of a Fin de Siècle.* Chicago: University of Chicago Press, 1997.

de Man, Paul. *Blindness and Insight: Essays in the Rhetoric of Contemporary Criticism.* 1971. Reprint, Minneapolis: University of Minnesota Press, 1983.

Despringre, André-Marie. "Démarche, concepts et méthodes pour l'étude des relations *musique/langue* examinées dans la poésie chantée de tradition orale." *Revue d'ethnolinguistique (Cahiers du LACITO)* 5 (1990): 165–202.

Diaz, Brigitte. "Portrait de l'artiste en maçon: La Correspondance entre George Sand et Charles Poncy (1842–1876)." In *Le Siècle de George Sand,* edited by David A. Powell, 309–20. Amsterdam: Rodopi, 1998.

Didier, Béatrice. "Femme/Identité/Écriture. A propos de l'*Histoire de ma vie* de

George Sand." *Revue des sciences humaines* 77 (October-December 1977): 561–76.

———. "George Sand, *Consuelo* et la création féminine." *La Quinzaine littéraire* 240 (15–30 September 1976): 16–17.

———. "George Sand critique musical dans ses lettres." *Présence de George Sand* 12 (Oct. 1981): 22–27.

———. *George Sand écrivain: "Un grand fleuve d'Amérique."* Paris: Presses Universitaires de France, 1998.

———. "George Sand et *Don Giovanni*." *Revue des sciences humaines* 226 (1992–2): 37–53.

———. "Problèmes de sémiologie musicale dans *Consuelo*." In *La Porporina*, edited by Léon Cellier, 131–39. Grenoble: Presses Universitaires de Grenoble, 1976.

———. "Sexe, société et création: *Consuelo* et *La Comtesse de Rudolstadt*." *Romantisme* 13–14 (1976): 155–66.

———. "Le Souvenir musical dans *Histoire de ma vie* et l'ombre de Rousseau." *Présence de George Sand* 8 (May 1980): 48–52.

Dindinaud, G. "Notes sur les sociétés secrètes dans le sud du département du Cher en 1851." *Cahier d'archéologie et d'histoire du Berry* 26 (September 1971): 75–78.

DuBellis, Mark. "The Representational Context of Musical Experience." *Philosophy and Phenomenological Research* 51, no. 2 (June 1991): 303–24.

Eco, Umberto. *A Theory of Semiotics*. Bloomington: Indiana University Press, 1976.

Einstein, Alfred. *Music in the Romantic Era*. New York: Norton, 1947.

Escal, Françoise. *Espaces sociaux, espaces musicaux*. Paris: Payot, 1979.

Feder, Lillian. *Madness in Literature*. Princeton: Princeton University Press, 1980.

Felman, Shoshana. *La "Folie" dans l'œuvre romanesque de Stendhal*. Paris: José Corti, 1971.

Ferrá, Bertolomé. *Chopin and George Sand in Majorca*. Translated by James Webb. New York: Haskell House, 1974.

Fischer-Dieskau, Dietrich. *Quand le musique nourrit l'amour: Études biographiques du XIXe sièle*. Translated by Léa Marcou. Paris: Buchet/Chastel, 1995.

FitzLyon, April. *Maria Malibran: Diva of the Romantic Age*. London: Souvenir Press, 1987.

———. *The Price of Genius: A Life of Pauline Viardot*. New York: Appleton-Century, 1964.

Foucault, Michel. *Madness and Civilization: A History of Insanity in the Age of Reason*. Translated by Richard Howard. New York: Vintage, 1973.

Frappier-Mazur, Lucienne. "Code romantique et ressurgences du féminin dans *La Comtesse de Rudolstadt*." In *Le Récit amoureux*, edited by Didier Coste and Michel Zénaffa, 53–70. Paris: Editions du Champ Vallon, 1984.

———. "Desire, Writing, and Identity in the Romantic Mystical Novel: Notes for a Definition of the Feminine." *Style* 18, no. 3 (summer 1984): 328–54.

Freud, Sigmund. "The Uncanny"(1919). In *Studies in Parapsychology*, translated by Alix Strachey, 17:217–52. London: Hogarth Press, 1955.

Gaulmier, Jean. "Un Exemple d'utilisation immédiate du folklore: Genèse et structure des *Maîtres Sonneurs*.” *Actes du VIe Congrès national de la Société française de littérature comparée* (1965): 143–50.

Geiringer, Karl, and Irene Geiringer. *Haydn: A Creative Life in Music*. Berkeley: University of California Press, 1982.

Genevray, Françoise. “Le Personnage de Don Juan dans *Lélia* et *Le Château des Désertes*.” *Présence de George Sand* 10 (February 1981): 26–31.

Glasgow, Janis. “ ‘*Mouny-Robin*,’ nouvelle fantastique de George Sand.” *George Sand Studies* 10, nos. 1–2 (1990–91): 3–10.

———. “Sand’s Imaginary Travels in ‘Carl’.” In *The Traveler in the Life and Works of George Sand*, edited by Tamara Alvarez-Detrell, 97–107. Troy, N.Y.: Whitston, 1994.

Godwin, Joscelyn. *Music and the Occult: French Musical Philosophies, 1750–1950*. Rochester: University of Rochester Press, 1995.

Goldin, Jeanne. “Le Saint-Simonisme.” In *Une Correspondance*, edited by Nicole Mozet, 163–91. St-Cyr-sur-Loire: Christian Pirot, 1994.

Grey, Thomas. “Metaphorical Modes in Nineteenth-Century Music Criticism: Image, Narrative, and Idea.” In *Music and Text: Critical Inquiries*, edited by Steven Paul Scher, 93–117. Cambridge: Cambridge University Press, 1992.

Grimm, Friedrich Melchior von. *Le Petit Prophète de Boehmischbroda*. In *Correspondance littéraire, philosophique et critique par Grimm, Diderot, Raynal, Meister, etc.*, edited by Maurice Tourneux, 16: 313–36. 1882. Reprint, Nendeln: Draus, 1968.

Guichard, Léon. *La Musique et les lettres au temps du romantisme*. 1955. Reprint, Paris: Editions d’Aujourd’hui, 1984.

Guillaume, G. “*Les Maîtres Sonneurs*, mythe sandien ou réalité régionale?” In *À la croisée des chemins: Musiques savantes—musiques populaires, Hommage à George Sand*, edited by Joseph LeFloc’h, 122–35. Saint-Jouin-de-Milly: FAMDT, 1999.

Hamburger, Klára. *Liszt*. Translated by Paul Merrick. Budapest: Kossuth, 1987.

Hamilton, James F. “From Art to Nature in George Sand’s *La Mare au diable*.” In *French Literature and the Arts*, edited by Phillip Crant. Columbia: University of South Carolina Press, 1978.

Hanslick, Eduard. *On the Musically Beautiful*. Translated by Geoggrey Payzant. Indianapolis: Hackett Publishing, 1986.

Harnoncourt, Nikolaus. *Baroque Music Today: Music as Speech: Ways to a New Understanding of Music*. Translated by Mary O’Neill. Portland, Ore.: Amadeus Press, 1988.

Hecquet, Michèle. *Poétique de la parabole: Les Romans socialistes de George Sand, 1840–1845*. Paris: Klincksieck, 1992.

———. “Roman populaire: *Consuelo*.” In *George Sand et l’écriture du roman*, edited by Jeanne Goldin, 197–206. Montréal: Paragraphes, 1996.

Hegel, Georg Wilhelm Friedrich. *Aesthetics: Lectures on Fine Art*. 2 vols. Translated by T. M. Knox. Oxford: Clarendon Press, 1975.

Heintzen, J.-F. “A la recherche de monsieur Marsillat: Vie et mœurs des cornemuseux en Centre-France au XIXe siècle.” In *Les Cornemuses de George Sand*, edited by Sylvia Douce de la Salle, 22–7. Montluçom: Mame, 1996.

———. “Bourbonnais, la plus récente des traditions.” In *Vielle à roue, territoires illimités*. Saint-Jouin de Milly: Collection Modal, FAMDT, 1996.

————. "La Musique pousse dans les bois." In *À la croisée des chemins: Musiques savantes—musiques populaires, Hommage à George Sand*, edited by Joseph LeFloc'h, 136–47. Saint-Jouin-de-Milly: FAMDT, 1999.

Helgeson, James S. *Ensemble discors: Musica speculativa et subjectivité poétique chez Maurice Scève*. Geneva: Droz, 2001.

Hermand, Jost, and Michael Gilbert, eds. *German Essays on Music*. New York: Continuum, 1994.

Hertz, David Michael. *The Tuning of the Word: The Musico-Literary Poetics of the Symbolist Movement*. Carbondale: Southern Illinois University Press, 1987.

Higonnet, Margaret. "Speaking Silences: Women's Suicide." In *The Female Body in Western Culture: Comtemporary Perspectives*, edited by Susan Rubin Suleiman, 68–83. Cambridge: Harvard University Press, 1986.

Hines, Thomas Jensen. *Collaborative Form: Studies in the Relations of the Arts*. Kent: Kent State University Press, 1991.

Hoffmann, E. T. A. *Selected Writings of E. T. A. Hoffmann*. 2 vols. Edited and translated by Leonard J. Kent and Elizabeth C. Knight. Chicago: University of Chicago Press, 1969.

Hofstadter, Albert, and Richard Kuhns, eds. *Philosophies of Art and Beauty: Selected Readings in Aesthetics from Plato to Heidegger*. New York: Modern Library, 1964.

Hoog, Marie-Jacques. "L'Improvisatrice ou la prise de la parole féminine." *Bulletin de la Société des professeurs français en Amérique*, 1983–84: 37–46.

Howard, Patricia. *Gluck: An Eighteenth-Century Portrait in Letters and Documents*. Oxford: Clarendon Press, 1995.

Huf, Linda. *Portrait of the Artist as a Young Woman: The Writer as Heroine in American Literature*. New York: Frederick Ungar, 1983.

Hunt, Lynn. *Politics, Culture, and Class in the French Revolution*. Berkeley: University of California Press, 1984.

Jakobson, Roman. "About the Relation between Visual and Auditory Signs." In *Models for the Perception of Speech and Visual Form*, edited by Wiant Wathen-Dunn, 1–7. Cambridge: MIT Press, 1967.

————. "Le Folklore, forme spécifique de création." In *Questions de poétique*. Paris: Seuil, 1973.

Jaubert, comte H. François. *Glossaire du centre de la France*. 2 vols. Paris: Chaix, 1855.

————. *Supplément au glossaire du centre de la France*. Paris: Chaix, 1869.

————. *Vocabulaire du Berry et de quelques cantons voisins*. Paris: Roret, 1842.

Joeres, Ruth-Ellen B., and Mary Jo Maynes. *German Women in the Eighteenth and Nineteenth Centuries: A Social and Literary History*. Bloomington: Indiana University Press, 1986.

Jordan, William. "Augustine on Music." In *Grace, Politics and Desire: Essays on Augustine*, edited by Hugo A. Meynell, 123–35. Calgary: University of Calgary Press, 1990.

Juden, Brian. "L'Esthétique: 'L'Harmonie immense qui dit tout'." *Romantisme* 5 (1973): 4–17.

————. "Que la théorie des correspondances ne dérive pas de Swedenborg." *Travaux de linguistique et de littérature* 11, no. 2 (1973): 33–46.

————. *Traditions orphiques et tendances mystiques dans le romantisme français (1800–1855)*. Paris: Klincksieck, 1971.

Kallberg, Jeffrey. *Chopin at the Boundaries: Sex, History, and Musical Genre.* Cambridge: Harvard University Press, 1996.

Kaminsky, Jack. *Hegel on Art: An Interpretation of Hegel's Aesthetics.* New York: University Publishers, 1962.

Kennedy, George A., trans. and intro. *Sept Cordes de la lyre, A Woman's Version of the Faust Legend: "The Seven Strings of the Lyre" by George Sand.* Chapel Hill: University of North Carolina Press, 1989.

Kivy, Peter. *Music Alone: Philosophical Reflections on the Purely Musical Experience.* Ithaca: Cornell University Press, 1990.

————. *Sound and Semblance: Reflections on Musical Representation.* Princeton: Princeton University Press, 1984.

Knox, Israel. "Schopenhauer's Aesthetic Theory." In *Schopenhauer: His Philosophical Achievement*, edited by Michael Fox. Brighton: Harvester Press, 1980.

Kontje, Todd. *The German Bildungsroman: History of a National Genre.* Columbia, S.C.: Camden House, 1993.

————. *Private Lives in the Public Sphere: The German "Bildungsroman" as Metafiction.* University Park: Pennsylvania State University Press, 1992.

Kramer, Lawrence. *Music and Poetry: The Nineteenth Century and After.* Berkeley: University of California Press, 1984.

————. *Music as Cultural Practice, 1800–1900.* Berkeley: University of California Press, 1990.

Kreitman, Lenore. "George Sand's Symbolic Vision: A Fading Yet Future Fantastic." Ph.D. diss., University of Pennsylvania, 1976.

Kristeva, Julia. *The Kristeva Reader*, edited by Toril Moi. New York: Columbia University Press, 1986.

Lacassagne, J.-P. *Histoire d'une amitié. Leroux et Sand. D'après une correspondance inédite, 1836–1866.* Paris: Klincksieck, 1973.

Laforge, François. "Structure et fonction du mythe d'Orphée dans *Consuelo* de George Sand." *Revue d'histoire littéraire de la France* 84 (1984): 53–66.

Langer, Suzanne. *Feeling and Form. A Theory of Art.* New York: Scribner's, 1953.

Le Huray, Peter, and James Day, eds. *Music and Aesthetics in the Eighteenth and Early-Nineteenth Centuries.* Cambridge: Cambridge University Press, 1981.

Leonardi, Susan J., and Rebecca A. Pope. *The Diva's Mouth: Body, Voice, Prima Donna Politics.* New Brunswick: Rutgers University Press, 1996.

Lesure, F. "La Communauté des 'joueurs d'instruments' au XVIe siècle." *Revue historique de droit français et étranger* 4 (1953): 79–109.

Lévi-Strauss, Claude. *Myth and Meaning.* New York: Schocken Books, 1979.

————. *The Raw and the Cooked: Introduction to a Science of Mythology: 1.* Translated by John and Doreen Weightman. New York: Harper and Row, 1969.

Le Vot, Gérard. "Berlioz écrivain et les musiques 'autres' en France à l'époque romantique." In *À la croisée des chemins: Musiques savantes—musiques populaires, Hommage à George Sand*, edited by Joseph LeFloc'h, 50–69. Saint-Jouin-de-Milly: FAMDT, 1999.

L'Hopital, Madeleine. *La Notion de l'artiste chez George Sand.* Paris: Boivin, 1946.

Lippman, Edward. *A History of Western Musical Aesthetics.* Lincoln: University of Nebraska Press, 1992.

Liszt, Franz. *An Artist's Journey.* Translated by Charles Suttoni. Chicago: University of Chicago Press, 1989.

———. "De la situation des artistes et de leur condition dans la société." *Gazette musicale de Paris,* 2d year (May–November 1835).

———. *Pages romantiques.* Edited by Jean Cantavoine. Paris: Félix Alcan, 1912.

———. *Rondeau fantastique, sur un thème espagnol.* Piano score, 1839. Département de Musique, Bibliothèque Nationale, Paris. B.L. 1031.

Lloyd, Rosemary. *Baudelaire et Hoffmann: Affinités et influences.* Cambridge: Cambridge University Press, 1979.

Locatelli, Aude. "Musique et roman de formation." *Revue de littérature comparée* 68, no. 2 (April–June 1994): 169–82.

Locke, Ralph P. "Liszt's Saint-Simonian Adventure." *Nineteenth-Century Music* 4 (1980): 209–27; 5 (1981): 281.

———. *Music, Musicians and the Saint-Simonians.* Chicago: University of Chicago Press, 1986.

Longyear, Rey M. *Nineteenth-Century Romanticism in Music.* Englewood Cliffs, N.J.: Prentice-Hall, 1969.

Lubin, Georges. "Le nom de Podiebrad et la famille de George Sand." *Présence de George Sand* 16 (February 1983), 12–13.

Mallet, Francine. *George Sand.* Paris: Grasset, 1976.

———. "George Sand et la musique." *Présence de George Sand* 10 (February 1981): 32–38.

Manifold, Gay. *George Sand's Theatre Career.* Ann Arbor: UMI, 1985.

Marix, Thérèse. "La musique naturelle et la musique populaire." *Revue musicale* 9 (1 July 1926): 33–45.

Marix-Spire, Thérèse. "Du piano à l'action sociale: Franz Liszt et George Sand, militante socialiste." *Renaissance* 2–3 (1945): 187–216.

———. *Lettres inédites de Sand et de Pauline Viardot (1839–1849), recueillies, annotées et précédées d'une introduction.* Paris: Nouvelles Editions Latines, 1959.

———. "Naissance d'une passion: George Sand et Chopin." *Cahier de l'Association Internationale des Etudes Françaises* 28 (May 1976): 263–77.

———. *Les Romantiques et la musique: Le Cas George Sand, 1804–1838.* Paris: Nouvelles Editions Latines, 1954.

———. "Vicissitudes d'un opéra-comique: *La Mare au diable* de George Sand et de Pauline Viardot." *Romanic Review* 35, no. 2 (April 1944): 125–46.

Marrone, Claire. "Male and Female *Bildung*: The *Memoires de Céleste Mogador.*" *Nineteenth-Century French Studies* 25, nos. 3–4 (spring–summer 1997): 335–47.

Michel, Arlette. "Musique et poésie: Sand et Balzac lecteurs des *Kreisleriana.*" *Présence de George Sand* 13 (February 1982): 23–31.

Milner, Max. *Le Diable dans la littérature française, de Cazotte à Baudelaire (1772–1861).* 2 vols. Paris: Corti, 1960.

———. *La Fantasmagorie: Essai sur l'optique fantastique.* Paris: Presses Universitaires de France, 1982.

———. *Le Romantisme, I: 1820–1843*. Paris: Arthaud, 1973.

Minehan, John A. *Word Like a Bell: John Keats, Music and the Romantic Poet.* Kent: Kent State University Press, 1992.

Moses, Claire Goldberg. *French Feminism in the Nineteenth Century.* Albany: SUNY Press, 1984.

Moses, Claire Goldberg, and Leslie Wahl Rabine. *Feminism, Socialism, and French Romanticism.* Bloomington: Indiana University Press, 1993.

Mozet, Nicole, ed. *Une correspondance.* St-Cyr-sur-Loire: Christian Pirot, 1994.

———. *George Sand: Écrivain de romans.* St-Cyr-sur-Loire: Christian Pirot, 1997.

———. "Signé le voyageur: George Sand et l'invention de l'artiste." *Romantisme* 55 (1987): 23–32.

———. "Le voyageur sandien en quête d'un lieu d'écriture." *George Sand: Voyage et écriture. Études françaises* 24, no. 1 (spring 1988): 41–55.

Naginski, Isabelle Hoog. "La Comédie féminine: Constance et mouvance dans l'œuvre sandienne." In *George Sand et l'écriture du roman*, edited by Jeanne Goldin, 231–39. Montréal: Paragraphes, 1996.

———. *George Sand: Writing for Her Life.* New Brunswick: Rutgers University Press, 1991.

Nattiez, Jean-Jacques. *Fondements d'une sémiologie de la musique.* Paris: Union Générale d'Edition, 1975.

———. "La Linguistique: Voie nouvelle pour l'analyse musicale?" *Les Cahiers canadiens de musique* 4 (January 1972): 101–15.

———. *Proust as Musician.* Translated by Derrick Puffett. New York: Cambridge University Press, 1989.

Neubauer, John. *The Emancipation of Music from Language: Departure from Mimesis in Eighteenth-Century Aesthetics.* New Haven: Yale University Press, 1986.

———. "Music and Literature: The Institutional Dimensions." In *Music and Text: Critical Inquiries*, edited by Steven Paul Scher, 3–20. Cambridge: Cambridge University Press, 1992.

Nisard, Charles. *Des Chansons populaires chez les Anciens et chez les Français: Essai historique suivi d'une étude sur la chanson des rues contemporaines.* Paris: Dentu, 1867.

Nodier, Charles. "Du fantastique en littérature," In *Œuvres complètes.* Vol. 5. Geneva: Slatkine Reprints, 1968.

Onega, Susana, and José Ángel García Landa, eds. *Narratology: An Introduction.* New York: Longman, 1996.

Osburne, Charles. *The Bel Canto Operas of Rossini, Donizetti and Bellini.* Portland, Ore.: Amadeus Press, 1994.

Pagnini, Marcello. *Lingua e musica: Proposta per un'indagine strutturalistic-semiotica.* Bologna: Il Mulino, 1974.

Parent, Monique. "George Sand et le patois berrichon." *Bulletin de la Faculté des Lettres de Strasbourg* (May–June 1954): 17–23.

Pearson, Carol, and Katherine Pope. *The Female Hero in American and British Literature.* New York: R. R. Bowker, 1981.

Pekacz, Jolanta T. "The Salonnières and the Philosophes in Old Regime France:

The Authority of Aesthetic Judgment." *Journal of the History of Ideas* 60, no. 2 (1999): 277–97.

Pellisier. "Avant-Garde Theater and Musical Forms: Jean Tardieu's Attempt at Fusion of the Arts." In *French Literature and the Arts*, edited by Phillip Crant. Columbia: University of South Carolina Press, 1978.

Perrot, Michelle. *George Sand: Politique et polémiques*. Paris: Imprimerie nationale, 1997.

Poli, Annarosa. *George Sand et les années terribles*. Paris: Nizet, 1975.

———. "Incidenze faustiane nell'opera di George Sand." *Francofonia* 2 (spring 1982): 71–83.

———. *L'Italie dans la vie et l'œuvre de Sand*. Paris: Colin, 1960.

Pousseur, Henri. *Musique, sémantique, société*. Brussels: Casterman, 1972.

Powell, David A. "Discord, Dissension, and Dissonance: The Initiation in Sand's *Les Maîtres Sonneurs*." *Friends of George Sand Newsletter* 6, nos. 3–4 (1987): 54–61.

———. "Une fausse note: La Parodie d'une leçon de musique dans *Consuelo* de George Sand." In *Corps/Décor: Femmes, Orgie, Parodie*, edited by Catherine Nesci, with Gerald Prince and Gretchen van Slyke, 269–83. Amsterdam: Rodopi, 1999.

———. *George Sand*. Boston: Twayne, 1990.

———. " 'Histoire du rêveur', ou le 'rêve de mélodie': Le Fantastique musical chez George Sand." In *George Sand et son temps: Hommage à Annarosa Poli*, edited by Elio Mosele, 2: 505–22. Geneva: Slatkine, 1993.

———. "Improvisation(s) dans *Consuelo*." *La Revue des sciences humaines* 226 (April–June 1992): 116–34.

———. " 'La langue de l'infini': George Sand et la langue musicale." In *Les Langues du XIXe siècle*, edited by Graham Falconer, Andrew Oliver, and Dorothy Speirs, 139–53. Toronto: Centre d'Études Romantiques Joseph Sablé, 1998.

———. "Musical-Literary Intertextuality: George Sand and Franz Liszt." In *Correspondances: Studies in Literature, History, and the Arts in Nineteenth-Century France*, edited by Keith Busby, 165–76. Amsterdam: Rodopi, 1992.

———. " 'Music Conducive to Dream': Sand and the Musical Fantastic." In *Le Siècle de George Sand*, edited by David A. Powell, 321–33. Amsterdam: Rodopi, 1998.

———. "Musique et musiquette: George Sand et la valeur de la musique." In *À la croisée des chemins: Musiques savantes—musiques populaires, Hommage à George Sand*, edited by Joseph LeFloc'h, 12–25. Saint-Jouin-de-Milly: FAMDT, 1999.

———. "Nous et Eux: Le Narrateur français dans un texte italien: 'La Prima donna.' " In *Le Chantier de George Sand/George Sand et l'étranger*, edited by Tivador Gorilovics and Anna Szabó, 285–93. Debrecen, Hungary: Kossuth Lajos Tudományegyetem, 1993.

———, ed. *Le Siècle de George Sand*. Amsterdam: Rodopi, 1998.

Présence de George Sand 12 (1981), devoted to "George Sand et la musique."

Prince, Gerald. *Narratology: The Form and Functioning of Narrative*. New York: Mouton, 1982.

Quignard, Pascal. *La Haine de la musique*. Paris: Calmann-Lévy, 1996.

Rabine, Leslie Wahl. *Reading the Romantic Heroine: Text, History, Ideology.* Ann Arbor: University of Michigan Press, 1985.

Ramant-Chevassus, Béatrice. "Le Postminimalisme comme volonté de dialogue entre le 'majeur' et le 'mineur': 'L'Exemple de Steve Reich." In *À la croisée des chemins: Musiques savantes—musiques populaires, Hommage à George Sand,* edited by Joseph LeFloc'h, 164–73. Saint-Jouin-de-Milly: FAMDT, 1999.

Rambeau, Marie-Paule. *Chopin dans la vie et l'œuvre de George Sand.* Paris: Les Belles Lettres, 1985.

———. "Fallait-il accommoder Aristophane à la sauce berrichonne? Le *Plutus* de George Sand." *Les Amis de George Sand,* n.s., 13 (July 1992): 26–30.

———. "Maladie mentale et folie dans l'œuvre de George Sand." In *George Sand et son temps: Hommage à Annarosa Poli,* edited by Elio Mosele, 2: 523–38.

Rea, Annabelle. "*La Filleule*: An Apolitical Sand?" In *Le Siècle de George Sand,* edited by David A. Powell, 45–54. Amsterdam: Rodopi, 1998.

Reid, Martine. "Troubadoureries." In *Une Correspondance,* edited by Nicole Mozet, 254–68. St-Cyr-sur-Loire: Christian Pirot, 1994.

Rhodes, Willard. "Folk Music, Old and New." In *Folklore and Society: Essays in Honor of Benjamin A. Botkin,* edited by Bruce Jackson, 11–19. Hatboro, Pa.: Folklore Associates, 1966.

Rousseau, Jean-Jacques. *Dictionnaire de musique.* In *Écrits sur la musique, la langue et le théâtre.* Vol. 5. of *Œuvres complètes.* Paris: Gallimard/Pléiade, 1995.

———. *Discours sur l'origine des langues.* In *Écrits sur la musique, la langue et le théâtre.* Vol. 5. of *Œuvres complètes.* Paris: Gallimard/Pléiade, 1995.

———. *Écrits sur la musique.* Edited by Catherine Kintzler. Paris: Stock/Musique, 1979.

———. *Écrits sur la musique, la langue et le théâtre.* Vol. 5 of *Œuvres complètes.* Paris: Gallimard/Pléiade, 1995.

———. *Lettre sur la musique françoise. Écrits sur la musique, la langue et le théâtre.* Vol. 5 of *Œuvres complètes.* Paris: Gallimard/Pléiade, 1995.

Ruwet, Nicolas. *Langage, musique, poésie.* Paris: Seuil, 1972.

Said, Edward W. *Musical Elaborations.* New York: Columbia University Press, 1991.

Saint-Gérand, Jacques-Philippe. "Métaphores correspondancielles du début du XIXe siècle: Linguistique, style, synesthésies." *Nineteenth-Century French Studies* 26, nos. 1–2 (fall–winter 1997–98): 1–23.

Saint-Simon, Henri. *Selected Writings on Science, Industry and Social Organisation.* Edited and translated by Keith Taylor. New York: Holmes and Meier Publishers, 1975.

Saloman, O. Frishberg. "Chabanon and Chastellux on Music and Language, 1764–1773." *International Review of the Aesthetics and Sociology of Music* 20, no. 2 (1989): 109–20.

Salomon, Pierre. *George Sand.* 1953. Reprint, Meylan: Editions de l'Aurore, 1984.

———. "George Sand et Don Juan." *Présence de George Sand* 11 (May 1981): 47–48.

Salomon, Pierre, and J. Mallion. "Présentation." In *La Mare au diable* et *François le champi,* by George Sand, iii–xxviii. Paris: Garnier, 1981.

Schafer, R. Murray. *E. T. A. Hoffmann and Music.* Toronto: University of Toronto Press, 1975.

Schelling, Friedrich Wilhelm Joseph. *The Philosophy of Art.* Edited and translated by Douglas W. Scott. Minneapolis: University of Minnesota Press, 1989.

Scher, Steven Paul, ed. *Music and Text: Critical Inquiries.* Cambridge: Cambridge University Press, 1992.

Schneider, Marcel. *La Littérature fantastique en France.* Paris: Fayard, 1964.

Schor, Naomi. "Le Féminisme et George Sand: *Lettres à Marcie.*" *Revue des sciences humaines* 226 (April–June 1992): 21–35.

———. *George Sand and Idealism.* New York: Columbia University Press, 1993.

———. "Reading Double: Sand's Difference." In *The Poetics of Gender*, edited by Nancy Miller, 236–45. New York: Columbia University Press, 1986.

Schuerewegen, Franc. "Histoire de pieds: Gautier, Lorrain et le fantastique." *Nineteenth-Century French Studies* 13, no. 4 (summer 1985): 200–10.

Schwab, Gail M. "Mother's Body, Father's Tongue." In *Engaging with Irigaray*, edited by Carolyn Burke, Naomi Schor, and Margaret Whitford, 351–78. New York: Columbia University Press, 1993.

Scott, John T. "The Harmony between Rousseau's Musical Theory and His Philosophy." *Journal of the History of Ideas* 59, no. 2 (1998): 287–308.

Seillière, Ernest. *George Sand: Mystique de la passion, de la politique et de l'art.* Paris: Félix Alcan, 1920.

Sessions, Roger. *The Musical Experience of Composer, Performer, Listener.* Princeton: Princeton University Press, 1950.

———. *Questions about Music.* Cambridge: Harvard University Press, 1970.

Seybert, Gislinde. "George Sand und die Musik. Zur Vermittlung von Music im Text: 'Symphonie pastorale de Beethoven.' " In *Musik und Literatur*, edited by Albert Bier and Gerold W. Gruber, 159–68. Frankfurt: Peter Lang, 1995.

Siebers, Tobin. *The Romantic Fantastic.* Ithaca: Cornell University Press, 1984.

Sonnenfeld, Albert. "George Sand: Music and Sexualities." *Nineteenth-Century French Studies* 16, nos. 3–4 (spring–summer 1988): 310–21.

Sourian, Eve. "Les Opinions religieuses de George Sand: Pourquoi Consuelo a-t-elle perdu sa voix?" In *George Sand: Collected Essays*, edited by Janis Glasgow, 127–38. Troy, N.Y.: Whitston, 1985.

Springer, George P. "Language and Music: Parallels and Divergencies." In *For Roman Jakobson: Essays on the Occasion of His Sixtieth Birthday*, edited by Morris Halle, 504–13. The Hague: Mouton, 1956.

Standring, Enid. "George Sand and the Romantic Composers of France." In *West Virginia George Sand Conference Papers*, edited by Armand E. Singer, Mary W. Sinber, and Janice S. Spleth, 75–83. Morgantown: Department of Foreign Languages of West Virginia University, 1981.

———. "Rossini and His Music in the Life and Works of George Sand." *Nineteenth-Century French Studies* 10, nos. 1–2 (1981–82): 17–27.

Steiner, Wendy, ed. *The Sign in Music and Literature.* Austin: University of Texas Press, 1981.

Storr, Anthony. *Music and the Mind.* New York: Free Press, 1992.

Swales, Martin. *The German Bildungsroman from Wieland to Hesse.* Princeton: Princeton University Press, 1978.

Szabó, Anna. *Le Personnage sandien: Constantes et variations*. Debrecen, Hungary: Kossuth Lajos Tudományegyetem, 1991.

———. *Les Préfaces de George Sand*. 2 vols. Debrecen, Hungary: Kossuth Lajos Tudományegyetem, 1997.

Taviani, Ferdinando, and Mirella Schino. *Le Secret de la commedia dell'arte*. Translated by Yves Libert. Paris: Editions Bouffonneries, 1984.

Thibert, Marguerite. *Le Rôle social de l'art d'après les Saint-Simoniens*. Paris: Marcel Rivère, 1926.

Tiersot, Julien. *La Chanson populaire et les écrivains romantiques*. Paris: Plon, 1931.

———. *Histoire de la chanson populaire en France*. Paris: Plon, 1889. Reprint, Geneva: Minkoff Reprint, 1978.

———. *La Musique aux temps romantiques*. Paris: Félix Alcan, 1930.

Toch, Ernst. *The Shaping Forces in Music: An Inquiry into the Nature of Harmony, Melody, Counterpoint, Form*. Translated by Lawrence Weschler. 1948. Reprint, New York: Dover, 1977.

Todorov, Tzvetan. *Introduction à la littérature fantastique*. Paris: Seuil, 1970.

———. *Theories of the Symbol*. Translated by Catherine Porter. Ithaca: Cornell University Press, 1982.

Tourgenev, Ivan. *Quelques lettres d'Ivan Tourguénev à Pauline Viardot*. Edited by Henri Granjard. Paris: Mouton, 1974.

Treitler, Leo. *Music and the Historical Imagination*. Cambridge: Harvard University Press, 1989.

Van Gennep, A. "George Sand folkloriste." *Mercure de France* (1 June 1926): 371–84.

Van Slyke, Gretchen. "History in Her Story: Historical Referents in Sand's *La Petite Fadette*." *Romanic Review* 82 (1991): 49–69.

Vierne, Simone. "George Sand, Pauline Viardot et la chanson populaire." *Cahiers Tourgueniev-Viardot-Malibran* 3 (October 1979): 43–55.

———. *Jules Verne et le roman initiatique*. Paris: Editions du Sirac, 1973.

———. "Music in the Heart of the World: The Challenge of Music to Literature." *George Sand Studies* 7, nos. 1–2: 3–14.

———. "Musique au cœur du monde ou le défi de la musique à l'écriture." In *George Sand et son temps: Hommage à Annarosa Poli*, edited by Elio Mosele, 931–52. Geneva: Slatkine, 1993.

———. "Le Mythe de la femme dans *Consuelo*." In *La Porporina*, edited by Léon Cellier, 41–50. Grenoble: Presses Universitaires de Grenoble, 1976.

———. "Parole(s) et musique." *Recherches et travaux*. Grenoble: UER des Lettres, Bulletin 11 (April 1975), 10–13.

———. *Rite, roman, initiation*. Grenoble: Presses Universitaires de Grenoble, 1973.

———. "Venise, décor mythique." *Présence de George Sand* 18 (November 1983): 5–10.

———. "Voyage initiatique." *Romantisme* 4 (1972): 37–44.

———, ed. *George Sand: Colloque de Cerisy*. Paris: CDU-SEDES, 1983.

Vierne, Simone, and René Bourgeois. "Introduction" and "Lexicon." In *Con-*

suelo. La Comtesse de Rudolstadt, by George Sand, 1: 5–35; 2: 385–402. Meylan: Editions de l'Aurore, 1983.

Villemarqué, Théodore Hersart de la. *Baraz-Breiz: Chants populaires de la Bretagne.* 2 vols. Paris: Delloye, Crozet, Techener, 1839.

Vincent, Marie-Louise. *George Sand et le Berry.* 2 vols. Paris: Champion, 1919.

———. *La Langue et le style rustiques de George Sand dans les romans champêtres.* Paris: Champion, 1916.

Walker, Alan. *Franz Liszt.* 2 vols. New York: Knopf, 1983.

Walker, Hallam. "Music and Meaning in Baudelaire: The 'Thyrse' Image." In *French Literature and the Arts*, edited by Phillip Crant. Columbia: University of South Carolina Press, 1978.

Watzlawick, Paul, Janet Helmick Beauvin, and Don D. Jackson. *Une Logique de la communication.* 1967. Reprint, Paris: Seuil, 1972.

Wentz, Debra Linowitz. *Les Profils du "Théâtre de Nohant" de George Sand.* Paris: Nizet, 1978.

White, Hayden. "Form, Reference, and Ideology in Musical Discourse." In *Music and Text: Critical Inquiries*, edited by Steven Paul Scher, 288–319. Cambridge: Cambridge University Press, 1992.

Zuckerkandl, Victor. *Sound and Symbol. Vol. 1: Music and the External World.* Translated by Willard R. Trask. 1956. Reprint, Princeton: Princeton University Press, 1973.

———. *Sound and Symbol. Vol. 2: Man the Musician.* Translated by Norbert Buterman. Princeton: Princeton University Press, 1973.

♫♫ Index ♫♫